THE
HISTORY OF
ECONOMIC
THOUGHT

A Book of Readings

THE
HISTORY OF
ECONOMIC
THOUGHT

A Book of Readings

HOWARD D. MARSHALL
Vassar College

NATALIE J. MARSHALL
State University College, New Paltz, New York

Pitman Publishing Corporation

NEW YORK/LONDON/TORONTO

Copyright © 1968 by Pitman Publishing Corporation
All Rights Reserved
Library of Congress Catalog Card Number: 68–10260
Published in cooperation with Landsberger Publishing Corporation
Typography and binding design by Vincent Torre
MANUFACTURED IN THE UNITED STATES OF AMERICA
1.987654321

THE HISTORY OF ECONOMIC THOUGHT:
A BOOK OF READINGS
is one of a series of textbooks
published in cooperation with
E. K. Georg Landsberger.

To Alison and Fred

CONTENTS

Thomas Robert Malthus (1766–1834) 59

David Ricardo (1772–1823) 85

John Stuart Mill (1806–1873) 131

Karl Marx (1818–1883)   187

DAS KAPITAL

William Stanley Jevons (1835–1881)   231

THE THEORY OF POLITICAL ECONOMY

Alfred Marshall (1842–1924)   259

PRINCIPLES OF ECONOMICS

Joan Robinson (1903–   )   313

THE ECONOMICS OF IMPERFECT COMPETITION

John Maynard Keynes (1887–1946)   353

THE GENERAL THEORY OF EMPLOYMENT,
INTEREST AND MONEY

INTRODUCTION

Few economists, even those possessed with the fiercest of nationalistic prides, would deny that nineteenth-century economic thought belonged to England. Starting a quarter of a century earlier with Adam Smith and his Wealth of Nations, the hundred years that followed witnessed England's absolute domination of the field. Only toward the end of the nineteenth century did major writers from other countries begin to challenge England's supremacy. This elevation of others in no way should be interpreted to mean that the excellence of English economists came to an end at that time; any such statement would be sheer nonsense. A nation which in the twentieth century has produced John Maynard Keynes, John Hicks, Dennis H. Robertson, and Joan Robinson, to mention but a few, needs no apologies. What happened, of course, was that other countries began to produce a number of top-flight economic theorists of their own.

There were both a number of advantages and disadvantages attached to this degree of concentration of economic thought in one country. Among the more obvious disadvantages for a number of years was the tendency of economic theory to be unduly ethnocentric and confined to a given era in time. Most of these early English political economists were convinced that the principles they had uncovered were equally applicable to all other countries as well. Supporting this judgment was a natural inclination of the English economists to see England's problems as of paramount importance. Insufficient recognition was also accorded to the fact that a theory is an abstract pictorial sketch of the real world as it exists and may become a less and less accurate picture as the real world changes. Finally, the attractiveness of Ricardo's deductive approach to economic reasoning led many scholars to neglect the importance of empirical research and the inductive method. The influence of the German Historical School which criticized Classical economists on all three counts came to England only late in the century and never completely corrected these deficiencies.

Even after granting these and other possible blemishes, however, we are forced to admire the monumental edifice erected by these writers. They were masters of economic thought, and the beginning student today can still learn a great deal about the subject of economics and the proper way to approach it by carefully reading these early writings. The writers' proximity to each other both in time and space enabled them to build a unified model based upon each other's work. In contrast, other European economists like Karl Menger (founder of the Austrian School of marginal utility) either had little or no knowledge of the work of the great English economic theorists or else studied the works of these economists with teachers who had little or no first-hand knowledge of them. The result in England was the establishment of a substantial body of economic thought known as the Classical School to which even such twentieth-century theorists as Joan Robinson and John Maynard Keynes in large measure continued to subscribe.

One of the central issues that has plagued thinkers since early times is the question of value. What determines the worth of a commodity in relation to the host of other commodities also on the market? Although the question had been of interest to philosophers such as Aristotle and Plato and to medieval church leaders such as St. Thomas Aquinas, the question assumed greater significance with the beginning of the industrial revolution and the development of a market economy. Despite John Stuart Mill's confident assurance (see p. 163) that by his time all that needed to be said on the subject had already been written, the problem has continued to trouble economists down to the present day.

Given this preoccupation by economists with the topic of value, it is not surprising that a substantial part of the following selections deal with the question. For many of the economists you are about to study, the question was of importance not only in and of itself, but as a tool for answering other questions. For Adam Smith it was a means by which to study the wealth of a nation; for Ricardo it was a device for analyzing distribution; for Malthus, Mill, and Marshall both goals were sought; while for Marx the theory of value became the key by which he explained surplus value and the exploitation of labor. Even Jevons, who wished to emphasize the difference between his explanation of value and that of those who had gone before, saw a practical application of his theory of value as a guide to how much and why people worked. The question of value will acquire a greater importance to the reader if he looks for the applications in the passages which follow.

Value is not the only subject to have intrigued English economists for the past two hundred years. As England began to industrialize and grow, its population, which had remained virtually stationary for several centuries, suddenly began to expand. The views of the Reverend Thomas Robert Malthus on population not only helped to shape the treatment by him and others of the subject of value, but provoked a controversy over population policy that continues to this day.

Two major changes came to English economic theory during the first third of the twentieth century. The first of these involved a consideration of The Economics of Imperfect Competition by Joan Robinson. This book was a product of the growing recognition by economists that the perfect market formulated by their predecessors no longer provided (if it ever had) a reasonable model for the real world.

The other change in economic theory, which was even more dramatic, was prompted by the faltering of the economic system and the existence of unemployment and depression. Not only did they exist, but they showed no inclination to go away. The early warnings by Malthus that an economy might not always generate sufficient demand to assure full employment had been brushed away by David Ricardo and his followers. In the twentieth century fresh doubts were raised with the publication of Keynes' General Theory of Employment, Interest and Money.

Although both Robinson and Keynes were dissenters from certain aspects of the Classical and Neo-Classical tradition, it is important to note that in many respects they remained loyal to the school. Joan Robinson in her preface noted that her book on imperfect competition was built on a foundation laid down by Alfred Marshall. Keynes took little exception to the bulk of Classical value theory and in many respects remained an integral part of the Classical tradition.

Enough then by way of introduction; it is time to let the distinguished economists we have selected speak for themselves as they have been doing so ably for more than one hundred years.

A Note on the Text

Instructors will inevitably disagree when asked to choose the most important selections to be included in any book that does not reproduce in toto the books from which the selections were drawn. Given the limitations of space and reprint rights, however, we have tried to include sufficiently large excerpts to give the student an appreciation of the writer's style and his main ideas. We have avoided, as much as possible, deleting passages within the selections, except where references were made to other parts of the original work not included in this volume. We have exercised greater freedom in the cutting of footnotes although the most important ones have been retained.

A Note on the Text

THE
HISTORY OF
ECONOMIC
THOUGHT
A Book of Readings

ADAM SMITH

(1 7 2 5 – 1 7 9 0)

Adam Smith began his university training at Glasgow at the age of fourteen. Three years later he went to Oxford where he remained for a number of years. Later he returned to Glasgow as professor of logic and still later as professor of moral philosophy, appointments brought about by his book The Theory of Moral Sentiments. Following a tour in Europe where he served as tutor for Lord Townshend's son, Smith returned to Scotland and began concentrated work on his magnum opus—a task which took ten years to complete, but proved to be worth all of the effort expended.

Although Adam Smith has frequently been called the "father of political economy" and provides us with our first set of readings, it would be a mistake to assume that the study of economics began with him. As noted in the introduction, one can find consideration of economic questions in the writings of Plato and Aristotle as well as among the early Catholic thinkers such as St. Thomas Aquinas. Smith's own views were influenced to some extent by the doctrines of the Mercantilists and to a lesser (and to some degree unknown) extent by the ideas of the French Physiocrats.

The latter group preached the doctrine of laissez-faire and emphasized the need for the individual to pursue his own self-interest without government interference. While this doctrine appealed to Smith, he rejected the Physiocratic belief that all wealth emanated from agriculture. Nevertheless, the careful reader can find a certain fondness for agriculture in Smith's writing. With this one major qualification as to the true source of a nation's wealth, Smith found much to admire in Physiocratic economics.

The Mercantilists were an inspiration to Smith in a quite different fashion—Smith found little to praise in the Mercantilists' economics, and much with which he was in sharp disagreement. The Mercantilists in England and elsewhere had espoused a strong case for government intervention in economic affairs both on the domestic scene and in

international trade. All adherents of Mercantilist thinking saw the
gains from international trade as a kind of "dog eat dog" relationship
with one country gaining in wealth only at the expense of the others.
A nation's wealth was to be measured in terms of its stockpile of gold,
and to protect and augment that stockpile it was necessary for a nation
to impose trade restrictions on its imports from other nations while
at the same time subsidizing its own exports.

Smith's Inquiry into the Nature and Cause of the Wealth of Nations rejected the Mercantilist prescription. Trade restrictions, Smith
said, fostered the development of uneconomic production and limited the scope of the market. The latter failure was a fatal one in
its consequences since without a broad market the opportunity to
engage in further subdivision of labor was destroyed. As the opening chapters of the following selection make evident, Smith felt that
the true path to increasing a nation's wealth lay in the opportunity to
continue constantly the division of labor. Equally repugnant to Smith
were any internal interferences. The economic system could best function if it were left to its own devices, with businessmen forced to
compete with each other for the consumers' favor. The possibility that
monopoly might arise even in the absence of governmental efforts to
foster it was alien to Smith's thinking.

Although the attack on Mercantilism won Smith's book much of its
immediate attention and has served as a partial basis for its enduring
fame, The Wealth of Nations is far more than just an attack on Mercantilism. It is a big book embracing a wide variety of subjects, ranging
from the question of value to the problems of capital accumulation,
distribution, and determination of wages, profits, and rents. The role
each of those played was then related to the question of value.

Smith subdivided his book into five separate books: Book I dealt
with the sources of the wealth of nations; Book II with the process
of accumulation; Book III with varying degrees of opulence in various
countries; Book IV with Mercantilism; and Book V with taxes and the
role of government. Our selections are drawn from the first and fourth
books.

Book II which is not included here is of interest among other things
for the distinction Smith drew between productive and unproductive
labor. Only labor that produced tangible material goods could be considered productive, Smith said, thereby excluding all of the services
and professions. It is in Book III that one discovers Smith's fondness
for agriculture along with his firm rejection of the Physiocratic notion
that all wealth and progress stem from that sector of the economy.

Book V contained Smith's famous four canons of taxation. A good
tax, Smith argued, should have the following attributes. It should be
based on principles of equality of burden, should be certain in its

burden, convenient to pay, and economical to collect. Although Smith, true to his opposition to government intervention in the affairs of the economy, believed that taxes should be kept to a minimum, his principle of equality (what would today be termed equity) in taxation set the stage for justification for the progressive income tax.

Smith remained generally faithful to his philosophy that only a minimum amount of government intervention was desirable, and he even toyed with the idea that education would be improved if more effort were made in the direction of private education, even at the lower grades. On the other hand, government was not without its proper duties, including the provision of internal improvements in order to foster trade and increase the possibilities for the further division of labor.

Although Smith did not provide a strong theoretical model of how the economy functioned, he was the first economist to bring the wide range of economic issues together in an orderly and well-organized fashion. Many of his observations and ideas served as models for economists who were to follow him for the next hundred years. If Smith has sometimes been misused by those who quote his doctrine as a defense against all forms of government intervention, he himself was too keen an observer of the world around him to fall into any such trap. Any writer is to some degree limited by the times in which he lives, and Smith's example of a pin factory shows the rudimentary stage of industrial development at the time he was writing. A study of current economic journals will reveal, however, that Smith provided later scholars with a rich feast upon which to chew—a meal which is by no means completely tasteless, even by modern standards.

AN INQUIRY INTO THE NATURE AND CAUSES OF THE WEALTH OF NATIONS

BOOK I / Of the Causes of Improvement in the production Powers of Labour, and of the Order according to which its Produce is naturally distributed among the different Ranks of the People

Chapter 1: OF THE DIVISION OF LABOUR

The greatest improvement in the productive powers of labour, and the greater part of the skill, dexterity, and judgment with which it is any where directed, or applied, seem to have been the effects of the division of labour.

The effects of the division of labour, in the general business of society, will be more easily understood, by considering in what manner it operates in some particular manufactures. It is commonly supposed to be carried furthest in some very trifling ones: not perhaps that it really is carried further in them than in others of more importance: but in those trifling manufactures which are destined to supply the small wants of but a small number of people, the whole number of workmen must necessarily be small; and those employed in every different branch of the work can often be collected into the same workhouse, and placed at once under the view of the spectator. In those great manufactures, on the contrary, which are destined to supply the great wants of the great body of the people, every different branch of the work employs so great a number of workmen, that it is impossible to collect them all into the same workhouse. We can seldom see more, at one time, than those employed in one single branch. Though in such manufactures, therefore, the work may really be divided into a much greater number of parts, than in those of a more trifling nature, the division is not near so obvious, and has accordingly been much less observed.

To take an example, therefore, from a very trifling manufacture; but one in which the division of labour has been very often taken notice of, the trade of the pin-maker; a workman not educated to this business (which the division of labour has rendered a distinct trade), nor acquainted with the use of the machinery employed in it (to the invention of which the same division of labour has probably given occasion), could scarce, perhaps, with his utmost industry, make one pin in a day, and certainly could not make twenty. But in the way in which this business is now carried on, not only the whole work is a peculiar trade, but it is divided into a number of branches, of which the greater part are likewise peculiar trades. One man draws out the wire, another straights it, a third cuts it, a fourth points it, a fifth grinds it at the top for receiving the head; to make the head requires two or three distinct operations; to put it on, is a peculiar business, to whiten the pins is another; it is even a trade by itself to put them into the paper; and the important business of making a pin is, in this manner, divided into about eighteen distinct operations, which, in some manufactories, are all performed by distinct hands, though in others the same man will sometimes perform two or three of them. I have seen a small manufactory of this kind where ten men only were employed, and where some of them consequently performed two or three distinct operations. But though they were very poor, and therefore but indifferently accommodated with the necessary machinery, they could, when they exerted themselves, make among them about twelve pounds of pins in a day. There are in a pound upwards of four thousand pins of a middling size. Those ten persons, therefore, could make among them upwards of forty-eight thousand pins in a day. Each person, therefore, making a tenth part of forty-eight thousand pins, might be considered as making four thousand eight hundred pins in a day. But if they had all wrought separately and independently, and without any of them having been educated to this peculiar business, they certainly could not each of them have made twenty, perhaps not one pin in a day; that is, certainly, not the two hundred and fortieth, perhaps not the four thousand eight hundredth part of what they are at present capable of performing, in consequence of a proper division and combination of their different operations.

In every other art and manufacture, the effects of the division of labour are similar to what they are in this very trifling one; though, in many of them, the labour can neither be so much subdivided, nor reduced to so great a simplicity of operation. The division of labour, however, so far as it can be introduced, occasions, in every art, a proportionable increase of the productive powers of labour. The separation of different trades and employments from one another, seems to have taken place, in consequence of this advantage. This separation too is generally carried furthest in those countries which enjoy the highest degree of industry and improvement; what is the work of one man in a rude state of society, being generally that of several in an improved one. In every improved society, the farmer is generally nothing but a farmer; the manufacturer, nothing but a manufacturer. The labour too which is necessary to produce any one complete manufacture, is almost always divided among a great number of hands. How many different trades are employed in each branch of the linen and woollen manufactures, from the growers of the flax and the wool, to the bleachers and smoothers of the linen, or to the dyers and dressers of the cloth! The nature of agriculture, indeed, does not admit of so many subdivisions of labour, nor of so complete a separation of one business from another, as manufactures. It is impossible to separate so entirely, the business of the grazier from that of the corn-farmer, as the trade of the carpenter is commonly separated from that of the smith. The spinner is almost always a distinct person from the weaver; but the ploughman, the harrower, the sower of the seed, and the reaper of the corn, are often the same. The occasions for those different sorts of labour returning with the different seasons of the year, it is impossible that one man should be constantly employed in any one of them. This impossibility of making so complete and entire a separation of all the different branches of labour employed in agriculture, is perhaps the reason why the improvement of the productive powers of labour in this art, does not always keep pace with their improvement in manufactures. The most opulent nations, indeed, generally excel all their neighbours in agriculture as well as in manufactures; but they are commonly more distinguished by their superiority in the latter than in the former. Their lands are in general better cultivated, and having more labour and expence bestowed upon them, produce more in proportion to the extent and natural fertility of the ground. But this superiority of produce is seldom much more than in proportion to the superiority of labour and expence. In agriculture, the labour of the rich country is not always much more productive than that of the poor; or, at least, it is never so much more productive, as it commonly is in manufactures. The corn of the rich country, therefore, will not always, in the same degree of goodness, come cheaper to market than that of the poor. The corn of Poland, in the same degree of goodness, is as cheap as that of France, notwithstanding the superior opulence and improvement of the latter country. The corn of France is, in the corn provinces, fully as good, and in most years nearly about the same price with the corn of England, though, in opulence and improvement, France is perhaps inferior to England. The corn-lands of England, however, are better cultivated than those of France, and the corn-lands of France are said to be much better cultivated than those of Poland. But though the poor country, notwithstanding the inferiority of its cultivation, can, in some measure, rival the rich in the cheapness and goodness of its corn, it can pretend to no such competition in its manufactures; at least if those manufactures suit the soil, climate, and situation of the rich country. The silks of France are better and cheaper than those of England, because the silk manufacture, at least under the present high duties upon the importation of raw silk, does not so well suit the climate of England as that of France. But the hard-ware and the coarse woollens of England are beyond all comparison superior to those of France, and much cheaper too in the same degree of goodness. In Poland there are said to be scarce any manufactures of any kind, a few of those coarser household manufactures excepted, without which no country can well subsist.

This great increase of the quantity of work, which, in consequence of the division of labour, the same number of people are capable of performing, is owing to three different circumstances; first, to the increase of dexterity in every particular workman; secondly, to the saving of the time which is commonly lost in passing from one species of work to another; and lastly, to the invention of a great number of machines which facilitate and abridge labour, and enable one man to do the work of many.

First, the improvement of the dexterity of the workman necessarily increases the quantity of the work he can perform; and the division of labour, by reducing every man's business to some one simple operation, and by making this operation the sole employment of his life, necessarily increases very much the dexterity of the workman. A common smith, who, though accustomed to handle the hammer, has never been used to make nails, if upon some particular occasion he is obliged to attempt it, will scarce, I am assured, be able to make above two or three hundred nails in a day, and those too very bad ones. A smith who has been accustomed to make nails, but whose sole or principal business has not been that of a nailer, can seldom with his utmost diligence make more than eight hundred or a thousand nails in a day. I have seen several boys under twenty years of age who had never exercised any other trade but that of making nails, and who, when they exerted themselves, could make, each of them, upwards of two thousand three hundred nails in a day. The making of a nail, however, is by no means one of the simplest operations. The same person blows the bellows, stirs or mends the fire as there is occasion, heats the iron, and forges every part of the nail: In forging the head too he is obliged to change his tools. The different operations into which the making of a pin, or of a metal button, is subdivided, are all of them much more simple, and the dexterity of the person, of whose life it has been the sole business to perform them, is usually much greater. The rapidity with which some of the operations of those manufactures are performed, exceeds what the human hand could, by those who had never seen them, be supposed capable of acquiring.

Secondly, the advantage which is gained by saving the time commonly lost in passing from one sort of work to another, is much greater than we should at first view be apt to imagine it. It is impossible to pass very quickly from one kind of work to another, that is carried on in a different place, and with quite different tools. A country weaver, who cultivates a small farm, must lose a good deal of time in passing from his loom to the field, and from the field to his loom. When the two trades can be carried on in the same workhouse, the loss of time is no doubt much less. It is even in this case, however, very considerable. A man commonly saunters a little in turning his hand from one sort of employment to another. When he first begins the new work he is seldom very keen and hearty; his mind, as they say, does not go to it, and for some time he rather trifles than applies to good purpose. The habit of sauntering and of indolent careless application, which is naturally, or rather necessarily acquired by every country workman who is obliged to change his work and his tools every half hour, and to apply his hand in twenty different ways almost every day of his life; renders him almost always slothful and lazy, and incapable of any vigorous application even on the most pressing occasions. Independent, therefore, of his deficiency in point of dexterity, this cause alone must always reduce considerably the quantity of work which he is capable of performing.

Thirdly, and lastly, every body must be sensible how much labour is facilitated and abridged by the application of proper machinery. It is unnecessary to give any example. I shall only observe, therefore, that the invention of all those machines by which labour is so much facilitated and abridged, seems to have been originally owing to the division of labour. Men are much more likely to discover easier and readier methods of attaining any object, when the whole attention of their minds is directed towards that single object, than when it is dissipated among a great variety of things. But in consequence of the division of labour, the whole of every man's attention comes naturally to be directed towards some one very simple object. It is naturally to be expected, therefore, that some one or other of those who are employed in each particular branch of labour should soon find out easier and readier methods of performing their own particular work, wherever the nature of it admits of such improvement. A greater part of the machines made use of in those manufactures in which labour is most subdivided, were originally the inventions of common workmen, who, being each of them employed in some very simple operation, naturally turned their thoughts towards finding out easier and readier methods of performing it. Whoever has been much accustomed to visit such manufactures, must frequently have been shewn very pretty machines, which were the inventions of such workmen, in order to facilitate and quicken their own particular part of the work. In the first fire-engines, a boy was constantly employed to open and shut alternately the communication between the boiler and the cylinder, according as the piston either ascended or descended. One of those boys, who loved to play with his companions, observed that, by tying a string from the handle of the valve which opened this communication to another part of the machine, the valve would open and shut without his assistance, and leave him at liberty to divert himself with his play-fellows. One of the greatest improvements that has been made upon this machine, since it was first invented, was in this manner the discovery of a boy who wanted to save his own labour.

All the improvements in machinery, however, have by no means been the inventions of those who had occasion to use the machines. Many improvements have been made by the ingenuity of the makers of the machines, when to make them became the business of a peculiar trade; and some by that of those who are called philosophers or men of speculation, whose trade it is not to do any thing, but to observe every thing; and who, upon that account, are often capable of combining together the powers of the most distant and dissimilar objects. In the progress of society, philosophy or speculation becomes, like every other employment, the principal or sole trade and occupation of a particular class of citizens. Like every other employment too, it is subdivided into a great number of different branches, each of which affords occupation to a peculiar tribe or class of philosophers; and this subdivision of employment in philosophy, as well as in every other business, improves dexterity, and saves time. Each individual becomes more expert in his own peculiar branch, more·work is done upon the whole, and the quantity of science is considerably increased by it.

It is the great multiplication of the productions of all the different arts, in consequence of the division of labour, which occasions, in a well-governed society, that universal opulence which extends itself to the lowest ranks of the people. Every workman has a great quantity of his own work to dispose of beyond what he himself has occasion for; and every other workman being exactly in the same situation, he is enabled to exchange a great quantity of his own goods for a great quantity, or, what comes to the same thing, for the price of a great quantity of theirs. He supplies them abundantly with what they have occasion for, and they accommodate him as amply with what he has occasion for, and a general plenty diffuses itself through all the different ranks of the society.

Observe the accommodation of the most common artificer or day-labourer in a civilized and thriving country, and you will perceive that the number of people of whose industry a part, though but a small part, has been employed in procuring him this accommodation, exceeds all computation. The woollen coat, for example, which covers the day-labourer, as coarse and rough as it may appear, is the produce of the joint labour of a great multitude of workmen. The shepherd, the sorter of the wool, the wool-comber or carder, the dyer, the scribbler, the spinner, the weaver, the fuller, the dresser, with many others, must all join their different arts in order to complete even this homely production. How many merchants and carriers, besides, must have been employed in transporting the materials from some of those workmen to others who often live in a very distant part of the country! how much commerce and navigation in particular, how many ship-builders, sailors, sail-makers, rope-makers, must have been employed in order to bring together the different drugs made use of by the dyer, which often come from the remotest corners of the world! What a variety of labour too is necessary in order to produce the tools of the meanest of those workmen! To say nothing of such complicated machines as the ship of the sailor, the mill of the fuller, or even the loom of the weaver, let us consider only what a variety of labour is requisite in order to form that very simple machine, the shears with which the shepherd clips the wool. The miner, the builder of the furnace for smelting the ore, the feller of the timber, the burner of the charcoal to be made use of in the smelting-house, the brick-maker, the brick-layer, the workmen who attend the furnace, the mill-wright, the forger, the smith, must all of them join their different arts in order to produce them. Were we to examine, in the same manner, all the different parts of his dress and household furniture, the coarse linen shirt which he wears next his skin, the shoes which cover his feet, the bed which he lies on, and all the different parts which compose it, the kitchen-grate at which he prepares his victuals, the coals which he makes use of for that purpose, dug from the bowels of the earth, and brought to him perhaps by a long sea and a long land carriage, all the other utensils of his kitchen, all the furniture of his table, the knives and forks, the earthen or pewter plates upon which he serves up and divides his victuals, the different hands employed in preparing his bread and his beer, the glass window which lets in the heat and the light, and keeps out the wind and the rain, with all the knowledge and art requisite for preparing that beautiful and happy invention, without which these northern parts of the world could scarce have afforded a very comfortable habitation, together with the tools of all the different workmen employed in producing those different conveniencies; if we examine, I say, all these things, and consider what a variety of labour is employed about each of them, we shall be sensible that without the assistance and co-operation of many thousands, the very meanest person in a civilized country could not be provided, even according to, what we very falsely imagine, the easy and simple manner in which he is commonly accommodated. Compared, indeed, with the more extravagant luxury of the great, his accommodation must no doubt appear extremely simple and easy; and yet it may be true, perhaps, that the accommodation of an European prince does not always so much exceed that of an industrious and frugal peasant, as the accommodation of the latter exceeds that of many an African king, the absolute master of the lives and liberties of ten thousand naked savages.

Chapter 2: OF THE PRINCIPLE WHICH GIVES OCCASION TO
THE DIVISION OF LABOUR

This division of labour, from which so many advantages are derived, is not originally the effect of any human wisdom, which foresees and intends that general opulence to which it gives occasion. It is the necessary, though very slow and gradual, consequence of a certain propensity in human nature which has in view no such extensive utility; the propensity to truck, barter, and exchange one thing for another.

Whether this propensity be one of those original principles in human nature, of which no further account can be given; or whether, as seems more probable, it be the necessary consequence of the faculties of reason and speech, it belongs not to our present subject to enquire. It is common to all men, and to be found in no other race of animals, which seem to know neither this nor any other species of contracts. Two greyhounds, in running down the same hare, have sometimes the appearance of acting in some sort of concert. Each turns her towards his companion, or endeavours to intercept her when his companion turns her towards himself. This, however, is not the effect of any contract, but of the accidental concurrence of their passions in the same object at that particular time. Nobody ever saw a dog make a fair and deliberate exchange of one bone for another with another dog. Nobody ever saw one animal by its gestures and natural cries signify to another, this is mine, that yours; I am willing to give this for that. When an animal wants to obtain something either of a man or of another animal, it has no other means of persuasion but to gain the favour of those whose service it requires. A puppy fawns upon its dam, and a spaniel endeavours by a thousand attractions to engage the attention of its master who is at dinner, when it wants to be fed by him. Man sometimes uses the same arts with his brethren, and when he has no other means of engaging them to act according to his inclinations, endeavours by every servile and fawning attention to obtain their good will. He has not time, however, to do this upon every occasion. In civilized society he stands at all times in need of the co-operation and assistance of great multitudes, while his whole life is scarce sufficient to gain the friendship of a few persons. In almost every other race of animals each individual, when it is grown up to maturity, is entirely independent, and in its natural state has occasion for the assistance of no other living creature. But man has almost constant occasion for the help of his brethren, and it is in vain for him to expect it from their benevolence only. He will be more likely to prevail if he can interest their self-love in his favour, and shew them that it is for their own advantage to do for him what he requires of them. Whoever offers to another a bargain of any kind, proposes to do this. Give me that which I want, and you shall have this which you want, is the meaning of every such offer; and it is in this manner that we obtain from one another the far greater part of those good offices which we stand in need of. It is not from the benevolence of the butcher, the brewer, or the baker, that we expect our dinner, but from their regard to their own interest. We address ourselves, not to their humanity but to their self-love, and never talk to them of our own necessities but of their advantages. Nobody but a beggar chuses to depend chiefly upon the benevolence of his fellow-citizens. Even a beggar does not depend upon it entirely. The charity of well-disposed people, indeed, supplies him with the whole fund of his subsistence. But though this principle ultimately provides him with all the necessaries of life which he has occasion for, it neither does nor can provide him with them as he has occasion for them. The greater part of his occasional wants are supplied in the same manner as those of other people, by treaty, by barter, and by purchase. With the money which one man gives him he purchases food. The old cloaths which another bestows upon him he exchanges for other old cloaths which suit him better, or for lodging, or for food, or for money, with which he can buy either food, cloaths, or lodging, as he has occasion.

As it is by treaty, by barter, and by purchase, that we obtain from one another the greater part of those mutual good offices which we stand in need of, so it is this same trucking disposition which originally gives occasion to the division of labour. In a tribe of hunters or shepherds a particular person makes bows and arrows, for example, with more readiness and dexterity than any other. He frequently exchanges them for cattle or for venison with his companions; and he finds at last that he can in this manner get more cattle and venison, than if he himself went to the field to catch them. From a regard to his own interest, therefore, the making of bows and arrows grows to be his chief business, and he becomes a sort of armourer. Another excels in making the frames and covers of their little huts or moveable houses. He is accustomed to be of use in this way to his neighbours, who reward him in the same manner with cattle and with venison, till at last he finds it his interest to dedicate himself entirely to this employment, and to become a sort of house-carpenter. In the same manner a third becomes a smith or a brazier; a fourth a tanner or dresser of hides or skins, the principal part of the clothing of savages. And thus the certainty of being able to exchange all that surplus part of the produce of his own labour, which is over and above his own consumption, for such parts of the produce of other men's labour as he may have occasion for, encourages every man to apply himself to a particular occupation, and to cultivate and bring to perfection whatever talent or genius he may possess for that particular species of business.

The difference of natural talents in different men is, in reality, much less than we are aware of; and the very different genius which appears to distinguish men of different professions, when grown up to maturity, is not upon many occasions so much the cause, as the effect of the division of labour. The difference between the most dissimilar characters, between a philosopher and a common street porter, for example, seems to arise not so much from nature, as from habit, custom, and education. When they came into the world, and for the first six or eight years of their existence, they were, perhaps, very much alike, and neither their parents nor play-fellows could perceive any remarkable difference. About that age, or soon after, they come to be employed in very different occupations. The difference of talents comes then to be taken notice of, and widens by degrees, till at last the vanity of the philosopher is willing to acknowledge scarce any resemblance. But without the disposition to truck, barter, and exchange, every man must have procured to himself every necessary and conveniency of life which he wanted. All must have had the same duties to perform, and the same work to do, and there could have been no such difference of employment as could alone give occasion to any great difference of talents.

As it is this disposition which forms that difference of talents, so remarkable among men of different professions, so it is this same disposition which renders that difference useful. Many tribes of animals acknowledged to be all of the same species, derive from nature a much more remarkable distinction of genius, than what, antecedent to custom and education, appears to take place among men. By nature a philosopher is not in genius and disposition half so different from a street porter, as a mastiff is from a greyhound, or a greyhound from a spaniel, or this last from a shepherd's dog. Those different tribes of animals, however, though all of the same species, are of scarce any use to one another. The strength of the mastiff is not in the least supported either by the swiftness of the greyhound, or by the sagacity of the spaniel, or by the docility of the shepherd's dog. The effects of those different geniuses and talents, for want of the power or disposition to barter and exchange, cannot be brought into a common stock, and do not in the least contribute to the better accommodation and conveniency of the species. Each animal is still obliged to support and defend itself, separately and independently, and derives no sort of advantage from that variety of talents with which nature has distinguished its fellows. Among men, on the contrary, the most dissimilar geniuses are of use to one another; the different produces of their respective talents, by the general disposition to truck, barter, and exchange, being brought, as it were, into a common stock, where every man may purchase whatever part of the produce of other men's talents he has occasion for.

Chapter 3: THAT THE DIVISION OF LABOUR IS LIMITED BY THE
EXTENT OF THE MARKET

As it is the power of exchanging that gives occasion to the division of labour, so the extent of this division must always be limited by the extent of that power, or, in other words, by the extent of the market. When the market is very small, no person can have any encouragement to dedicate himself entirely to one employment, for want of the power to exchange all that surplus part of the produce of his own labour, which is over and above his own consumption, for such parts of the produce of other men's labour as he has occasion for.

There are some sorts of industry, even of the lowest kind, which can be carried on no where but in a great town. A porter, for example, can find employment and subsistence in no other place. A village is by much too narrow a sphere for him; even an ordinary market town is scarce large enough to afford him constant occupation. In the lone houses and very small villages which are scattered about in so desert a country as the Highlands of Scotland, every farmer must be butcher, baker and brewer for his own family. In such situations we can scarce expect to find even a smith, a carpenter, or a mason, within less than twenty miles of another of the same trade. The scattered families that live at eight or ten miles distance from the nearest of them, must learn to perform themselves a great number of little pieces of work, for which, in more populous countries, they would call in the assistance of those workmen. Country workmen are almost every where obliged to apply themselves to all the different branches of industry that have so much affinity to one another as to be employed about the same sort of materials. A country carpenter deals in every sort of work that is made of wood: a country smith in every sort of work that is made of iron. The former is not only a carpenter, but a joiner, a cabinet maker, and even a carver in wood, as well as a wheelwright, a ploughwright, a cart and waggon maker. The employments of the latter are still more various. It is impossible there should be such a trade as even that of a nailer in the remote and inland parts of the Highlands of Scotland. Such a workman at the rate of a thousand nails a day, and three hundred working days in the year, will make three hundred thousand nails in the year. But in such a situation it would be impossible to dispose of one thousand, that is, of one day's work in the year.

As by means of water-carriage a more extensive market is opened to every sort of industry than what land-carriage alone can afford it, so it is upon the sea-coast, and along the banks of navigable rivers, that industry of every kind naturally begins to subdivide and improve itself, and it is frequently not till a long time after that those improvements extend themselves to the inland parts of the country. A broad-wheeled waggon, attended by two men, and drawn by eight horses, in about six weeks time carries and brings back between London and Edinburgh near four ton weight of goods. In about the same time a ship navigated by six or eight men, and sailing between the ports of London and Leith, frequently carries and brings back two hundred ton weight of goods. Six or eight men, therefore, by the help of water-carriage, can carry and bring back in the same time the same quantity of goods between London and Edinburgh, as fifty broad-wheeled waggons, attended by a hundred men, and drawn by four hundred horses. Upon two hundred tons of goods, therefore, carried by the cheapest land-carriage from London to Edinburgh, there must be charged the mainte-nance of a hundred men for three weeks, and both the maintenance, and, what is nearly equal to the maintenance, the wear and tear of four hundred horses as well as of fifty great waggons. Whereas, upon the same quantity of goods carried by water, there is to be charged only the maintenance of six or eight men, and the wear and tear of a ship of two hundred tons burthen, together with the value of the superior risk, or the difference of the insur-ance between land and water-carriage. Were there no other communication between those two places, therefore, but by land-carriage, as no goods could be transported from the one to the other, except such whose price was very considerable in proportion to their weight, they could carry on but a small part of that commerce which at present subsists between them, and conse-quently could give but a small part of that encouragement which they at present mutually afford to each other's industry. There could be little or no commerce of any kind between the distant parts of the world. What goods could bear the expence of land-carriage between London and Cal-cutta? Or if there were any so precious as to be able to support this expence, with what safety could they be transported through the territories of so many barbarous nations? Those two cities, however, at present carry on a very considerable commerce with each other, and by mutually affording a market, give a good deal of encouragement to each other's industry.

. . .

Chapter 5: OF THE REAL AND NOMINAL PRICE OF COMMODITIES,
OR OF THEIR PRICE IN LABOUR, AND THEIR PRICE IN
MONEY

Every man is rich or poor according to the degree in which he can afford to enjoy the necessaries, conveniencies, and amusements of human life. But after the division of labour has once thoroughly taken place, it is but a very small part of these with which a man's own labour can supply him. The far greater part of them he must derive from the labour of other people, and he must be rich or poor according to the quantity of that labour which he can command, or which he can afford to purchase. The value of any commodity, therefore, to the person who possesses it, and who means not to use or consume it himself, but to exchange it for other commodities, is equal to the quantity of labour which it enables him to purchase or com-mand. Labour, therefore, is the real measure of the exchangeable value of all commodities.

The real price of every thing, what every thing really costs to the man who wants to acquire it, is the toil and trouble of acquiring it. What every thing is really worth to the man who has acquired it, and who wants to dispose of it or exchange it for something else, is the toil and trouble which it can save to himself, and which it can impose upon other people. What is bought with money or with goods is purchased by labour, as much as what we acquire by the toil of our own body. That money or those goods indeed save us this toil. They contain the value of a certain quantity of labour which we exchange for what is supposed at the time to contain the value of an equal quantity. Labour was the first price, the original purchase-money that was paid for all things. It was not by gold or by silver, but by labour, that all the wealth of the world was originally purchased; and its value, to those who possess it, and who want to exchange it for some new productions, is precisely equal to the quantity of labour which it can enable them to purchase or command.

Wealth, as Mr. Hobbes says, is power. But the person who either acquires, or succeeds to a great fortune, does not necessarily acquire or succeed to any political power, either civil or military. His fortune may, perhaps, afford him the means of acquiring both, but the mere possession of that fortune does not necessarily convey to him either. The power which that possession immediately and directly conveys to him, is the power of purchasing; a certain command over all the labour, or over all the produce of labour which is then in the market. His fortune is greater or less, precisely in proportion to the extent of this power; or to the quantity either of other men's labour, or, what is the same thing, of the produce of other men's labour, which it enables him to purchase or command. The exchangeable value of every thing must always be precisely equal to the extent of this power which it conveys to its owner.

But though labour be the real measure of the exchangeable value of all commodities, it is not that by which their value is commonly estimated. It is often difficult to ascertain the proportion between two different quantities of labour. The time spent in two different sorts of work will not always alone determine this proportion. The different degrees of hardship endured, and of ingenuity exercised, must likewise be taken into account. There may be more labour in an hour's hard work than in two hours easy business; or in an hour's application to a trade which it cost ten years labour to learn, than in a month's industry at an ordinary and obvious employment. But it is not easy to find any accurate measure either of hardship or ingenuity. In exchanging indeed the different productions of different sorts of labour for one another, some allowance is commonly made for both. It is adjusted, however, not by any accurate measure, but by the higgling and bargaining of the market, according to that sort of rough equality which, though not exact, is sufficient for carrying on the business of common life.

Every commodity besides, is more frequently exchanged for, and thereby compared with, other commodities than with labour. It is more natural therefore, to estimate its exchangeable value by the quantity of some other commodity than by that of the labour which it can purchase. The greater part of people too understand better what is meant by a quantity of a particular commodity, than by a quantity of labour. The one is a plain palpable object; the other an abstract notion, which, though it can be made sufficiently intelligible, is not altogether so natural and obvious.

But when barter ceases, and money has become the common instrument of commerce, every particular commodity is more frequently exchanged for money than for any other commodity. The butcher seldom carries his beef or his mutton to the baker, or the brewer, in order to exchange them for bread or for beer; but he carries them to the market, where he exchanges them for money, and afterwards exchanges that money for bread and for beer. The quantity of money which he gets for them regulates too the quantity of bread and beer which he can afterwards purchase. It is more natural and obvious to him, therefore, to estimate their value by the quantity of money, the commodity for which he immediately exchanges them, than by that of bread and beer, the commodities for which he can exchange them only by the intervention of another commodity; and rather to say that his butcher's meat is worth threepence or fourpence a pound, than that it is worth three or four pounds of bread, or three or four quarts of small beer. Hence it comes to pass, that the exchangeable value of every commodity is more frequently estimated by the quantity of money, than by the quantity either of labour or of any other commodity which can be had in exchange for it.

Gold and silver, however, like every other commodity, vary in their value, are sometimes cheaper and sometimes dearer, sometimes of easier and sometimes of more difficult purchase. The quantity of labour which any particular quantity of them can purchase or command, or the quantity of other goods which it will exchange for, depends always upon the fertility or barrenness of the mines which happen to be known about the time when such exchanges are made. The discovery of the abundant mines of America reduced, in the sixteenth century, the value of gold and silver in Europe to about a third of what it had been before. As it cost less labour to bring those metals from the mine to the market, so when they were brought thither they could purchase or command less labour; and this revolution in their value, though perhaps the greatest, is by no means the only one of which history gives some account. But as a measure of quantity, such as the natural foot, fathom, or handful, which is continually varying in its own quantity, can never be an accurate measure of the quantity of other things; so a commodity which is itself continually varying in its own value, can never be an accurate measure of the value of other commodities. Equal quantities of labour, at all times and places, may be said to be of equal value to the labourer. In his ordinary state of health, strength and spirits; in the ordinary degree of his skill and dexterity, he must always lay down the same portion of his ease, his liberty, and his happiness. The price which he pays must always be the same, whatever may be the quantity of goods which he receives in return for it. Of these, indeed, it may sometimes purchase a greater and sometimes a smaller quantity; but it is their value which varies, not that of the labour which purchases them. At all times and places that is dear which it is difficult to come at, or which it costs much labour to acquire; and that cheap which is to be had easily, or with very little labour. Labour alone, therefore, never varying in its own value, is alone the ultimate and real standard by which the value of all commodities can at all times and places be estimated and compared. It is their real price; money is their nominal price only.

But though equal quantities of labour are always of equal value to the labourer, yet to the person who employs him they appear sometimes to be of greater and sometimes of smaller value. He purchases them sometimes with a greater and sometimes with a smaller quantity of goods, and to him the price of labour seems to vary like that of all other things. It appears to him dear in the one case, and cheap in the other. In reality, however, it is the goods which are cheap in the one case, and dear in the other.

In this popular sense, therefore, labour, like commodities, may be said to have a real and a nominal price. Its real price may be said to consist in the quantity of the necessaries and conveniencies of life which are given for it; its nominal price, in the quantity of money. The labourer is rich or poor, is well or ill rewarded, in proportion to the real, not to the nominal price of his labour.

The distinction between the real and the nominal price of commodities and labour, is not a matter of mere speculation, but may sometimes be of considerable use in practice. The same real price is always of the same value; but on account of the variations in the value of gold and silver, the same nominal price is sometimes of very different values. When a landed estate, therefore, is sold with a reservation of a perpetual rent, if it is intended that this rent should always be of the same value, it is of importance to the family in whose favour it is reserved, that it should not consist in a particular sum of money. Its value would in this case be liable to variations of two different kinds; first, to those which arise from the different quantities of gold and silver which are contained at different times in coin of the same denomination; and, secondly, to those which arise from the different values of equal quantities of gold and silver at different times.

Princes and sovereign states have frequently fancied that they had a temporary interest to diminish the quantity of pure metal contained in their coins; but they seldom have fancied that they had any to augment it. The quantity of metal contained in the coins, I believe of all nations, has, accordingly, been almost continually diminishing, and hardly ever augment-ing. Such variations therefore tend almost always to diminish the value of a money rent.

. . .

Equal quantities of labour will at distant times be purchased more nearly with equal quantities of corn, the subsistence of the labourer, than with equal quantities of gold and silver, or perhaps of any other commodity. Equal quantities of corn, therefore, will, at distant times, be more nearly of the same real value, or enable the possessor to purchase or command more nearly the same quantity of the labour of other people. They will do this, I say, more nearly than equal quantities of almost any other com-modity; for even equal quantities of corn will not do it exactly. The subsistence of the labourer, or the real price of labour, as I shall endeavour to show hereafter, is very different upon different occasions; more liberal in a society advancing to opulence, than in one that is standing still; and in one that is standing still, than in one that is going backwards. Every other commodity, however, will at any particular time purchase a greater or smaller quantity of labour in proportion to the quantity of subsistence which it can purchase at that time. A rent therefore reserved in corn is liable only to the variations in the quantity of labour which a certain quan-tity of corn can purchase. But a rent reserved in any other commodity is liable, not only to the variations in the quantity of labour which any par-ticular quantity of corn can purchase, but to the variations in the quantity of corn which can be purchased by any particular quantity of that commodity.

Though the real value of a corn rent, it is to be observed however, varies much less from century to century than that of a money rent, it varies much more from year to year. The money price of labour, as I shall en-deavour to show hereafter, does not fluctuate from year to year with the money price of corn, but seems to be every where accommodated, not to the temporary or occasional, but to the average or ordinary price of that necessary of life. The average or ordinary price of corn again is regulated, as I shall likewise endeavour to show hereafter, by the value of silver, by the richness or barrenness of the mines which supply the market with that metal, or by the quantity of labour which must be employed, and consequently of corn which must be consumed, in order to bring any particular quantity of silver from the mine to the market. But the value of silver, though it sometimes varies greatly from century to century, seldom varies much from year to year, but frequently continues the same, or very nearly the same, for half a century or a century together. The ordinary or average money price of corn, therefore, may, during so long a period, con-tinue the same or very nearly the same too, and along with it the money price of labour, provided, at least, the society continues, in other respects, in the same or nearly in the same condition. In the mean time the temporary and occasional price of corn may frequently be double, one year, of what it had been the year before, or fluctuate, for example, from five and twenty to fifty shillings the quarter. But when corn is at the latter price, not only the nominal, but the real value of a corn rent will be double of what it is when at the former, or will command double the quantity either of labour or of the greater part of other commodities; the money price of labour, and along with it that of most other things, continuing the same during all these fluctuations.

Labour, therefore, it appears evidently, is the only universal, as well as the only accurate measure of value, or the only standard by which we can compare the values of different commodities at all times and at all places. We cannot estimate, it is allowed, the real value of different commodities from century to century by the quantities of silver which were given for them. We cannot estimate it from year to year by the quantities of corn. By the quantities of labour we can, with the greatest accuracy, estimate it both from century to century and from year to year. From century to century, corn is a better measure than silver, because from century to century, equal quantities of corn will command the same quantity of labour more nearly than equal quantities of silver. From year to year, on the contrary, silver is a better measure than corn, because equal quantities of it will more nearly command the same quantity of labour.

But though in establishing perpetual rents, or even in letting very long leases, it may be of use to distinguish between real and nominal price; it is of none in buying and selling, the more common and ordinary transactions of human life.

At the same time and place the real and the nominal price of all commodities are exactly in proportion to one another. The more or less money you get for any commodity, in the London market, for example, the more or less labour it will at that time and place enable you to purchase or command. At the same time and place, therefore, money is the exact measure of the real exchangeable value of all commodities. It is so, however, at the same time and place only.

Though at distant places, there is no regular proportion between the real and the money price of commodities, yet the merchant who carries goods from the one to the other has nothing to consider but their money price, or the difference between the quantity of silver for which he buys them, and that for which he is likely to sell them. Half an ounce of silver at Canton in China may command a greater quantity both of labour and of the necessaries and conveniencies of life, than an ounce at London. A commodity, therefore, which sells for half an ounce of silver at Canton may there be really dearer, of more real importance to the man who possesses it there, than a commodity which sells for an ounce at London is to the man who possesses it at London. If a London merchant, however, can buy at Canton for half an ounce of silver, a commodity which he can afterwards sell at London for an ounce, he gains a hundred per cent. by the bargain, just as much as if an ounce of silver was at London exactly of the same value as at Canton. It is of no importance to him that half an ounce of silver at Canton would have given him the command of more labour and of a greater quantity of the necessaries and conveniencies of life than an ounce can do at London. An ounce at London will always give him the command of double the quantity of all these, which half an ounce could have done there, and this is precisely what he wants.

As it is the nominal or money price of goods, therefore, which finally determines the prudence or imprudence of all purchases and sales, and thereby regulates almost the whole business of common life in which price is concerned, we cannot wonder that it should have been so much more attended to than the real price.

In such a work as this, however, it may sometimes be of use to compare the different real values of a particular commodity at different times and places, or the different degrees of power over the labour of other people which it may, upon different occasions, have given to those who possessed it. We must in this case compare, not so much the different quantities of silver for which it was commonly sold, as the different quantities of labour which those different quantities of silver could have purchased. But the current prices of labour at distant times and places can scarce ever be known with any degree of exactness. Those of corn, though they have in few places been regularly recorded, are in general better known and have been more frequently taken notice of by historians and other writers. We must generally, therefore, content ourselves with them, not as being always exactly in the same proportion as the current prices of labour, but as being the nearest approximation which can commonly be had to that proportion. I shall hereafter have occasion to make several comparisons of this kind.

In the progress of industry, commercial nations have found it convenient to coin several different metals into money; gold for larger payments, silver for purchases of moderate value, and copper, or some other coarse metal, for those of still smaller consideration. They have always, however, considered one of those metals as more peculiarly the measure of value than any of the other two; and this preference seems generally to have been given to the metal which they happened first to make use of as the instrument of commerce. Having once begun to use it as their standard, which they must have done when they had no other money, they have generally continued to do so even when the necessity was not the same.

· · ·

Chapter 6: OF THE COMPONENT PARTS OF THE PRICE OF
            COMMODITIES

In that early and rude state of society which precedes both the accumulation of stock and the appropriation of land, the proportion between the
quantities of labour necessary for acquiring different objects seems to be
the only circumstance which can afford any rule for exchanging them for
one another. If among a nation of hunters, for example, it usually costs
twice the labour to kill a beaver which it does to kill a deer, one beaver
should naturally exchange for or be worth two deer. It is natural that what
is usually the produce of two days or two hours labour, should be worth
double of what is usually the produce of one day's or one hour's labour.

If the one species of labour should be more severe than the other, some
allowance will naturally be made for this superior hardship; and the produce of one hour's labour in the one way may frequently exchange for that
of two hours labour in the other.

Or if the one species of labour requires an uncommon degree of dexterity
and ingenuity, the esteem which men have for such talents, will naturally
give a value to their produce, superior to what would be due to the time
employed about it. Such talents can seldom be acquired but in consequence
of long application, and the superior value of their produce may frequently
be no more than a reasonable compensation for the time and labour which
must be spent in acquiring them. In the advanced state of society, allow-
ances of this kind, for superior hardship and superior skill, are commonly
made in the wages of labour; and something of the same kind must probably have taken place in its earliest and rudest period.

In this state of things, the whole produce of labour belongs to the
labourer; and the quantity of labour commonly employed in acquiring
or producing any commodity, is the only circumstance which can regulate
the quantity of labour which it ought commonly to purchase, command,
or exchange for.

As soon as stock has accumulated in the hands of particular persons,
some of them will naturally employ it in setting to work industrious people,
whom they will supply with materials and subsistence, in order to make
a profit by the sale of their work, or by what their labour adds to the value
of the materials. In exchanging the complete manufacture either for
money, for labour, or for other goods, over and above what may be sufficient
to pay the price of the materials, and the wages of the workmen, something
must be given for the profits of the undertaker of the work who hazards his
stock in this adventure. The value which the workmen add to the materials,
therefore, resolves itself in this case into two parts, of which the one pays
their wages, the other the profits of their employer upon the whole stock
of materials and wages which he advanced. He could have no interest to

employ them, unless he expected from the sale of their work something more than what was sufficient to replace his stock to him; and he could have no interest to employ a great stock rather than a small one, unless his profits were to bear some proportion to the extent of his stock.

The profits of stock, it may perhaps be thought, are only a different name for the wages of a particular sort of labour, the labour of inspection and direction. They are, however, altogether different, are regulated by quite sufficient principles, and bear no proportion to the quantity, the hardship, or the ingenuity of this supposed labour of inspection and direction. They are regulated altogether by the value of the stock employed, and are greater or smaller in proportion to the extent of this stock. Let us suppose, for example, that in some particular place, where the common annual profits of manufacturing stock are ten per cent. there are two different manufactures, in each of which twenty workmen are employed at the rate of fifteen pounds a year each, or at the expence of three hundred a year in each manufactory. Let us suppose too, that the coarse materials annually wrought up in the one cost only seven hundred pounds, while the finer materials in the other cost seven thousand. The capital annually employed in the one will in this case amount only to one thousand pounds; whereas that employed in the other will amount to seven thousand three hundred pounds. At the rate of ten per cent. therefore, the undertaker of the one will expect a yearly profit of about one hundred pounds only; while that of the other will expect about seven hundred and thirty pounds. But though their profits are so very different, their labour of inspection and direction may be either altogether or very nearly the same. In many great works, almost the whole labour of this kind is committed to some principal clerk. His wages properly express the value of this labour of inspection and direction. Though in settling them some regard is had commonly, not only to his labour and skill, but to the trust which is reposed in him, yet they never bear any regular proportion to the capital of which he oversees the management; and the owner of this capital, though he is thus discharged of almost all labour, still expects that his profits should bear a regular proportion to his capital. In the price of commodities, therefore, the profits of stock constitute a component part altogether different from the wages of labour, and regulated by quite different principles.

In this state of things, the whole produce of labour does not always belong to the labourer. He must in most cases share it with the owner of the stock which employs him. Neither is the quantity of labour commonly employed in acquiring or producing any commodity, the only circumstance which can regulate the quantity which it ought commonly to purchase, command, or exchange for. An additional quantity, it is evident, must be due for the profits of the stock which advanced the wages and furnished the materials of that labour.

As soon as the land of any country has all become private property, the landlords, like all other men, love to reap where they never sowed, and demand a rent even for its natural produce. The wood of the forest, the grass of the field, and all the natural fruits of the earth, which, when land was in common, cost the labourer only the trouble of gathering them, come, even to him, to have an additional price fixed upon them. He must give up to the landlord a portion of what his labour either collects or produces. This portion, or, what comes to the same thing, the price of this portion, constitutes the rent of land, and in the price of the greater part of commodities makes a third component part.

The real value of all the different component parts of price, it must be observed, is measured by the quantity of labour which they can, each of them, purchase or command. Labour measures the value not only of that part of price which resolves itself into labour, but of that which resolves itself into rent, and of that which resolves itself into profit.

In every society the price of every commodity finally resolves itself into some one or other, or all of those three parts; and in every improved society, all the three enter more or less, as component parts, into the price of the far greater part of commodities.

In the price of corn, for example, one part pays the rent of the landlord, another pays the wages or maintenance of the labourers and labouring cattle employed in producing it, and the third pays the profit of the farmer. These three parts seem either immediately or ultimately to make up the whole price of corn. A fourth part, it may perhaps be thought, is necessary for replacing the stock of the farmer, or for compensating the wear and tear of his labouring cattle, and other instruments of husbandry. But it must be considered that the price of any instrument of husbandry, such as a labouring horse, is itself made up of the same three parts; the rent of the land upon which he is reared, the labour of tending and rearing him, and the profits of the farmer who advances both the rent of this land, and the wages of this labour. Though the price of the corn, therefore, may pay the price as well as the maintenance of the horse, the whole price still resolves itself either immediately or ultimately into the same three parts of rent, labour, and profit.

In the price of flour or meal, we must add to the price of the corn, the profits of the miller, and the wages of his servants; in the price of bread, the profits of the baker, and the wages of his servants; and in the price of both, the labour of transporting the corn from the house of the farmer to that of the miller, and from that of the miller to that of the baker, together with the profits of those who advance the wages of that labour.

The price of flax resolves itself into the same three parts as that of corn. In the price of linen we must add to this price the wages of the flax-dresser, of the spinner, of the weaver, of the bleacher, &c. together with the profits of their respective employers.

As any particular commodity comes to be more manufactured, that part of the price which resolves itself into wages and profit, comes to be greater in proportion to that which resolves itself into rent. In the progress of the manufacture, not only the number of profits increase, but every subsequent profit is greater than the foregoing; because the capital from which it is derived must always be greater. The capital which employs the weavers, for example, must be greater than that which employs the spinners; because it not only replaces that capital with its profits, but pays, besides, the wages of the weavers; and the profits must always bear some proportion to the capital.

In the most improved societies, however, there are always a few commodities of which the price resolves itself into two parts only, the wages of labour, and the profits of stock; and a still smaller number, in which it consists altogether in the wages of labour. In the price of sea-fish, for example, one part pays the labour of the fishermen, and the other the profits of the capital employed in the fishery. Rent very seldom makes any part of it, though it does sometimes, as I shall shew hereafter. It is otherwise, at least through the greater part of Europe, in river fisheries. A salmon fisher pays a rent, and rent, though it cannot well be called the rent of land, makes a part of the price of a salmon as well as wages and profit. In some parts of Scotland a few poor people make a trade of gathering, along the sea-shore, those little variegated stones commonly known by the name of Scotch Pebbles. The price which is paid to them by the stone-cutter is altogether the wages of their labour; neither rent nor profit make any part of it.

But the whole price of any commodity must still finally resolve itself into some one or other, or all of those three parts; as whatever part of it remains after paying the rent of the land, and the price of the whole labour employed in raising, manufacturing, and bringing it to market, must necessarily be profit to somebody.

As the price or exchangeable value of every particular commodity, taken separately, resolves itself into some one or other, or all of those three parts; so that of all the commodities which compose the whole annual produce of the labour of every country, taken complexly, must resolve itself into the same three parts, and be parcelled out among different inhabitants of the country, either as the wages of their labour, the profits of their stock, or the rent of their land. The whole of what is annually either collected or produced by the labour of every society, or what comes to the same thing, the whole price of it, is in this manner originally distributed among some of its different members. Wages, profit, and rent, are the three original sources of all revenue as well as of all exchangeable value. All other revenue is ultimately derived from some one or other of these.

Whoever derives his revenue from a fund which is his own, must draw it either from his labour, from his stock, or from his land. The revenue derived from labour is called wages. That derived from stock, by the person who manages or employs it, is called profit. That derived from it by the person who does not employ it himself, but lends it to another, is called the interest or the use of money. It is the compensation which the borrower pays to the lender, for the profit which he has an opportunity of making by the use of the money. Part of that profit naturally belongs to the borrower, who runs the risk and takes the trouble of employing it; and part to the lender, who affords him the opportunity of making this profit. The interest of money is always a derivative revenue, which, if it is not paid from the profit which is made by the use of the money, must be paid from some other source of revenue, unless perhaps the borrower is a spendthrift, who contracts a second debt in order to pay the interest of the first. The revenue which proceeds altogether from land, is called rent, and belongs to the land-lord. The revenue of the farmer is derived partly from his labour, and partly from his stock. To him, land is only the instrument which enables him to earn the wages of this labour, and to make the profits of this stock. All taxes, and all the revenue which is founded upon them, all salaries, pensions, and annuities of every kind, are ultimately derived from some one or other of those three original sources of revenue, and are paid either immediately or mediately from the wages of labour, the profits of stock, or the rent of land.

When those three different sorts of revenue belong to different persons, they are readily distinguished; but when they belong to the same they are sometimes confounded with one another, at least in common language.

A gentleman who farms a part of his own estate, after paying the expense of cultivation, should gain both the rent of the landlord and the profit of the farmer. He is apt to denominate, however, his whole gain, profit, and thus confounds rent with profit, at least in common language. The greater part of our North American and West Indian planters are in this situation. They farm, the greater part of them, their own estates, and accordingly we seldom hear of the rent of a plantation, but frequently of its profit.

Common farmers seldom employ any overseer to direct the general operations of the farm. They generally too work a good deal with their own hands, as ploughmen, harrowers, &c. What remains of the crop after paying the rent, therefore, should not only replace to them their stock employed in cultivation, together with its ordinary profits, but pay them the wages which are due to them, both as labourers and overseers. Whatever remains, however, after paying the rent and keeping up the stock, is called profit. But wages evidently make a part of it. The farmer, by saving these wages, must necessarily gain them. Wages, therefore, are in this case confounded with profit.

An independent manufacturer, who has stock enough both to purchase materials, and to maintain himself till he can carry his work to market, should gain both the wages of a journeyman who works under a master, and the profit which that master makes by the sale of the journeyman's work. His whole gains, however, are commonly called profit, and wages are, in this case too, confounded with profit.

A gardener who cultivates his own garden with his own hands, unites in his own person the three different characters, of landlord, farmer, and labourer. His produce, therefore, should pay him the rent of the first, the profit of the second, and the wages of the third. The whole, however, is commonly considered as the earnings of his labour. Both rent and profit are, in this case, confounded with wages.

As in a civilized country there are but few commodities of which the exchangeable value arises from labour only, rent and profit contributing largely to that of the far greater part of them, so the annual produce of its labour will always be sufficient to purchase or command a much greater quantity of labour than what was employed in raising, preparing, and bringing that produce to market. If the society were annually to employ all the labour which it can annually purchase, as the quantity of labour would increase greatly every year, so the produce of every succeeding year would be of vastly greater value than that of the foregoing. But there is no country in which the whole annual produce is employed in maintaining the industrious. The idle every where consume a great part of it; and according to the different proportions in which it is annually divided between those two different orders of people, its ordinary or average value must either annually increase, or diminish, or continue the same from one year to another.

Chapter 7: OF THE NATURAL AND MARKET PRICE OF
                    COMMODITIES

There is in every society or neighbourhood an ordinary or average rate both of wages and profit in every different employment of labour and stock. This rate is naturally regulated, as I shall show hereafter, partly by the general circumstances of the society, their riches or poverty, their advancing, stationary, or declining condition; and partly by the particular nature of each employment.

There is likewise in every society or neighbourhood an ordinary or average rate of rent, which is regulated too, as I shall show hereafter, partly by the general circumstances of the society or neighbourhood in which the land is situated, and partly by the natural or improved fertility of the land.

These ordinary or average rates may be called the natural rates of wages, profit, and rent, at the time and place in which they commonly prevail.

When the price of any commodity is neither more nor less than what is sufficient to pay the rent of the land, the wages of the labour, and the profits of the stock employed in raising, preparing, and bringing it to market, according to their natural rates, the commodity is then sold for what may be called its natural price.

The commodity is then sold precisely for what it is worth, or for what it really costs the person who brings it to market; for though in common language what is called the prime cost of any commodity does not comprehend the profit of the person who is to sell it again, yet if he sells it at a price which does not allow him the ordinary rate of profit in his neighbourhood, he is evidently a loser by the trade; since by employing his stock in some other way he might have made that profit. His profit, besides, is his revenue, the proper fund of his subsistence. As, while he is preparing and bringing the goods to market, he advances to his workmen their wages, or their subsistence; so he advances to himself, in the same manner, his own subsistence, which is generally suitable to the profit which he may reasonably expect from the sale of his goods. Unless they yield him this profit, therefore, they do not repay him what they may very properly be said to have really cost him.

Though the price, therefore, which leaves him this profit, is not always the lowest at which a dealer may sometimes sell his goods, it is the lowest at which he is likely to sell them for any considerable time; at least where there is perfect liberty, or where he may change his trade as often as he pleases.

The actual price at which any commodity is commonly sold is called its market price. It may either be above, or below, or exactly the same with its natural price.

The market price of every particular commodity is regulated by the proportion between the quantity which is actually brought to market, and the demand of those who are willing to pay the natural price of the commodity, or the whole value of the rent, labour, and profit, which must be paid in order to bring it thither. Such people may be called the effectual demanders, and their demand the effectual demand; since it may be sufficient to effectuate the bringing of the commodity to market. It is different from the absolute demand. A very poor man may be said in some sense to have a demand for a coach and six; he might like to have it; but his demand is not an effectual demand, as the commodity can never be brought to market in order to satisfy it.

When the quantity of any commodity which is brought to market falls short of the effectual demand, all those who are willing to pay the whole value of the rent, wages, and profit, which must be paid in order to bring it thither, cannot be supplied with the quantity which they want. Rather than want it altogether, some of them will be willing to give more. A competition will immediately begin among them, and the market price will rise more or less above the natural price, according as either the greatness of the deficiency, or the wealth and wanton luxury of the competitors, happen to animate more or less the eagerness of the competition. Among competitors of equal wealth and luxury the same deficiency will generally occasion a more or less eager competition, according as the acquisition of the commodity happens to be of more or less importance to them. Hence the exorbitant price of the necessaries of life during the blockade of a town or in a famine.

When the quantity brought to market exceeds the effectual demand, it cannot be all sold to those who are willing to pay the whole value of the rent, wages and profit, which must be paid in order to bring it thither. Some part must be sold to those who are willing to pay less, and the low price which they give for it must reduce the price of the whole. The market price will sink more or less below the natural price, according as the greatness of the excess increases more or less the competition of the sellers, or according as it happens to be more or less important to them to get immediately rid of the commodity. The same excess in the importation of perishables, will occasion a much greater competition than in that of durable commodities; in the importation of oranges, for example, than in that of old iron.

When the quantity brought to market is just sufficient to supply the effectual demand and no more, the market price naturally comes to be either exactly, or as nearly as can be judged of, the same with the natural price. The whole quantity upon hand can be disposed of for this price, and cannot be disposed of for more. The competition of the different dealers obliges them all to accept of this price, but does not oblige them to accept of less.

The quantity of every commodity brought to market naturally suits itself to the effectual demand. It is the interest of all those who employ their land, labour, or stock, in bringing any commodity to market, that the quantity never should exceed the effectual demand; and it is the interest of all other people that it never should fall short of that demand.

If at any time it exceeds the effectual demand, some of the component parts of its price must be paid below their natural rate. If it is rent, the interest of the landlords will immediately prompt them to withdraw a part of their land; and if it is wages or profit, the interest of the labourers in the one case, and of their employers in the other, will prompt them to withdraw a part of their labour or stock from this employment. The quantity brought to market will soon be no more than sufficient to supply the effectual demand. All the different parts of its price will rise to their natural rate, and the whole price to its natural price.

If, on the contrary, the quantity brought to market should at any time fall short of the effectual demand, some of the component parts of its price must rise above their natural rate. If it is rent, the interest of all other landlords will naturally prompt them to prepare more land for the raising of this commodity; if it is wages or profit, the interest of all other labourers and dealers will soon prompt them to employ more labour and stock in preparing and bringing it to market. The quantity brought thither will soon be sufficient to supply the effectual demand. All the different parts of its price will soon sink to their natural rate, and the whole price to its natural price.

The natural price, therefore, is, as it were, the central price, to which the prices of all commodities are continually gravitating. Different accidents may sometimes keep them suspended a good deal above it, and sometimes force them down even somewhat below it. But whatever may be the obstacles which hinder them from setting in this center of repose and continuance, they are constantly tending towards it.

. . .

Chapter 8: OF THE WAGES OF LABOUR

The produce of labour constitutes the natural recompence or wages of labour.

In that original state of things, which precedes both the appropriation of land and the accumulation of stock, the whole produce of labour belongs to the labourer. He has neither landlord nor master to share with him.

Had this state continued, the wages of labour would have augmented with all those improvements in its productive powers, to which the division of labour gives occasion. All things would gradually have become cheaper. They would have been produced by a smaller quantity of labour; and as the commodities produced by equal quantities of labour would naturally in this state of things be exchanged for one another, they would have been purchased likewise with the produce of a smaller quantity.

But though all things would have become cheaper in reality, in appearance many things might have become dearer than before, or have been exchanged for a greater quantity of other goods. Let us suppose, for example, that in the greater part of employments the productive powers of labour had been improved to tenfold, or that a day's labour could produce ten times the quantity of work which it had done originally; but that in a particular employment they had been improved only to double, or that a day's labour could produce only twice the quantity of work which it had done before. In exchanging the produce of a day's labour in the greater part of employments, for that of a day's labour in this particular one, ten times the original quantity of work in them would purchase only twice the original quantity in it. Any particular quantity in it, therefore, a pound weight, for example, would appear to be five times dearer than before. In reality, however, it would be twice as cheap. Though it required five times the quantity of other goods to purchase it, it would require only half the quantity of labour either to purchase or to produce it. The acquisition, therefore, would be twice as easy as before.

But this original state of things, in which the labourer enjoyed the whole produce of his own labour, could not last beyond the first introduction of the appropriation of land and the accumulation of stock. It was at an end, therefore, long before the most considerable improvements were made in the productive powers of labour, and it would be to no purpose to trace further what might have been its effects upon the recompence or wages of labour.

As soon as land becomes private property, the landlord demands a share of almost all the produce which the labourer can either raise, or collect from it. His rent makes the first deduction from the produce of the labour which is employed upon land.

It seldom happens that the person who tills the ground has wherewithal to maintain himself till he reaps the harvest. His maintenance is generally advanced to him from the stock of a master, the farmer who employs him, and who would have no interest to employ him, unless he was to share in the produce of his labour, or unless his stock was to be replaced to him with a profit. This profit makes a second deduction from the produce of the labour which is employed upon land.

The produce of almost all other labour is liable to the like deduction of profit. In all arts and manufactures the greater part of the workmen stand in need of a master to advance them the materials of their work, and their wages and maintenance till it be compleated. He shares in the produce of their labour, or in the value which it adds to the materials upon which it is bestowed; and in this share consists his profit.

It sometimes happens, indeed, that a single independent workman has stock sufficient both to purchase the materials of his work, and to maintain himself till it be compleated. He is both master and workman, and enjoys the whole produce of his own labour, or the whole value which it adds to the materials upon which it is bestowed. It includes what are usually two distinct revenues, belonging to two distinct persons, the profits of stock, and the wages of labour.

Such cases, however, are not very frequent, and in every part of Europe, twenty workmen serve under a master for one that is independent; and the wages of labour are every where understood to be, what they usually are, when the labourer is one person, and the owner of the stock which employs him another.

What are the common wages of labour, depends every where upon the contract usually made between those two parties, whose interests are by no means the same. The workmen desire to get as much, the masters to give as little as possible. The former are disposed to combine in order to raise, the latter in order to lower the wages of labour.

It is not, however, difficult to foresee which of the two parties must, upon all ordinary occasions, have the advantage in the dispute, and force the other into a compliance with their terms. The masters, being fewer in number, can combine much more easily; and the law, besides, authorises, or at least does not prohibit their combinations, while it prohibits those of the workmen. We have no acts of parliament against combining to lower the price of work; but many against combining to raise it. In all such disputes the masters can hold out much longer. A landlord, a farmer, a master manufacturer, or merchant, though they did not employ a single workman, could generally live a year or two upon the stocks which they have already acquired. Many workmen could not subsist a week, few could subsist a month, and scarce any a year without employment. In the long-run the workman may be as necessary to his master as his master is to him, but the necessity is not so immediate.

We rarely hear, it has been said, of the combinations of masters, though frequently of those of workmen. But whoever imagines, upon this account, that masters rarely combine, is as ignorant of the world as of the subject. Masters are always and every where in a sort of tacit, but constant and uniform combination, not to raise the wages of labour above their actual rate. To violate this combination is every where a most unpopular action, and a sort of reproach to a master among his neighbours and equals. We seldom, indeed, hear of this combination, because it is the usual, and one may say, the natural state of things which nobody ever hears of. Masters too sometimes enter into particular combinations to sink the wages of labour even below this rate. These are always conducted with the utmost silence and secrecy, till the moment of execution, and when the workmen yield, as they sometimes do, without resistance, though severely felt by them, they are never heard of by other people. Such combinations, however, are frequently resisted by a contrary defensive combination of the workmen; who sometimes too, without any provocation of this kind, combine of their own accord to raise the price of their labour. Their usual pretences are, sometimes the high price of provisions; sometimes the great profit which their masters make by their work. But whether their combinations be offensive or defensive, they are always abundantly heard of. In order to bring the point to a speedy decision, they have always recourse to the loudest clamour, and sometimes to the most shocking violence and outrage. They are desperate, and act with the folly and extravagance of desperate men, who must either starve, or frighten their masters into an immediate compliance with their demands. The masters upon these occasions are just as clamorous upon the other side, and never cease to call aloud for the assistance of the civil magistrate, and the rigorous execution of those laws which have been enacted with so much severity against the combinations of servants, labourers, and journeymen. The workmen, accordingly, very seldom derive any advantage from the violence of those tumultuous combinations, which, partly from the interposition of the civil magistrate, partly from the superior steadiness of the masters, partly from the necessity which the greater part of the workmen are under of submitting for the sake of present subsistence, generally end in nothing, but the punishment or ruin of the ring-leaders.

But though in disputes with their workmen, masters must generally have the advantage, there is however a certain rate below which it seems impossible to reduce, for any considerable time, the ordinary wages even of the lowest species of labour.

A man must always live by his work, and his wages must at least be sufficient to maintain him. They must even upon most occasions be somewhat more; otherwise it would be impossible for him to bring up a family, and the race of such workmen could not last beyond the first generation. Mr. Cantillon seems, upon this account, to suppose that the lowest species of common labourers must every where earn at least double their own maintenance, in order that one with another they may be enabled to bring up two children; the labour of the wife, on account of her necessary attendance on the children, being supposed no more than sufficient to provide for herself. But one-half the children born, it is computed, die before the age of manhood. The poorest labourers, therefore, according to this account, must, one with another, attempt to rear at least four children, in order that two may have an equal chance of living to that age. But the necessary maintenance of four children, it is supposed, may be nearly equal to that of one man. The labour of an able-bodied slave, the same author adds, is computed to be worth double his maintenance; and that of the meanest labourer, he thinks, cannot be worth less than that of an able-bodied slave. Thus far at least seems certain, that, in order to bring up a family, the labour of the husband and wife together must, even in the lowest species of common labour, be able to earn something more than what is precisely necessary for their own maintenance; but in what proportion, whether in that above mentioned, or in any other, I shall not take upon me to determine.

There are certain circumstances, however, which sometimes give the labourers an advantage, and enable them to raise their wages considerably above this rate; evidently the lowest which is consistent with common humanity.

When in any country the demand for those who live by wages; labourers, journeymen, servants of every kind, is continually increasing; when every year furnishes employment for a greater number than had been employed the year before, the workmen have no occasion to combine in order to raise their wages. The scarcity of hands occasions a competition among masters, who bid against one another, in order to get workmen, and thus voluntarily break through the natural combination of masters not to raise wages.

The demand for those who live by wages, it is evident, cannot increase but in proportion to the increase of the funds which are destined for the payment of wages. These funds are of two kinds; first, the revenue which is over and above what is necessary for the maintenance; and, secondly, the stock which is over and above what is necessary for the employment of their masters.

When the landlord, annuitant, or monied man, has a greater revenue than what he judges sufficient to maintain his own family, he employs either the whole or a part of the surplus in maintaining one or more menial servants. Increase this surplus, and he will naturally increase the number of those servants.

When an independent workman, such as a weaver or shoe-maker, has got more stock than what is sufficient to purchase the materials of his own work, and to maintain himself till he can dispose of it, he naturally employs one or more journeymen with the surplus, in order to make a profit by their work. Increase this surplus, and he will naturally increase the number of his journeymen.

The demand for those who live by wages, therefore, necessarily increases with the increase of the revenue and stock of every country, and cannot possibly increase without it. The increase of revenue and stock is the increase of national wealth. The demand for those who live by wages, therefore, naturally increases with the increase of national wealth, and cannot possibly increase without it.

It is not the actual greatness of national wealth, but its continual increase, which occasions a rise in the wages of labour. It is not, accordingly, in the richest countries, but in the most thriving, or in those which are growing rich the fastest, that the wages of labour are highest. England is certainly, in the present times, a much richer country than any part of North America. The wages of labour, however, are much higher in North America than in any part of England. In the province of New York, common labourers earn three shillings and sixpence currency, equal to two shillings sterling, a day; ship carpenters, ten shillings and sixpence currency, with a pint of rum worth sixpence sterling, equal in all to six shillings and sixpence sterling; house carpenters and bricklayers, eight shillings currency, equal to four shillings and sixpence sterling; journeymen taylors, five shillings currency, equal to about two shillings and ten pence sterling. These prices are all above the London price; and wages are said to be as high in the other colonies as in New York. The price of provisions is every where in North America much lower than in England. A dearth has never been known there. In the worst seasons, they have always had a sufficiency for themselves, though less for exportation. If the money price of labour, therefore, be higher than it is any where in the mother country, its real price, the real command of the necessaries and conveniencies of life which it conveys to the labourer, must be higher in a still greater proportion.

· · ·

Though the wealth of a country should be very great, yet if it has been long stationary, we must not expect to find the wages of labour very high in it. The funds destined for the payment of wages, the revenue and stock of its inhabitants, may be of the greatest extent; but if they have continued for several centuries of the same, or very nearly of the same extent, the number of labourers employed every year could easily supply, and even more than supply, the number wanted the following year. There could seldom be any scarcity of hands, nor could the masters be obliged to bid against one another in order to get them. The hands, on the contrary, would, in this case, naturally multiply beyond their employment. There would be a constant scarcity of employment, and the labourers would be obliged to bid against one another in order to get it. If in such a country the wages of labour had ever been more than sufficient to maintain the labourer, and to enable him to bring up a family, the competition of the labourers and the interest of the masters would soon reduce them to this lowest rate which is consistent with common humanity. China has been long one of the richest, that is, one of the most fertile, best cultivated, most industrious, and most populous countries in the world. It seems, however, to have been long stationary. . . .

.   .   .

In Great Britain the wages of labour seem, in the present times, to be evidently more than what is precisely necessary to enable the labourer to bring up a family. In order to satisfy ourselves upon this point it will not be necessary to enter into any tedious or doubtful calculation of what may be the lowest sum upon which it is possible to do this. There are many plain symptoms that the wages of labour are no-where in this country regulated by this lowest rate which is consistent with common humanity.

First, in almost every part of Great Britain there is a distinction, even in the lowest species of labour, between summer and winter wages. Summer wages are always highest. But on account of the extraordinary expence of fewel, the maintenance of a family is most expensive in winter. Wages, therefore, being highest when this expence is lowest, it seems evident that they are not regulated by what is necessary for this expence; but by the quantity and supposed value of the work. A labourer, it may be said indeed, ought to save part of his summer wages in order to defray his winter expence; and that through the whole year they do not exceed what is necessary to maintain his family through the whole year. A slave, however, or one absolutely dependent on us for immediate subsistence, would not be treated in this manner. His daily subsistence would be proportioned to his daily necessities.

Secondly, the wages of labour do not in Great Britain fluctuate with the price of provisions. These vary every-where from year to year, frequently from month to month. But in many places the money price of labour remains uniformly the same sometimes for half a century together. If in these places, therefore, the labouring poor can maintain their families in dear years, they must be at their ease in times of moderate plenty, and in affluence in those of extraordinary cheapness. The high price of provisions during these ten years past has not in many parts of the kingdom been accompanied with any sensible rise in the money price of labour. It has, indeed, in some; owing probably more to the increase of the demand for labour than to that of the price of provisions.

Thirdly, as the price of provisions varies more from year to year than the wages of labour, so, on the other hand, the wages of labour vary more from place to place than the price of provisions. The prices of bread and butcher's meat are generally the same or very nearly the same through the greater part of the United Kingdom. These and most other things which are sold by retail, the way in which the labouring poor buy all things, are generally fully as cheap or cheaper in great towns than in the remoter parts of the country, for reasons which I shall have occasion to explain hereafter. But the wages of labour in a great town and its neighbourhood are frequently a fourth or a fifth part, twenty or five-and-twenty per cent. higher than at a few miles distance. Eighteen pence a day may be reckoned the common price of labour in London and its neighbourhood. At a few miles distance it falls to fourteen and fifteen pence. Ten pence may be reckoned its price in Edinburgh and its neighbourhood. At a few miles distance it falls to eight pence, the usual price of common labour through the greater part of the low country of Scotland, where it varies a good deal less than in England. Such a difference of prices, which it seems is not always sufficient to transport a man from one parish to another, would necessarily occasion so great a transportation of the most bulky commodities, not only from one parish to another, but from one end of the kingdom, almost from one end of the world to the other, as would soon reduce them more nearly to a level. After all that has been said of the levity and inconstancy of human nature, it appears evidently from experience that a man is of all sorts of luggage the most difficult to be transported. If the labouring poor, therefore, can maintain their families in those parts of the kingdom where the price of labour is lowest, they must be in affluence where it is highest.

Fourthly, the variations in the price of labour not only do not correspond either in place or time with those in the price of provisions, but they are frequently quite opposite.

. . .

Is this improvement in the circumstances of the lower ranks of the people to be regarded as an advantage or as an inconveniency to the society? The answer seems at first sight abundantly plain. Servants, labourers and workmen of different kinds, make up the far greater part of every great political society. But what improves the circumstances of the greater part can never be regarded as an inconveniency to the whole. No society can surely be flourishing and happy, of which the far greater part of the members are poor and miserable. It is but equity, besides, that they who feed, cloath and lodge the whole body of the people, should have such a share of the produce of their own labour as to be themselves tolerably well fed, cloathed and lodged.

Poverty, though it no doubt discourages, does not always prevent marriage. It seems even to be favourable to generation. A half-starved Highland woman frequently bears more than twenty children, while a pampered fine lady is often incapable of bearing any, and is generally exhausted by two or three. Barrenness, so frequent among women of fashion, is very rare among those of inferior station. Luxury in the fair sex, while it inflames perhaps the passion for enjoyment, seems always to weaken, and frequently to destroy altogether, the powers of generation.

But poverty, though it does not prevent the generation, is extremely unfavourable to the rearing of children. The tender plant is produced, but in so cold a soil, and so severe a climate, soon withers and dies. It is not uncommon, I have been frequently told, in the Highlands of Scotland for a mother who has borne twenty children not to have two alive. Several officers of great experience have assured me, that so far from recruiting their regiment, they have never been able to supply it with drums and fifes from all the soldiers' children that were born in it. A greater number of fine children, however, is seldom seen any where than about a barrack of soldiers. Very few of them, it seems, arrive at the age of thirteen or fourteen. In some places one half the children born die before they are four years of age; in many places before they are seven; and in almost all places before they are nine or ten. This great mortality, however, will every where be found chiefly among the children of the common people, who cannot afford to tend them with the same care as those of better station. Though their marriages are generally more fruitful than those of people of fashion, a smaller proportion of their children arrive at maturity. In foundling hospitals, and among the children brought up by parish charities, the mortality is still greater than among those of the common people.

Every species of animals naturally multiplies in proportion to the means of their subsistence, and no species can ever multiply beyond it. But in civilized society it is only among the inferior ranks of people that the scantiness of subsistence can set limits to the further multiplication of the human species; and it can do so in no other way than by destroying a great part of the children which their fruitful marriages produce.

The liberal reward of labour, by enabling them to provide better for their children, and consequently to bring up a greater number, naturally tends to widen and extend those limits. It deserves to be remarked too, that it necessarily does this as nearly as possible in the proportion which the demand for labour requires. If this demand is continually increasing, the reward of labour must necessarily encourage in such a manner the marriage and multiplication of labourers, as may enable them to supply that continually increasing demand by a continually increasing population. If the reward should at any time be less than what was requisite for this purpose, the deficiency of hands would soon raise it; and if it should at any time be more, their excessive multiplication would soon lower it to this necessary rate. The market would be so much under-stocked with labour in the one case, and so much over-stocked in the other, as would soon force back its price to that proper rate which the circumstances of the society required. It is in this manner that the demand for men, like that for any other commodity, necessarily regulates the production of men; quickens it when it goes on too slowly, and stops it when it advances too fast. It is this demand which regulates and determines the state of propagation in all the different countries of the world, in North America, in Europe, and in China; which renders it rapidly progressive in the first, slow and gradual in the second, and altogether stationary in the last.

The wear and tear of a slave, it has been said, is at the expence of his master; but that of a free servant is at his own expence. The wear and tear of the latter, however, is, in reality, as much at the expence of his master as that of the former. The wages paid to journeymen and servants of every kind must be such as may enable them, one with another, to continue the race of journeymen and servants, according as the increasing, diminishing, or stationary demand of the society may happen to require. But though the wear and tear of a free servant be equally at the expence of his master, it generally costs him much less than that of a slave. The fund destined for replacing or repairing, if I may say so, the wear and tear of the slave, is commonly managed by a negligent master or careless overseer. That destined for performing the same office with regard to the free man, is managed by the free man himself. The disorders which generally prevail in the economy of the rich, naturally introduce themselves into the management of the former: The strict frugality and parsimonious attention of the poor as naturally establish themselves in that of the latter. Under such different management, the same purpose must require very different degrees of expence to execute it. It appears, accordingly, from the experience of all ages and nations, I believe, that the work done by freemen comes cheaper in the end than that performed by slaves. It is found to do so even at Boston, New York, and Philadelphia, where the wages of common labour are so very high.

The liberal reward of labour, therefore, as it is the effect of increasing wealth, so it is the cause of increasing population. To complain of it, is to lament over the necessary effect and cause of the greatest public prosperity.

It deserves to be remarked, perhaps, that it is in the progressive state, while the society is advancing to the further acquisition, rather than when it has acquired its full complement of riches, that the condition of the labouring poor, of the great body of the people, seems to be the happiest and the most comfortable. It is hard in the stationary, and miserable in the declining state. The progressive state is in reality the cheerful and the hearty state to all the different orders of the society. The stationary is dull; the declining melancholy.

The liberal reward of labour, as it encourages the propagation, so it increases the industry of the common people. The wages of labour are the encouragement of industry, which, like every other human quality, improves in proportion to the encouragement it receives. A plentiful subsistence increases the bodily strength of the labourer, and the comfortable hope of bettering his condition, and of ending his days perhaps in ease and plenty, animates him to exert that strength to the utmost. Where wages are high, accordingly, we shall always find the workmen more active, diligent, and expeditious, than where they are low; in England, for example, than in Scotland; in the neighbourhood of great towns, than in remote country places. Some workmen, indeed, when they can earn in four days what will maintain them through the week, will be idle the other three. This, however, is by no means the case with the greater part. Workmen, on the contrary, when they are liberally paid by the piece, are very apt to over-work themselves, and to ruin their health and constitutions in a few years.

. . .

In cheap years, it is pretended, workmen are generally more idle, and in dear ones more industrious than ordinary. A plentiful subsistence therefore, it has been concluded, relaxes, and a scanty one quickens their industry. That a little more plenty than ordinary may render some workmen idle, cannot well be doubted; but that it should have this effect upon the greater part, or that men in general should work better when they are ill fed than when they are well fed, when they are disheartened than when they are in good spirits, when they are frequently sick than when they are generally in good health, seems not very probable. Years of dearth, it is to be observed, are generally among the common people years of sickness and mortality, which cannot fail to diminish the produce of their industry.

. . .

BOOK IV / Of Systems of Political Economy

Chapter 1: OF THE PRINCIPLE OF THE COMMERCIAL OR
              MERCANTILE SYSTEM

That wealth consists in money, or in gold and silver, is a popular notion which naturally arises from the double function of money, as the instrument of commerce, and as the measure of value. In consequence of its being the instrument of commerce, when we have money we can more readily obtain whatever else we have occasion for, than by means of any other commodity. The great affair, we always find, is to get money. When that is obtained, there is no difficulty in making any subsequent purchase. In consequence of its being the measure of value, we estimate that of all other commodities by the quantity of money which they will exchange for. We say of a rich man that he is worth a great deal, and of a poor man that he is worth very little money. A frugal man, or a man eager to be rich, is said to love money; and a careless, a generous, or a profuse man, is said to be indifferent about it. To grow rich is to get money; and wealth and money, in short, are, in common language, considered as in every respect synonymous.

A rich country, in the same manner as a rich man, is supposed to be a country abounding in money; and to heap up gold and silver in any country is supposed to be the readiest way to enrich it. For some time after the discovery of America, the first enquiry of the Spaniards, when they arrived upon any unknown coast, used to be, if there was any gold or silver to be found in the neighbourhood? By the information which they received, they judged whether it was worth while to make a settlement there, or if the country was worth the conquering. Plano Carpino, a monk sent ambassador from the king of France to one of the sons of the famous Gengis Khan, says that the Tartars used frequently to ask him, if there was plenty of sheep and oxen in the kingdom of France? Their enquiry had the same object with that of the Spaniards. They wanted to know if the country was rich enough to be worth the conquering. Among the Tartars, as among all other nations of shepherds, who are generally ignorant of the use of money, cattle are the instruments of commerce and the measures of value. Wealth, therefore, according to them, consisted in cattle, as according to the Spaniards it consisted in gold and silver. Of the two, the Tartar notion, perhaps, was the nearest to the truth.

Mr. Locke remarks a distinction between money and other moveable goods. All other moveable goods, he says, are of so consumable a nature that the wealth which consists in them cannot be much depended on, and a nation which abounds in them one year may, without any exportation, but merely by their own waste and extravagance, be in great want of them the next. Money, on the contrary, is a steady friend, which, though it may travel about from hand to hand, yet if it can be kept from going out of the country, is not very liable to be wasted and consumed. Gold and silver, therefore, are, according to him, the most solid and substantial part of the moveable wealth of a nation, and to multiply those metals ought, he thinks, upon that account, to be the great object of its political economy.

Others admit that if a nation could be separated from all the world, it would be of no consequence how much, or how little money circulated in it. The consumable goods which were circulated by means of this money, would only be exchanged for a greater or a smaller number of pieces; but the real wealth or poverty of the country, they allow, would depend altogether upon the abundance or scarcity of those consumable goods. But it is otherwise, they think, with countries which have connections with foreign nations, and which are obliged to carry on foreign wars, and to maintain fleets and armies in distant countries. This, they say, cannot be done, but by sending abroad money to pay them with; and a nation cannot send much money abroad, unless it has a good deal at home. Every such nation, therefore, must endeavour in time of peace to accumulate gold and silver, that, when occasion requires, it may have wherewithal to carry on foreign wars.

In consequence of these popular notions, all the different nations of Europe have studied, though to little purpose, every possible means of accumulating gold and silver in their respective countries. Spain and Portugal, the proprietors of the principal mines which supply Europe with those metals, have either prohibited their exportation under the severest penalties, or subjected it to a considerable duty. The like prohibition seems anciently to have made a part of the policy of most other European nations. It is even to be found, where we should least of all expect to find it, in some old Scotch acts of parliament, which forbid under heavy penalties the carrying of gold or silver *forth of the kingdom*. The like policy anciently took place both in France and England.

When those countries became commercial, the merchants found this prohibition, upon many occasions, extremely inconvenient. They could frequently buy more advantageously with gold and silver than with any other commodity, the foreign goods which they wanted, either to import into their own, or to carry to some other foreign country. They remonstrated, therefore, against this prohibition as hurtful to trade.

They represented, first, that the exportation of gold and silver in order to purchase foreign goods, did not always diminish the quantity of those metals in the kingdom. That, on the contrary, it might frequently increase that quantity; because, if the consumption of foreign goods was not thereby increased in the country, those goods might be re-exported to foreign countries, and, being there sold for a large profit, might bring back much more treasure than was originally sent out to purchase them. Mr. Mun compares this operation of foreign trade to the seed-time and harvest of agriculture. "If we only behold," says he, "the actions of the husbandman in the seed-time, when he casteth away much good corn into the ground, we shall account him rather a madman than a husbandman. But when we consider his labours in the harvest, which is the end of his endeavours, we shall find the worth and plentiful increase of his actions."

They represented, secondly, that this prohibition could not hinder the exportation of gold and silver, which, on account of the smallness of their bulk in proportion to their value, could easily be smuggled abroad. That this exportation could only be prevented by a proper attention to, what they called, the balance of trade. That when the country exported to a greater value than it imported, a balance became due to it from foreign nations, which was necessarily paid to it in gold and silver, and thereby increased the quantity of those metals in the kingdom. But that when it imported to a greater value than it exported, a contrary balance became due to foreign nations, which was necessarily paid to them in the same manner, and thereby diminished that quantity. That in this case to prohibit the exportation of those metals could not prevent it, but only by making it more dangerous, render it more expensive. That the exchange was thereby turned more against the country which owed the balance, than it otherwise might have been; the merchant who purchased a bill upon the foreign country being obliged to pay the banker who sold it, not only for the natural risk, trouble and expence of sending the money thither, but for the extraordinary risk arising from the prohibition. But that the more the exchange was against any country, the more the balance of trade became necessarily against it; the money of that country becoming necessarily of so much less value, in comparison with that of the country to which the balance was due. That if the exchange between England and Holland, for example, was five per cent. against England, it would require a hundred and five ounces of silver in England to purchase a bill for a hundred ounces of silver in Holland: that a hundred and five ounces of silver in England, therefore, would be worth only a hundred ounces of silver in Holland, and would purchase only a proportionable quantity of Dutch goods: but that a hundred ounces of silver in Holland, on the contrary, would be worth a hundred and five ounces in England, and would purchase a proportionable quantity of English goods: that the English goods which were sold to Holland would be sold so much cheaper; and the Dutch goods which were sold to England, so much dearer, by the difference of the exchange; that the one would draw so much less Dutch money to England, and the other so much more English money to Holland, as this difference amounted to: and that the balance of trade, therefore, would necessarily be so much more against England, and would require a greater balance of gold and silver to be exported to Holland.

Those arguments were partly solid and partly sophistical. They were solid so far as they asserted that the exportation of gold and silver in trade might frequently be advantageous to the country. They were solid too, in asserting that no prohibition could prevent their exportation, when private people found any advantage in exporting them. But they were sophistical in supposing, that either to preserve or to augment the quantity of those metals required more the attention of government, than to preserve or to augment the quantity of any other useful commodities, which the freedom of trade, without any such attention, never fails to supply in the proper quantity. They were sophistical too, perhaps, in asserting that the high price of exchange necessarily increased, what they called, the unfavourable balance of trade, or occasioned the exportation of a greater quantity of gold and silver. That high price, indeed, was extremely disadvantageous to the merchants who had any money to pay in foreign countries. They paid so much dearer for the bills which their bankers granted them upon those countries. But though the risk arising from the prohibition might occasion some extraordinary expence to the bankers, it would not necessarily carry any more money out of the country. This expence would generally be all laid out in the country, in smuggling the money out of it, and could seldom occasion the exportation of a single six-pence beyond the precise sum drawn for. The high price of exchange too would naturally dispose the merchants to endeavour to make their exports nearly balance their imports, in order that they might have this high exchange to pay upon as small a sum as possible. The high price of exchange, besides, must necessarily have operated as a tax, in raising the price of foreign goods, and thereby diminishing their consumption. It would tend, therefore, not to increase, but to diminish, what they called, the unfavourable balance of trade, and consequently the exportation of gold and silver.

Such as they were, however, those arguments convinced the people to whom they were addressed. They were addressed by merchants to parliaments, and to the councils of princes, to nobles, and to country gentlemen; by those who were supposed to understand trade, to those who were conscious to themselves that they knew nothing about the matter. That foreign trade enriched the country, experience demonstrated to the nobles and country gentlemen, as well as to the merchants; but how, or in what manner, none of them well knew. The merchants knew perfectly in what manner it enriched themselves. It was their business to know it. But to know in what manner it enriched the country, was no part of their business. This subject never came into their consideration, but when they had occasion to apply to their country for some change in the laws relating to foreign trade. It then became necessary to say something about the beneficial effects of foreign trade, and the manner in which those effects were obstructed by the laws as they then stood. To the judges who were to decide the business, it appeared a most satisfactory account of the matter, when they were told that foreign trade brought money into the country, but that the laws in question hindered it from bringing so much as it otherwise would do. Those arguments therefore produced the wished-for effect. The prohibition of exporting gold and silver was in France and England confined to the coin of those respective countries. The exportation of foreign coin and of bullion was made free. In Holland, and in some other places, this liberty was extended even to the coin of the country. The attention of government was turned away from guarding against the exportation of gold and silver, to watch over the balance of trade, as the only cause which could occasion any augmentation or diminution of those metals. From one fruitless care it was turned away to another care much more intricate, much more embarrassing, and just equally fruitless. The title of Mun's book, England's Treasure in Foreign Trade, became a fundamental maxim in the political economy, not of England only, but of all other commercial countries. The inland or home trade, the most important of all, the trade in which an equal capital affords the greatest revenue, and creates the greatest employment to the people of the country, was considered as subsidiary only to foreign trade. It neither brought money into the country, it was said, nor carried any out of it. The country therefore could never become either richer or poorer by means of it, except so far as its prosperity or decay might indirectly influence the state of foreign trade.

A country that has no mines of its own must undoubtedly draw its gold and silver from foreign countries, in the same manner as one that has no vineyards of its own must draw its wines. It does not seem necessary, however, that the attention of government should be more turned towards the one than towards the other object. A country that has wherewithal to buy wine, will always get the wine which it has occasion for; and a country that has wherewithal to buy gold and silver, will never be in want of those metals. They are to be bought for a certain price like all other commodities, and as they are the price of all other commodities, so all other commodities are the price of those metals. We trust with perfect security that the freedom of trade, without any attention of government, will always supply us with the wine which we have occasion for: and we may trust with equal security that it will always supply us with all the gold and silver which we can afford to purchase or to employ, either in circulating our commodities, or in other uses.

The quantity of every commodity which human industry can either purchase or produce, naturally regulates itself in every country according to the effectual demand, or according to the demand of those who are willing to pay the whole rent, labour and profits which must be paid in order to prepare and bring it to market. But no commodities regulate themselves more easily or more exactly according to this effectual demand than gold and silver; because, on account of the small bulk and great value of those metals, no commodities can be more easily transported from one place to another, from the places where they are cheap, to those where they are dear, from the places where they exceed, to those where they fall short of this effectual demand. If there were in England, for example, an effectual demand for an additional quantity of gold, a packet-boat could bring from Lisbon, or from wherever else it was to be had, fifty tons of gold, which could be coined into more than five millions of guineas. But if there were an effectual demand for grain to the same value, to import it would require, at five guineas a ton, a million of tons of shipping, or a thousand ships of a thousand tons each. The navy of England would not be sufficient.

When the quantity of gold and silver imported into any country exceeds the effectual demand, no vigilance of government can prevent their exportation. All the sanguinary laws of Spain and Portugal are not able to keep their gold and silver at home. The continual importations from Peru and Brazil exceed the effectual demand of those countries, and sink the price of those metals there below that in the neighbouring countries. If, on the contrary, in any particular country their quantity fell short of the effectual demand, so as to raise their price above that of the neighbouring countries, the government would have no occasion to take any pains to import them. If it were even to take pains to prevent their importation, it would not be able to effectuate it. Those metals, when the Spartans had got wherewithal to purchase them, broke through all the barriers which the laws of Lycurgus opposed to their entrance into Lacedemon. All the sanguinary laws of the customs are not able to prevent the importation of the teas of the Dutch and Gottenburgh East India companies; because somewhat cheaper than those of the British company. A pound of tea, however, is about a hundred times the bulk of one of the highest prices, sixteen shillings, that is commonly paid for it in silver, and more than two thousand times the bulk of the same price in gold, and consequently just so many times more difficult to smuggle.

It is partly owing to the easy transportation of gold and silver from the places where they abound to those where they are wanted, that the price of those metals does not fluctuate continually like that of the greater part of other commodities, which are hindered by their bulk from shifting their situation, when the market happens to be either over or under-stocked with them. The price of those metals, indeed, is not altogether exempted from variation, but the changes to which it is liable are generally slow, gradual, and uniform. In Europe, for example, it is supposed, without much foundation, perhaps, that, during the course of the present and preceding century, they have been constantly, but gradually, sinking in their value, on account of the continual importations from the Spanish West Indies. But to make any sudden change in the price of gold and silver, so as to raise or lower at once, sensibly and remarkably, the money price of all other commodities, requires such a revolution in commerce as that occasioned by the discovery of America.

If, notwithstanding all this, gold and silver should at any time fall short in a country which has wherewithal to purchase them, there are more expedients for supplying their place, than that of almost any other commodity. If the materials of manufacture are wanted, industry must stop. If provisions are wanted, the people must starve. But if money is wanted, barter will supply its place, though with a good deal of inconveniency. Buying and selling upon credit, and the different dealers compensating their credits with one another, once a month or once a year, will supply it with less inconveniency. A well-regulated paper money will supply it, not only without any inconveniency, but, in some cases, with some advantages. Upon every account, therefore, the attention of government never was so unnecessarily employed, as when directed to watch over the preservation or increase of the quantity of money in any country.

. . .

It would be too ridiculous to go about seriously to prove, that wealth does not consist in money, or in gold and silver; but in what money purchases, and is valuable only for purchasing. Money, no doubt, makes always a part of the national capital; but it has already been shown that it generally makes but a small part, and always the most unprofitable part of it.

It is not because wealth consists more essentially in money than in goods, that the merchant finds it generally more easy to buy goods with money, than to buy money with goods; but because money is the known and established instrument of commerce, for which every thing is readily given in exchange, but which is not always with equal readiness to be got in exchange for every thing. The greater part of goods besides are more perishable than money, and he may frequently sustain a much greater loss by keeping them. When his goods are upon hand too, he is more liable to such demands for money as he may not be able to answer, than when he has got their price in his coffers. Over and above all this, his profit arises more directly from selling than from buying, and he is upon all these accounts generally much more anxious to exchange his goods for money, than his money for goods. But though a particular merchant, with abundance of goods in his warehouse, may sometimes be ruined by not being able to sell them in time, a nation or country is not liable to the same accident. The whole capital of a merchant frequently consists in perishable goods destined for purchasing money. But it is but a very small part of the annual produce of the land and labour of a country which can ever be destined for purchasing gold and silver from their neighbours. The far greater part is circulated and consumed among themselves; and even of the surplus which is sent abroad, the greater part is generally destined for the purchase of other foreign goods. Though gold and silver, therefore, could not be had in exchange for the goods destined to purchase them, the nation would not be ruined. It might, indeed, suffer some loss and inconveniency, and be forced upon some of those expedients which are necessary for supplying the place of money. The annual produce of its land and labour, however, would be the same, or very nearly the same, as usual, because the same, or very nearly the same consumable capital would be employed in maintaining it. And though goods do not always draw money so readily as money draws goods, in the long-run they draw it more necessarily than even it draws them. Goods can serve many other purposes besides purchasing money, but money can serve no other purpose besides purchasing goods. Money, therefore, necessarily runs after goods, but goods do not always or necessarily run after money. The man who buys, does not always mean to sell again, but frequently to use or to consume; whereas he who sells, always means to buy again. The one may frequently have done the whole, but the other can never have done more than the one-half of his business. It is not for its own sake that men desire money, but for the sake of what they can purchase with it.

. . .

Chapter 2: OF RESTRAINTS UPON THE IMPORTATION FROM FOREIGN COUNTRIES OF SUCH GOODS AS CAN BE PRODUCED AT HOME

By restraining, either by high duties, or by absolute prohibitions, the importation of such goods from foreign countries as can be produced at home, the monopoly of the home market is more or less secured to the domestic industry employed in producing them. Thus the prohibition of importing either live cattle or salt provisions from foreign countries secures to the graziers of Great Britain the monopoly of the home market for butcher's meat. The high duties upon the importation of corn, which in times of moderate plenty amount to a prohibition, give a like advantage to the growers of that commodity. The prohibition of the importation of foreign woollens is equally favourable to the woollen manufacturers. The silk manufacture, though altogether employed upon foreign materials, has lately obtained the same advantage. The linen manufacture has not yet obtained it, but is making great strides towards it. Many other sorts of manufacturers have, in the same manner, obtained in Great Britain, either altogether, or very nearly a monopoly against their countrymen. The variety of goods of which the importation into Great Britain is prohibited, either absolutely, or under certain circumstances, greatly exceeds what can easily be suspected by those who are not well acquainted with the laws of the customs.

That this monopoly of the home-market frequently gives great encouragement to that particular species of industry which enjoys it, and frequently turns towards that employment a greater share of both the labour and stock of the society than would otherwise have gone to it, cannot be doubted. But whether it tends either to increase the general industry of the society, or to give it the most advantageous direction, is not, perhaps, altogether so evident.

The general industry of the society never can exceed what the capital of the society can employ. As the number of workmen that can be kept in employment by any particular person must bear a certain proportion to his capital, so the number of those that can be continually employed by all the members of a great society, must bear a certain proportion to the whole capital of that society, and never can exceed that proportion. No regulation of commerce can increase the quantity of industry in any society beyond what its capital can maintain. It can only divert a part of it into a direction into which it might not otherwise have gone; and it is by no means certain that this artificial direction is likely to be more advantageous to the society than that into which it would have gone of its own accord.

Every individual is continually exerting himself to find out the most advantageous employment for whatever capital he can command. It is his own advantage, indeed, and not that of the society, which he has in view. But the study of his own advantage naturally, or rather necessarily leads him to prefer that employment which is most advantageous to the society.

First, every individual endeavours to employ his capital as near home as he can, and consequently as much as he can in the support of domestic industry; provided always that he can thereby obtain the ordinary, or not a great deal less than the ordinary profits of stock.

Thus, upon equal or nearly equal profits, every wholesale merchant naturally prefers the home-trade to the foreign trade of consumption, and the foreign trade of consumption to the carrying trade. In the home-trade his capital is never so long out of his sight as it frequently is in the foreign trade of consumption. He can know better the character and situation of the persons whom he trusts, and if he should happen to be deceived, he knows better the laws of the country from which he must seek redress. In the carrying trade, the capital of the merchant is, as it were, divided between two foreign countries, and no part of it is ever necessarily brought home, or placed under his own immediate view and command. The capital which an Amsterdam merchant employs in carrying corn from Konnigsberg to Lisbon, and fruit and wine from Lisbon to Konnigsberg, must generally be the one-half of it at Konnigsberg and the other half at Lisbon. No part of it need ever come to Amsterdam. The natural residence of such a merchant should either be at Konnigsberg or Lisbon, and it can only be some very particular circumstances which can make him prefer the residence of Amsterdam. The uneasiness, however, which he feels at being separated so far from his capital, generally determines him to bring part both of the Konnigsberg goods which he destines for the market of Lisbon, and of the Lisbon goods which he destines for that of Konnigsberg, to Amsterdam: and though this necessarily subjects him to a double charge of loading and unloading, as well as to the payment of some duties and customs, yet for the sake of having some part of his capital always under his own view and command, he willingly submits to this extraordinary charge; and it is in this manner that every country which has any considerable share of the carrying trade, becomes always the emporium, or general market, for the goods of all the different countries whose trade it carries on. The merchant, in order to save a second loading and unloading, endeavours always to sell in the home-market as much of the goods of all those different countries as he can, and thus, so far as he can, to convert his carrying trade into a foreign trade of consumption. A merchant, in the same manner, who is engaged in the foreign trade of consumption, when he collects goods for foreign markets, will always be glad, upon equal or nearly equal profits, to sell as great a part of them at home as he can. He saves himself the risk and trouble of exportation, when, so far as he can, he thus converts his foreign trade of consumption into a home-trade. Home is in this manner the center, if I may say so, round which the capitals of the inhabitants of every country are continually circulating, and towards which they are always tending, though by particular causes they may sometimes be driven off and repelled from it towards more distant employments. But a capital employed in the home-trade, it has already been shown, necessarily puts into motion a greater quantity of domestic industry, and gives revenue and employment to a greater number of the inhabitants of the country, than an equal capital employed in the foreign trade of consumption: and one employed in the foreign trade of consumption has the same advantage over an equal capital employed in the carrying trade. Upon equal, or only nearly equal profits, therefore, every individual naturally inclines to employ his capital in the manner in which it is likely to afford the greatest support to domestic industry, and to give revenue and employment to the greatest number of people of his own country.

Secondly, every individual who employs his capital in the support of domestic industry, necessarily endeavours so to direct that industry, that its produce may be of the greatest possible value.

The produce of industry is what it adds to the subject or materials upon which it is employed. In proportion as the value of this produce is great or small, so will likewise be the profits of the employer. But it is only for the sake of profit that any man employs a capital in the support of industry; and he will always, therefore, endeavour to employ it in the support of that industry of which the produce is likely to be of the greatest value, or to exchange for the greatest quantity either of money or of other goods.

But the annual revenue of every society is always precisely equal to the exchangeable value of the whole annual produce of its industry, or rather is precisely the same thing with that exchangeable value. As every individual, therefore, endeavours as much as he can both to employ his capital in the support of domestic industry, and so to direct that industry that its produce may be of the greatest value; every individual necessarily labours to render the annual revenue of the society as great as he can. He generally, indeed, neither intends to promote the public interest, nor knows how much he is promoting it. By preferring the support of domestic to that of foreign industry, he intends only his own security; and by directing that industry in such a manner as its produce may be of the greatest value, he intends only his own gain, and he is in this, as in many other cases, led by an invisible hand to promote an end which was no part of his intention. Nor is it always the worse for the society that it was no part of it. By pursuing his own interest he frequently promotes that of the society more effectually than when he really intends to promote it. I have never known much good done by those who affected to trade for the public good. It is an affectation, indeed, not very common among merchants, and very few words need be employed in dissuading them from it.

What is the species of domestic industry which his capital can employ, and of which the produce is likely to be of the greatest value, every individual, it is evident, can, in his local situation, judge much better than any statesman or lawgiver can do for him. The statesman, who should attempt to direct private people in what manner they ought to employ their capitals, would not only load himself with a most unnecessary attention, but assume an authority which could safely be trusted, not only to no single person, but to no council or senate whatever, and which would nowhere be so dangerous as in the hands of a man who had folly and presumption enough to fancy himself fit to exercise it.

To give the monopoly of the home-market to the produce of domestic industry, in any particular art or manufacture, is in some measure to direct private people in what manner they ought to employ their capitals, and must, in almost all cases, be either a useless or a hurtful regulation. If the produce of domestic can be brought there as cheap as that of foreign industry, the regulation is evidently useless. If it cannot, it must generally be hurtful. It is the maxim of every prudent master of a family, never to attempt to make at home what it will cost him more to make than to buy. The taylor does not attempt to make his own shoes, but buys them of the shoemaker. The shoemaker does not attempt to make his own clothes, but employs a taylor. The farmer attempts to make neither the one nor the other, but employs those different artificers. All of them find it for their interest to employ their whole industry in a way in which they have some advantage over their neighbours, and to purchase with a part of its produce, or what is the same thing, with the price of a part of it, whatever else they have occasion for.

What is prudence in the conduct of every private family, can scarce be folly in that of a great kingdom. If a foreign country can supply us with a commodity cheaper than we ourselves can make it, better buy it of them with some part of the produce of our own industry, employed in a way in which we have some advantage. The general industry of the country, being always in proportion to the capital which employs it, will not thereby be diminished, no more than that of the above-mentioned artificers; but only left to find out the way in which it can be employed with the greatest advantage. It is certainly not employed to the greatest advantage, when it is thus directed towards an object which it can buy cheaper than it can make. The value of its annual produce is certainly more or less diminished, when it is thus turned away from producing commodities evidently of more value than the commodity which it is directed to produce. According to the supposition, that commodity could be purchased from foreign countries cheaper than it can be made at home. It could, therefore, have been purchased with a part only of the commodities, or, what is the same thing, with a part only of the price of the commodities, which the industry employed by an equal capital would have produced at home, had it been left to follow its natural course. The industry of the country, therefore, is thus turned away from a more, to a less advantageous employment, and the exchangeable value of its annual produce, instead of being increased, according to the intention of the lawgiver, must necessarily be diminished by every such regulation.

By means of such regulations, indeed, a particular manufacture may sometimes be acquired sooner than it could have been otherwise, and after a certain time may be made at home as cheap or cheaper than in the foreign country. But though the industry of the society may be thus carried with advantage into a particular channel sooner than it could have been otherwise, it will by no means follow that the sum total, either of its industry, or of its revenue, can ever be augmented by any such regulation. The industry of the society can augment only in proportion as its capital augments, and its capital can augment only in proportion to what can be gradually saved out of its revenue. But the immediate effect of every such regulation is to diminish its revenue, and what diminishes its revenue is certainly not very likely to augment its capital faster than it would have augmented of its own accord, had both capital and industry been left to find out their natural employments.

Though for want of such regulations the society should never acquire the proposed manufacture, it would not, upon that account, necessarily be the poorer in any one period of its duration. In every period of its duration its whole capital and industry might still have been employed, though upon different objects, in the manner that was most advantageous at the time. In every period its revenue might have been the greatest which its capital could afford, and both capital and revenue might have been augmented with the greatest possible rapidity.

The natural advantages which one country has over another in producing particular commodities are sometimes so great, that it is acknowledged by all the world to be in vain to struggle with them. By means of glasses, hotbeds, and hotwalls, very good grapes can be raised in Scotland, and very good wine too can be made of them at about thirty times the expence for which at least equally good can be brought from foreign countries. Would it be a reasonable law to prohibit the importation of all foreign wines, merely to encourage the making of claret and burgundy in Scotland? But if there would be a manifest absurdity in turning towards any employment, thirty times more of the capital and industry of the country, than would be necessary to purchase from foreign countries an equal quantity of the commodities wanted, there must be an absurdity, though not altogether so glaring, yet exactly of the same kind, in turning towards any such employment a thirtieth, or even a three hundredth part more of either. Whether the advantages which one country has over another, be natural or acquired, is in this respect of no consequence. As long as the one country has those advantages, and the other wants them, it will always be more advantageous for the latter, rather to buy of the former than to make. It is an acquired advantage only, which one artificer has over his neighbour, who exercises another trade; and yet they both find it more advantageous to buy of one another, than to make what does not belong to their particular trades.

Merchants and manufacturers are the people who derive the greatest advantage from this monopoly of the home-market. The prohibition of the importation of foreign cattle, and of salt provisions, together with the high duties upon foreign corn, which in times of moderate plenty amount to a prohibition, are not near so advantageous to the graziers and farmers of Great Britain, as other regulations of the same kind are to its merchants and manufacturers. Manufactures, those of the finer kind especially, are more easily transported from one country to another than corn or cattle. It is in the fetching and carrying manufactures, accordingly, that foreign trade is chiefly employed. In manufactures, a very small advantage will enable foreigners to undersell our own workmen, even in the home market. It will require a very great one to enable them to do so in the rude produce of the soil. If the free importation of foreign manufactures were permitted, several of the home manufactures would probably suffer, and some of them, perhaps, go to ruin altogether, and a considerable part of the stock and industry at present employed in them, would be forced to find out some other employment. But the freest importation of the rude produce of the soil could have no such effect upon the agriculture of the country.

. . .

There seem, however, to be two cases in which it will generally be advantageous to lay some burden upon foreign, for the encouragement of domestic industry.

The first is, when some particular sort of industry is necessary for the defence of the country. The defence of Great Britain, for example, depends very much upon the number of its sailors and shipping. The act of navigation, therefore, very properly endeavours to give the sailors and shipping of Great Britain the monopoly of the trade of their own country, in some cases, by absolute prohibitions, and in others by heavy burdens upon the shipping of foreign countries. . . .

. . .

The second case, in which it will generally be advantageous to lay some burden upon foreign for the encouragement of domestic industry, is, when some tax is imposed at home upon the produce of the latter. In this case, it seems reasonable that an equal tax should be imposed upon the like produce of the former. This would not give the monopoly of the home market to domestic industry, nor turn towards a particular employment a greater share of the stock and labour of the country, than what would naturally go to it. It would only hinder any part of what would naturally go to it from being turned away by the tax, into a less natural direction, and would leave the competition between foreign and domestic industry, after the tax, as nearly as possible upon the same footing as before it. In Great Britain, when any such tax is laid upon the produce of domestic industry, it is usual at the same time, in order to stop the clamorous complaints of our merchants and manufacturers, that they will be undersold at home, to lay a much heavier duty upon the importation of all foreign goods of the same kind.

This second limitation of the freedom of trade according to some people should, upon some occasions, be extended much farther than to the precise foreign commodities which could come into competition with those which had been taxed at home. When the necessaries of life have been taxed in any country, it becomes proper, they pretend, to tax not only the like necessaries of life imported from other countries, but all sorts of foreign goods which can come into competition with any thing that is the produce of domestic industry. Subsistence, they say, becomes necessarily dearer in consequence of such taxes; and the price of labour must always rise with the price of the labourers subsistence. Every commodity, therefore, which is the produce of domestic industry, though not immediately taxed itself, becomes dearer in consequence of such taxes, because the labour which produces it becomes so. Such taxes, therefore, are really equivalent, they say, to a tax upon every particular commodity produced at home. In order to put domestic upon the same footing with foreign industry, therefore, it becomes necessary, they think, to lay some duty upon every foreign commodity, equal to this enhancement of the price of the home commodities with which it can come into competition.

Whether taxes upon the necessaries of life, such as those in Great Britain upon soap, salt, leather, candles, &c. necessarily raise the price of labour, and consequently that of all other commodities, I shall consider hereafter, when I come to treat of taxes. Supposing, however, in the mean time, that they have this effect, and they have it undoubtedly, this general enhancement of the price of all commodities, in consequence of that of labour, is a case which differs in the two following respects from that of a particular commodity, of which the price was enhanced by a particular tax immediately imposed upon it.

First, it might always be known with great exactness how far the price of such a commodity could be enhanced by such a tax: but how far the general enhancement of the price of labour might affect that of every different commodity about which labour was employed, could never be known with any tolerable exactness. It would be impossible, therefore, to proportion with any tolerable exactness the tax upon every foreign, to this enhancement of the price of every home commodity.

Secondly, taxes upon the necessaries of life have nearly the same effect upon the circumstances of the people as a poor soil and a bad climate. Provisions are thereby rendered dearer in the same manner as if it required extraordinary labour and expence to raise them. As in the natural scarcity arising from soil and climate, it would be absurd to direct the people in what manner they ought to employ their capitals and industry, so is it likewise in the artificial scarcity arising from such taxes. To be left to accommodate, as well as they could, their industry to their situation, and to find out those employments in which, notwithstanding their unfavourable circumstances, they might have some advantage either in the home or in the foreign market, is what in both cases would evidently be most for their advantage. To lay a new tax upon them, because they are already overburdened with taxes, and because they already pay too dear for the necessaries of life, to make them likewise pay too dear for the greater part of other commodities, is certainly a most absurd way of making amends.

Such taxes, when they have grown up to a certain height, are a curse equal to the barrenness of the earth and the inclemency of the heavens; and yet it is in the richest and most industrious countries that they have been most generally imposed. No other countries could support so great a disorder. As the strongest bodies only can live and enjoy health, under an unwholesome regimen; so the nations only, that in every sort of industry have the greatest natural and acquired advantages, can subsist and prosper under such taxes. Holland is the country in Europe in which they abound most, and which from peculiar circumstances continues to prosper, not by means of them, as has been most absurdly supposed, but in spite of them.

As there are two cases in which it will generally be advantageous to lay some burden upon foreign, for the encouragement of domestic industry; so there are two others in which it may sometimes be a matter of deliberation; in the one, how far it is proper to continue the free importation of certain foreign goods; and in the other, how far, or in what manner, it may be proper to restore that free importation after it has been for some time interrupted.

The case in which it may sometimes be a matter of deliberation how far it is proper to continue the free importation of certain foreign goods, is, when some foreign nation restrains by high duties or prohibitions the importation of some of our manufactures into their country. Revenge in this case naturally dictates retaliation, and that we should impose the like duties and prohibitions upon the importation of some or all of their manufactures into ours. Nations accordingly seldom fail to retaliate in this manner. The French have been particularly forward to favour their own manufactures by restraining the importation of such foreign goods as could come into competition with them. In this consisted a great part of the policy of Mr. Colbert, who, notwithstanding his great abilities, seems in this case to have been imposed upon by the sophistry of merchants and manufacturers, who are always demanding a monopoly against their countrymen. It is at present the opinion of the most intelligent men in France that his operations of this kind have not been beneficial to his country. That minister, by the tariff of 1667, imposed very high duties upon a great number of foreign manufactures. Upon his refusing to moderate them in favour of the Dutch, they in 1671 prohibited the importation of the wines, brandies and manufactures of France. The war of 1672 seems to have been in part occasioned by this commercial dispute. The peace of Nimeguen put an end to it in 1678, by moderating some of those duties in favour of the Dutch, who in consequence took off their prohibition. It was about the same time that the French and English began mutually to oppress each other's industry, by the like duties and prohibitions, of which the French, however, seem to have set the first example. The spirit of hostility which has subsisted between the two nations ever since, has hitherto hindered them from being moderated on either side. In 1697 the English prohibited the importation of bonelace, the manufacture of Flanders. The government of that country, at that time under the dominion of Spain, prohibited in return the importation of English woollens. In 1700, the prohibition of importing bonelace into England, was taken off upon condition that the importation of English woollens into Flanders should be put on the same footing as before.

There may be good policy in retaliations of this kind, when there is a probability that they will procure the repeal of the high duties or prohibitions complained of. The recovery of a great foreign market will generally more than compensate the transitory inconveniency of paying dearer during a short time for some sorts of goods. To judge whether such retaliations are likely to produce such an effect, does not, perhaps, belong so much to the science of a legislator, whose deliberations ought to be governed by general principles which are always the same, as to the skill of that insidious and crafty animal, vulgarly called a statesman or politician, whose councils are directed by the momentary fluctuations of affairs. When there is no probability that any such repeal can be procured, it seems a bad method of compensating the injury done to certain classes of our people, to do another injury ourselves, not only to those classes, but to almost all the other classes of them. When our neighbours prohibit some manufacture of ours, we generally prohibit, not only the same, for that alone would seldom affect them considerably, but some other manufacture of theirs. This may no doubt give encouragement to some particular class of workmen among ourselves, and by excluding some of their rivals, may enable them to raise their price in the home-market. Those workmen, however, who suffered by our neighbours' prohibition will not be benefited by ours. On the contrary, they and almost all the other classes of our citizens will thereby be obliged to pay dearer than before for certain goods. Every such law, therefore, imposes a real tax upon the whole country, not in favour of that particular class of workmen who were injured by our neighbours' prohibition, but of some other class.

. . .

THOMAS ROBERT MALTHUS

(1766–1834)

Few, if any, economists are as well known or as frequently cited as the Reverend T. R. Malthus. Inspired in part by conversations with his father, in part from his reading of The Wealth of Nations, and in part by a rejection of the dreams of social reformers such as William Godwin and Condorcet who envisioned an eventual perfectibility of man here on earth, Malthus published an anonymous essay warning of the tendency of the population to outstrip the means of subsistence. The first version of the now celebrated Law of Population was a terse polemic, proclaiming the dangers of overpopulation and denouncing those who foresaw an ultimate earth-bound utopia. The fear of over-population had been raised many times before, but never with such pungency and spirit. The targets of Malthus' attack were prompt to response in kind, and on the basis of the criticism the first essay received, Malthus set about solidifying his position.

Subsequent editions, which appeared with the author's name fully revealed—a poorly kept secret even for the first edition—contained three striking changes. The first was that the Essay ceased to be primarily an attack upon those who espoused the perfectibility of mankind; subsequent editions of the Essay make far less exciting reading and give one cause to wonder whether the impact of Malthus' writing would have been as great if the first edition had appeared in the same form as later editions.

The remaining two changes were designed to answer the criticisms of Malthus' opponents. Before offering a second version, Malthus spent three years studying at first hand the various restraints upon population imposed by nations around the world. His travels provided him with empirical and statistical evidence with which to buttress his original argument. Finally, to those critics who said that Malthus was too pessimistic or who argued that Malthus pictured God as a being who left man no chance to save himself, Malthus offered the possibility of moral restraint. In addition to the positive checks of war, famine, and disease originally listed in the first edition as forces holding population down, Malthus now suggested that man could, by postponing marriage and practicing continence, save himself from a fate worse than death—too many births. As the excerpt from Book IV, Chapter III makes evident, however, Malthus was never completely convinced of the efficacy of this solution.

With the exception of the passage just cited, all of our selection is drawn from the opening pages of Malthus' revised Essay. Here he developed his famous Law of Population. A substantial portion of the remaining chapters in the book was devoted to a study of how population had been controlled in various societies around the world. The reader was alternately exposed to the population problem as seen by the American Indians, the natives of Africa and the South Seas, the inhabitants of China, Japan, and Tibet, as well as the peoples of ancient and contemporary (to Malthus) Europe.

Only when the reader came to Book III (nearly four hundred pages from the beginning) did he find Malthus repeating his attack on William Godwin and Condorcet. Here too Malthus restated his opposition to the Poor Laws and warned that emigration assistance would provide only a temporary palliative to the problem of overpopulation. Malthus attacked the Poor Laws because they encouraged the poor to continue to have large families and further weakened the sense of responsibility of the head of the family for the care of his numerous offspring. For one who had been so pessimistic throughout much of his book, Malthus ended on a surprisingly cheery note. The poor were not really to blame for their tendency to have unduly large families; they had never been educated to another course! Perhaps education might lead them to be more prudent (he was still not overly optimistic on this score), or at least make them aware that the blame for their poverty was their own. Such a realization would prevent them from seeking panaceas from the government (such as more liberal Poor Laws) that would do more harm than good.

Although Malthus was an ordained minister, he established his reputation as a professional economist and spent the major part of his life in academic circles. His other major work, Principles of Political Economy, evoked both praise and sharp disagreement from his friend, David Ricardo. Among the points upon which the two disagreed was the question of repeal of the Corn Laws—Malthus upheld them as a needed protection to the landlords and as a means of preserving agriculture as a major element in the nation's economy, while, as we shall see, Ricardo sought the abolition of the Corn Laws. The two friends also disagreed as to the nature of rent—Ricardo supported a differential explanation (see the selection from Ricardo) while Malthus offered a more eclectic approach which attributed rent to the bountifulness of nature or the scarcity of fertile land or the fact that food was the only commodity where supply created its own demand.

This latter explanation is perhaps the most interesting since it marked another major difference between the two economists. Whereas Ricardo was willing to accept Say's Law of the Markets (named after its formulator, the French economist, Jean Baptiste Say) whereby supply created its own demand for all products and where there thus could never be generalized overproduction, Malthus had doubts and questioned the belief that the economy could never be plagued by gluts of nonfood goods. The existence of profits, said Malthus, meant that the workers did not receive sufficient purchasing power to buy back all of the items of consumption produced for them. The solution, he suggested, was to encourage unproductive consumption by having a substantial number of unproductive members of the society such as clergymen, doctors, lawyers, and landlords.

Malthus' reservations about Say's Law are particularly interesting in light of the work (in a similar vein) by John Maynard Keynes nearly a century later.

AN ESSAY ON THE
PRINCIPLE OF POPULATION

BOOK I / Of the Checks to Population in the Less Civilised Parts of the World and in Past Times

Chapter 1: STATEMENT OF THE SUBJECT—RATIOS OF THE
INCREASE OF POPULATION AND FOOD

In an inquiry concerning the improvement of society, the mode of conducting the subject which naturally presents itself, is,

1. To investigate the causes that have hitherto impeded the progress of mankind towards happiness; and,

2. To examine the probability of the total or partial removal of these causes in future.

To enter fully into this question, and to enumerate all the causes that have hitherto influenced human improvement, would be much beyond the power of an individual. The principal object of the present essay is to examine the effects of one great cause intimately united with the very nature of man; which, though it has been constantly and powerfully operating since the commencement of society, has been little noticed by the writers who have treated this subject. The facts which establish the existence of this cause have, indeed, been repeatedly stated and acknowledged; but its natural and necessary effects have been almost totally overlooked; though probably among these effects may be reckoned a very considerable portion of that vice and misery, and of that unequal distribution of the bounties of nature, which it has been the unceasing object of the enlightened philanthropist in all ages to correct.

The cause to which I allude is the constant tendency in all animated life to increase beyond the nourishment prepared for it.

It is observed by Dr. Franklin that there is no bound to the prolific

nature of plants or animals but what is made by their crowding and inter-
fering with each other's means of subsistence. Were the face of the earth,
he says, vacant of other plants, it might be gradually sowed and overspread
with one kind only, as for instance with fennel: and were it empty of other
inhabitants, it might in a few ages be replenished from one nation only, as
for instance with Englishmen.

This is incontrovertibly true. Through the animal and vegetable kingdoms nature has scattered the seeds of life abroad with the most profuse
and liberal hand; but has been comparatively sparing in the room and the
nourishment necessary to rear them. The germs of existence contained in
this earth, if they could freely develop themselves, would fill millions of
worlds in the course of a few thousand years. Necessity, that imperious, all
pervading law of nature, restrains them within the prescribed bounds. The
race of plants and the race of animals shrink under this great restrictive law;
and man cannot by any efforts of reason escape from it.

In plants and irrational animals, the view of the subject is simple. They
are all impelled by a powerful instinct to the increase of their species; and
this instinct is interrupted by no doubts about providing for their offspring.
Wherever therefore there is liberty, the power of increase is exerted; and
the superabundant effects are repressed afterwards by want of room and
nourishment.

The effects of this check on man are complicated. Impelled to the
increase of his species by an equally powerful instinct, reason interrupts his
career, and asks him whether he may not bring beings into the world for
whom he cannot provide the means of support. If he attend to this natural
suggestion, the restriction too frequently produces vice. If he hear it not,
the human race will be constantly endeavouring to increase beyond the
means of subsistence. But as, by that law of our nature which makes food
necessary to the life of man, population can never actually increase beyond
the lowest nourishment capable of supporting it, a strong check on population, from the difficulty of acquiring food, must be constantly in operation.
This difficulty must fall somewhere, and must necessarily be severely felt
in some or other of the various forms of misery, or the fear of misery, by
a large portion of mankind.

That population has this constant tendency to increase beyond the
means of subsistence, and that it is kept to its necessary level by these
causes, will sufficiently appear from a review of the different states of
society in which man has existed. But, before we proceed to this review,
the subject will, perhaps, be seen in a clearer light if we endeavour to
ascertain what would be the natural increase of population if left to exert
itself with perfect freedom; and what might be expected to be the rate
of increase in the productions of the earth under the most favourable
circumstances of human industry.

It will be allowed that no country has hitherto been known where the manners were so pure and simple, and the means of subsistence so abundant, that no check whatever has existed to early marriages from the difficulty of providing for a family, and that no waste of the human species has been occasioned by vicious customs, by towns, by unhealthy occupations, or too severe labour. Consequently in no state that we have yet known has the power of population been left to exert itself with perfect freedom.

Whether the law of marriage be instituted, or not, the dictate of nature and virtue seems to be an early attachment to one woman; and where there were no impediments of any kind in the way of an union to which such an attachment would lead, and no causes of depopulation afterwards, the increase of the human species would be evidently much greater than any increase which has been hitherto known.

In the northern states of America, where the means of subsistence have been more ample, the manners of the people more pure, and the checks to early marriages fewer than in any of the modern states of Europe, the population has been found to double itself, for above a century and a half successively, in less than twenty-five years.[1] Yet, even during these periods, in some of the towns, the deaths exceeded the births, a circumstance which clearly proves that, in those parts of the country which supplied this deficiency, the increase must have been much more rapid than the general average.

In the back settlements, where the sole employment is agriculture, and vicious customs and unwholesome occupations are little known, the population has been found to double itself in fifteen years. Even this extraordinary rate of increase is probably short of the utmost power of population. Very severe labour is requisite to clear a fresh country; such situations are not in general considered as particularly healthy; and the inhabitants, probably, are occasionally subject to the incursions of the Indians, which may destroy some lives, or at any rate diminish the fruits of industry.

According to a table of Euler, calculated on a mortality of 1 in 36, if the births be to the deaths in the proportion of 3 to 1, the period of doubling will be only 12 years and 4/5ths. And this proportion is not only a possible supposition, but has actually occurred for short periods in more countries than one.

Sir William Petty supposes a doubling possible in so short a time as ten years.

But, to be perfectly sure that we are far within the truth, we will take the slowest of these rates of increase, a rate in which all concurring testimonies agree, and which has been repeatedly ascertained to be from procreation only.

---

[1] It appears, from some recent calculations and estimates, that from the first settlement of America to the year 1800, the periods of doubling have been but very little above twenty years.

It may safely be pronounced, therefore, that population, when un-checked, goes on doubling itself every twenty-five years, or increases in a geometrical ratio.

The rate according to which the productions of the earth may be sup-posed to increase, it will not be so easy to determine. Of this, however, we may be perfectly certain, that the ratio of their increase in a limited terri-tory must be of a totally different nature from the ratio of the increase of population. A thousand millions are just as easily doubled every twenty-five years by the power of population as a thousand. But the food to support the increase from the greater number will by no means be obtained with the same facility. Man is necessarily confined in room. When acre has been added to acre till all the fertile land is occupied, the yearly increase of food must depend upon the melioration of the land already in possession. This is a fund, which, from the nature of all soils, instead of increasing, must be gradually diminishing. But population, could it be supplied with food, would go on with unexhausted vigour; and the increase of one period would furnish the power of a greater increase the next, and this without any limit.

From the accounts we have of China and Japan, it may be fairly doubted whether the best-directed efforts of human industry could double the produce of these countries even once in any number of years. There are many parts of the globe, indeed, hitherto uncultivated, and almost unoc-cupied; but the right of exterminating, or driving into a corner where they must starve, even the inhabitants of these thinly-peopled regions, will be questioned in a moral view. The process of improving their minds and directing their industry would necessarily be slow; and during this time, as population would regularly keep pace with the increasing produce, it would rarely happen that a great degree of knowledge and industry would have to operate at once upon rich unappropriated soil. Even where this might take place, as it does sometimes in new colonies, a geometrical ratio increases with such extraordinary rapidity, that the advantage could not last long. If the United States of America continue increasing, which they certainly will do, though not with the same rapidity as formerly, the Indians will be driven further and further back into the country, till the whole race is ultimately exterminated, and the territory is incapable of further extension.

These observations are, in a degree, applicable to all the parts of the earth where the soil is imperfectly cultivated. To exterminate the inhabi-tants of the greatest part of Asia and Africa is a thought that could not be admitted for a moment. To civilise and direct the industry of the various tribes of Tartars and Negroes would certainly be a work of considerable time and of variable and uncertain success.

Europe is by no means so fully peopled as it might be. In Europe there is the fairest chance that human industry may receive its best direction.

The science of agriculture has been much studied in England and Scotland; and there is still a great portion of uncultivated land in these countries. Let us consider at what rate the produce of this island might be supposed to increase under circumstances the most favourable to improvement.

If it be allowed that by the best possible policy, and great encouragements to agriculture, the average produce of the island could be doubled in the first twenty-five years, it will be allowing, probably, a greater increase than could with reason be expected.

In the next twenty-five years, it is impossible to suppose that the produce could be quadrupled. It would be contrary to all our knowledge of the properties of land. The improvement of the barren parts would be a work of time and labour; and it must be evident to those who have the slightest acquaintance with agricultural subjects that, in proportion as cultivation extended, the additions that could yearly be made to the former average produce must be gradually and regularly diminishing. That we may be the better able to compare the increase of population and food, let us make a supposition, which, without pretending to accuracy, is clearly more favourable to the power of production in the earth than any experience we have had of its qualities will warrant.

Let us suppose that the yearly additions which might be made to the former average produce, instead of decreasing, which they certainly would do, were to remain the same; and that the produce of this island might be increased every twenty-five years by a quantity equal to what it at present produces. The most enthusiastic speculator cannot suppose a greater increase than this. In a few centuries it would make every acre of land in the island like a garden.

If this supposition be applied to the whole earth, and if it be allowed that the subsistence for man which the earth affords might be increased every twenty-five years by a quantity equal to what it at present produces, this will be supposing a rate of increase much greater than we can imagine that any possible exertions of mankind could make it.

It may be fairly pronounced, therefore, that, considering the present average state of the earth, the means of subsistence, under circumstances the most favourable to human industry, could not possibly be made to increase faster than in an arithmetical ratio.

The necessary effects of these two different rates of increase, when brought together, will be very striking. Let us call the population of this island eleven millions; and suppose the present produce equal to the easy support of such a number. In the first twenty-five years the population would be twenty-two millions, and the food being also doubled, the means of subsistence would be equal to this increase. In the next twenty-five years, the population would be forty-four millions, and the means of subsistence only equal to the support of thirty-three millions. In the next period the population would be eighty-eight millions, and the means of subsistence just equal to the support of half that number. And, at the conclusion of the first century, the population would be a hundred and seventy-six millions, and the means of subsistence only equal to the support of fifty-five millions, leaving a population of a hundred and twenty-one millions totally unprovided for.

Taking the whole earth, instead of this island, emigration would of course be excluded; and, supposing the present population equal to a thousand millions, the human species would increase as the numbers, 1, 2, 4, 8, 16, 32, 64, 128, 256, and subsistence as 1, 2, 3, 4, 5, 6, 7, 8, 9. In two centuries the population would be to the means of subsistence as 256 to 9; in three centuries as 4096 to 13, and in two thousand years the difference would be almost incalculable.

In this supposition no limits whatever are placed to the produce of the earth. It may increase for ever and be greater than any assignable quantity; yet still the power of population being in every period so much superior, the increase of the human species can only be kept down to the level of the means of subsistence by the constant operation of the strong law of necessity, acting as a check upon the greater power.

Chapter 2: OF THE GENERAL CHECKS TO POPULATION, AND THE
MODE OF THEIR OPERATION

The ultimate check to population appears then to be a want of food, arising necessarily from the different ratios according to which population and food increase. But this ultimate check is never the immediate check, except in cases of actual famine.

The immediate check may be stated to consist in all those customs, and all those diseases, which seem to be generated by a scarcity of the means of subsistence; and all those causes, independent of this scarcity, whether of a moral or physical nature, which tend prematurely to weaken and destroy the human frame.

These checks to population, which are constantly operating with more or less force in every society, and keep down the number to the level of the means of subsistence, may be classed under two general heads—the preventive and the positive checks.

The preventive check, as far as it is voluntary, is peculiar to man, and arises from that distinctive superiority in his reasoning faculties which enables him to calculate distant consequences. The checks to the indefinite increase of plants and irrational animals are all either positive, or, if preventive, involuntary. But man cannot look around him and see the distress which frequently presses upon those who have large families; he cannot contemplate his present possessions or earnings, which he now nearly consumes himself, and calculate the amount of each share, when with very little addition they must be divided, perhaps, among seven or eight, without feeling a doubt whether, if he follow the bent of his inclinations, he may be able to support the offspring which he will probably bring into the world. In a state of equality, if such can exist, this would be the simple question. In the present state of society other considerations occur. Will he not lower his rank in life, and be obliged to give up in great measure his former habits? Does any mode of employment present itself by which he may reasonably hope to maintain a family? Will he not at any rate subject himself to greater difficulties, and more severe labour, than in his single state? Will he not be unable to transmit to his children the same advantages of education and improvement that he had himself possessed? Does he even feel secure that, should he have a large family, his utmost exertions can save them from rags and squalid poverty, and their consequent degradation in the community? And may he not be reduced to the grating necessity of forfeiting his independence, and of being obliged to the sparing hand of Charity for support?

These considerations are calculated to prevent, and certainly do prevent, a great number of persons in all civilised nations from pursuing the dictate of nature in an early attachment to one woman.

If this restraint does not produce vice, it is undoubtedly the least evil that can arise from the principle of population. Considered as a restraint on a strong natural inclination, it must be allowed to produce a certain degree of temporary unhappiness; but evidently slight, compared with the evils which result from any of the other checks to population; and merely of the same nature as many other sacrifices of temporary to permanent gratification, which it is the business of a moral agent continually to make.

When this restraint produces vice, the evils which follow are but too conspicuous. A promiscuous intercourse to such a degree as to prevent the birth of children seems to lower, in the most marked manner, the dignity of human nature. It cannot be without its effect on men, and nothing can be more obvious than its tendency to degrade the female character, and to destroy all its most amiable and distinguishing characteristics. Add to which, that among those unfortunate females, with which all great towns abound, more real distress and aggravated misery are, perhaps, to be found than in any other department of human life.

When a general corruption of morals, with regard to the sex, pervades all the classes of society, its effects must necessarily be to poison the springs of domestic happiness, to weaken conjugal and parental affection, and to lessen the united exertions and ardour of parents in the care and education of their children—effects which cannot take place without a decided diminution of the general happiness and virtue of the society; particularly as the necessity of art in the accomplishment and conduct of intrigues, and in the concealment of their consequences, necessarily leads to many other vices.

The positive checks to population are extremely various, and include every cause, whether arising from vice or misery, which in any degree contributes to shorten the natural duration of human life. Under this head, therefore, may be enumerated all unwholesome occupations, severe labour and exposure to the seasons, extreme poverty, bad nursing of children, great towns, excesses of all kinds, the whole train of common diseases and epidemics, wars, plague, and famine.

On examining these obstacles to the increase of population which I have classed under the heads of preventive and positive checks, it will appear that they are all resolvable into moral restraint, vice, and misery.

Of the preventive checks, the restraint from marriage which is not followed by irregular gratifications may properly be termed moral restraint.[1]

Promiscuous intercourse, unnatural passions, violations of the marriage bed, and improper arts to conceal the consequences of irregular connections, are preventive checks that clearly come under the head of vice.

Of the positive checks, those which appear to arise unavoidably from the laws of nature, may be called exclusively misery; and those which we obviously bring upon ourselves, such as wars, excesses, and many others which it would be in our power to avoid, are of a mixed nature. They are brought upon us by vice, and their consequences are misery.[2]

The sum of all these preventive and positive checks, taken together, forms the immediate check to population; and it is evident that, in every

---

[1] It will be observed that I here use the term *moral* in its most confined sense. By moral restraint I would be understood to mean a restraint from marriage from prudential motives, with a conduct strictly moral during the period of this restraint; and I have never intentionally deviated from this sense. When I have wished to consider the restraint from marriage unconnected with its consequences, I have either called it prudential restraint, or a part of the preventive check, of which indeed it forms the principal branch.

In my review of the different stages of society, I have been accused of not allowing sufficient weight in the prevention of population to moral restraint; but when the confined sense of the term, which I have here explained, is adverted to, I am fearful that I shall not be found to have erred much in this respect. I should be very glad to believe myself mistaken.

[2] As the general consequence of vice is misery, and as this consequence is the precise reason why an action is termed vicious, it may appear that the term misery alone would be here sufficient, and that it is superfluous to use both. But the rejection of the term vice would introduce a considerable confusion into our language and ideas. We want it particularly to distinguish those actions, the general tendency of which is to produce misery, and which are therefore prohibited by the commands of the Creator, and the precepts of the moralist, although, in their immediate or individual effects, they may produce perhaps exactly the contrary. The gratification of all our passions in its immediate effect is happiness, not misery; and, in individual instances, even the remote consequences (at least in this life) may possibly come under the same denomination. There may have been some irregular connections with women, which have added to the happiness of both parties, and have injured no one. These individual actions, therefore, cannot come under the head of misery. But they are still evidently vicious, because an action is so denominated, which violates an express precept, founded upon its general tendency to produce misery, whatever may be its individual effect; and no person can doubt the general tendency of an illicit intercourse between the sexes to injure the happiness of society.

country where the whole of the procreative power cannot be called into action, the preventive and the positive checks must vary inversely as each other; that is, in countries either naturally unhealthy, or subject to a great mortality, from whatever cause it may arise, the preventive check will prevail very little. In those countries, on the contrary, which are naturally healthy, and where the preventive check is found to prevail with considerable force, the positive check will prevail very little, or the mortality be very small.

In every country some of these checks are, with more or less force, in constant operation; yet, notwithstanding their general prevalence, there are few states in which there is not a constant effort in the population to increase beyond the means of subsistence. This constant effort as constantly tends to subject the lower classes of society to distress, and to prevent any great permanent melioration of their condition.

These effects, in the present state of society, seem to be produced in the following manner. We will suppose the means of subsistence in any country just equal to the easy support of its inhabitants. The constant effort towards population, which is found to act even in the most vicious societies, increases the number of people before the means of subsistence are increased. The food, therefore, which before supported eleven millions, must now be divided among eleven millions and a half. The poor consequently must live much worse, and many of them be reduced to severe distress. The number of labourers also being above the proportion of work in the market, the price of labour must tend to fall, while the price of provisions would at the same time tend to rise. The labourer therefore must do more work to earn the same as he did before. During this season of distress, the discouragements to marriage and the difficulty of rearing a family are so great that the progress of population is retarded. In the meantime, the cheapness of labour, the plenty of labourers, and the necessity of an increased industry among them, encourage cultivators to employ more labour upon their land, to turn up fresh soil, and to manure and improve more completely what is already in tillage, till ultimately the means of subsistence may become in the same proportion to the population as at the period from which we set out. The situation of the labourer being then again tolerably comfortable, the restraints to population are in some degree loosened; and, after a short period, the same retrograde and progressive movements, with respect to happiness, are repeated.

This sort of oscillation will not probably be obvious to common view; and it may be difficult even for the most attentive observer to calculate its periods. Yet that, in the generality of old states, some alternation of this kind does exist though in a much less marked, and in a much more irregular manner, than I have described it, no reflecting man, who considers the subject deeply, can well doubt.

One principal reason why this oscillation has been less remarked, and less decidedly confirmed by experience than might naturally be expected, is, that the histories of mankind which we possess are, in general, histories only of the higher classes. We have not many accounts that can be depended upon of the manners and customs of that part of mankind where these retrograde and progressive movements chiefly take place. A satisfactory history of this kind, of one people and of one period, would require the constant and minute attention of many observing minds in local and general remarks on the state of the lower classes of society, and the causes that influenced it; and to draw accurate inferences upon this subject, a succession of such historians for some centuries would be necessary. This branch of statistical knowledge has, of late years, been attended to in some countries,[3] and we may promise ourselves a clearer insight into the internal structure of human society from the progress of these inquiries. But the science may be said yet to be in its infancy, and many of the objects, on which it would be desirable to have information, have been either omitted or not stated with sufficient accuracy. Among these, perhaps, may be reckoned the proportion of the number of adults to the number of marriages; the extent to which vicious customs have prevailed in consequence of the restraints upon matrimony; the comparative mortality among the children of the most distressed part of the community and of those who live rather more at their ease; the variations in the real price of labour; the observable differences in the state of the lower classes of society, with respect to ease and happiness, at different times during a certain period; and very accurate registers of births, deaths, and marriages, which are of the utmost importance in this subject.

A faithful history, including such particulars, would tend greatly to elucidate the manner in which the constant check upon population acts; and would probably prove the existence of the retrograde and progressive movements that have been mentioned; though the times of their vibration must necessarily be rendered irregular from the operation of many interrupting causes; such as, the introduction or failure of certain manufactures; a greater or less prevalent spirit of agricultural enterprise; years of plenty or

---

[3] The judicious questions which Sir John Sinclair circulated in Scotland, and the valuable accounts which he has collected in that part of the island, do him the highest honour; and these accounts will ever remain an extraordinary monument of the learning, good sense, and general information of the clergy of Scotland. It is to be regretted that the adjoining parishes are not put together in the work, which would have assisted the memory both in attaining and recollecting the state of particular districts. The repetitions and contradictory opinions which occur are not in my opinion so objectionable, as, to the result of such testimony, more faith may be given than we could possibly give to the testimony of any individual. Even were this result drawn for us by some master hand, though much valuable time would undoubtedly be saved, the information would not be so satisfactory. If, with a few subordinate improvements, this work had contained accurate and complete registers for the last 150 years, it would have been inestimable, and would have exhibited a better picture of the internal state of a country than has yet been presented to the world. But this last most essential improvement no diligence could have effected.

years of scarcity; wars, sickly seasons, poor laws, emigrations, and other causes of a similar nature.

A circumstance which has, perhaps, more than any other, contributed to conceal this oscillation from common view is the difference between the nominal and real price of labour. It very rarely happens that the nominal price of labour universally falls; but we well know that it frequently remains the same while the nominal price of provisions has been gradually rising. This, indeed, will generally be the case if the increase of manufactures and commerce be sufficient to employ the new labourers that are thrown into the market, and to prevent the increased supply from lowering the money-price.[4] But an increased number of labourers receiving the same money-wages will necessarily, by their competition, increase the money-price of corn. This is, in fact, a real fall in the price of labour; and, during this period, the condition of the lower classes of the community must be gradually growing worse. But the farmers and capitalists are growing rich from the real cheapness of labour. Their increasing capitals enable them to employ a greater number of men; and, as the population had probably suffered some check from the greater difficulty of supporting a family, the demand for labour, after a certain period, would be great in proportion to the supply, and its price would of course rise, if left to find its natural level; and thus the wages of labour, and consequently the condition of the lower classes of society, might have progressive and retrograde movements, though the price of labour might never nominally fall.

In savage life, where there is no regular price of labour, it is little to be doubted that similar oscillations took place. When population has increased nearly to the utmost limits of the food, all the preventive and the positive checks will naturally operate with increased force. Vicious habits with respect to the sex will be more general, the exposing of children more frequent, and both the probability and fatality of wars and epidemics will be considerably greater; and these causes will probably continue their operation till the population is sunk below the level of the food; and then the return to comparative plenty will again produce an increase, and, after a certain period, its further progress will again be checked by the same causes.[5]

But without attempting to establish these progressive and retrograde

---

[4] If the new labourers thrown yearly into the market should find no employment but in agriculture, their competition might so lower the money-price of labour as to prevent the increase of population from occasioning an effective demand for more corn; or, in other words, if the landlords and farmers could get nothing but an additional quantity of agricultural labour in exchange for any additional produce which they could raise, they might not be tempted to raise it.

[5] Sir James Stuart very justly compares the generative faculty to a spring loaded with a variable weight (*Political Economy*, Vol. I, Bk. I, Chap. 4, p. 20), which would of course produce exactly that kind of oscillation which has been mentioned. In the first book of his Political Economy, he has explained many parts of the subject of population very ably.

movements in different countries, which would evidently require more minute histories than we possess, and which the progress of civilisation naturally tends to counteract, the following propositions are intended to be proved:—

1. Population is necessarily limited by the means of subsistence.

2. Population invariably increases where the means of subsistence increase, unless prevented by some very powerful and obvious checks.[6]

3. These checks, and the checks which repress the superior power of population, and keep its effects on a level with the means of subsistence, are all resolvable into moral restraint, vice, and misery.

The first of these propositions scarcely needs illustration. The second and third will sufficiently be established by a review of the immediate checks to population in the past and present state of society.

BOOK IV / Of Our Future Prospects Respecting the Removal or Mitigation of the Evils Arising from the Principle of Population

Chapter 3: OF THE ONLY EFFECTUAL MODE OF IMPROVING THE CONDITION OF THE POOR

He who publishes a moral code, or system of duties, however firmly he may be convinced of the strong obligation on each individual strictly to conform to it, has never the folly to imagine that it will be universally or even generally practised. But this is no valid objection against the publication of the code. If it were, the same objection would always have applied; we should be totally without general rules; and to the vices of mankind arising from temptation would be added a much longer list than we have at present of vices from ignorance.

Judging merely from the light of nature, if we feel convinced of the misery arising from a redundant population on the one hand, and of the evils and unhappiness, particularly to the female sex, arising from promiscuous intercourse, on the other, I do not see how it is possible for any

---

[6] I have expressed myself in this cautious manner, because I believe there are some instances where population does not keep up to the level of the means of subsistence. But these are extreme cases; and, generally speaking, it might be said that,

2. Population always increases where the means of subsistence increase.

3. The checks which repress the superior power of population, and keep its effects on a level with the means of subsistence, are all resolvable into moral restraint, vice, and misery.

It should be observed that, by an increase in the means of subsistence is here meant such an increase as will enable the mass of the society to command more food. An increase might certainly take place, which in the actual state of a particular society would not be distributed to the lower classes, and consequently would give no stimulus to population.

person who acknowledges the principle of utility as the great criterion of moral rules to escape the conclusion that moral restraint, or the abstaining from marriage till we are in a condition to support a family, with a perfectly moral conduct during that period, is the strict line of duty; and when revelation is taken into question, this duty undoubtedly receives very powerful confirmation. At the same time I believe that few of my readers can be less sanguine that I am in their expectations of any sudden and great change in the general conduct of men on this subject: and the chief reason why in the last chapter I allowed myself to suppose the universal prevalence of this virtue was, that I might endeavour to remove any imputation on the goodness of the Deity, by showing that the evils arising from the principle of population were exactly of the same nature as the generality of other evils which excite fewer complaints: that they were increased by human ignorance and indolence, and diminished by human knowledge and virtue; and on the supposition that each individual strictly fulfilled his duty would be almost totally removed; and this without any general diminution of those sources of pleasure, arising from the regulated indulgence of the passions, which have been justly considered as the principal ingredients of human happiness.

. . .

PRINCIPLES OF
POLITICAL ECONOMY

BOOK II

Chapter 1: ON THE PROGRESS OF WEALTH

§ Section 3. Of Accumulation, or the Saving from Revenue to Add to
Capital, Considered as a Stimulus to the Increase of Wealth

Those who reject mere population as an adequate stimulus to the increase
of wealth, are generally disposed to make every thing depend upon accumulation. It is certainly true that no permanent and continued increase of
wealth can take place without a continued increase of capital; and I cannot agree with Lord Lauderdale in thinking that this increase can be
effected in any other way than by saving from the stock which might
have been destined for immediate consumption, and adding it to that
which is to yield a profit; or in other words, by the conversion of revenue
into capital.[1]

But we have yet to inquire what is the state of things which generally
disposes a nation to accumulate; and further, what is the state of things
which tends to make that accumulation the most effective, and lead to a
further and continued increase of capital and wealth.

It is undoubtedly possible by parsimony to devote at once a much larger
share than usual of the produce of any country to the maintenance of productive labour; and suppose this to be done, it is quite true that the
labourers so employed are consumers as well as those engaged in personal

---

[1] See Lord Lauderdale's Chapter on Parsimony, in his *Inquiry into the Nature and
Origin of Public Wealth*, Chap. IV, p. 198, 2nd ed. Lord Lauderdale appears to have
gone as much too far in deprecating accumulation, as some other writers in recommend-
ing it. This tendency to extremes is one of the great sources of error in political economy,
where so much depends upon proportions.

services, and that as far as the labourers are concerned, there would be no diminution of consumption or demand. But it has already been shewn that the consumption and demand occasioned by the workmen employed in productive labour can never *alone* furnish a motive to the accumulation and employment of capital; and with regard to the capitalists themselves, together with the landlords and other rich persons, they have, by the supposition, agreed to be parsimonious, and by depriving themselves of their usual conveniencies and luxuries to save from their revenue and add to their capital. Under these circumstances, it is impossible that the increased quantity of commodities, obtained by the increased number of productive labourers, should find purchasers, without such a fall of price as would probably sink their value below that of the outlay, or, at least, so reduce profits as very greatly to diminish both the power and the will to save.

It has been thought by some very able writers, that although there may easily be a glut of particular commodities, there cannot possibly be a glut of commodities in general; because, according to their view of the subject, commodities being always exchanged for commodities, one half will furnish a market for the other half, and production being thus the sole source of demand, an excess in the supply of one article merely proves a deficiency in the supply of some other, and a general excess is impossible. M. Say, in his distinguished work on political economy, has indeed gone so far as to state that the consumption of a commodity by taking it out of the market diminishes demand, and the production of a commodity proportionably increases it.

This doctrine, however, as generally applied, appears to me to be utterly unfounded, and completely to contradict the great principles which regulate supply and demand.

It is by no means true, as a matter of fact, that commodities are always exchanged for commodities. An immense mass of commodities is exchanged directly, either for productive labour, or personal services: and it is quite obvious, that this mass of commodities, compared with the labour with which it is to be exchanged, may fall in value from a glut just as any one commodity falls in value from an excess of supply, compared either with labour or money.

In the case supposed there would evidently be an unusual quantity of commodities of all kinds in the market, owing to those who had been before engaged in personal services having been converted, by the accumulation of capital, into productive labourers; while the number of labourers altogether being the same, and the power and will to purchase for consumption among landlords and capitalists being by supposition diminished, commodities would necessarily fall in value compared with labour, so as very greatly to lower profits, and to check for a time further production.

But this is precisely what is meant by the term glut, which, in this case, is evidently general, not partial.

M. Say, Mr. Mill,[2] and Mr. Ricardo, the principal authors of these new doctrines, appear to me to have fallen into some fundamental errors in the view which they have taken of this subject.

In the first place, they have considered commodities as if they were so many mathematical figures, or arithmetical characters, the relations of which were to be compared, instead of articles of consumption, which must of course be referred to the numbers and wants of the consumers.

If commodities were only to be compared and exchanged with each other, then indeed it would be true that, if they were all increased in their proper proportions to any extent, they would continue to bear among themselves the same relative value; but, if we compare them, as we certainly ought to do, with the means of producing them, and with the numbers and wants of the consumers, then a great increase of produce with comparatively stationary numbers or with wants diminished by parsimony, must necessarily occasion a great fall of value estimated in labour, so that the same produce, though it might have *cost* the same quantity of labour as before, would no longer *command* the same quantity; and both the power of accumulation and the motive to accumulate would be strongly checked.

It is asserted that effectual demand is nothing more than the offering of one commodity in exchange for another which has cost the same quantity of labour. But is this all that is necessary to effectual demand? Though each commodity may have cost the same quantity of labour in its production, and they may be exactly equivalent to each other in exchange, yet why may not both be so plentiful as not to command more labour, than they have cost, that is, to yield no profit, and in this case, would the demand for them be effectual? Would it be such as to encourage their continued production? Unquestionably not. Their relation to each other may not have changed; but their relation to the wants of the society, and their relation to labour, may have experienced a most important change.[3]

---

[2] Mr. Mill, in a reply to Mr. Spence, published in 1808, has laid down very broadly the doctrine that commodities are only purchased by commodities, and that one half of them must always furnish a market for the other half. The same doctrine appears to be adopted in its fullest extent by the author of an able and useful article on the Corn Laws, in the supplement to the *Encyclopaedia Britannica*, which has been referred to in a previous chapter. These writers do not seem to be aware of what is unquestionably true, that demand is always determined by *value*, and supply by *quantity*. Two bushels of wheat are double the quantity of one in regard to supply; but in numerous cases, two bushels will not make so great a demand as one bushel.

[3] The variations which take place in the *general* rate of profits being common to all commodities, will not of course affect their *relative* values; that is, whether commodities *universally* rise to a higher price, or sink to a lower one, or even fall below their cost, they will continue to bear the same proportion to each other as they did before. But no one would ever think of saying, that the demand for them (in the ordinary sense of the word) was the same in both cases. When, therefore, Mr. Mill explains the equality

It will be readily allowed that a new commodity thrown into the market, which, in proportion to the labour employed upon it, is of higher exchangeable value than usual, is precisely calculated to increase demand; because it implies, not a mere increase of quantity, but an increase of value owing to a better adaptation of the produce to the tastes, wants and consumption of the society. But to fabricate or procure commodities of this kind is the grand difficulty; and they certainly do not naturally and necessarily follow an accumulation of capital and increase of commodities, most particularly when such accumulation and increase have been occasioned by economy of consumption, or a discouragement to the indulgence of those tastes and wants, which are the very elements of demand and of value.

Mr. Ricardo, though he maintains as a general position that capital cannot be redundant, is obliged to make the following concession. He says, "There is only one case, and that will be temporary, in which the accumulation of capital with a low price of food may be attended with a fall of profits; and that is, when the funds for the maintenance of labour increase much more rapidly than population;—wages will then be high and profits low. If every man were to forego the use of luxuries and be intent only on accumulation, a quantity of necessaries might be produced for which there

---

of demand and supply to consist in this;—"that goods which have been produced by a certain quantity of labour, exchange for goods which have been produced by an equal quantity of labour" (*Elements of Political Economy*, 3rd edit., p. 239), he uses the term *demand* in a sense quite different from that which is usually meant by it. The demand and supply, as he understands them, may be equal to each other, when, owing to a general slackness of trade, the mass of goods are selling at a price very much below their ordinary costs of production; or when, in consequence of unusual briskness, they are selling very much above their costs; that is, when, according to Adam Smith, and to the accustomed language of society, the supply would be said, either greatly to exceed the demand, or to fall considerably short of it.

Throughout the chapter from which the foregoing passage is taken, Mr. Mill uses the term *demand*, as if it were synonymous with *extent of consumption*. By an increase or diminution of the demand, he means to refer simply to the greater or less quantity of goods bought or sold. What is usually meant by it, is, the rise or fall in the value of any given quantity of them.

An error, not to the same extent, but somewhat similar in kind, pervades the writings of Col. Torrens.—He represents *effectual and profitable demand* as consisting in the power of exchanging commodities for a *greater* quantity of the ingredients of capital than have been expended in their production. (*Essay on Wealth*, p. 360.) This view of demand, though nearer to the truth than the foregoing one, is nevertheless incorrect. The chief ingredients of capital, and frequently by far the largest, are food and clothing; and this Col. Torrens admits, since he represents the costs of production, as consisting in the advance of a given number of quarters of corn and suits of clothing. Now, although a man should sell his commodity for more corn and clothing than it has cost him, he may, notwithstanding, find himself in this predicament, that, the corn and clothing when obtained, may not, owing to a change in their relation to labour, command the services of the same number of men as were employed in the production of the commodity for which they have been exchanged; in which case the *apparent* profit would be greatly reduced, or might even disappear altogether. It is then in vain for us to measure the demand for a commodity by the quantity of any other commodity which can be had in exchange for it, since we must at last resort to labour as the only standard of the real value of every thing, and of the effectual demand for it. *Ed.*

could not be any immediate consumption. Of commodities so limited in number, there might undoubtedly be an universal glut; and consequently there might neither be demand for an additional quantity of such commodities, nor profits on the employment of more capital. If men ceased to consume, they would cease to produce." Mr. Ricardo then adds, "This admission does not impugn the general principle."[4] In this last remark I can by no means agree with him. It appears to me most completely to impugn the general principle. Even if we suppose with Mr. Ricardo, what is not true, that an increase of population would certainly remedy the evil; yet as from the nature of a population, an increase of labourers cannot be brought into the market, in consequence of a particular demand, till after the lapse of sixteen or eighteen years, and the conversion of revenue into capital by saving, may take place much more rapidly; a country is always liable to an increase in the quantity of the funds for the maintenance of labour faster than the increase of population. But if, whenever this occurs, there may be an universal glut of commodities, how can it be maintained, as a general position, that capital is never redundant; and that because commodities may retain the same relative values, a glut can only be partial, not general?

Another fundamental error into which the writers above-mentioned and their followers appear to have fallen is, the not taking into consideration the influence of so general and important a principle in human nature, as indolence or love of ease.

It has been supposed that, if a certain number of farmers and a certain number of manufacturers had been exchanging their surplus food and clothing with each other, and their powers of production were suddenly so increased that both parties could, with the same labour, produce luxuries in addition to what they had before obtained, there could be no sort of difficulty with regard to demand, as part of the luxuries which the farmer produced would be exchanged against part of the luxuries produced by the manufacturer; and the only result would be, the happy one of both parties being better supplied and having more enjoyments.

But in this intercourse of mutual gratifications, two things are taken for granted, which are the very points in dispute. It is taken for granted that luxuries are always preferred to indolence, and that an adequate proportion of the profits of each party is consumed as revenue. What would be the effect of a desire to save under such circumstances, shall be considered presently. The effect of a preference of indolence to luxuries would evidently be to occasion a want of demand for the returns of the increased powers of production supposed, and to throw labourers out of employment. The cultivator, being now enabled to obtain the necessaries and conveniences to which he had been accustomed, with less toil and trouble, and his tastes for ribands, lace and velvet not being fully formed, might be

[4] David Ricardo, *Principles of Political Economy*, Chap. XXI, p. 343, 3rd edit.

very likely to indulge himself in indolence, and employ less labour on the land; while the manufacturer, finding his velvets rather heavy of sale, would be led to discontinue their manufacture, and to fall almost necessarily into the same indolent system as the farmer. That an efficient taste for luxuries and conveniences, that is, such a taste as will properly stimulate industry, instead of being ready to appear at the moment it is required, is a plant of slow growth, the history of human society sufficiently shows; and that it is a most important error to take for granted, that mankind will produce and consume all that they have the power to produce and consume, and will never prefer indolence to the rewards of industry, will sufficiently appear from a slight review of some of the nations with which we are acquainted. But I shall have occasion for a review of this kind in the next section; and to this I refer the reader.

It has been said, that it is specifically the deficiency of production on the part of the indolent, which occasions the want of demand for the products of the industrious; and that, if the idle were made to produce, the surplus would disappear. But this remark is evidently beside the question.[5] The real question is, whether under the actual habits and tastes of the society, any number of persons who might be inclined to save and produce, if they suited their produce to these habits and tastes, would be secure of finding such a demand for all they could bring into the market as to prevent the possibility of what is called a glut, or a great fall of profits in a large mass of commodities. What might happen under different tastes and habits is entirely a different question.

It has also been said, that there is never an indisposition to consume, that the indisposition is to produce. Yet, what is the disposition of those master manufacturers, and merchants who produce very largely and consume sparingly? Is their will to purchase commodities for their consumption proportioned to their power? Does not the use which they make of their capital clearly show that their will is to produce, not to consume? and in fact, if there were not in every country some who were indisposed to consume to the value of what they produced, how could the national capital ever be increased?

A third very serious error of the writers above referred to, and practically the most important of the three, consists in supposing that accumulation ensures demand; or that the consumption of the labourers employed by those whose object is to save, will create such an effectual demand for commodities as to encourage a continued increase of produce.

[5] This answer of the author will hardly be thought satisfactory. For if the allegation set up be a *true* one, it certainly falls within the limits of the question. The proper answer is, that it is *not a true* one. If the idle were to produce, it could only be by means of a larger accumulation, that is, of the conversion of more *revenue* into *capital*. But this, though it might make some alteration in the channels of demand, could not possibly increase the sum total of the demand.   *Ed.*

Mr. Ricardo observes, that "If £10,000 were given to a man having £100,000 per annum, he would not lock it up in a chest, but would either increase his expenses by £10,000, employ it himself productively, or lend it to some other person for that purpose; in either case demand would be increased, although it would be for different objects. If he increased his expenses, his effectual demand might probably be for buildings, furniture, or some such enjoyment. If he employed his £10,000 productively, his effectual demand would be for food, clothing, and raw materials, which might set new labourers to work. But still it would be *demand*."[6]

Upon this principle it is supposed that if the richer portion of society were to forego their accustomed conveniences and luxuries with a view to accumulation, the only effect would be a direction of nearly the whole capital of the country to the production of necessaries, which would lead to a great increase of cultivation and population. But this is precisely the case in which Mr. Ricardo distinctly allows that there might be a universal glut; for there would undoubtedly be more necessaries produced than would be sufficient for the existing demand. This state of things could not, however, continue; since, owing to the fall which would take place, cultivation would be checked, and accumulation be arrested in its progress.

It is therefore obvious that without an expenditure which will encourage commerce, manufactures, and personal services, the possessors of land would have no sufficient stimulus to cultivate well; and a country such as our own, which had been rich and populous, would, with too parsimonious habits, infallibly become poor and comparatively unpeopled.

This reasoning will obviously apply to the case noticed before. While the farmers were disposed to consume the luxuries produced by the manufacturers, and the manufacturers those produced by the farmers, all would go on smoothly; but if either one or both of the parties were disposed to save largely, with a view of bettering their condition, and providing for their families in future, the state of things would be very different. The farmer, instead of indulging himself in ribands, lace, and velvets, would be disposed to be satisfied with more simple clothing, but by this economy he would disable the manufacturer from purchasing the same amount of his produce; and for the returns of so much labour employed upon the land, and all greatly increased in productive power, there would evidently be no market. The manufacturer, in like manner, instead of indulging himself in sugar, grapes, and tobacco, might be disposed to save with a view to the future, but would be totally unable to do so, owing to the parsimony of the farmers and the want of demand for manufactures.[7]

---

6 *Principles of Political Economy*, Chap. XXI, p. 361, 2nd edit.

7 Theoretical writers in Political Economy, from the fear of appearing to attach too much importance to money, have perhaps been too apt to throw it out of their consideration in their reasonings. It is an abstract truth that we want commodities, not

An accumulation, to a certain extent, of common food and common clothing might take place on both sides; but the amount must necessarily be extremely confined. It would be no sort of use to the farmer to go on cultivating his land with a view merely to give food and clothing to his labourers. He would be doing nothing either for himself or family, if he neither consumed the surplus of what they produced himself, nor could realize it in a shape that might be transmitted to his descendants. If he were a tenant, such additional care and labour would be entirely thrown away; and if he were a landlord, and were determined, without reference to markets, to cultivate his estate in such a way as to make it yield the greatest neat surplus with a view to the future, it is quite certain that the large portion of this surplus which was not required either for his home consumption, or to purchase clothing for himself and his labourers, would be absolutely wasted. If he did not choose to use it in the purchase of luxuries or the maintenance of personal services, it might as well be thrown into the sea. To save it, that is to use it in employing more labourers upon the land, would be to impoverish both himself and his family, and render it impossible at a future time to obtain a large disposeable produce from his land, without retracing his steps and dismissing half his labourers, who might starve when their labour was no longer wanted.

It would be still more useless to the manufacturers to go on producing clothing beyond what was wanted by the agriculturists and themselves. Their numbers indeed would entirely depend upon the demands of the agriculturists, as they would have no means of purchasing subsistence, but in proportion as there was a reciprocal want of their manufactures. The population required to provide simple clothing for such a society with the assistance of good machinery would be inconsiderable, and would absorb but a small portion of the proper surplus of rich and well cultivated land. There would evidently therefore be a general want of demand, both for produce and population; and while it is quite certain that an adequate passion for consumption may fully keep up the proper proportion between supply and demand, whatever may be the powers of production, it appears

---

money. But, in reality, no commodity for which it is possible to sell our goods at once, can be an adequate substitute for a circulating medium, and enable us in the same manner to provide for children, to purchase an estate, or to command labour and provisions a year or two hence. A circulating medium is absolutely necessary to any considerable saving; and even the manufacturer would get on but slowly, if he were obliged to accumulate in kind all the wages of his workmen. We cannot therefore be surprised at his wanting money rather than other goods; and, in civilized countries, we may be quite sure that if the farmer or manufacturer cannot sell his products so as to give him a profit estimated in money, his industry will immediately slacken. The circulating medium bears so important a part in the distribution of wealth, and the encouragement of industry, that it is hardly ever safe to set it aside in our reasonings, and all attempts at illustration, by supposing advances of a certain quantity of corn and clothing, instead of a certain quantity of money, which every year practically represents a variable quantity of corn, cannot fail to lead us wrong.

to be quite as certain that an inordinate passion for accumulation must inevitably lead to a supply of commodities beyond what the structure and habits of such a society will permit to be profitably consumed.[8]

But if this be so, surely it is a most important error to couple the passion for expenditure and the passion for accumulation together, as if they were of the same nature; and to consider the demand for the food and clothing of the labourer, who is to be employed productively, as securing such a general demand for commodities and such a rate of profits for the capital employed in producing them, as will adequately call forth the powers of the soil, and the ingenuity of man in procuring the greatest quantity both of raw and manufactured produce.

If, in the process of saving, all that was lost by the capitalist was gained by the labourer, the check to the progress of wealth would be but temporary, as stated by Mr. Ricardo; and the consequences need not be apprehended. But if the conversion of revenue into capital pushed beyond a certain point must, by diminishing the effectual demand for produce, throw the labouring classes out of employment, it is obvious that the adoption of parsimonious habits beyond a certain point, may be accompanied by the most distressing effects at first, and by a marked depression of wealth and population afterwards.

It is not, of course, meant to be stated that parsimony, or even a temporary diminution of consumption,[9] is not often in the highest degree useful, and sometimes absolutely necessary to the progress of wealth. A state may certainly be ruined by extravagance; and a diminution of the actual expenditure may not only be necessary on this account, but when the capital of a country is deficient, compared with the demand for its products, a temporary economy of consumption is required, in order to provide that supply of capital which can alone furnish the means of an increased consumption in future. All that is contended for is, that no nation can *possibly* grow rich by an accumulation of capital, arising from a permanent diminution of consumption; because such accumulation being beyond what is wanted in order to supply the effectual demand for produce, a part of it would very soon lose both its use and its value, and cease to possess the character of wealth.

· · ·

[8] The reader must already know, that I do not share in the apprehensions of Mr. Owen about the permanent effects of machinery. But I am decidedly of opinion, that on this point he has the best of the argument with those who think that accumulation ensures effectual demand.

[9] Parsimony, or the conversion of revenue into capital, may take place without any diminution of consumption, if the revenue increases first.

DAVID RICARDO

(1 7 7 2 – 1 8 2 3)

Unlike the two preceding figures, Ricardo was self-educated in the field of economics and never held any academic position. Born the son of a banker, Ricardo broke with his family at an early age over his marriage to a gentile and proceeded to amass a fortune on his own. Despite the handicap of not being able to express himself clearly either verbally or in writing, Ricardo won widespread respect from his contemporaries and a seat in Parliament through the power of his analytic mind. His complete writings and correspondence have been assembled and edited by Professor Piero Sraffa in David Ricardo, The Works and Correspondence, Cambridge University Press, New york, 1951–1955.

Although they disagreed on a number of questions in economics, including some details concerning the danger of overpopulation, Ricardo and Malthus were good friends and Ricardo made considerable use of Malthus' Law of Population in formulating his own theories. Whereas Smith had seen the principal issue in economics as a question of production, Ricardo chose to focus on the problem of distribution.

The drive for profits led capitalists to accumulate capital, thus supplying them with funds with which to bid for labor. The resulting upward pressure on money wages led to an expansion in the population along Malthusian lines, thereby compelling the cultivation of inferior pieces of land to produce the means of supporting the enlarged population. The result, said Ricardo, since the rate of profit could not, due to competition, differ between different cultivators, was to produce a rising amount of rent on the more fertile pieces of land. As the cost of production of necessities grew increasingly great because less and less fertile pieces of land had to be cultivated, the cost of food and agricultural produce rose. The natural wage, which Ricardo defined as the subsistence wage, also had to rise to match the rise in the cost of agricultural produce. As the rate of wages rose, the rate of profits would decline until eventually no new accumulation of capital would take place and the economy would cease to grow as a stationary state arose.

The basis for Ricardo's reputation as a pessimist emerges from the above brief sketch of his system. Workers, according to the iron law of wages (although partially qualified by Ricardo, see p. 116), were condemned in the long run to a subsistence wage, while the economy itself ceased its economic growth. Even if landlords were to forego all of their rents, the same inevitable result would occur.

As is so often the case, Ricardo's pessimism was qualified by a big "if." If the government would follow his recommendations and eliminate the Corn Laws protecting domestic agricultural production, the rising cost of agricultural produce could be averted for a long time, the natural wage thus be prevented from rising, and the rate of profits preserved. Ricardo also provided a more sophisticated (compared to Smith) explanation of the gains from free trade in terms of comparative advantage.

Two aspects of Ricardo's economics which have been omitted from the following selection deserve a special word of attention at this point. The reader should note that the full title of Ricardo's book was The Principles of Political Economy and Taxation; nearly a third of the book dealt with the question of various taxes, their influence and their impact on the economy. In keeping with the Classical economic view that governments produced no real wealth, Ricardo saw cause to keep taxes at as low a level as possible. Furthermore, since with few exceptions all taxes eventually fell on profits, the effect of taxes was to divert capital abroad and check the pace of economic growth at home.

Somewhat surprising in light of Ricardo's general acceptance of the concept of Say's Law—one of the sources of contention between Malthus and himself—Ricardo warned that the employment of machinery might lead to the displacement of workers because capital funds which would otherwise be used in their employment would be tied up in machinery and thus be removed from the wage fund.

The book was not started as a book but as a collection of essays, and the chapters as originally set up followed in no logical sequence. The present editors have reorganized Ricardo's chapters somewhat so that they follow in a more logical sequence.

Ricardo's book is a difficult one to read and understand. Part of this difficulty stems from Ricardo's awkwardness of expression, but part of it is also due to the abstract, deductive style he employed in his analysis. Whatever the impediments in style which resulted, it remains true that Ricardo's method of analysis has served as a model for later generations of economists.

THE PRINCIPLES OF POLITICAL
ECONOMY AND TAXATION

Chapter 1: ON VALUE

§ Section 1

> *The value of a commodity, or the quantity of any other commodity for which it will exchange, depends on the relative quantity of labour which is necessary for its production, and not on the greater or less compensation which is paid for that labour.*

It has been observed by Adam Smith that "the word Value has two different meanings, and sometimes expresses the utility of some particular object, and sometimes the power of purchasing other goods which the possession of that object conveys. The one may be called *value in use*; the other *value in exchange*. The things," he continues, "which have the greatest value in use, have frequently little or no value in exchange; and, on the contrary, those which have the greatest value in exchange, have little or no value in use." Water and air are abundantly useful; they are indeed indispensable to existence, yet, under ordinary circumstances, nothing can be obtained in exchange for them. Gold, on the contrary, though of little use compared with air or water, will exchange for a great quantity of other goods.

Utility then is not the measure of exchangeable value, although it is absolutely essential to it. If a commodity were in no way useful—in other words, if it could in no way contribute to our gratification—it would be destitute of exchangeable value, however scarce it might be, or whatever quantity of labour might be necessary to procure it.

Possessing utility, commodities derive their exchangeable value from two sources: from their scarcity, and from the quantity of labour required to obtain them.

There are some commodities, the value of which is determined by their scarcity alone. No labour can increase the quantity of such goods, and therefore their value cannot be lowered by an increased supply. Some rare statues and pictures, scarce books and coins, wines of a peculiar quality, which can be made only from grapes grown on a particular soil, of which there is a very limited quantity, are all of this description. Their value is wholly independent of the quantity of labour originally necessary to produce them, and varies with the varying wealth and inclinations of those who are desirous to possess them.

These commodities, however, form a very small part of the mass of commodities daily exchanged in the market. By far the greatest part of those goods which are the objects of desire are procured by labour; and they may be multiplied, not in one country alone, but in many, almost without any assignable limit, if we are disposed to bestow the labour necessary to obtain them.

In speaking, then, of commodities, of their exchangeable value, and of the laws which regulate their relative prices, we mean always such commodities only as can be increased in quantity by the exertion of human industry, and on the production of which competition operates without restraint.

In the early stages of society, the exchangeable value of these commodities, or the rule which determines how much of one shall be given in exchange for another, depends almost exclusively on the comparative quantity of labour expended on each.

"The real price of everything," says Adam Smith, "what everything really costs to the man who wants to acquire it, is the toil and trouble of acquiring it. What everything is really worth to the man who has acquired it, and who wants to dispose of it, or exchange it for something else, is the toil and trouble which it can save to himself, and which it can impose upon other people." "Labour was the first price—the original purchase-money that was paid for all things." Again, "in that early and rude state of society which precedes both the accumulation of stock and the appropriation of land, the proportion between the quantities of labour necessary for acquiring different objects seems to be the only circumstance which can afford any rule for exchanging them for one another. If, among a nation of hunters, for example, it usually cost twice the labour to kill a beaver which it does to kill a deer, one beaver should naturally exchange for, or be worth, two deer. It is natural that what is usually the produce of two days' or two hours' labour should be worth double of what is usually the produce of one day's or one hour's labour."

That this is really the foundation of the exchangeable value of all things, excepting those which cannot be increased by human industry, is a doctrine of the utmost importance in political economy; for from no source do so many errors, and so much difference of opinion in that science proceed, as from the vague ideas which are attached to the word value.

If the quantity of labour realised in commodities regulate their exchangeable value, every increase of the quantity of labour must augment the value of that commodity on which it is exercised, as every diminution must lower it.

Adam Smith, who so accurately defined the original source of exchangeable value, and who was bound in consistency to maintain that all things became more or less valuable in proportion as more or less labour was bestowed on their production, has himself erected another standard measure of value, and speaks of things being more or less valuable in proportion as they will exchange for more or less of this standard measure. Sometimes he speaks of corn, at other times of labour, as a standard measure; not the quantity of labour bestowed on the production of any object, but the quantity which it can command in the market: as if these were two equivalent expressions, and as if, because a man's labour had become doubly efficient, and he could therefore produce twice the quantity of a commodity, he would necessarily receive twice the former quantity in exchange for it.

If this indeed were true, if the reward of the labourer were always in proportion to what he produced, the quantity of labour bestowed on a commodity, and the quantity of labour which that commodity would purchase, would be equal, and either might accurately measure the variations of other things; but they are not equal; the first is under many circumstances an invariable standard, indicating correctly the variations of other things; the latter is subject to as many fluctuations as the commodities compared with it. Adam Smith, after most ably showing the insufficiency of a variable medium, such as gold and silver, for the purpose of determining the varying value of other things, has himself, by fixing on corn or labour, chosen a medium no less variable.

Gold and silver are no doubt subject to fluctuations from the discovery of new and more abundant mines; but such discoveries are rare, and their effects, though powerful, are limited to periods of comparatively short duration. They are subject also to fluctuation from improvements in the skill and machinery with which the mines may be worked; as in consequence of such improvements a greater quantity may be obtained with the same labour. They are further subject to fluctuation from the decreasing produce of the mines, after they have yielded a supply to the world for a succession of ages. But from which of these sources of fluctuation is corn exempted? Does not that also vary, on one hand, from improvements in agriculture, from improved machinery and implements used in husbandry, as well as from the discovery of new tracts of fertile land, which in other countries may be taken into cultivation, and which will affect the value of corn in every market where importation is free? Is it not on the other hand subject to be enhanced in value from prohibitions of importation, from increasing population and wealth, and the greater difficulty of obtaining the increased supplies, on account of the additional quantity of labour which the cultivation of inferior land requires? Is not the value of labour equally variable; being not only affected, as all other things are, by the proportion between the supply and demand, which uniformly varies with every change in the condition of the community, but also by the varying price of food and other necessaries, on which the wages of labour are expended?

In the same country double the quantity of labour may be required to produce a given quantity of food and necessaries at one time that may be necessary at another and a distant time; yet the labourer's reward may possibly be very little diminished. If the labourer's wages at the former period were a certain quantity of food and necessaries, he probably could not have subsisted if that quantity had been reduced. Food and necessaries in this case will have risen 100 per cent. if estimated by the *quantity* of labour necessary to their production, while they will scarcely have increased in value if measured by the quantity of labour for which they will *exchange*.

The same remark may be made respecting two or more countries. In America and Poland, on the land last taken into cultivation, a year's labour of any given number of men will produce much more corn than on land similarly circumstanced in England. Now, supposing all other necessaries to be equally cheap in those three countries, would it not be a great mistake to conclude that the quantity of corn awarded to the labourer would in each country be in proportion to the facility of production?

If the shoes and clothing of the labourer could, by improvements in machinery, be produced by one-fourth of the labour now necessary to their production, they would probably fall 75 per cent.; but so far is it from being true that the labourer would thereby be enabled permanently to consume four coats, or four pair of shoes, instead of one, that it is probable his wages would in no long time be adjusted by the effects of competition, and the stimulus to population, to the new value of the necessaries on which they were expended. If these improvements extended to all the objects of the labourer's consumption, we should find him probably, at the end of a very few years, in possession of only a small, if any, addition to his enjoyments, although the exchangeable value of those commodities, compared with any other commodity, in the manufacture of which no such improvement were made, had sustained a very considerable reduction; and though they were the produce of a very considerably diminished quantity of labour.

It cannot then be correct to say with Adam Smith, "that as labour may sometimes *purchase* a greater and sometimes a smaller quantity of goods, it is their value which varies, not that of the labour which purchases them;" and therefore, "that labour, *alone never varying in its own value*, is alone the ultimate and real standard by which the value of all commodities can at all times and places be estimated and compared;"—but it is correct to say, as Adam Smith had previously said, "that the proportion between the quantities of labour necessary for acquiring different objects seems to be the only circumstance which can afford any rule for exchanging them for one another;" or in other words that it is the comparative quantity of commodities which labour will produce that determines their present or past relative value, and not the comparative quantities of commodities which are given to the labourer in exchange for his labour.

Two commodities vary in relative value, and we wish to know in which the variation has really taken place. If we compare the present value of one with shoes, stockings, hats, iron, sugar, and all other commodities, we find that it will exchange for precisely the same quantity of all these things as before. If we compare the other with the same commodities, we find it has varied with respect to them all: we may then with great probability infer that the variation has been in this commodity, and not in the commodities with which we have compared it. If on examining still more particularly into all the circumstances connected with the production of these various commodities, we find that precisely the same quantity of labour and capital are necessary to the production of the shoes, stockings, hats, iron, sugar, etc.; but that the same quantity as before is not necessary to produce the single commodity whose relative value is altered, probability is changed into certainty, and we are sure that the variation is in the single commodity: we then discover also the cause of its variation.

If I found that an ounce of gold would exchange for a less quantity of all the commodities above enumerated and many others; and if, moreover, I found that by the discovery of a new and more fertile mine, or by the employment of machinery to great advantage, a given quantity of gold could be obtained with a less quantity of labour, I should be justified in saying that the cause of the alteration in the value of gold relatively to other commodities was the greater facility of its production, or the smaller quantity of labour necessary to obtain it. In like manner, if labour fell very considerably in value, relatively to all other things, and if I found that its fall was in consequence of an abundant supply, encouraged by the great facility with which corn, and the other necessaries of the labourer, were produced, it would, I apprehend, be correct for me to say that corn and necessaries had fallen in value in consequence of less quantity of labour being necessary to produce them, and that this facility of providing for the support of the labourer had been followed by a fall in the value of labour. No, say Adam Smith and Mr. Malthus, in the case of the gold you were correct in calling its variation a fall of its value, because corn and labour had not then varied; and as gold would command a less quantity of them, as well as of all other things, than before, it was correct to say that all things had remained stationary and that gold only had varied; but when corn and labour fall, things which we have selected to be our standard measure of value, notwithstanding all the variations to which we acknowledge they are subject, it would be highly improper to say so; the

correct language will be to say that corn and labour have remained stationary, and all other things have risen in value.

Now it is against this language that I protest. I find that precisely, as in
the case of the gold, the cause of the variation between corn and other
things is the smaller quantity of labour necessary to produce it, and therefore, by all just reasoning, I am bound to call the variation of corn and
labour a fall in their value, and not a rise in the value of the things with
which they are compared. If I have to hire a labourer for a week, and instead of ten shillings I pay him eight, no variation having taken place in
the value of money, the labourer can probably obtain more food and necessaries with his eight shillings than he before obtained for ten: but this is
owing, not to a rise in the real value of his wages, as stated by Adam Smith,
and more recently by Mr. Malthus, but to a fall in the value of the things
on which his wages are expended, things perfectly distinct; and yet for
calling this a fall in the real value of wages, I am told that I adopt new and
unusual language, not reconcilable with the true principles of the science.
To me it appears that the unusual and, indeed, inconsistent language is
that used by my opponents.

Suppose a labourer to be paid a bushel of corn for a week's work when
the price of corn is 80s. per quarter, and that he is paid a bushel and a
quarter when the price falls to 40s. Suppose, too, that he consumes half
a bushel of corn a week in his own family, and exchanges the remainder
for other things, such as fuel, soap, candles, tea, sugar, salt, etc. etc.; if the
three-fourths of a bushel which will remain to him, in one case, cannot
procure him as much of the above commodities as half a bushel did in the
other, which it will not, will labour have risen or fallen in value? Risen,
Adam Smith must say, because his standard is corn, and the labourer receives more corn for a week's labour. Fallen, must the same Adam Smith
say, "because the value of a thing depends on the power of purchasing
other goods which the possession of that object conveys," and labour has
a less power of purchasing such other goods.

§ Section 2

> *Labour of different qualities differently re-
> warded. This no cause of variation in the rela-
> tive value of commodities.*

In speaking, however, of labour, as being the foundation of all value,
and the relative quantity of labour as almost exclusively determining the
relative value of commodities, I must not be supposed to be inattentive to
the different qualities of labour, and the difficulty of comparing an hour's
or a day's labour in one employment with the same duration of labour in
another. The estimation in which different qualities of labour are held

comes soon to be adjusted in the market with sufficient precision for all practical purposes, and depends much on the comparative skill of the labourer and intensity of the labour performed. The scale, when once formed, is liable to little variation. If a day's labour of a working jeweller be more valuable than a day's labour of a common labourer, it has long ago been adjusted and placed in its proper position in the scale of value.[1]

In comparing, therefore, the value of the same commodity at different periods of time, the consideration of the comparative skill and intensity of labour required for that particular commodity needs scarcely to be attended to, as it operates equally at both periods. One description of labour at one time is compared with the same description of labour at another; if a tenth, a fifth, or a fourth has been added or taken away, an effect proportioned to the cause will be produced on the relative value of the commodity.

If a piece of cloth be now of the value of two pieces of linen, and if, in ten years hence, the ordinary value of a piece of cloth should be four pieces of linen, we may safely conclude that either more labour is required to make the cloth, or less to make the linen, or that both causes have operated.

As the inquiry to which I wish to draw the reader's attention relates to the effect of the variations in the relative value of commodities, and not in their absolute value, it will be of little importance to examine into the comparative degree of estimation in which the different kinds of human labour are held. We may fairly conclude that whatever inequality there might originally have been in them, whatever the ingenuity, skill, or time necessary for the acquirement of one species of manual dexterity more than another, it continues nearly the same from one generation to another; or at least that the variation is very inconsiderable from year to year, and therefore can have little effect, for short periods, on the relative value of commodities.

"The proportion between the different rates both of wages and profit in the different employments of labour and stock seems not to be much affected, as has already been observed, by the riches or poverty, the advancing, stationary, or declining state of the society. Such revolutions in the

1 "But though labour be the real measure of the exchangeable value of all commodities, it is not that by which their value is commonly estimated. It is often difficult to ascertain the proportion between two different quantities of labour. The time spent in two different sorts of work will not always alone determine this proportion. The different degrees of hardship endured, and of ingenuity exercised, must likewise be taken into account. There may be more labour in an hour's hard work than in two hours' easy business; or in an hour's application to a trade, which it costs ten years' labour to learn, than in a month's industry at an ordinary and obvious employment. But it is not easy to find any accurate measure, either of hardship or ingenuity. In exchanging, indeed, the different productions of different sorts of labour from one another, some allowance is commonly made for both. It is adjusted, however, not by any accurate measure, but by the higgling and bargaining of the market, according to that sort of rough equality which, though not exact, is sufficient for carrying on the business of common life." Adam Smith, Wealth of Nations, Book I, Chap. 10.

public welfare, though they affect the general rates both of wages and profit, must in the end affect them equally in all different employments. The proportion between them therefore must remain the same, and cannot well be altered, at least for any considerable time, by any such revolutions."[2]

§ Section 3

> *Not only the labour applied immediately to commodities affect their value, but the labour also which is bestowed on the implements, tools, and buildings, with which such labour is assisted.*

Even in that early state to which Adam Smith refers, some capital, though possibly made and accumulated by the hunter himself, would be necessary to enable him to kill his game. Without some weapon, neither the beaver nor the deer could be destroyed, and therefore the value of these animals would be regulated, not solely by the time and labour necessary to their destruction, but also by the time and labour necessary for providing the hunter's capital, the weapon, by the aid of which their destruction was effected.

Suppose the weapon necessary to kill the beaver was constructed with much more labour than that necessary to kill the deer, on account of the greater difficulty of approaching near to the former animal, and the consequent necessity of its being more true to its mark; one beaver would naturally be of more value than two deer, and precisely for this reason, that more labour would, on the whole, be necessary to its destruction. Or suppose that the same quantity of labour was necessary to make both weapons, but that they were of very unequal durability; of the durable implement only a small portion of its value would be transferred to the commodity, a much greater portion of the value of the less durable implement would be realised in the commodity which it contributed to produce.

All the implements necessary to kill the beaver and deer might belong to one class of men, and the labour employed in their destruction might be furnished by another class; still, their comparative prices would be in proportion to the actual labour bestowed, both on the formation of the capital and on the destruction of the animals. Under different circumstances of plenty or scarcity of capital, as compared with labour, under different circumstances of plenty or scarcity of the food and necessaries essential to the support of men, those who furnished an equal value of capital for either one employment or for the other might have a half, a fourth, or an eighth of the produce obtained, the remainder being paid as wages to those who furnished the labour; yet this division could not affect the relative value of these commodities, since whether the profits of capital were greater or

[2] *Wealth of Nations*, Book I, Chap. 10.

less, whether they were 50, 20, or 10 per cent., or whether the wages of labour were high or low, they would operate equally on both employments.

If we suppose the occupations of the society extended, that some provide canoes and tackle necessary for fishing, others the seed and rude machinery first used in agriculture, still the same principle would hold true, that the exchangeable value of the commodities produced would be in proportion to the labour bestowed on their production; not on their immediate production only, but on all those implements or machines required to give effect to the particular labour to which they were applied.

If we look to a state of society in which greater improvements have been made, and in which arts and commerce flourish, we shall still find that commodities vary in value conformably with this principle: in estimating the exchangeable value of stockings, for example, we shall find that their value, comparatively with other things, depends on the total quantity of labour necessary to manufacture them and bring them to market. First, there is the labour necessary to cultivate the land on which the raw cotton is grown; secondly, the labour of conveying the cotton to the country where the stockings are to be manufactured, which includes a portion of the labour bestowed in building the ship in which it is conveyed, and which is charged in the freight of the goods; thirdly, the labour of the spinner and weaver; fourthly, a portion of the labour of the engineer, smith, and carpenter, who erected the buildings and machinery, by the help of which they are made; fifthly, the labour of the retail dealer, and of many others, whom it is unnecessary further to particularise. The aggregate sum of these various kinds of labour determines the quantity of other things for which these stockings will exchange, while the same consideration of the various quantities of labour which have been bestowed on those other things will equally govern the portion of them which will be given for the stockings.

To convince ourselves that this is the real foundation of exchangeable value, let us suppose any improvement to be made in the means of abridging labour in any one of the various processes through which the raw cotton must pass before the manufactured stockings come to the market to be exchanged for other things, and observe the effects which will follow. If fewer men were required to cultivate the raw cotton, or if fewer sailors were employed in navigating, or shipwrights in constructing the ship, in which it was conveyed to us; if fewer hands were employed in raising the buildings and machinery, or if these, when raised, were rendered more efficient, the stockings would inevitably fall in value, and consequently command less of other things. They would fall, because a less quantity of labour was necessary to their production, and would therefore exchange for a smaller quantity of those things in which no such abridgment of labour had been made.

Economy in the use of labour never fails to reduce the relative value of a commodity, whether the saving be in the labour necessary to the manufacture of the commodity itself, or in that necessary to the formation of the capital by the aid of which it is produced. In either case the price of stockings would fall, whether there were fewer men employed as bleachers, spinners, and weavers, persons immediately necessary to their manufacture; or as sailors, carriers, engineers, and smiths, persons more indirectly concerned. In the one case, the whole saving of labour would fall on the stockings, because that portion of labour was wholly confined to the stockings; in the other, a portion only would fall on the stockings, the remainder being applied to all those other commodities, to the production of which the buildings, machinery, and carriage were subservient.

Suppose that, in the early stages of society, the bows and arrows of the hunter were of equal value, and of equal durability, with the canoe and implements of the fisherman, both being the produce of the same quantity of labour. Under such circumstances the value of the deer, the produce of the hunter's day's labour, would be exactly equal to the value of the fish, the produce of the fisherman's day's labour. The comparative value of the fish and the game would be entirely regulated by the quantity of labour realised in each, whatever might be the quantity of production or however high or low general wages or profits might be. If, for example, the canoes and implements of the fisherman were of the value of £100, and were calculated to last for ten years, and he employed ten men, whose annual labour cost £100, and who in one day obtained by their labour twenty salmon: If the weapons employed by the hunter were also of £100 value, and calculated to last ten years, and if he also employed ten men, whose annual labour cost £100, and who in one day produced him ten deer; then the natural price of a deer would be two salmon, whether the proportion of the whole produce bestowed on the men who obtained it were large or small. The proportion which might be paid for wages is of the utmost importance in the question of profits; for it must at once be seen that profits would be high or low exactly in proportion as wages were low or high; but it could not in the least affect the relative value of fish and game, as wages would be high or low at the same time in both occupations. If the hunter urged the plea of his paying a large proportion, or the value of a large proportion of his game for wages, as an inducement to the fisherman to give him more fish in exchange for his game, the latter would state that he was equally affected by the same cause; and therefore, under all variations of wages and profits, under all the effects of accumulation of capital, as long as they continued by a day's labour to obtain respectively the same quantity of fish and the same quantity of game, the natural rate of exchange would be one deer for two salmon.

If with the same quantity of labour a less quantity of fish or a greater quantity of game were obtained, the value of fish would rise in comparison with that of game. If, on the contrary, with the same quantity of labour a less quantity of game or a greater quantity of fish was obtained, game would rise in comparison with fish.

If there were any other commodity which was invariable in its value, we should be able to ascertain, by comparing the value of fish and game with this commodity, how much of the variation was to be attributed to a cause which affected the value of fish, and how much to a cause which affected the value of game.

Suppose money to be that commodity. If a salmon were worth £1 and a deer £2, one deer would be worth two salmon. But a deer might become of the value of three salmon, for more labour might be required to obtain the deer, or less to get the salmon, or both these causes might operate at the same time. If we had this invariable standard, we might easily ascertain in what degree either of these causes operated. If salmon continued to sell for £1 whilst deer rose to £3, we might conclude that more labour was required to obtain the deer. If deer continued at the same price of £2 and salmon sold for 13s. 4d., we might then be sure that less labour was required to obtain the salmon; and if deer rose to £2 10s. and salmon fell to 16s. 8d., we should be convinced that both causes had operated in producing the alteration of the relative value of these commodities.

No alteration in the wages of labour could produce any alteration in the relative value of these commodities; for suppose them to rise, no greater quantity of labour would be required in any of these occupations but it would be paid for at a higher price, and the same reasons which should make the hunter and fisherman endeavour to raise the value of their game and fish would cause the owner of the mine to raise the value of his gold. This inducement acting with the same force on all these three occupations, and the relative situation of those engaged in them being the same before and after the rise of wages, the relative value of game, fish, and gold would continue unaltered. Wages might rise twenty per cent., and profits consequently fall in a greater or less proportion, without occasioning the least alteration in the relative value of these commodities.

Now suppose that, with the same labour and fixed capital, more fish could be produced, but no more gold or game, the relative value of fish would fall in comparison with gold or game. If, instead of twenty salmon, twenty-five were the produce of one day's labour, the price of a salmon would be sixteen shillings instead of a pound, and two salmon and a half, instead of two salmon, would be given in exchange for one deer, but the price of deer would continue at £2 as before. In the same manner, if fewer fish could be obtained with the same capital and labour, fish would rise in comparative value. Fish then would rise or fall in exchangeable value, only because more or less labour was required to obtain a given quantity; and it never could rise or fall beyond the proportion of the increased or diminished quantity of labour required.

If we had then an invariable standard, by which we could measure the variàtion in other commodities, we should find that the utmost limit to which they could permanently rise, if produced under the circumstances supposed, was proportioned to the additional quantity of labour required for their production; and that unless more labour were required for their production they could not rise in any degree whatever. A rise of wages would not raise them in money value, nor relatively to any other commodities, the production of which required no additional quantity of labour, which employed the same proportion of fixed and circulating capital, and fixed capital of the same durability. If more or less labour were required in the production of the other commodity, we have already stated that this will immediately occasion an alteration in its relative value, but such alteration is owing to the altered quantity of requisite labour, and not to the rise of wages.

§ Section 4

The principle that the quantity of labour bestowed on the production of commodities regulates their relative value considerably modified by the employment of- machinery and other fixed and durable capital.

In the former section we have supposed the implements and weapons necessary to kill the deer and salmon to be equally durable, and to be the result of the same quantity of labour, and we have seen that the variations in the relative value of deer and salmon depended solely on the varying quantities of labour necessary to obtain them, but in every state of society, the tools, implements, buildings, and machinery employed in different trades may be of various degrees of durability, and may require different portions of labour to produce them. The proportions, too, in which the capital that is to support labour, and the capital that is invested in tools, machinery, and buildings, may be variously combined. This difference in the degree of durability of fixed capital, and this variety in the proportions in which the two sorts of capital may be combined, introduce another cause, besides the greater or less quantity of labour necessary to produce commodities, for the variations in their relative value—this cause is the rise or fall in the value of labour.

The food and clothing consumed by the labourer, the buildings in which he works, the implements with which his labour is assisted, are all of a perishable nature. There is, however, a vast difference in the time for which these different capitals will endure: a steam-engine will last longer than a ship, a ship than the clothing of the labourer, and the clothing of the labourer longer than the food which he consumes.

According as capital is rapidly perishable, and requires to be frequently reproduced, or is of slow consumption, it is classed under the heads of circulating or of fixed capital.[3] A brewer whose buildings and machinery are valuable and durable is said to employ a large portion of fixed capital: on the contrary, a shoemaker, whose capital is chiefly employed in the payment of wages, which are expended on food and clothing, commodities more perishable than buildings and machinery, is said to employ a large proportion of his capital as circulating capital.

It is also to be observed that the circulating capital may circulate, or be returned to its employer, in very unequal times. The wheat bought by a farmer to sow is comparatively a fixed capital to the wheat purchased by a baker to make into loaves. One leaves it in the ground and can obtain no return for a year; the other can get it ground into flour, sell it as bread to his customers, and have his capital free to renew the same or commence any other employment in a week.

Two trades then may employ the same amount of capital; but it may be very differently divided with respect to the portion which is fixed and that which is circulating.

In one trade very little capital may be employed as circulating capital, that is to say, in the support of labour—it may be principally invested in machinery, implements, buildings, etc., capital of a comparatively fixed and durable character. In another trade the same amount of capital may be used, but it may be chiefly employed in the support of labour, and very little may be invested in implements, machines, and buildings. A rise in the wages of labour cannot fail to affect unequally commodities produced under such different circumstances.

Again, two manufacturers may employ the same amount of fixed and the same amount of circulating capital; but the durability of their fixed capitals may be very unequal. One may have steam-engines of the value of £10,000, the other, ships of the same value.

If men employed no machinery in production but labour only, and were all the same length of time before they brought their commodities to market, the exchangeable value of their goods would be precisely in proportion to the quantity of labour employed.

If they employed fixed capital of the same value and of the same durability, then, too, the value of the commodities produced would be the same, and they would vary with the greater or less quantity of labour employed on their production.

But although commodities produced under similar circumstances would not vary with respect to each other from any cause but an addition or diminution of the quantity of labour necessary to produce one or other of them, yet, compared with others not produced with the same proportionate quantity of fixed capital, they would vary from the other cause also which

[3] A division not essential, and in which the line of demarcation cannot be accurately drawn.

I have before mentioned, namely, a rise in the value of labour, although neither more nor less labour were employed in the production of either of them. Barley and oats would continue to bear the same relation to each other under any variation of wages. Cotton goods and cloth would do the same, if they also were produced under circumstances precisely similar to each other, but yet with a rise or fall of wages barley might be more or less valuable compared with cotton goods and oats compared with cloth.

Suppose two men employ one hundred men each for a year in the construction of two machines, and another man employs the same number of men in cultivating corn, each of the machines at the end of the year will be of the same value as the corn, for they will each be produced by the same quantity of labour. Suppose one of the owners of one of the machines to employ it, with the assistance of one hundred men, the following year in making cloth, and the owner of the other machine to employ his also, with the assistance likewise of one hundred men, in making cotton goods, while the farmer continues to employ one hundred men as before in the cultivation of corn. During the second year they will all have employed the same quantity of labour, but the goods and machine together of the clothier, and also of the cotton manufacturer, will be the result of the labour of two hundred men employed for a year; or, rather, of the labour of one hundred men for two years; whereas the corn will be produced by the labour of one hundred men for one year, consequently if the corn be of the value of £500, the machine and cloth of the clothier together ought to be of the value of £1000, and the machine and cotton goods of the cotton manufacturer ought to be also of twice the value of the corn. But they will be of more than twice the value of the corn, for the profit on the clothier's and cotton manufacturer's capital for the first year has been added to their capitals, while that of the farmer has been expended and enjoyed. On account then of the different degrees of durability of their capitals, or, which is the same thing, on account of the time which must elapse before one set of commodities can be brought to market, they will be valuable, not exactly in proportion to the quantity of labour bestowed on them—they will not be as two to one, but something more, to compensate for the greater length of time which must elapse before the most valuable can be brought to market.

Suppose that for the labour of each workman £50 per annum were paid, or that £5000 capital were employed and profits were 10 per cent., the value of each of the machines as well as of the corn, at the end of the first year, would be £5500. The second year the manufacturers and farmers will again employ £5000 each in the support of labour, and will therefore again sell their goods for £5500; but the men using the machines, to be on a par with the farmer, must not only obtain £5500 for the equal capitals of £5000 employed on labour, but they must obtain a further sum of £550 for the profit on £5500, which they have invested in machinery, and consequently their goods must sell for £6050. Here, then, are capitalists employing precisely the same quantity of labour annually on the production of their commodities, and yet the goods they produce differ in value on account of the different quantities of fixed capital, or accumulated labour, employed by each respectively. The cloth and cotton goods are of the same value, because they are the produce of equal quantities of labour and equal quantities of fixed capital; but corn is not of the same value as these commodities, because it is produced, as far as regards fixed capital, under different circumstances.

But how will their relative value be affected by a rise in the value of labour? It is evident that the relative values of cloth and cotton goods will undergo no change, for what affects one must equally affect the other under the circumstances supposed; neither will the relative values of wheat and barley undergo any change, for they are produced under the same circumstances as far as fixed and circulating capital are concerned; but the relative value of corn to cloth, or to cotton goods, must be altered by a rise of labour.

There can be no rise in the value of labour without a fall of profits. If the corn is to be divided between the farmer and the labourer, the larger the proportion that is given to the latter the less will remain for the former. So, if cloth or cotton goods be divided between the workman and his employer, the larger the proportion given to the former the less remains for the latter. Suppose then, that owing to a rise of wages, profits fall from 10 to 9 per cent., instead of adding £550 to the common price of their goods (to £5500) for the profits on their fixed capital, the manufacturers would add only 9 per cent. on that sum, or £495, consequently the price would be £5995 instead of £6050. As the corn would continue to sell for £5500 the manufactured goods in which more fixed capital was employed would fall relatively to corn or to any other goods in which a less portion of fixed capital entered. The degree of alteration in the relative value of goods, on account of a rise or fall of labour, would depend on the proportion which the fixed capital bore to the whole capital employed. All commodities which are produced by very valuable machinery, or in very valuable buildings, or which require a great length of time before they can be brought to market, would fall in relative value, while all those which were chiefly produced by labour, or which would be speedily brought to market, would rise in relative value.

The reader, however, should remark that this cause of the variation of commodities is comparatively slight in its effects. With such a rise of wages as should occasion a fall of 1 per cent. in profits, goods produced under the circumstances I have supposed vary in relative value only 1 per cent.; they fall with so great a fall of profits from £6050 to £5995. The greatest effects which could be produced on the relative prices of these goods from a rise of wages could not exceed 6 or 7 per cent.; for profits could not, probably, under any circumstances, admit of a greater general and permanent depression than to that amount.

Not so with the other great cause of the variation in the value of commodities, namely, the increase or diminution in the quantity of labour necessary to produce them. If to produce the corn, eighty, instead of one hundred men, should be required, the value of the corn would fall 20 per cent., or from £5500 to £4400. If to produce the cloth, the labour of eighty instead of one hundred men would suffice, cloth would fall from £6050 to £4950. An alteration in the permanent rate of profits, to any great amount, is the effect of causes which do not operate but in the course of years, whereas alterations in the quantity of labour necessary to produce commodities are of daily occurrence. Every improvement in machinery, in tools, in buildings, in raising the raw material, saves labour, and enables us to produce the commodity to which the improvement is applied with more facility, and consequently its value alters. In estimating, then, the causes of the variations in the value of commodities, although it would be wrong wholly to omit the consideration of the effect produced by a rise or fall of labour, it would be equally incorrect to attach much importance to it; and consequently, in the subsequent part of this work, though I shall occasionally refer to this cause of variation, I shall consider all the great variations which take place in the relative value of commodities to be produced by the greater or less quantity of labour which may be required from time to time to produce them.

It is hardly necessary to say that commodities which have the same quantity of labour bestowed on their production will differ in exchangeable value if they cannot be brought to market in the same time.

Suppose I employ twenty men at an expense of £1000 for a year in the production of a commodity, and at the end of the year I employ twenty men again for another year, at a further expense of £1000 in finishing or perfecting the same commodity, and that I bring it to market at the end of two years, if profits be 10 per cent., my commodity must sell for £2310; for I have employed £1000 capital for one year, and £2100 capital for one year more. Another man employs precisely the same quantity of labour, but he employs it all in the first year; he employs forty men at an expense of £2000, and at the end of the first year he sells it with 10 per cent. profit, or for £2200. Here, then, are two commodities having precisely the same quantity of labour bestowed on them, one of which sells for £2310—the other for £2200.

This case appears to differ from the last, but is, in fact, the same. In both cases the superior price of one commodity is owing to the greater length of time which must elapse before it can be brought to market. In the former case the machinery and cloth were more than double the value of the corn, although only double the quantity of labour was bestowed on them. In the second case, one commodity is more valuable than the other, although no more labour was employed on its production. The difference in value arises in both cases from the profits being accumulated as capital, and is only a just compensation for the time that the profits were withheld.

It appears, then, that the division of capital into different proportions of fixed and circulating capital, employed in different trades, introduces a considerable modification to the rule, which is of universal application when labour is almost exclusively employed in production; namely, that commodities never vary in value unless a greater or less quantity of labour be bestowed on their production, it being shown in this section that, without any variation in the quantity of labour, the rise of its value merely will occasion a fall in the exchangeable value of those goods in the production of which fixed capital is employed; the larger the amount of fixed capital, the greater will be the fall.

Chapter 30: ON THE INFLUENCE OF DEMAND AND SUPPLY ON
            PRICES

It is the cost of production which must ultimately regulate the price of commodities, and not, as has been often said, the proportion between the supply and demand: the proportion between supply and demand may, indeed, for a time, affect the market value of a commodity, until it is supplied in greater or less abundance, according as the demand may have increased or diminished; but this effect will be only of temporary duration.

Diminish the cost of production of hats, and their price will ultimately fall to their new natural price, although the demand should be doubled, trebled, or quadrupled. Diminish the cost of subsistence of men, by diminishing the natural price of the food and clothing by which life is sustained, and wages will ultimately fall, notwithstanding that the demand for labourers may very greatly increase.

The opinion that the price of commodities depends solely on the proportion of supply to demand, or demand to supply, has become almost an axiom in political economy, and has been the source of much error in that science. It is this opinion which has made Mr. Buchanan maintain that wages are not influenced by a rise or fall in the price of provisions, but solely by the demand and supply of labour; and that a tax on the wages of labour would not raise wages, because it would not alter the proportion of the demand of labourers to the supply.

The demand for a commodity cannot be said to increase if no additional quantity of it be purchased or consumed; and yet under such circumstances its money value may rise. Thus, if the value of money were to fall, the price of every commodity would rise, for each of the competitors would be willing to spend more money than before on its purchase; but though its price rose 10 or 20 per cent., if no more were bought than before, it would not, I apprehend, be admissible to say that the variation in the price of the commodity was caused by the increased demand for it. Its natural price, its money cost of production, would be really altered by the altered value of money; and without any increase of demand, the price of the commodity would be naturally adjusted to that new value.

"We have seen," says M. Say, "that the cost of production determines the lowest price to which things can fall: the price below which they cannot remain for any length of time, because production would then be either entirely stopped or diminished."[1]

He afterwards says that the demand for gold having increased in a still greater proportion than the supply, since the discovery of the mines, "its price in goods, instead of falling in the proportion of ten to one, fell only in the proportion of four to one;" that is to say, instead of falling in proportion as its natural price had fallen, fell in proportion as the supply exceeded the demand.[2]—*"The value of every commodity rises always in a direct ratio to the demand, and in an inverse ratio to the supply."*

The same opinion is expressed by the Earl of Lauderdale.

"With respect to the variations in value, of which everything valuable is susceptible, if we could for a moment suppose that any substance possessed intrinsic and fixed value, so as to render an assumed quantity of it constantly, under all circumstances, of an equal value, then the degree of value of all things, ascertained by such a fixed standard, would vary according to the proportion *betwixt the quantity of them* and the demand for them, and every commodity would, of course, be subject to a variation in its value, from four different circumstances:

1. "It would be subject to an increase of its value, from a diminution of its quantity.

2. "To a diminution of its value, from an augmentation of its quantity.

3. "It might suffer an augmentation in its value, from the circumstance of an increased demand.

4. "Its value might be diminished by a failure of demand.

"As it will, however, clearly appear that no commodity can possess fixed and intrinsic value, so as to qualify it for a measure of the value of other commodities, mankind are induced to select, as a practical measure of value, that which appears the least liable to any of these four sources of variations, *which are the sole causes of alteration of value.*

"When, in common language, therefore, we express the *value* of any

---

[1] J. B. Say, *Economie Politique*, Vol. II, p. 26.

[2] If, with the quantity of gold and silver which actually exists, these metals only served for the manufacture of utensils and ornaments, they would be abundant, and would be much cheaper than they are at present: in other words, in exchanging them for any other species of goods, we should be obliged to give proportionally a greater quantity of them. But as a large quantity of these metals is used for money, and as this portion is used for no other purpose, there remains less to be employed in furniture and jewellery; now this scarcity adds to their value. Say, Vol. II, p. 316.

commodity, it may vary at one period from what it is at another, in consequence of eight different contingencies:—

1. "From the four circumstances above stated, in relation to the commodity of which we mean to express the value.

2. "From the same four circumstances, in relation to the commodity we have adopted as a measure of value."[3]

This is true of monopolised commodities, and, indeed, of the market price of all other commodities for a limited period. If the demand for hats should be doubled, the price would immediately rise, but that rise would be only temporary, unless the cost of production of hats or their natural price were raised. If the natural price of bread should fall 50 per cent. from some great discovery in the science of agriculture, the demand would not greatly increase, for no man would desire more than would satisfy his wants, and as the demand would not increase, neither would the supply; for a commodity is not supplied merely because it can be produced, but because there is a demand for it. Here, then, we have a case where the supply and demand have scarcely varied, or, if they have increased, they have increased in the same proportion; and yet the price of bread will have fallen 50 per cent., at a time, too, when the value of money had continued invariable.

Commodities which are monopolised, either by an individual or by a company, vary according to the law which Lord Lauderdale has laid down: they fall in proportion as the sellers augment their quantity, and rise in proportion to the eagerness of the buyers to purchase them; their price has no necessary connection with their natural value: but the prices of commodities which are subject to competition, and whose quantity may be increased in any moderate degree, will ultimately depend, not on the state of demand and supply, but on the increased or diminished cost of their production.

Chapter 2: ON RENT

It remains however to be considered whether the appropriation of land, and the consequent creation of rent, will occasion any variation in the relative value of commodities independently of the quantity of labour necessary to production. In order to understand this part of the subject we must inquire into the nature of rent, and the laws by which its rise or fall is regulated.

Rent is that portion of the produce of the earth which is paid to the landlord for the use of the original and indestructible powers of the soil. It is often, however, confounded with the interest and profit of capital, and, in popular language, the term is applied to whatever is annually paid by a farmer to his landlord. If, of two adjoining farms of the same extent,

---

[3] *An Inquiry into the Nature and Origin of Public Wealth*, p. 13.

and of the same natural fertility, one had all the conveniences of farming buildings, and, besides, were properly drained and manured, and advantageously divided by hedges, fences, and walls, while the other had none of these advantages, more remuneration would naturally be paid for the use of one than for the use of the other; yet in both cases this remuneration would be called rent. But it is evident that a portion only of the money annually to be paid for the improved farm would be given for the original and indestructible powers of the soil; the other portion would be paid for the use of the capital which had been employed in ameliorating the quality of the land, and in erecting such buildings as were necessary to secure and preserve the produce. Adam Smith sometimes speaks of rent in the strict sense to which I am desirous of confining it, but more often in the popular sense in which the term is usually employed. He tells us that the demand for timber, and its consequent high price, in the more southern countries of Europe caused a rent to be paid for forests in Norway which could before afford no rent. Is it not, however, evident that the person who paid what he thus calls rent, paid it in consideration of the valuable commodity which was then standing on the land, and that he actually repaid himself with a profit by the sale of the timber? If, indeed, after the timber was removed, any compensation were paid to the landlord for the use of the land, for the purpose of growing timber or any other produce, with a view to future demand, such compensation might justly be called rent, because it would be paid for the productive powers of the land; but in the case stated by Adam Smith, the compensation was paid for the liberty of removing and selling the timber, and not for the liberty of growing it. He speaks also of the rent of coal mines, and of stone quarries, to which the same observation applies—that the compensation given for the mine or quarry is paid for the value of the coal or stone which can be removed from them, and has no connection with the original and indestructible powers of the land. This is a distinction of great importance in an inquiry concerning rent and profits; for it is found that the laws which regulate the progress of rent are widely different from those which regulate the progress of profits, and seldom operate in the same direction. In all improved countries, that which is annually paid to the landlord, partaking of both characters, rent and profit, is sometimes kept stationary by the effects of opposing causes; at other times advances or recedes as one or the other of these causes preponderates. In the future pages of this work, then, whenever I speak of the rent of land, I wish to be understood as speaking of that compensation which is paid to the owner of land for the use of its original and indestructible powers.

On the first settling of a country in which there is an abundance of rich and fertile land, a very small proportion of which is required to be cultivated for the support of the actual population, or indeed can be cultivated with the capital which the population can command, there will be no rent;

for no one would pay for the use of land when there was an abundant quantity not yet appropriated, and, therefore, at the disposal of whosoever might choose to cultivate it.

On the common principles of supply and demand, no rent could be paid for such land, for the reason stated why nothing is given for the use of air and water, or for any other of the gifts of nature which exist in boundless quantity. With a given quantity of materials, and with the assistance of the pressure of the atmosphere, and the elasticity of steam, engines may perform work, and abridge human labour to a very great extent; but no charge is made for the use of these natural aids, because they are inexhaustible and at every man's disposal. In the same manner, the brewer, the distiller, the dyer, make incessant use of the air and water for the production of their commodities; but as the supply is boundless, they bear no price.[1] If all land had the same properties, if it were unlimited in quantity, and uniform in quality, no charge could be made for its use, unless where it possessed peculiar advantages of situation. It is only, then, because land is not unlimited in quantity and uniform in quality, and because, in the progress of population, land of an inferior quality, or less advantageously situated, is called into cultivation, that rent is ever paid for the use of it. When, in the progress of society, land of the second degree of fertility is taken into cultivation, rent immediately commences on that of the first quality, and the amount of that rent will depend on the difference in the quality of these two portions of land.

When land of the third quality is taken into cultivation, rent immediately commences on the second, and it is regulated as before by the difference in their productive powers. At the same time, the rent of the first quality will rise, for that must always be above the rent of the second by the difference between the produce which they yield with a given quantity of capital and labour. With every step in the progress of population, which shall oblige a country to have recourse to land of a worse quality, to enable it to raise its supply of food, rent, on all the more fertile land, will rise.

Thus suppose land—No. 1, 2, 3—to yield, with an equal employment of capital and labour, a net produce of 100, 90, and 80 quarters of corn. In a new country, where there is an abundance of fertile land compared with the population, and where therefore it is only necessary to cultivate No. 1, the whole net produce will belong to the cultivator, and will be the profits

[1] "The earth, as we have already seen, is not the only agent of nature which has a productive power; but it is the only one, or nearly so, that one set of men take to themselves to the exclusion of others; and of which, consequently, they can appropriate the benefits. The waters of rivers, and of the sea, by the power which they have of giving movement to our machines, carrying our boats, nourishing our fish, have also a productive power; the wind which turns our mills, and even the heat of the sun, work for us; but happily no one has yet been able to say, the 'wind and the sun are mine, and the service which they render must be paid for.'" J. B. Say, *Economie Politique*, Vol. II, p. 124.

of the stock which he advances. As soon as population had so far increased as to make it necessary to cultivate No. 2, from which ninety quarters only can be obtained after supporting the labourers, rent would commence on No. 1; for either there must be two rates of profit on agricultural capital, or ten quarters, or the value of ten quarters must be withdrawn from the produce of No. 1 for some other purpose. Whether the proprietor of the land, or any other person, cultivated No. 1, these ten quarters would equally constitute rent; for the cultivator of No. 2 would get the same result with his capital whether he cultivated No. 1, paying ten quarters for rent, or continued to cultivate No. 2, paying no rent. In the same manner it might be shown that when No. 3 is brought into cultivation, the rent of No. 2 must be ten quarters, or the value of ten quarters, whilst the rent of No. 1 would rise to twenty quarters; for the cultivator of No. 3 would have the same profits whether he paid twenty quarters for the rent of No. 1, ten quarters for the rent of No. 2, or cultivated No. 3 free of all rent.

It often, and, indeed, commonly happens, that before No. 2, 3, 4, or 5, or the inferior lands are cultivated, capital can be employed more productively on those lands which are already in cultivation. It may perhaps be found that by doubling the original capital employed on No. 1, though the produce will not be doubled, will not be increased by 100 quarters, it may be increased by eighty-five quarters, and that this quantity exceeds what could be obtained by employing the same capital on land No. 3.

In such case, capital will be preferably employed on the old land, and will equally create a rent; for rent is always the difference between the produce obtained by the employment of two equal quantities of capital and labour. If, with a capital of £1000 a tenant obtain 100 quarters of wheat from his land, and by the employment of a second capital of £1000 he obtain a further return of eighty-five, his landlord would have the power, at the expiration of his lease, of obliging him to pay fifteen quarters or an equivalent value for additional rent; for there cannot be two rates of profit. If he is satisfied with a diminution of fifteen quarters in the return for his second £1000, it is because no employment more profitable can be found for it. The common rate of profit would be in that proportion, and if the original tenant refused, some other person would be found willing to give all which exceeded that rate of profit to the owner of the land from which he derived it.

In this case, as well as in the other, the capital last employed pays no rent. For the greater productive powers of the first £1000, fifteen quarters, is paid for rent, for the employment of the second £1000 no rent whatever is paid. If a third £1000 be employed on the same land, with a return of seventy-five quarters, rent will then be paid for the second £1000, and will be equal to the difference between the produce of these two, or ten quarters; and at the same time the rent for the first £1000 will rise from fifteen to twenty-five quarters; while the last £1000 will pay no rent whatever.

If, then, good land existed in a quantity much more abundant than the production of food for an increasing population required, or if capital could be indefinitely employed without a diminished return on the old land, there could be no rise of rent; for rent invariably proceeds from the employment of an additional quantity of labour with a proportionally less return.

The most fertile and most favourably situated land will be first cultivated, and the exchangeable value of its produce will be adjusted in the same manner as the exchangeable value of all other commodities, by the total quantity of labour necessary in various forms, from first to last, to produce it and bring it to market. When land of an inferior quality is taken into cultivation, the exchangeable value of raw produce will rise, because more labour is required to produce it.

The exchangeable value of all commodities, whether they be manufactured, or the produce of the mines, or the produce of land, is always regulated, not by the less quantity of labour that will suffice for their production under circumstances highly favourable, and exclusively enjoyed by those who have peculiar facilities of production; but by the greater quantity of labour necessarily bestowed on their production by those who have no such facilities; by those who continue to produce them under the most unfavourable circumstances; meaning—by the most unfavourable circumstances, the most unfavourable under which the quantity of produce required renders it necessary to carry on the production.

Thus, in a charitable institution, where the poor are set to work with the funds of benefactors, the general prices of the commodities, which are the produce of such work, will not be governed by the peculiar facilities afforded to these workmen, but by the common, usual, and natural difficulties which every other manufacturer will have to encounter. The manufacturer enjoying none of these facilities might indeed be driven altogether from the market if the supply afforded by these favoured workmen were equal to all the wants of the community; but if he continued the trade, it would be only on condition that he should derive from it the usual and general rate of profits on stock; and that could only happen when his commodity sold for a price proportioned to the quantity of labour bestowed on its production.[2]

---

[2] Has not M. Say forgotten, in the following passage, that it is the cost of production which ultimately regulates price? "The produce of labour employed on the land has this peculiar property, that it does not become more dear by becoming more scarce, because population always diminishes at the same time that food diminishes, and consequently the quantity of these products *demanded* diminishes at the same time as the quantity supplied. Besides, it is not observed that corn is more dear in those places where there is plenty of uncultivated land, than in completely cultivated countries. England and France were much more imperfectly cultivated in the middle ages than they are now; they produced much less raw produce: nevertheless, from all that we can judge by a comparison with the value of other things, corn was not sold at a dearer price. If the produce was less, so was the population; the weakness of the demand compensated the feebleness of the supply" (Vol. II, 338). M. Say being impressed with the opinion that

It is true, that on the best land, the same produce would still be obtained with the same labour as before, but its value would be enhanced in consequence of the diminished returns obtained by those who employed fresh labour and stock on the less fertile land. Notwithstanding, then, that the advantages of fertile over inferior lands are in no case lost, but only transferred from the cultivator, or consumer, to the landlord, yet, since more labour is required on the inferior lands, and since it is from such land only that we are enabled to furnish ourselves with the additional supply of raw produce, the comparative value of that produce will continue permanently above its former level, and make it exchange for more hats, cloth, shoes, etc., etc., in the production of which no such additional quantity of labour is required.

The reason, then, why raw produce rises in comparative value is because more labour is employed in the production of the last portion obtained, and not because a rent is paid to the landlord. The value of corn is regulated by the quantity of labour bestowed on its production on that quality of land, or with that portion of capital, which pays no rent. Corn is not high because a rent is paid, but a rent is paid because corn is high; and it has been justly observed that no reduction would take place in the price of corn although landlords should forego the whole of their rent. Such a measure would only enable some farmers to live like gentlemen, but would not diminish the quantity of labour necessary to raise raw produce on the least productive land in cultivation.

Nothing is more common than to hear of the advantages which the land possesses over every other source of useful produce, on account of the surplus which it yields in the form of rent. Yet when land is most abundant, when most productive, and most fertile, it yields no rent; and it is only when its powers decay, and less is yielded in return for labour, that a share of the original produce of the more fertile portions is set apart for rent. It is singular that this quality in the land, which should have been noticed as an imperfection compared with the natural agents by which manufacturers are assisted, should have been pointed out as constituting its peculiar preeminence. If air, water, the elasticity of steam, and the pressure of the atmosphere were of various qualities; if they could be appropriated, and each quality existed only in moderate abundance, they, as well as the land, would afford a rent, as the successive qualities were brought into use. With every worse quality employed, the value of the commodities in the manufacture of which they were used would rise, because equal quantities of labour would be less productive. Man would do more by the sweat of his

the price of commodities is regulated by the price of labour, and justly supposing that charitable institutions of all sorts tend to increase the population beyond what it otherwise would be, and therefore to lower wages, says, "I suspect that the cheapness of the goods which come from England is partly caused by the numerous charitable institutions which exist in that country" (Vol. II, 277). This is a consistent opinion in one who maintains that wages regulate price.

brow and nature perform less; and the land would be no longer pre-eminent for its limited powers.

If the surplus produce which land affords in the form of rent be an advantage, it is desirable that, every year, the machinery newly constructed should be less efficient than the old, as that would undoubtedly give a greater exchangeable value to the goods manufactured, not only by that machinery but by all the other machinery in the kingdom; and a rent would be paid to all those who possessed the most productive machinery.[3]

The rise of rent is always the effect of the increasing wealth of the coun-

---

[3] "In agriculture, too," says Adam Smith, "nature labours along with man; and though her labour costs no expense, its produce has its value, as well as that of the most expensive workman." The labour of nature is paid, not because she does much, but because she does little. In proportion as she becomes niggardly in her gifts she exacts a greater price for her work. Where she is munificently beneficent she always works gratis. "The labouring cattle employed in agriculture not only occasion, like the workmen in manufactures, the reproduction of a value equal to their own consumption, or to the capital which employs them, together with its owner's profits, but of a much greater value. Over and above the capital of the farmer and all its profits, they regularly occasion the reproduction of the rent of the landlord. This rent may be considered as the produce of those powers of nature, the use of which the landlord lends to the farmer. It is greater or smaller according to the supposed extent of those powers, or, in other words, according to the supposed natural or improved fertility of the land. It is the work of nature which remains, after deducting or compensating everything which can be regarded as the work of man. It is seldom less than a fourth, and frequently more than a third of the whole produce. No equal quantity of productive labour employed in manufactures can ever occasion so great a reproduction. *In them nature does nothing, man does all*; and the reproduction must always be in proportion to the strength of the agents that occasion it. The capital employed in agriculture, therefore, not only puts into motion a greater quantity of productive labour than any equal capital employed in manufactures, but in proportion, too, to the quantity of the productive labour which it employs it adds a much greater value to the annual produce of the land and labour of the country, to the *real* wealth and revenue of its inhabitants. Of all the ways in which a capital can be employed, it is by far the most advantageous to the society." Book II, Chap. v, p. 15.

Does nature do nothing for man in manufactures? Are the powers of wind and water, which move our machinery and assist navigation, nothing? The pressure of the atmosphere and the elasticity of steam, which enable us to work the most stupendous engines —are they not the gifts of nature? To say nothing of the effects of the matter of heat in softening and melting metals, of the decomposition of the atmosphere in the process of dyeing and fermentation. There is not a manufacture which can be mentioned in which nature does not give her assistance to man, and give it, too, generously and gratuitously.

In remarking on the passage which I have copied from Adam Smith, Mr. Buchanan observes, "I have endeavoured to show, in the observations on productive and unproductive labour, contained in the fourth volume, that agriculture adds no more to the national stock than any other sort of industry. In dwelling on the reproduction of rent as so great an advantage to society, Dr. Smith does not reflect that rent is the effect of high price, and that what the landlord gains in this way he gains at the expense of the community at large. There is no absolute gain to the society by the reproduction of rent; it is only one class profiting at the expense of another class. The notion of agriculture yielding a produce, and a rent in consequence, because nature concurs with human industry in the process of cultivation, is a mere fancy. It is not from the produce, but from the price at which the produce is sold, that the rent is derived; and this price is got not because nature assists in the production, but because it is the price which suits the consumption to the supply.

try, and of the difficulty of providing food for its augmented population. It is a symptom, but it is never a cause of wealth; for wealth often increases most rapidly while rent is either stationary, or even falling. Rent increases most rapidly as the disposable land decreases in its productive powers. Wealth increases most rapidly in those countries where the disposable land is most fertile, where importation is least restricted, and where, through agricultural improvements, productions can be multiplied without any increase in the proportional quantity of labour, and where consequently the progress of rent is slow.

If the high price of corn were the effect, and not the cause of rent, price would be proportionally influenced as rents were high or low, and rent would be a component part of price. But that corn which is produced by the greatest quantity of labour is the regulator of the price of corn; and rent does not and cannot enter in the least degree as a component part of its price.[4] Adam Smith, therefore, cannot be correct in supposing that the original rule which regulated the exchangeable value of commodities, namely, the comparative quantity of labour by which they were produced, can be at all altered by the appropriation of land and the payment of rent. Raw material enters into the composition of most commodities, but the value of that raw material, as well as corn, is regulated by the productiveness of the portion of capital last employed on the land and paying no rent; and therefore rent is not a component part of the price of commodities.

We have been hitherto considering the effects of the natural progress of wealth and population on rent in a country in which the land is of variously productive powers, and we have seen that with every portion of additional capital which it becomes necessary to employ on the land with a less productive return rent would rise. It follows from the same principles that any circumstances in the society which should make it unnecessary to employ the same amount of capital on the land, and which should therefore make the portion last employed more productive, would lower rent. Any great reduction in the capital of a country which should materially diminish the funds destined for the maintenance of labour, would naturally have this effect. Population regulates itself by the funds which are to employ it, and therefore always increases or diminishes with the increase or diminution of capital. Every reduction of capital is therefore necessarily followed by a less effective demand for corn, by a fall of price, and by diminished cultivation. In the reverse order to that in which the accumulation of capital raises rent will the diminution of it lower rent. Land of a less unproductive quality will be in succession relinquished, the exchangeable value of produce will fall, and land of a superior quality will be the land last cultivated, and that which will then pay no rent.

---

[4] The clear understanding of this principle is, I am persuaded, of the utmost importance to the science of political economy.

The same effects may, however, be produced when the wealth and population of a country are increased, if that increase is accompanied by such marked improvements in agriculture as shall have the same effect of diminishing the necessity of cultivating the poorer lands, or of expending the same amount of capital on the cultivation of the more fertile portions.

If a million of quarters of corn be necessary for the support of a given population, and it be raised on land of the qualities of No. 1, 2, 3; and if an improvement be afterwards discovered by which it can be raised on No. 1 and 2, without employing No. 3, it is evident that the immediate effect must be a fall of rent; for No. 2, instead of No. 3, will then be cultivated without paying any rent; and the rent of No. 1, instead of being the difference between the produce of No. 3 and No. 1, will be the difference only between No. 2 and 1. With the same population, and no more, there can be no demand for any additional quantity of corn; the capital and labour employed on No. 3 will be devoted to the production of other commodities desirable to the community, and can have no effect in raising rent, unless the raw material from which they are made cannot be obtained without employing capital less advantageously on the land, in which case No. 3 must again be cultivated.

It is undoubtedly true that the fall in the relative price of raw produce, in consequence of the improvement in agriculture, or rather in consequence of less labour being bestowed on its production, would naturally lead to increased accumulation; for the profits of stock would be greatly augmented. This accumulation would lead to an increased demand for labour, to higher wages, to an increased population, to a further demand for raw produce, and to an increased cultivation. It is only, however, after the increase in the population that rent would be as high as before; that is to say, after No. 3 was taken into cultivation. A considerable period would have elapsed, attended with a positive diminution of rent.

But improvements in agriculture are of two kinds: those which increase the productive powers of the land and those which enable us, by improving our machinery, to obtain its produce with less labour. They both lead to a fall in the price of raw produce; they both affect rent, but they do not affect it equally. If they did not occasion a fall in the price of raw produce they would not be improvements; for it is the essential quality of an improvement to diminish the quantity of labour before required to produce a commodity; and this diminution cannot take place without a fall of its price or relative value.

The improvements which increased the productive powers of the land are such as the more skilful rotation of crops or the better choice of manure. These improvements absolutely enable us to obtain the same produce from a smaller quantity of land. If, by the introduction of a course of turnips, I can feed my sheep besides raising my corn, the land on which the sheep were before fed becomes unnecessary, and the same quantity of raw produce is raised by the employment of a less quantity of land. If I discover a manure which will enable me to make a piece of land produce 20 per cent. more corn, I may withdraw at least a portion of my capital from the most unproductive part of my farm. But, as I before observed, it is not necessary that land should be thrown out of cultivation in order to reduce rent: to produce this effect, it is sufficient that successive portions of capital are employed on the same land with different results, and that the portion which gives the least result should be withdrawn. If, by the introduction of the turnip husbandry, or by the use of a more invigorating manure, I can obtain the same produce with less capital, and without disturbing the difference between the productive powers of the successive portions of capital, I shall lower rent; for a different and more productive portion will be that which will form the standard from which every other will be reckoned. If, for example, the successive portions of capital yielded 100, 90, 80, 70; whilst I employed these four portions, my rent would be 60, or the difference between

$$
\left.\begin{array}{l}
70 \text{ and } 100 = 30 \\
70 \text{ and } 90 = 20 \\
70 \text{ and } 80 = 10 \\
\overline{60}
\end{array}\right\}
\text{ whilst the produce would be } 340
\left\{\begin{array}{l}
100 \\
90 \\
80 \\
70 \\
\overline{340}
\end{array}\right.
$$

and while I employed these portions, the rent would remain the same, although the produce of each should have an equal augmentation. If, instead of 100, 90, 80, 70, the produce should be increased to 125, 115, 105, 95, the rent would still be 60, or the difference between

$$
\left.\begin{array}{l}
95 \text{ and } 125 = 30 \\
95 \text{ and } 115 = 20 \\
95 \text{ and } 105 = 10 \\
\overline{60}
\end{array}\right\}
\begin{array}{c}
\text{whilst the produce would be} \\
\text{increased to } 440
\end{array}
\left\{\begin{array}{l}
125 \\
115 \\
105 \\
95 \\
\overline{440}
\end{array}\right.
$$

But with such an increase of produce, without an increase of demand,[5] there could be no motive for employing so much capital on the land; one portion would be withdrawn, and consequently the last portion of capital would yield 105 instead of 95, and rent would fall to 30, or the difference between

$$
\left.\begin{array}{l}
105 \text{ and } 125 = 20 \\
105 \text{ and } 115 = 10 \\
\overline{30}
\end{array}\right\}
\begin{array}{l}
\text{whilst the produce will be still ade-} \\
\text{quate to the wants of the population,} \\
\text{for it would be } 345 \text{ quarters, or}
\end{array}
\left\{\begin{array}{l}
125 \\
115 \\
105 \\
\overline{345}
\end{array}\right.
$$

---

[5] I hope I am not understood as undervaluing the importance of all sorts of improvements in agriculture to landlords—their immediate effect is to lower rent; but as they

the demand being only for 340 quarters.—But there are improvements which may lower the relative value of produce without lowering the corn rent, though they will lower the money rent of land. Such improvements do not increase the production powers of the land, but they enable us to obtain its produce with less labour. They are rather directed to the formation of the capital applied to the land than to the cultivation of the land itself. Improvements in agricultural implements, such as the plough and the threshing machine, economy in the use of horses employed in husbandry, and a better knowledge of the veterinary art, are of this nature. Less capital, which is the same thing as less labour, will be employed on the land; but to obtain the same produce, less land cannot be cultivated. Whether improvements of this kind, however, affect corn rent, must depend on the question whether the difference between the produce obtained by the employment of different portions of capital be increased, stationary, or diminished. If four portions of capital, 50, 60, 70, 80, be employed on the land, giving each the same results, and any improvement in the formation of such capital should enable me to withdraw 5 from each, so that they should be 45, 55, 65, and 75, no alteration would take place in the corn rent; but if the improvements were such as to enable me to make the whole saving on that portion of capital which is least productively employed, corn rent would immediately fall, because the difference between the capital most productive and the capital least productive would be diminished; and it is this difference which constitutes rent.

Without multiplying instances, I hope enough has been said to show that whatever diminishes the inequality in the produce obtained from successive portions of capital employed on the same or on new land tends to lower rent; and that whatever increases that inequality, necessarily produces an opposite effect, and tends to raise it.

In speaking of the rent of the landlord, we have rather considered it as the proportion of the produce, obtained with a given capital on any given farm, without any reference to its exchangeable value; but since the same cause, the difficulty of production, raises the exchangeable value of raw produce, and raises also the proportion of raw produce paid to the landlord for rent, it is obvious that the landlord is doubly benefited by difficulty of production. First, he obtains a greater share, and, secondly, the commodity in which he is paid is of greater value.[6]

---

give a great stimulus to population, and at the same time enable us to cultivate poorer lands with less labour, they are ultimately of immense advantage to landlords. A period, however, must elapse during which they are positively injurious to him.

[6] To make this obvious, and to show the degrees in which corn and money rent will vary, let us suppose that the labour of ten men will, on land of a certain quality, obtain 180 quarters of wheat, and its value to be £4 per quarter, or £720; and that the labour of ten additional men will, on the same or any other land, produce only 170 quarters in addition; wheat would rise from £4 to £4 4s. 8d. for 170:180: :£4:£4 4s. 8d.; or, as in

Chapter 5: ON WAGES

Labour, like all other things which are purchased and sold, and which may be increased or diminished in quantity, has its natural and its market price. The natural price of labour is that price which is necessary to enable the labourers, one with another, to subsist and to perpetuate their race, without either increase or diminution.

The power of the labourer to support himself, and the family which may be necessary to keep up the number of labourers, does not depend on the quantity of money which he may receive for wages, but on the quantity of food, necessaries, and conveniences become essential to him from habit which that money will purchase. The natural price of labour, therefore, depends on the price of the food, necessaries, and conveniences required for the support of the labourer and his family. With a rise in the price of food and necessaries, the natural price of labour will rise; with the fall in their price, the natural price of labour will fall.

With the progress of society the natural price of labour has always a tendency to rise, because one of the principal commodities by which its natural price is regulated has a tendency to become dearer from the greater difficulty of producing it. As, however, the improvements in agriculture, the discovery of new markets, whence provisions may be imported, may for a time counteract the tendency to a rise in the price of necessaries, and may even occasion their natural price to fall, so will the same causes produce the correspondent effects on the natural price of labour.

The natural price of all commodities, excepting raw produce and labour, has a tendency to fall in the progress of wealth and population; for though, on one hand, they are enhanced in real value, from the rise in the natural price of the raw material of which they are made, this is more than counterbalanced by the improvements in machinery, by the better division and

---

the production of 170 quarters, the labour of 10 men is necessary in one case, and only of 9.44 in the other, the rise would be as 9.44 to 10, or as £4 to £4 4s. 8d. If 10 men be further employed, and the return be

160 the price will rise to	£4	10	0
150 " "	4	16	0
140 " "	5	2	10

Now, if no rent was paid for the land which yielded 180 quarters, when corn was at £4 per quarter, the value of 10 quarters would be paid as rent when only 170 could be procured, which at £4 4s. 8d. would be £42 7s. 6d.

20 quarters when 160 were produced, which at £4 10 0 would be £90 0 0
30 quarters when 150 were produced, which at 4 16 0 would be 144 0 0
40 quarters when 140 were produced, which at 5 2 10 would be 205 13 4

Corn rent would increase in the proportion of $\begin{Bmatrix} 100 \\ 200 \\ 300 \\ 400 \end{Bmatrix}$ and money rent in the proportion of $\begin{Bmatrix} 100 \\ 212 \\ 340 \\ 485 \end{Bmatrix}$

distribution of labour, and by the increasing skill, both in science and art, of the producers.

The market price of labour is the price which is really paid for it, from the natural operation of the proportion of the supply to the demand; labour is dear when it is scarce and cheap when it is plentiful. However much the market price of labour may deviate from its natural price, it has, like commodities, a tendency to conform to it.

It is when the market price of labour exceeds its natural price that the condition of the labourer is flourishing and happy, that he has it in his power to command a greater proportion of the necessaries and enjoyments of life, and therefore to rear a healthy and numerous family. When, however, by the encouragement which high wages give to the increase of population, the number of labourers is increased, wages again fall to their natural price, and indeed from a reaction sometimes fall below it.

When the market price of labour is below its natural price, the condition of the labourers is most wretched: then poverty deprives them of those comforts which custom renders absolute necessaries. It is only after their privations have reduced their number, or the demand for labour has increased, that the market price of labour will rise to its natural price, and that the labourer will have the moderate comforts which the natural rate of wages will afford.

Notwithstanding the tendency of wages to conform to their natural rate, their market rate may, in an improving society, for an indefinite period, be constantly above it; for no sooner may the impulse which an increased capital gives to a new demand for labour be obeyed, than another increase of capital may produce the same effect; and thus, if the increase of capital be gradual and constant, the demand for labour may give a continued stimulus to an increase of people.

Capital is that part of the wealth of a country which is employed in production, and consists of food, clothing, tools, raw materials, machinery, etc., necessary to give effect to labour.

Capital may increase in quantity at the same time that its value rises. An addition may be made to the food and clothing of a country at the same time that more labour may be required to produce the additional quantity than before; in that case not only the quantity but the value of capital will rise.

Or capital may increase without its value increasing, and even while its value is actually diminishing; not only may an addition be made to the food and clothing of a country, but the addition may be made by the aid of machinery, without any increase, and even with an absolute diminution in the proportional quantity of labour required to produce them. The quantity of capital may increase, while neither the whole together, nor any part of it singly, will have a greater value than before, but may actually have a less.

In the first case, the natural price of labour, which always depends on the price of food, clothing, and other necessaries, will rise; in the second, it will remain stationary or fall; but in both cases the market rate of wages will rise, for in proportion to the increase of capital will be the increase in the demand for labour; in proportion to the work to be done will be the demand for those who are to do it.

In both cases, too, the market price of labour will rise above its natural price; and in both cases it will have a tendency to conform to its natural price, but in the first case this agreement will be most speedily effected. The situation of the labourer will be improved, but not much improved; for the increased price of food and necessaries will absorb a large portion of his increased wages; consequently a small supply of labour, or a trifling increase in the population, will soon reduce the market price to the then increased natural price of labour.

In the second case, the condition of the labourer will be very greatly improved; he will receive increased money wages without having to pay any increased price, and perhaps even a diminished price for the commodities which he and his family consume; and it will not be till after a great addition has been made to the population that the market price of labour will again sink to its then low and reduced natural price.

Thus, then, with every improvement of society, with every increase in its capital, the market wages of labour will rise; but the permanence of their rise will depend on the question whether the natural price of labour has also risen; and this again will depend on the rise in the natural price of those necessaries on which the wages of labour are expended.

It is not to be understood that the natural price of labour, estimated even in food and necessaries, is absolutely fixed and constant. It varies at different times in the same country, and very materially differs in different countries.[1] It essentially depends on the habits and customs of the people. An English labourer would consider his wages under their natural rate, and too scanty to support a family, if they enabled him to purchase no other food than potatoes, and to live in no better habitation than a mud cabin; yet these moderate demands of nature are often deemed sufficient in countries where "man's life is cheap" and his wants easily satisfied. Many of the conveniences now enjoyed in an English cottage would have been thought luxuries at an earlier period of our history.

From manufactured commodities always falling and raw produce always

---

[1] "The shelter and the clothing which are indispensable in one country may be no way necessary in another; and a labourer in Hindostan may continue to work with perfect vigour, though receiving, as his natural wages, only such a supply of covering as would be insufficient to preserve a labourer in Russia from perishing. Even in countries situated in the same climate, different habits of living will often occasion variations in the natural price of labour as considerable as those which are produced by natural causes." R. Torrens, Esq., *An Essay on the External Corn Trade*, p. 68.

The whole of this subject is most ably illustrated by Colonel Torrens.

rising, with the progress of society, such a disproportion in their relative value is at length created, that in rich countries a labourer, by the sacrifice of a very small quantity only of his food, is able to provide liberally for all his other wants.

Independently of the variations in the value of money, which necessarily affect money wages, but which we have here supposed to have no operation, as we have considered money to be uniformly of the same value, it appears then that wages are subject to a rise or fall from two causes:—

First, the supply and demand of labourers.

Secondly, the price of the commodities on which the wages of labour are expended.

In different stages of society, the accumulation of capital, or of the means of employing labour, is more or less rapid, and must in all cases depend on the productive powers of labour. The productive powers of labour are generally greatest when there is an abundance of fertile land: at such periods accumulation is often so rapid that labourers cannot be supplied with the same rapidity as capital.

It has been calculated that under favourable circumstances population may be doubled in twenty-five years; but under the same favourable circumstances the whole capital of a country might possibly be doubled in a shorter period. In that case, wages during the whole period would have a tendency to rise, because the demand for labour would increase still faster than the supply.

In new settlements, where the arts and knowledge of countries far advanced in refinement are introduced, it is probable that capital has a tendency to increase faster than mankind; and if the deficiency of labourers were not supplied by more populous countries, this tendency would very much raise the price of labour. In proportion as these countries become populous, and land of a worse quality is taken into cultivation, the tendency to an increase of capital diminishes; for the surplus produce remaining, after satisfying the wants of the existing population, must necessarily be in proportion to the facility of production, viz. to the smaller number of persons employed in production. Although, then, it is probable that, under the most favourable circumstances, the power of production is still greater than that of population, it will not long continue so; for the land being limited in quantity, and differing in quality, with every increased portion of capital employed on it there will be a decreased rate of production, whilst the power of population continues always the same.

In those countries where there is abundance of fertile land, but where, from the ignorance, indolence, and barbarism of the inhabitants, they are exposed to all the evils of want and famine, and where it has been said that population presses against the means of subsistence, a very different remedy should be applied from that which is necessary in long settled countries, where, from the diminishing rate of the supply of raw produce, all the evils of a crowded population are experienced. In the one case, the evil proceeds from bad government, from the insecurity of property, and from a want of education in all ranks of the people. To be made happier they require only to be better governed and instructed, as the augmentation of capital, beyond the augmentation of people, would be the inevitable result. No increase in the population can be too great, as the powers of production are still greater. In the other case, the population increases faster than the funds required for its support. Every exertion of industry, unless accompanied by a diminished rate of increase in the population, will add to the evil, for production cannot keep pace with it.

With a population pressing against the means of subsistence, the only remedies are either a reduction of people or a more rapid accumulation of capital. In rich countries, where all the fertile land is already cultivated, the latter remedy is neither very practical nor very desirable, because its efforts would be, if pushed very far, to render all classes equally poor. But in poor countries, where there are abundant means of production in store, from fertile land not yet brought into cultivation, it is the only safe and efficacious means of removing the evil, particularly as its effect would be to elevate all classes of the people.

The friends of humanity cannot but wish that in all countries the labouring classes should have a taste for comforts and enjoyments, and that they should be stimulated by all legal means in their exertions to procure them. There cannot be a better security against a superabundant population. In those countries where the labouring classes have the fewest wants, and are contented with the cheapest food, the people are exposed to the greatest vicissitudes and miseries. They have no place of refuge from calamity; they cannot seek safety in a lower station; they are already so low that they can fall no lower. On any deficiency of the chief article of their subsistence there are few substitutes of which they can avail themselves and dearth to them is attended with almost all the evils of famine.

In the natural advance of society, the wages of labour will have a tendency to fall, as far as they are regulated by supply and demand; for the supply of labourers will continue to increase at the same rate, whilst the demand for them will increase at a slower rate. If, for instance, wages were regulated by a yearly increase of capital at the rate of 2 per cent., they would fall when it accumulated only at the rate of 1½ per cent. They would fall still lower when it increased only at the rate of 1 or ½ per cent., and would continue to do so until the capital became stationary, when wages also would become stationary, and be only sufficient to keep up the numbers of the actual population. I say that, under these circumstances, wages would fall if they were regulated only by the supply and demand of labourers; but we must not forget that wages are also regulated by the prices of the commodities on which they are expended.

As population increases, these necessaries will be constantly rising in price, because more labour will be necessary to produce them. If, then, the money wages of labour should fall, whilst every commodity on which the wages of labour were expended rose, the labourer would be doubly affected, and would be soon totally deprived of subsistence. Instead, therefore, of the money wages of labour falling, they would rise; but they would not rise sufficiently to enable the labourer to purchase as many comforts and necessaries as he did before the rise in the price of those commodities. If his annual wages were before £24, or six quarters of corn when the price was £4 per quarter, he would probably receive only the value of five quarters when corn rose to £5 per quarter. But five quarters would cost £25; he would, therefore, receive an addition in his money wages, though with that addition he would be unable to furnish himself with the same quantity of corn and other commodities which he had before consumed in his family.

Notwithstanding, then, that the labourer would be really worse paid, yet this increase in his wages would necessarily diminish the profits of the manufacturer; for his goods would sell at no higher price, and yet the expense of producing them would be increased. This, however, will be considered in our examination into the principles which regulate profits.

It appears, then, that the same cause which raises rent, namely, the increasing difficulty of providing an additional quantity of food with the same proportional quantity of labour, will also raise wages; and therefore, if money be of an unvarying value, both rent and wages will have a tendency to rise with the progress of wealth and population.

But there is this essential difference between the rise of rent and the rise of wages. The rise in the money value of rent is accompanied by an increased share of the produce; not only is the landlord's money rent greater, but his corn rent also; he will have more corn, and each defined measure of that corn will exchange for a greater quantity of all other goods which have not been raised in value. The fate of the labourer will be less happy; he will receive more money wages, it is true, but his corn wages will be reduced; and not only his command of corn, but his general condition will be deteriorated, by his finding it more difficult to maintain the market rate of wages above their natural rate. While the price of corn rises 10 per cent., wages will always rise less than 10 per cent., but rent will always rise more; the condition of the labourer will generally decline, and that of the landlord will always be improved.

· · ·

When wages rise it is generally because the increase of wealth and capital have occasioned a new demand for labour, which will infallibly be attended with an increased production of commodities. To circulate these additional commodities, even at the same prices as before, more money is required, more of this foreign commodity from which money is made, and which can only be obtained by importation. Whenever a commodity is required in greater abundance than before, its relative value rises comparatively with those commodities with which its purchase is made. If more hats were wanted, their price would rise, and more gold would be given for them. If more gold were required, gold would rise, and hats would fall in price, as a greater quantity of hats and of all other things would then be necessary to purchase the same quantity of gold. But in the case supposed, to say that commodities will rise because wages rise, is to affirm a positive contradiction; for we, first, say that gold will rise in relative value in consequence of demand, and, secondly, that it will fall in relative value because prices will rise, two effects which are totally incompatible with each other. To say that commodities are raised in price is the same thing as to say that money is lowered in relative value; for it is by commodities that the relative value of gold is estimated. If, then, all commodities rose in price, gold could not come from abroad to purchase those dear commodities, but it would go from home to be employed with advantage in purchasing the comparatively cheaper foreign commodities. It appears, then, that the rise of wages will not raise the prices of commodities, whether the metal from which money is made be produced at home or in a foreign country. All commodities cannot rise at the same time without an addition to the quantity of money. This addition could not be obtained at home, as we have already shown; nor could it be imported from abroad. To purchase any additional quantity of gold from abroad, commodities at home must be cheap, not dear. The importation of gold, and a rise in the price of all home-made commodities with which gold is purchased or paid for, are effects absolutely incompatible. The extensive use of paper money does not alter this question, for paper money conforms, or ought to conform, to the value of gold, and therefore its value is influenced by such causes only as influence the value of that metal.

These, then, are the laws by which wages are regulated, and by which the happiness of far the greatest part of every community is governed. Like all other contracts, wages should be left to the fair and free competition of the market, and should never be controlled by the interference of the legislature.

The clear and direct tendency of the poor laws is in direct opposition to these obvious principles: it is not, as the legislature benevolently intended, to amend the condition of the poor, but to deteriorate the condition of both poor and rich; instead of making the poor rich, they are calculated to make the rich poor; and whilst the present laws are in force, it is quite in the natural order of things that the fund for the maintenance of the poor should progressively increase till it has absorbed all the net revenue of the country, or at least so much of it as the state shall leave to us, after satisfying its own never-failing demands for the public expenditure.[2]

[2] With Mr. Buchanan, in the following passage, if it refers to temporary states of misery, I so far agree, that "the great evil of the labourer's condition is poverty, arising

This pernicious tendency of these laws is no longer a mystery, since it has been fully developed by the able hand of Mr. Malthus; and every friend to the poor must ardently wish for their abolition. Unfortunately, however, they have been so long established, and the habits of the poor have been so formed upon their operation, that to eradicate them with safety from our political system requires the most cautious and skilful management. It is agreed by all who are most friendly to a repeal of these laws that, if it be desirable to prevent the most overwhelming distress to those for whose benefit they were erroneously enacted, their abolition should be effected by the most gradual steps.

It is a truth which admits not a doubt that the comforts and well-being of the poor cannot be permanently secured without some regard on their part, or some effort on the part of the legislature, to regulate the increase of their numbers, and to render less frequent among them early and improvident marriages. The operation of the system of poor laws has been directly contrary to this. They have rendered restraint superfluous, and have invited imprudence, by offering it a portion of the wages of prudence and industry.[3]

The nature of the evil points out the remedy. By gradually contracting the sphere of the poor laws; by impressing on the poor the value of independence, by teaching them that they must look not to systematic or casual charity, but to their own exertions for support, that prudence and forethought are neither unnecesary nor unprofitable virtues, we shall by degrees approach a sounder and more healthful state.

No scheme for the amendment of the poor laws merits the least attention which has not their abolition for its ultimate object; and he is the best friend of the poor, and to the cause of humanity, who can point out how this end can be attained with the most security, and at the same time with the least violence. It is not by raising in any manner different from the present the fund from which the poor are supported that the evil can be mitigated. It would not only be no improvement, but it would be an aggravation of the distress which we wish to see removed, if the fund were increased in amount or were levied according to some late proposals, as a

---

either from a scarcity of food or of work; and in all countries laws without number have been enacted for his relief. But there are miseries in the social state which legislation cannot relieve; and it is useful therefore to know its limits, that we may not, by aiming at what is impracticable, miss the good which is really in our power."

[3] The progress of knowledge manifested upon this subject in the House of Commons since 1796 has happily not been very small, as may be seen by contrasting the late report of the committee on the poor laws and the following sentiments of Mr. Pitt in that year: "Let us," said he, "make relief in cases where there are a number of children a matter of right and honour, instead of a ground of opprobrium and contempt. This will make a large family a blessing and not a curse; and this will draw a proper line of distinction between those who are able to provide for themselves by their labour, and those who, after having enriched their country with a number of children, have a claim upon its assistance for support." Hansard's *Parliamentary History*, Vol. XXXII, p. 710.

general fund from the country at large. The present mode of its collection and application has served to mitigate its pernicious effects. Each parish raises a separate fund for the support of its own poor. Hence it becomes an object of more interest and more practicability to keep the rates low than if one general fund were raised for the relief of the poor of the whole kingdom. A parish is much more interested in an economical collection of the rate, and a sparing distribution of relief, when the whole saving will be for its own benefit, than if hundreds of other parishes were to partake of it.

It is to this cause that we must ascribe the fact of the poor laws not having yet absorbed all the net revenue of the country; it is to the rigour with which they are applied that we are indebted for their not having become overwhelmingly oppressive. If by law every human being wanting support could be sure to obtain it, and obtain it in such a degree as to make life tolerably comfortable, theory would lead us to expect that all other taxes together would be light compared with the single one of poor rates. The principle of gravitation is not more certain than the tendency of such laws to change wealth and power into misery and weakness; to call away the exertions of labour from every object, except that of providing mere subsistence; to confound all intellectual distinction; to busy the mind continually in supplying the body's wants; until at last all classes should be infected with the plague of universal poverty. Happily these laws have been in operation during a period of progressive prosperity, when the funds for the maintenance of labour have regularly increased, and when an increase of population would be naturally called for. But if our progress should become more slow; if we should attain the stationary state, from which I trust we are yet far distant, then will the pernicious nature of these laws become more manifest and alarming; and then, too, will their removal be obstructed by many additional difficulties.

Chapter 6: on profits

The profits of stock, in different employments, having been shown to bear a proportion to each other, and to have a tendency to vary all in the same degree and in the same direction, it remains for us to consider what is the cause of the permanent variations in the rate of profit, and the consequent permanent alterations in the rate of interest.

We have seen that the price[1] of corn is regulated by the quantity of labour necessary to produce it, with that portion of capital which pays no rent. We have seen, too, that all manufactured commodities rise and fall in price in proportion as more or less labour becomes necessary to their

---

[1] The reader is desired to bear in mind that, for the purpose of making the subject more clear, I consider money to be invariable in value, and therefore every variation of price to be referable to an alteration in the value of the commodity.

production. Neither the farmer who cultivates that quantity of land which regulates price, nor the manufacturer who manufactures goods, sacrifice any portion of the produce for rent. The whole value of their commodities is divided into two portions only: one constitutes the profits of stock, the other the wages of labour.

Supposing corn and manufactured goods always to sell at the same price, profits would be high or low in proportion as wages were low or high. But suppose corn to rise in price because more labour is necessary to produce it; that cause will not raise the price of manufactured goods in the production of which no additional quantity of labour is required. If, then, wages continued the same, the profits of manufacturers would remain the same; but if, as is absolutely certain, wages should rise with the rise of corn, then their profits would necessarily fall.

If a manufacturer always sold his goods for the same money, for £1000, for example, his profits would depend on the price of the labour necessary to manufacture those goods. His profits would be less when wages amounted to £800 than when he paid only £600. In proportion then as wages rose would profits fall. But if the price of raw produce would increase, it may be asked whether the farmer at least would not have the same rate of profits, although he should pay an additional sum for wages? Certainly not: for he will not only have to pay, in common with the manufacturer, an increase of wages to each labourer he employs, but he will be obliged either to pay rent, or to employ an additional number of labourers to obtain the same produce; and the rise in the price of raw produce will be proportioned only to that rent, or that additional number, and will not compensate him for the rise of wages.

If both the manufacturer and farmer employed ten men, on wages rising from £24 to £25 per annum per man, the whole sum paid by each would be £250 instead of £240. This is, however, the whole addition that would be paid by the manufacturer to obtain the same quantity of commodities; but the farmer on new land would probably be obliged to employ an additional man, and therefore to pay an additional sum of £25 for wages; and the farmer on the old land would be obliged to pay precisely the same additional sum of £25 for rent; without which additional labour corn would not have risen nor rent have been increased. One will therefore have to pay £275 for wages alone, the other for wages and rent together; each £25 more than the manufacturer: for this latter £25 the farmer is compensated by the addition to the price of raw produce, and therefore his profits still conform to the profits of the manufacturer. As this proposition is important, I will endeavour still further to elucidate it.

We have shown that in early stages of society, both the landlord's and the labourer's share of the *value* of the produce of the earth would be but small; and that it would increase in proportion to the progress of wealth and the difficulty of procuring food. We have shown, too, that although the value of the labourer's portion will be increased by the high value of food, his real share will be diminished; whilst that of the landlord will not only be raised in value, but will also be increased in quantity.

The remaining quantity of the produce of the land, after the landlord and labourer are paid, necessarily belongs to the farmer, and constitutes the profits of his stock. But it may be alleged, that though, as society advances, his proportion of the whole produce will be diminished, yet as it will rise in value, he, as well as the landlord and labourer, may, notwithstanding, receive a greater value.

It may be said, for example, that when corn rose from £4 to £10, the 180 quarters obtained from the best land would sell for £1800 instead of £720; and, therefore, though the landlord and labourer be proved to have a greater value for rent and wages, still the value of the farmer's profit might also be augmented. This, however, is impossible, as I shall now endeavour to show.

In the first place, the price of corn would rise only in proportion to the increased difficulty of growing it on land of a worse quality.

It has been already remarked, that if the labour of ten men will, on land of a certain quality, obtain 180 quarters of wheat, and its value be £4 per quarter, or £720; and if the labour of ten additional men will, on the same or any other land, produce only 170 quarters in addition, wheat would rise from £4 to £4 4s. 8d.; for 170 : 180 : : £4 : £4 4s. 8d. In other words, as for the production of 170 quarters the labour of ten men is necessary in the one case, and only that of 9.44 in the other, the rise would be as 9.44 to 10, or as £4 to £4 4s. 8d. In the same manner it might be shown that, if the labour of ten additional men would only produce 160 quarters, the price would further rise to £4 10s.; if 150, to £4 16s., etc., etc.

But when 180 quarters were produced on the land paying no rent,
    and its price was £4 per quarter, it is sold for £720
And when 170 quarters were produced on the land paying no rent,
    and the price rose to £4 4s. 8d., it still sold for 720
So 160 quarters at £4 10s. produce 720
And 150 quarters at £4 16s. produce the same sum of . . . 720

Now, it is evident that if, out of these equal values, the farmer is at one time obliged to pay wages regulated by the price of wheat at £4, and at other times at higher prices, the rate of his profits will diminish in proportion to the rise in the price of corn.

In this case, therefore, I think it is clearly demonstrated that a rise in the price of corn, which increases the money wages of the labourer, diminishes the money value of the farmer's profits.

But the case of the farmer of the old and better land will be in no way different; he also will have increased wages to pay, and will never retain more of the value of the produce, however high may be its price, than £720 to be divided between himself and his always equal number of labourers; in proportion therefore as they get more, he must retain less.

When the price of corn was at £4, the whole 180 quarters belonged to the cultivator, and he sold it for £720. When corn rose to £4 4s. 8d., he was obliged to pay the value of ten quarters out of his 180 for rent, consequently the remaining 170 yielded him no more than £720: when it rose further to £4 10s., he paid twenty quarters, or their value, for rent, and consequently only retained 160 quarters, which yielded the same sum of £720.

It will be seen, then, that whatever rise may take place in the price of corn, in consequence of the necessity of employing more labour and capital to obtain a given additional quantity of produce, such rise will always be equalled in value by the additional rent or additional labour employed; so that whether corn sells for £4, £4 10s., or £5 2s. 10d., the farmer will obtain for that which remains to him, after paying rent, the same real value. Thus we see that whether the produce belonging to the farmer be 180, 170, 160, or 150 quarters, he always obtains the same sum of £720 for it; the price increasing in an inverse proportion to the quantity.

Rent, then, it appears, always falls on the consumer, and never on the farmer; for if the produce of his farm should uniformly be 180 quarters, with the rise of price he would retain the value of a less quantity for himself, and give the value of a larger quantity to his landlord; but the deduction would be such as to leave him always the same sum of £720.

It will be seen too, that, in all cases, the same sum of £720 must be divided between wages and profits. If the value of the raw produce from the land exceed this value it belongs to rent, whatever may be its amount. If there be no excess, there will be no rent. Whether wages or profits rise or fall, it is this sum of £720 from which they must both be provided. On the one hand, profits can never rise so high as to absorb so much of this £720 that enough will not be left to furnish the labourers with absolute necessaries; on the other hand, wages can never rise so high as to leave no portion of this sum for profits.

Thus in every case, agricultural as well as manufacturing profits are lowered by a rise in the price of raw produce, if it be accompanied by a rise of wages.[2] If the farmer gets no additional value for the corn which remains to him after paying rent, if the manufacturer gets no additional value for the goods which he manufactures, and if both are obliged to pay a greater value in wages, can any point be more clearly established than that profits must fall with a rise of wages?

The farmer, then, although he pays no part of his landlord's rent, that being always regulated by the price of produce, and invariably falling on

[2] The reader is aware that we are leaving out of our consideration the accidental variations arising from bad and good seasons, or from the demand increasing or diminishing by any sudden effect on the state of population. We are speaking of the natural and constant, not of the accidental and fluctuating, price of corn.

the consumers, has however a very decided interest in keeping rent low, or rather in keeping the natural price of produce low. As a consumer of raw produce, and of those things into which raw produce enters as a component part, he will, in common with all other consumers, be interested in keeping the price low. But he is most materially concerned with the high price of corn as it affects wages. With every rise in the price of corn, he will have to pay, out of an equal and unvarying sum of £720, an additional sum for wages to the ten men whom he is supposed constantly to employ. We have seen, in treating on wages, that they invariably rise with the rise in the price of raw produce. On a basis assumed for the purpose of calculation, it will be seen that if when wheat is at £4 per quarter, wages should be £24 per annum,

	£	s.	d.			£	s.	d.
When wheat is at	4	4	8	wages would be		24	14	0
	4	10	0			25	10	0
	4	16	0			26	8	0
	5	2	10			27	8	6

Now, of the unvarying fund of £720 to be distributed between labourers and farmers,

	£	s.	d.		£	s.	d.		£	s.	d.
When the	4	0	0	the	240	0	0	the farmer	480	0	0
price of	4	4	8	labourers	247	0	0	will	473	0	0
wheat is at	4	10	0	will receive	255	0	0	receive	465	0	0
	4	16	0		264	0	0		456	0	0
	5	2	10		274	5	0		445	15	[3]

And supposing that the original capital of the farmer was £3000, the profits of his stock being in the first instance £480, would be at the rate of 16 per

---

[3] The 180 quarters of corn would be divided in the following proportions between landlords, farmers, and labourers, with the above-named variations in the value of corn.

Price per qr.			Rent.	Profit.	Wages.	Total.
£	s.	d.	In Wheat.	In Wheat.	In Wheat.	
4	0	0	None.	120 qrs.	60 qrs.	
4	4	8	10 qrs.	111.7	58.3	
4	10	0	20	103.4	56.6	180
4	16	0	30	95	55	
5	2	10	40	86.7	53.3	

and, under the same circumstances, money rent, wages, and profit would be as follows:

Price per qr.			Rent.			Profit.			Wages.			Total.		
£	s.	d.	£	s.	d.	£	s.	d.	£	s.	d.	£	s.	d.
4	0	0	None.			480	0	0	240	0	0	720	0	0
4	4	8	42	7	6	473	0	0	247	0	0	762	7	6
4	10	0	90	0	0	465	0	0	255	0	0	810	0	0
4	16	0	144	0	0	456	0	0	264	0	0	864	0	0
5	2	10	205	13	4	445	15	0	274	5	0	925	13	4

cent. When his profits fell to £473, they would be at the rate of 15.7 per cent.

£465	.	.	.	.	.	15.5
£456	.	.	.	.	.	15.2
£445	.	.	.	.	.	14.8

But the *rate* of profits will fall still more, because the capital of the farmer, it must be recollected, consists in a great measure of raw produce, such as his corn and hay-ricks, his unthreshed wheat and barley, his horses and cows, which would all rise in price in consequence of the rise of produce. His absolute profits would fall from £480 to £445 15s.; but if, from the cause which I have just stated, his capital should rise from £3000 to £3200, the rate of his profits would, when corn was at £5 2s. 10d., be under 14 per cent.

If a manufacturer had also employed £3000 in his business, he would be obliged, in consequence of the rise of wages, to increase his capital, in order to be enabled to carry on the same business. If his commodities sold before for £720 they would continue to sell at the same price; but the wages of labour, which were before £240, would rise, when corn was at £5 2s. 10d., to £274 5s. In the first case he would have a balance of £480 as profit on £3000, in the second he would have a profit only of £445 15s., on an increased capital, and therefore his profits would conform to the altered rate of those of the farmer.

There are few commodities which are not more or less affected in their price by the rise of raw produce, because some raw material from the land enters into the composition of most commodities. Cotton goods, linen, and cloth will all rise in price with the rise of wheat; but they rise on account of the greater quantity of labour expended on the raw material from which they are made, and not because more was paid by the manufacturer to the labourers whom he employed on those commodities.

In all cases, commodities rise because more labour is expended on them, and not because the labour which is expended on them is at a higher value. Articles of jewellery, of iron, of plate, and of copper, would not rise, because none of the raw produce from the surface of the earth enters into their composition.

It may be said that I have taken it for granted that money wages would rise with a rise in the price of raw produce, but that this is by no means a necessary consequence, as the labourer may be contented with fewer enjoyments. It is true that the wages of labour may previously have been at a high level, and that they may bear some reduction. If so, the fall of profits will be checked; but it is impossible to conceive that the money price of wages should fall or remain stationary with a gradually increasing price of necessaries; and therefore it may be taken for granted that, under ordinary circumstances, no permanent rise takes place in the price of necessaries without occasioning, or having been preceded by, a rise in wages.

The effects produced on profits would have been the same, or nearly the same, if there had been any rise in the price of those other necessaries, besides food, on which the wages of labour are expended. The necessity which the labourer would be under of paying an increased price for such necessaries would oblige him to demand more wages; and whatever increases wages, necessarily reduces profits. But suppose the price of silks, velvets, furniture, and any other commodities, not required by the labourer, to rise in consequence of more labour being expended on them, would not that affect profits? Certainly not: for nothing can affect profits but a rise in wages; silks and velvets are not consumed by the labourer, and therefore cannot raise wages.

.   .   .

JOHN STUART MILL

(1 8 0 6 – 1 8 7 3)

Each of the three giants we have reviewed thus far made a major contribution to the field of economics. Adam Smith provided us with the first complete treatise relating all of the various issues with which economics was concerned, Malthus introduced the problem of overpopulation and the principle of diminishing returns, while Ricardo added a rigorous and abstract analytical approach. Compared to these three, John Stuart Mill's contribution to economics was far less revolutionary. But even though Mill was a better political than economic theorist, to view his approach to economic theory as completely lacking in originality would be a grave mistake. However, it was Mill's command of the English language, his ability to express the most complex and difficult concepts in a way that could be easily understood by his readers, that has endeared him to succeeding generations of students of the history of economic thought.

Mill's ability as a writer stood him in good stead in other areas of study as well. In addition to his work as a political economist, Mill is also known for writing in the fields of ethics, politics, and philosophy. As a philosopher, he amended and extended the Utilitarianism of Jeremy Bentham. The mental acuteness demonstrated by this breadth of interest was fostered at an early age by Mill's father who was himself an economist and who started his son on the study of Greek at the age of three. Through his father, John Stuart Mill came to know David Ricardo, and he spent many long evenings at the home of the master discussing knotty economic problems.

His exposure to economics under the guidance of his father and Ricardo left the younger Mill imbued with a rather pessimistic outlook. Although this attitude led him in some ways to exceed Malthus in foreboding about the problem of population, and to define the law of diminishing returns as the "most important law in political economy," John Stuart Mill's economics was nevertheless of a quite different quality than that of his predecessors. Always threatening to destroy this strain of pessimism was Mill's basically optimistic view of life!

Many times the inherent conflict in these two varying attitudes appears to have gone unrecognized by Mill himself. At other points where the discrepancy became too great, Mill sought some kind of reconciliation. It was Mill who declared that the laws of production were immutable, but that the laws of distribution were subject to the wishes of society. When the contradiction between this view and his espousal of a wages-fund doctrine became increasingly apparent to him under the attacks of opponents of the doctrine, Mill abandoned the latter theory (see p. 148 for Mill's statement setting forth the idea of wages-fund).

One can cite many instances where Mill's analysis improved greatly on the thinking of his predecessors. Notable among these is his solution to the division of the gains to be made from international trade (determined by the nature of the demand of each country for the other's products), and his exposition of a cost of production theory of value where wages as a cost do enter into the determination of value.

Mill's Principles was consciously patterned after Smith's Wealth of Nations and was in part an effort to bring the latter book up-to-date. Like Smith's, Mill's was a big book, and like Smith, Mill sketched the role of land, labor, and capital in contributing to a nation's output. Mill also distinguished between productive and unproductive consumption. The latter consisted of all that consumption which adds nothing to workers' ability to produce. However, Mill noted that even some luxuries could be considered productive since they might be necessary to keep workers performing efficiently.

In Book III, Mill gave an extensive treatment of the role of money and credit and their relationship to prices.

Despite the generally gloomy outlook on the world inherited from his father and Ricardo, Mill was optimistic about the future of the English economy. Unlike Ricardo, he felt that machinery might better the economic position of the laboring class and he saw the arrival of the stationary state as an opportunity to devote more time to cultural pursuits and the finer things of life.

The concluding chapter of his book focused on the role of government and paralleled the observations made by Adam Smith. It was difficult to generalize about the proper scope of government, Mill declared, and clearly there were many instances where government action was necessary. True to his laissez-faire philosophy, Mill was fearful lest government become too large and infringe on personal liberty. Not unexpectedly, therefore, he cautioned against the government incurring much in the way of debt.

Although Mill's views on government marked no radical departure from the views of the political economists who came before him, on one issue Mill's thinking lay in a quite different direction from that of his predecessors. Always convinced that economic theory should be used to correct the social and economic ills of society, Mill grew increasingly sympathetic to socialism in his later years. Mill's brand of socialism, however, was one which deemphasized the role of the state; as stated above, Mill was too firm an opponent of undue state power ever to wish to accord control of the economy to an all-powerful government. Until some form of guild socialism could be achieved, Mill was inclined to support a modified laissez-faire model despite all the faults he believed it contained. The very fact that he was willing to see a possible end to private property, however, marks a sharp break with his predecessors. This attitude, plus his denial that there are laws of distribution which are forever immutable, has meant that for many Mill represented the close of the Classical system.

PRINCIPLES OF POLITICAL ECONOMY

BOOK I / Production

Chapter 10: OF THE LAW OF THE INCREASE OF LABOR

. . . What prevents the population of hares and rabbits from overstocking the earth? Not want of fecundity, but causes very different: many enemies, and insufficient subsistence; not enough to eat, and liability to being eaten. In the human race, which is generally not subject to the latter inconvenience, the equivalents for it are war and disease. If the multiplication of mankind proceeded only, like that of the other animals, from a blind instinct, it would be limited in the same manner with theirs; the birds would be as numerous as the physical constitution of the species admitted of, and the population would be kept down by deaths.[1] But the conduct of human creatures is more or less influenced by foresight of consequences, and by impulses superior to mere animal instincts: and they do not, therefore, propagate like swine, but are capable, though in very unequal degrees, of being withheld by prudence, or by the social affections, from giving existence to beings born only to misery and premature death. In proportion as mankind rise above the condition of the beasts, population is restrained

[1] Mr. Carey expatiates on the absurdity of supposing that matter tends to assume the highest form of organization, the human, at a more rapid rate than it assumes the lower forms which compose human food; that human beings multiply faster than turnips and cabbages. But the limit to the increase of mankind, according to the doctrine of Mr. Malthus, does not depend on the power of increase of turnips and cabbages, but on the limited quantity of the land on which they can be grown. So long as the quantity of land is practically unlimited, which it is in the United States, and food, consequently, can be increased at the highest rate which is natural to it, mankind also may, without augmented difficulty in obtaining subsistence, increase at their highest rate. When Mr. Carey can show, not that turnips and cabbages but that the soil itself, or the nutritive elements contained in it, tend naturally to multiply, and that, too, at a rate exceeding the most rapid possible increase of mankind, he will have said something to the purpose. Till then, this part, at least, of his argument may be considered as non-existent. (Editor's note: Carey was a contemporary American economist.)

by the fear of want, rather than by want itself. Even where there is no question of starvation, many are similarly acted upon by the apprehension of losing what have come to be regarded as the decencies of their situation in life. Hitherto no other motives than these two have been found strong enough, in the generality of mankind, to counteract the tendency to increase. It has been the practice of a great majority of the middle and the poorer classes, whenever free from external control, to marry as early, and in most countries to have as many children, as was consistent with maintaining themselves in the condition of life which they were born to, or were accustomed to consider as theirs. Among the middle classes, in many individual instances, there is an additional restraint exercised from the desire of doing more than maintaining their circumstances—of improving them; but such a desire is rarely found, or rarely has that effect, in the laboring classes. If they can bring up a family as they were themselves brought up, even the prudent among them are usually satisfied. Too often they do not think even of that, but rely on fortune, or on the resources to be found in legal or voluntary charity.

In a very backward state of society, like that of Europe in the Middle Ages, and many parts of Asia at present, population is kept down by actual starvation. The starvation does not take place in ordinary years, but in seasons of scarcity, which in those states of society are much more frequent and more extreme than Europe is now accustomed to. In these seasons actual want, or the maladies consequent on it, carry off numbers of the population, which in a succession of favorable years again expands, to be again cruelly decimated. In a more improved state, few, even among the poorest of the people, are limited to actual necessaries, and to a bare sufficiency of those: and the increase is kept within bounds, not by excess of deaths, but by limitation of births. The limitation is brought about in various ways. In some countries, it is the result of prudent or conscientious self-restraint. There is a condition to which the laboring people are habituated; they perceive that by having too numerous families, they must sink below that condition, or fail to transmit it to their children; and this they do not choose to submit to. The countries in which, so far as is known, a great degree of voluntary prudence has been longest practised on this subject, are Norway and parts of Switzerland. Concerning both, there happens to be unusually authentic information; many facts were carefully brought together by Mr. Malthus, and much additional evidence has been obtained since his time. In both these countries the increase of population is very slow; and what checks it, is not multitude of deaths, but fewness of births. Both the births and the deaths are remarkably few in proportion to the population; the average duration of life is the longest in Europe; the population contains fewer children, and a greater proportional number of persons in the vigor of life, than is known to be the case in any other part of the world. The paucity of births tends directly to prolong life, by keeping the people in comfortable circumstances; and the same prudence is doubt-less exercised in avoiding causes of disease, as in keeping clear of the prin-cipal cause of poverty. It is worthy of remark that the two countries thus honorably distinguished, are countries of small landed proprietors.

There are other cases in which the prudence and forethought, which perhaps might not be exercised by the people themselves, are exercised by the state for their benefit; marriage not being permitted until the contract-ing parties can show that they have the prospect of a comfortable support. Under these laws, of which I shall speak more fully hereafter, the condition of the people is reported to be good, and the illegitimate births not so numerous as might be expected. There are places, again, in which the restraining cause seems to be not so much individual prudence, as some general and perhaps even accidental habit of the country. In the rural dis-tricts of England, during the last century, the growth of population was very effectually repressed by the difficulty of obtaining a cottage to live in. It was the custom for unmarried laborers to lodge and board with their employers; it was the custom for married laborers to have a cottage: and the rule of the English poor laws by which a parish was charged with the support of its unemployed poor, rendered landowners averse to promote marriage. About the end of the century, the great demand for men in war and manufactures, made it be thought a patriotic thing to encourage popu-lation: and about the same time the growing inclination of farmers to live like rich people, favored as it was by a long period of high prices, made them desirous of keeping inferiors at a greater distance, and pecuniary motives arising from abuses of the poor laws being superadded, they gradu-ally drove their laborers into cottages, which the landlords now no longer refused permission to build. In some countries an old standing custom that a girl should not marry until she had spun and woven for herself an ample *trousseau* (destined for the supply of her whole subsequent life), is said to have acted as a substantial check to population. In England, at present, the influence of prudence in keeping down multiplication is seen by the diminished number of marriages in the manufacturing districts in years when trade is bad.

But whatever be the causes by which the population is anywhere limited to a comparatively slow rate of increase, an acceleration of the rate very speedily follows any diminution of the motives to restraint. It is but rarely that improvements in the condition of the laboring classes do anything more than give a temporary margin, speedily filled up by an increase of their numbers. The use they commonly choose to make of any advanta-geous change in their circumstances, is to take it out in the form which, by augmenting the population, deprives the succeeding generation of the benefit. Unless, either by their general improvement in intellectual and moral culture, or at least by raising their habitual standard of comfortable living, they can be taught to make a better use of favorable circumstances, nothing permanent can be done for them; the most promising schemes end only in having a more numerous, but not a happier people. By their habitual standard, I mean that (when any such there is) down to which they will multiply, but not lower. Every advance they make in education, civilization, and social improvement, tends to raise this standard; and there is no doubt that it is gradually, though slowly, rising in the more advanced countries of Western Europe. Subsistence and employment in England have never increased more rapidly than in the last forty years, but every census since 1821 showed a smaller proportional increase of population than that of the period preceding; and the produce of French agriculture and industry is increasing in a progressive ratio, while the population exhibits, in every quinquennial census, a smaller proportion of births to the population.

The subject, however, of population, in its connection with the condition of the laboring classes, will be considered in another place: in the present, we have to do with it solely as one of the elements of Production: and in that character we could not dispense with pointing out the unlimited extent of its natural powers of increase, and the causes owing to which so small a portion of that unlimited power is for the most part actually exercised. After this brief indication, we shall proceed to the other elements.

Chapter 11: OF THE LAW OF THE INCREASE OF CAPITAL

§ 1. The requisites of production being labor, capital, and land, it has been seen from the preceding chapter that the impediments to the increase of production do not arise from the first of these elements. On the side of labor there is no obstacle to an increase of production, indefinite in extent and of unslackening rapidity. Population has the power of increasing in a uniform and rapid geometrical ratio. If the only essential condition of production were labor, the produce might, and naturally would, increase in the same ratio; and there would be no limit, until the numbers of mankind were brought to a stand from actual want of space.

But production has other requisites, and of these, the one which we shall next consider is Capital. There cannot be more people in any country, or in the world, that can be supported from the produce of past labor until that of present labor comes in. There will be no greater number of productive laborers in any country, or in the world, than can be supported from that portion of the produce of past labor, which is spared from the enjoyments of its possessor for purposes of reproduction, and is termed Capital. We have next, therefore, to inquire into the conditions of the increase of capital; the causes by which the rapidity of its increase is determined, and the necessary limitations of that increase.

Since all capital is the product of saving, that is, of abstinence from present consumption for the sake of a future good, the increase of capital must depend upon two things—the amount of the fund from which saving can be made, and the strength of the dispositions which prompt to it.

The fund from which saving can be made, is the surplus of the produce of labor, after supplying the necessaries of life to all concerned in the production (including those employed in replacing the materials, and keeping the fixed capital in repair). More than this surplus cannot be saved under any circumstances. As much as this, though it never is saved, always might be. This surplus is the fund from which the enjoyments, as distinguished from the necessaries of the producers, are provided; it is the fund from which all are subsisted, who are not themselves engaged in production; and from which all additions are made to capital. It is the real net produce of the country. The phrase, net produce, is often taken in a more limited sense, to denote only the profits of the capitalist and the rent of the landlord, under the idea that nothing can be included in the net produce of capital, but what is returned to the owner of the capital after replacing his expenses. But this is too narrow an acceptation of the term. The capital of the employer forms the revenue of the laborers, and if this exceeds the necessaries of life, it gives them a surplus which they may either expend in enjoyments or save. For every purpose for which there can be occasion to speak of the net produce of industry, this surplus ought to be included in it. When this is included, and not otherwise, the net produce of the country is the measure of its effective power; of what it can spare for any purposes of public utility, or private indulgence; the portion of its produce of which it can dispose at pleasure; which can be drawn upon to attain any ends, or gratify any wishes, either of the government or of individuals; which it can either spend for its satisfaction, or save for future advantage.

The amount of this fund, this net produce, this excess of production above the physical necessaries of the producers, is one of the elements that determine the amount of saving. The greater the produce of labor after supporting the laborers, the more there is which *can* be saved. The same thing also partly contributes to determine how much *will* be saved. A part of the motive to saving consists in the prospect of deriving an income from savings; in the fact that capital, employed in production, is capable of not only reproducing itself but yielding an increase. The greater the profit that can be made from capital, the stronger is the motive to its accumulation. That indeed which forms the inducement to save, is not the whole of the fund which supplies the means of saving, not the whole net produce of the land, capital, and labor of the country, but only a part of it, the part which forms the remuneration of the capitalist, and is called profit of stock. It will, however, be readily enough understood, even previously to the explanations which will be given hereafter, that when the general productiveness of labor and capital is great, the returns to the capitalist are likely to be large, and that some proportion, though not a uniform one, will commonly obtain between the two.

§ 2. But the disposition to save does not wholly depend on the external inducement to it; on the amount of profit to be made from savings. With the same pecuniary inducement, the inclination is very different, in different persons, and in different communities. The effective desire of accumulation is of unequal strength, not only according to the varieties of individual character, but to the general state of society and civilization. Like all other moral attributes, it is one in which the human race exhibits great differences, conformably to the diversity of its circumstances and the stage of its progress.

On topics which if they were to be fully investigated would exceed the bounds that can be allotted to them in this treatise, it is satisfactory to be able to refer to other works in which the necessary developments have been presented more at length. On the subject of Population this valuable service has been rendered by the celebrated Essay of Mr. Malthus; and on the point which now occupies us I can refer with equal confidence to another, though a less known work, "New Principles of Political Economy," by Dr. Rae.[1] In no other book known to me is so much light thrown, both from principle and history, on the causes which determine the accumulation of capital.

All accumulation involves the sacrifice of a present, for the sake of a future good. But the expediency of such a sacrifice varies very much in different states of circumstances; and the willingness to make it, varies still more.

In weighing the future against the present, the uncertainty of all things future is a leading element; and that uncertainty is of very different degrees. "All circumstances," therefore, "increasing the probability of the provision we make for futurity being enjoyed by ourselves or others, tend" justly and reasonably "to give strength to the effective desire of accumulation. Thus a healthy climate or occupation, by increasing the probability of life, has

---

[1] This treatise is an example, such as not unfrequently presents itself, how much more depends on accident, than on the qualities of a book, in determining its reception. Had it appeared at a suitable time, and been favored by circumstances, it would have had every requisite for great success. The author, a Scotchman settled in the United States, unites much knowledge, an original vein of thought, a considerable turn for philosophic generalities, and a manner of exposition and illustration calculated to make ideas tell not only for what they are worth, but for more than they are worth, and which sometimes, I think, has that effect in the writer's own mind. The principal fault of the book is the position of antagonism in which, with the controversial spirit apt to be found in those who have new thoughts on old subjects, he has placed himself towards Adam Smith. I call this a fault (though I think many of the criticisms just, and some of them farseeing), because there is much less real difference of opinion than might be supposed from Dr. Rae's animadversions; and because what he has found vulnerable in his great predecessor is chiefly the "human too-much" in his premises; the portion of them that is over and above what was either required or is actually used for the establishment of his conclusions.

a tendency to add to this desire. When engaged in safe occupations, and living in healthy countries, men are much more apt to be frugal than in unhealthy or hazardous occupations, and in climates pernicious to human life. Sailors and soldiers are prodigals. In the West Indies, New Orleans, the East Indies, the expenditure of the inhabitants is profuse. The same people, coming to reside in the healthy parts of Europe, and not getting into the vortex of extravagant fashion, live economically. War and pestilence have always waste and luxury among the other evils that follow in their train. For similar reasons, whatever gives security to the affairs of the community is favorable to the strength of this principle. In this respect the general prevalence of law and order, and the prospect of the continuance of peace and tranquillity, have considerable influence." The more perfect the security, the greater will be the effective strength of the desire of accumulation. Where property is less safe, or the vicissitudes ruinous to fortunes are more frequent and severe, fewer persons will save at all, and of those who do, many will require the inducement of a higher rate of profit on capital, to make them prefer a doubtful future to the temptation of present enjoyment.

These are considerations which affect the expediency, in the eye of reason, of consulting future interests at the expense of present. But the inclination to make this sacrifice does not solely depend upon its expediency. The disposition to save is often far short of what reason would dictate: and at other times is liable to be in excess of it.

Deficient strength of the desire of accumulation may arise from improvidence, or from want of interest in others. Improvidence may be connected with intellectual as well as moral causes. Individuals and communities of a very low state of intelligence are always improvident. A certain measure of intellectual development seems necessary to enable absent things, and especially things future, to act with any force on the imagination and will. The effect of want of interest in others in diminishing accumulation, will be admitted, if we consider how much saving at present takes place, which has for its object the interest of others, rather than of ourselves; the education of children, their advancement in life, the future interests of other personal connections, the power of promoting by the bestowal of money or time, objects of public or private usefulness. If mankind were generally in the state of mind to which some approach was seen in the declining period of the Roman empire—caring nothing for their heirs, as well as nothing for friends, the public, or any object which survived them—they would seldom deny themselves any indulgence for the sake of saving, beyond what was necessary for their own future years; which they would place in life annuities, or in some other form which would make its existence and their lives terminate together. . . .

§ 4. We have hitherto spoken of countries in which the average strength of the desire to accumulate is short of that which, in circumstances of any tolerable security, reason and sober calculation would approve. We have now to speak of others in which it decidedly surpasses that standard. In the more prosperous countries of Europe, there are to be found abundance of prodigals; in some of them (and in none more than England) the ordinary degree of economy and providence among those who live by manual labor cannot be considered high; still, in a very numerous portion of the community, the professional, manufacturing, and trading classes, being those who, generally speaking, unite more of the means with more of the motives for saving than any other class, the spirit of accumulation is so strong, that the signs of rapidly increasing wealth meet every eye: and the great amount of capital seeking investment excites astonishment, whenever peculiar circumstances turning much of it into some one channel, such as railway construction or foreign speculative adventure, bring the largeness of the total amount into evidence.

There are many circumstances, which, in England, give a peculiar force to the accumulating propensity. The long exemption of the country from the ravages of war, and the far earlier period than elsewhere at which property was secure from military violence or arbitrary spoliation, have produced a long-standing and hereditary confidence in the safety of funds when trusted out of the owner's hands, which in most other countries is of much more recent origin, and less firmly established. The geographical causes which have made industry rather than war the natural source of power and importance to Great Britain, have turned an unusual proportion of the most enterprising and energetic characters into the direction of manufactures and commerce; into supplying their wants and gratifying their ambition by producing and saving, rather than by appropriating what has been produced and saved. Much also depended on the better political institutions of this country, which by the scope they have allowed to individual freedom of action, have encouraged personal activity and self-reliance, while by the liberty they confer of association and combination, they facilitate industrial enterprise on a large scale. The same institutions in another of their aspects, give a most direct and potent stimulus to the desire of acquiring wealth. The earlier decline of feudalism having removed or much weakened invidious distinctions between the originally trading classes and those who had been accustomed to despise them; and a polity having grown up which made wealth the real source of political influence; its acquisition was invested with a factitious value, independent of its intrinsic utility. It became synonymous with power; and since power with the common herd of mankind gives power, wealth became the chief source of personal consideration, and the measure and stamp of success in life. To get out of one rank in society into the next above it, is the great aim of English middle-class life, and the acquisition of wealth the means. And inasmuch as to be rich without industry, has always hitherto constituted a step in the social scale above those who are rich by means of industry, it becomes the object of ambition to save not merely as much as will afford a large income while in business, but enough to retire from business and live in affluence on realized gains. These causes have in England been greatly aided by that extreme incapacity of the people for personal enjoyment, which is a characteristic of countries over which Puritanism has passed. But if accumulation is, on one hand, rendered easier by the absence of a taste for pleasure, it is, on the other, made more difficult by the presence of a very real taste for expense. So strong is the association between personal consequence and the signs of wealth, that the silly desire for the appearance of a large expenditure has the force of a passion, among large classes of a nation which derive less pleasure than perhaps any other in the world from what it spends. Owing to this circumstance, the effective desire of accumulation has never reached so high a pitch in England as it did in Holland, where, there being no rich idle class to set the example of a reckless expenditure, and the mercantile classes, who possessed the substantial power on which social influence always waits, being left to establish their own scale of living and standard of propriety, their habits remained frugal and unostentatious.

In England and Holland, then, for a long time past, and now in most other countries in Europe (which are rapidly following England in the same race), the desire of accumulation does not require, to make it effective, the copious returns which it requires in Asia, but is sufficiently called into action by a rate of profit so low, that instead of slackening, accumulation seems now to proceed more rapidly than ever; and the second requisite of increased production, increase of capital, shows no tendency to become deficient. So far as that element is concerned, production is susceptible of an increase without any assignable bounds.

The progress of accumulation would no doubt be considerably checked, if the returns to capital were to be reduced still lower than at present. But why should any possible increase of capital have that effect? This question carries the mind forward to the remaining one of the three requisites of production. The limitation to production, not consisting in any necessary limit to the increase of the other two elements, labor and capital, must turn upon the properties of the only element which is inherently, and in itself, limited in quantity. It must depend on the properties of land.

Chapter 12: OF THE LAW OF THE INCREASE OF PRODUCTION FROM LAND

§ 1. Land differs from the other elements of production, labor and capital, in not being susceptible of indefinite increase. Its extent is limited, and the extent of the more productive kinds of it more limited still. It is also evident that the quantity of produce capable of being raised on any given piece of land is not indefinite. This limited quantity of land, and limited productiveness of it, are the real limits to the increase of production.

That they are the ultimate limits, must always have been clearly seen. But since the final barrier has never in any instance been reached; since there is no country in which all the land, capable of yielding food, is so highly cultivated that a larger produce could not (even without supposing any fresh advance in agricultural knowledge) be obtained from it, and since a large portion of the earth's surface still remains entirely uncultivated; it is commonly thought, and is very natural at first to suppose, that for the present all limitation of production or population from this source is at an indefinite distance, and that ages must elapse before any practical necessity arises for taking the limiting principle into serious consideration.

I apprehend this to be not only an error, but the most serious one, to be found in the whole field of political economy. The question is more important and fundamental than any other; it involves the whole subject of the causes of poverty, in a rich and industrious community; and unless this one matter be thoroughly understood, it is to no purpose proceeding any further in our inquiry.

§ 2. The limitation to production from the properties of the soil, is not like the obstacle opposed by a wall, which stands immovable in one particular spot, and offers no hindrance to motion short of stopping it entirely. We may rather compare it to a highly elastic and extensible band, which is hardly ever so violently stretched that it could not possibly be stretched any more, yet the pressure of which is felt long before the final limit is reached, and felt more severely the nearer that limit is approached.

After a certain, and not very advanced, stage in the progress of agriculture, it is the law of production from the land, that in any given state of agricultural skill and knowledge, by increasing the labor, the produce is not increased in an equal degree; doubling the labor does not double the produce; or, to express the same thing in other words, every increase of produce is obtained by a more than proportional increase in the application of labor to the land.

This general law of agricultural industry is the most important proposition in political economy. Were the law different, nearly all the phenomena of the production and distribution of wealth would be other than they are. The most fundamental errors which still prevail on our subject, result from not perceiving this law at work underneath the more superficial agencies on which attention fixes itself; but mistaking these agencies for the ultimate causes of effects of which they may influence the form and mode, but of which it alone determines the essence.

When, for the purpose of raising an increase of produce, recourse is had to inferior land, it is evident that, so far, the produce does not increase in the same proportion with the labor. The very meaning of inferior land, is land which with equal labor returns a smaller amount of produce. Land may be inferior either in fertility or in situation. The one requires a greater proportional amount of labor for growing the produce, the other for carrying it to market. If the land A yields a thousand quarters of wheat, to a given outlay in wages, manure, etc., and in order to raise another thousand recourse must be had to the land B, which is either less fertile or more distant from the market, the two thousand quarters will cost more than twice as much labor as the original thousand, and the produce of agriculture will be increased in a less ratio than the labor employed in procuring it.

Instead of cultivating the land B, it would be possible, by higher cultivation, to make the land A produce more. It might be ploughed or harrowed twice instead of once, or three times instead of twice; it might be dug instead of being ploughed; after ploughing, it might be gone over with a hoe instead of a harrow, and the soil more completely pulverized; it might be oftener or more thoroughly weeded; the implements used might be of higher finish, or more elaborate construction; a greater quantity or more expensive kinds of manure might be applied, or when applied, they might be more carefully mixed and incorporated with the soil. These are some of the modes by which the same land may be made to yield a greater produce; and when a greater produce must be had, some of these are among the means usually employed for obtaining it. But, that it is obtained at a more than proportional increase of expense, is evident from the fact that inferior lands are cultivated. Inferior lands, or lands at a greater distance from the market, of course yield an inferior return, and an increasing demand cannot be supplied from them unless at an augmentation of cost, and therefore of price. If the additional demand could continue to be supplied from the superior lands, by applying additional labor and capital, at no greater proportional cost than that at which they yield the quantity first demanded of them, the owners or farmers of those lands could undersell all others, and engross the whole market. Lands of a lower degree of fertility or in a more remote situation, might indeed be cultivated by their proprietors, for the sake of subsistence or independence; but it never could be the interest of anyone to farm them for profit. That a profit can be made from them, sufficient to attract capital to such an investment, is a proof that cultivation on the more eligible lands has reached a point, beyond which any greater application of labor and capital would yield, at the best, no greater return than can be obtained at the same expense from less fertile or less favorably situated lands.

The careful cultivation of a well-farmed district of England or Scotland is a symptom and an effect of the more unfavorable terms which the land has begun to exact for any increase of its fruits. Such elaborate cultivation costs much more in proportion, and requires a higher price to render it profitable, than farming on a more superficial system; and would not be adopted if access could be had to land of equal fertility, previously unoccupied. Where there is the choice of raising the increasing supply which society requires, from fresh land of as good quality as that already culti-vated, no attempt is made to extract from land anything approaching to what it will yield on what are esteemed the best European modes of culti-vating. The land is tasked up to the point at which the greatest return is obtained in proportion to the labor employed, but no further: any addi-tional labor is carried elsewhere. "It is long," says an intelligent traveller in the United States, "before an English eye becomes reconciled to the light-ness of the crops and the careless farming (as we should call it) which is apparent. One forgets that where land is so plentiful and labor so dear as it is here, a totally different principle must be pursued to that which prevails in populous countries, and that the consequences will of course be a want of tidiness, as it were, and finish, about everything which requires labor." Of the two causes mentioned, the plentifulness of land seems to me the true explanation, rather than the dearness of labor; for, however dear labor may be, when food is wanted, labor will always be applied to producing it in preference to anything else. But this labor is more effective for its end by being applied to fresh soil, than if it were employed in bringing the soil already occupied into higher cultivation. Only when no soils remain to be broken up but such as either from distance or inferior quality require a considerable rise of price to render their cultivation profitable, can it become advantageous to apply the high farming of Europe to any American lands; except, perhaps, in the immediate vicinity of towns, where saving in cost of carriage may compensate for great inferiority in the return from the soil itself. As American farming is to English, so is the ordinary English to that of Flanders, Tuscany, or the Terra di Lavoro; where by the applica-tion of a far greater quantity of labor there is obtained a considerably larger gross produce, but on such terms as would never be advantageous to a mere speculator for profit, unless made so by much higher prices of agricultural produce.

The principle which has now been stated must be received, no doubt, with certain explanations and limitations. Even after the land is so highly cultivated that the mere application of additional labor, or of an additional amount of ordinary dressing, would yield no return proportioned to the expense, it may still happen that the application of a much greater addi-tional labor and capital to improving the soil itself, by draining or perma-nent manures, would be as liberally remunerated by the produce, as any portion of the labor and capital already employed. It would sometimes be much more amply remunerated. This could not be, if capital always sought and found the most advantageous employment; but if the most advanta-geous employment has to wait longest for its remuneration, it is only in a rather advanced stage of industrial development that the preference will be given to it; and even in that advanced stage, the laws or usages connected with property in land and the tenure of farms, are often such as to prevent the disposable capital of the country from flowing freely into the channel of agricultural improvement: and hence the increased supply, required by increasing population, is sometimes raised at an augmenting cost by higher cultivation, when the means of producing it without increase of cost are known and accessible. There can be no doubt, that if capital were forthcoming to execute, within the next year, all known and recognized improvements in the land of the United Kingdom which would pay at the existing prices, that is, which would increase the produce in as great or a greater ratio than the expense; the result would be such (especially if we include Ireland in the supposition) that inferior land would not for a long time require to be brought under tillage: probably a considerable part of the less productive lands now cultivated, which are not particularly favored by situation, would go out of culture; or (as the improvements in question are not so much applicable to good land, but operate rather by converting bad land into good) the contraction of cultivation might principally take place by a less high dressing and less elaborate tilling of land generally; a falling back to something nearer the character of American farming; such only of the poor lands being altogether abandoned as were not found susceptible of improvement. And thus the aggregate of the whole cultivated land would bear a larger proportion than before to the labor expended on it; and the general law of diminishing return from land would have undergone, to that extent, a temporary supersession. No one, however, can suppose that even in these circumstances, the whole produce required for the country could be raised exclusively from the best lands, together with those possessing advantages of situation to place them on a par with the best. Much would undoubtedly continue to be produced under less advantageous conditions, and with a smaller proportional return, than that obtained from the best soils and situations. And in proportion as the further increase of population required a still greater addition to the supply, the general law would resume its course, and the further augmentation would be obtained at a more than proportionate expense of labor and capital.

. . .

. . . I do not assert that the cost of production and consequently the price, of agricultural produce, always and necessarily rises as population increases. It tends to do so, but the tendency may be, and sometimes is, even during long periods, held in check. The effect does not depend on a single principle, but on two antagonizing principles. There is another agency, in habitual antagonism to the law of diminishing return from land; and to the consideration of this we shall now proceed. It is no other than the progress of civilization. I use this general and somewhat vague expression, because the things to be included are so various, that hardly any term of a more restricted signification would comprehend them all.

Of these, the most obvious is the progress of agricultural knowledge, skill, and invention. Improved processes of agriculture are of two kinds: some enable the land to yield a greater absolute produce, without an equivalent increase of labor; others have not the power of increasing the produce, but have that of diminishing the labor and expense by which it is obtained. Among the first are to be reckoned the disuse of fallows, by means of the rotation of crops; and the introduction of new articles of cultivation capable of entering advantageously into the rotation. The change made in British agriculture toward the close of the last century, by the introduction of turnip husbandry, is spoken of as amounting to a revolution. These improvements operate not only by enabling the land to produce a crop every year instead of remaining idle one year in every two or three to renovate its powers, but also by direct increase of its productiveness; since the great addition made to the number of cattle by the increase of their food, affords more abundant manure to fertilize the corn lands. Next in order comes the introduction of new articles of food containing a greater amount of sustenance, like the potato, or more productive species or varieties of the same plant, such as the Swedish turnip. In the same class of improvements must be placed a better knowledge of the properties of manures, and of the most effective modes of applying them; the introduction of new and more powerful fertilizing agents, such as guano, and the conversion to the same purpose, of substances previously wasted; inventions like subsoil-ploughing or tile-draining; improvements in the breed or feeding of laboring cattle; augmented stock of the animals which consume and convert into human food what would otherwise be wasted; and the like. The other sort of improvements, those which diminish labor, but without increasing the capacity of the land to produce, are such as the improved construction of tools; the introduction of new instruments which spare manual labor, as the winnowing and threshing machines; a more skilful and economical application of muscular exertion, such as the introduction, so slowly accomplished in England, of Scotch ploughing, with two horses abreast and one man, instead of three or four horses in a team and two men, etc. These improvements do not add to the productiveness of the land, but they are equally calculated with the former to counteract the tendency in the cost of production of agricultural produce, to rise with the progress of population and demand.

Analogous in effect to this second class of agricultural improvements, are improved means of communication. Good roads are equivalent to good tools. It is of no consequence whether the economy of labor takes place in extracting the produce from the soil, or in conveying it to the place where it is to be consumed. Not to say in addition, that the labor of cultivation itself is diminished by whatever lessens the cost of bringing manure from a distance, or facilitates the many operations of transport from place to place which occur within the bounds of the farm. Railways and canals are virtually a diminution of the cost of production of all things sent to market by them; and literally so of all those, the appliances and aids for producing which, they serve to transmit. By their means land can be cultivated, which would not otherwise have remunerated the cultivators without a rise of price. Improvements in navigation have, with respect to food or materials brought from beyond sea, a corresponding effect.

. . .

BOOK II / Distribution

Chapter 11: OF WAGES

§ 1. Under the head of Wages are to be considered, first, the causes which determine or influence the wages of labor generally, and secondly, the differences that exist between the wages of different employments. It is convenient to keep these two classes of consideration separate; and in discussing the law of wages, to proceed in the first instance as if there were no other kind of labor than common unskilled labor, of the average degree of hardness and disagreeableness.

Wages, like other things, may be regulated either by competition or by custom. In this country there are few kinds of labor of which the remuneration would not be lower than it is, if the employer took the full advantage of competition. Competition, however, must be regarded, in the present state of society, as the principal regulator of wages, and custom or individual character only as a modifying circumstance, and that in a comparatively slight degree.

Wages, then, depend mainly upon the demand and supply of labor; or as it is often expressed, on the proportion between population and capital. By population is here meant the number only of the laboring class, or rather of those who work for hire; and by capital, only circulating capital, and not even the whole of that, but the part which is expended in the direct purchase of labor. To this, however, must be added all funds which, without forming a part of capital, are paid in exchange for labor, such as the wages of soldiers, domestic servants, and all other unproductive laborers. There is unfortunately no mode of expressing by one familiar term, the aggregate of what may be called the wages-fund of a country: and as the wages of productive labor form nearly the whole of that fund, it is usual to overlook the smaller and less important part, and to say that wages depend on population and capital. It will be convenient to employ this expression, remembering, however, to consider it as elliptical, and not as a literal statement of the entire truth.

With these limitations of the terms, wages not only depend upon the relative amount of capital and population, but cannot, under the rule of competition, be affected by anything else. Wages (meaning, of course, the general rate) cannot rise, but by an increase of the aggregate funds employed in hiring laborers, or a diminution in the number of the competitors for hire; nor fall, except either by a diminution of the funds devoted to paying labor, or by an increase in the number of laborers to be paid.

§ 2. There are, however, some facts in apparent contradiction to this doctrine, which it is incumbent on us to consider and explain.

For instance, it is a common saying that wages are high when trade is good. The demand for labor in any particular employment is more pressing, and higher wages are paid, when there is a brisk demand for the commodity produced; and the contrary when there is what is called a stagnation: then work-people are dismissed, and those who are retained must submit to a reduction of wages: though in these cases there is neither more nor less capital than before. This is true; and is one of those complications in the concrete phenomena, which obscure and disguise the operation of general causes; but it is not really inconsistent with the principles laid down. Capital which the owner does not employ in purchasing labor, but keeps idle in his hands, is the same thing to the laborers, for the time being, as if it did not exist. All capital is, from the variations of trade, occasionally in this state. A manufacturer, finding a slack demand for his commodity, forbears to employ laborers in increasing a stock which he finds it difficult to dispose of; or if he goes on until all his capital is locked up in unsold goods, then at least he must of necessity pause until he can get paid for some of them. But no one expects either of these states to be permanent; if he did, he would at the first opportunity remove his capital to some other occupation, in which it would still continue to employ labor. The capital remains unemployed for a time, during which the labor market is overstocked, and wages fall. Afterwards the demand revives, and perhaps becomes unusually brisk, enabling the manufacturer to sell his commodity even faster than he can produce it: his whole capital is then brought into complete efficiency, and if he is able, he borrows capital in addition, which would otherwise have gone into some other employment. At such times wages, in his particular occupation, rise. If we suppose, what in strictness is not absolutely impossible, that one of these fits of briskness or of stagnation should affect all occupations at the same time, wages altogether might undergo a rise or a fall. These, however, are but temporary fluctuations: the capital now lying idle will next year be in active employment, that which is this year unable to keep up with the demand will in its turn be locked up in crowded warehouses; and wages in these several departments will ebb and flow accordingly: but nothing can permanently alter general wages, except an increase or a diminution of capital itself (always meaning by the term, the funds of all sorts, destined for the payment of labor) compared with the quantity of labor offering itself to be hired.

Again, it is another common notion that high prices make high wages; because the producers and dealers, being better off, can afford to pay more to their laborers. I have already said that a brisk demand, which causes temporary high prices, causes also temporary high wages. But high prices, in themselves, can only raise wages if the dealers, receiving more, are induced to save more, and make an addition to their capital, or at least to their purchases of labor. This is indeed likely enough to be the case; and if the high prices came direct from heaven, or even from abroad, the laboring class might be benefited, not by the high prices themselves, but by the increase of capital occasioned by them. The same effect, however, is often attributed to a high price which is the result of restrictive laws, or which is in some way or other to be paid by the remaining members of the community; they having no greater means than before to pay it with. High prices of this sort, if they benefit one class of laborers, can only do so at the expense of others; since if the dealers by receiving high prices are enabled to make greater savings, or otherwise increase their purchases of labor, all other people by paying those high prices, have their means of saving, or of purchasing labor, reduced in an equal degree; and it is a matter of accident whether the one alteration or the other will have the greatest effect on the labor market. Wages will probably be temporarily higher in the employment in which prices have risen, and somewhat lower in other employments: in which case, while the first half of the phenomenon excites notice, the other is generally overlooked, or if observed, is not ascribed to the cause which really produced it. Nor will the partial rise of wages last long: for though the dealers in that one employment gain more, it does not follow that there is room to employ a greater amount of savings in their own business: their increasing capital will probably flow over into other employments, and there counterbalance the diminution previously made in the demand for labor by the diminished savings of other classes.

Another opinion often maintained is, that wages (meaning of course money wages) vary with the price of food; rising when it rises, and falling when it falls. This opinion is, I conceive, only partially true: and in so far as true, in no way affects the dependence of wages on the proportion between capital and labor: since the price of food, when it affects wages at all, affects them through that law. Dear or cheap food caused by variety of seasons does not affect wages (unless they are artificially adjusted to it by law or charity): or rather, it has some tendency to affect them in the contrary way to that supposed; since in times of scarcity people generally compete more violently for employment, and lower the labor market against themselves. But dearness or cheapness of food, when of a permanent character, and capable of being calculated on beforehand, may affect wages. In the first place, if the laborers have, as is often the case, no more than enough to keep them in working condition, and enable them barely to support the ordinary number of children, it follows that if food grows permanently dearer without a rise of wages, a greater number of the children will prematurely die; and thus wages will ultimately be higher, but only because the number of people will be smaller, than if food had remained cheap. But, secondly, even though wages were high enough to admit of food's becoming more costly without depriving the laborers and their families of necessaries; though they could bear, physically speaking, to be worse off, perhaps they would not consent to be so. They might have habits of comfort which were to them as necessaries, and sooner than forego which, they would put an additional restraint on their power of multiplication; so that wages would rise, not by increase of deaths but by diminution of births. In these cases, then, wages do adapt themselves to the price of food, though after an interval of almost a generation. Mr. Ricardo considers these two cases to comprehend all cases. He assumes, that there is everywhere a minimum rate of wages: either the lowest with which it is physically possible to keep up the population, or the lowest with which the people will choose to do so. To this minimum he assumes that the general rate of wages always tends; that they can never be lower, beyond the length of time required for a diminished rate of increase to make itself felt, and can never long continue higher. This assumption contains sufficient truth to render it admissible for the purposes of abstract science; and the conclusion which Mr. Ricardo draws from it, namely, that wages in the long run rise and fall with the permanent rise of food, is, like almost all his conclusions, true hypothetically, that is, granting the suppositions from which he sets out. But in the application to practice, it is necessary to consider that the minimum of which he speaks, especially when it is not a physical, but what may be termed a moral minimum, is itself liable to vary. If wages were previously so high that they could bear reduction, to which the obstacle was a high standard of comfort habitual among the laborers, a rise of the price of food, or any other disadvantageous change in their circumstances, may operate in two ways: it may correct itself by a rise of wages, brought about through a gradual effect on the prudential check of population; or it may permanently lower the standard of living of the class, in case their previous habits in respect of population prove stronger than their previous habits in respect of comfort. In that case the injury done to them will be permanent, and their deteriorated condition will become a new minimum, tending to perpetuate itself as the more ample minimum did before. It is to be feared that of the two modes in which the cause may operate, the last is the most frequent, or at all events sufficiently so, to render all propositions ascribing a self-repairing quality to the calamities which befall the laboring classes, practically of no validity. There is considerable evidence that the circumstances of the agricultural laborers in England have more than once in our history sustained great permanent deterioration, from causes which operated by diminishing the demand for labor, and which, if population had exercised its power of self-adjustment in obedience to the previous standard of comfort, could only have had a temporary effect: but unhappily the poverty in which the class was plunged during a long series of years, brought that previous standard into disuse; and the next generation, growing up without having possessed those pristine comforts, multiplied in turn without any attempt to retrieve them.[1]

The converse case occurs when, by improvements in agriculture, the repeal of corn laws, or other such causes, the necessaries of the laborers are cheapened, and they are enabled with the same wages, to command greater comforts than before. Wages will not fall immediately; it is even possible that they may rise; but they will fall at last, so as to leave the laborers no better off than before, unless, during this interval of prosperity, the standard of comfort regarded as indispensable by the class, is permanently raised. Unfortunately this salutary effect is by no means to be counted upon: it is a much more difficult thing to raise, than to lower, the scale of living which the laborers will consider as more indispensable than marrying and having a family. If they content themselves with enjoying the greater comfort while it lasts, but do not learn to require it, they will people down to their old scale of living. If from poverty their children had previously been insufficiently fed or improperly nursed, a greater number will now be reared, and the competition of these, when they grow up, will depress wages, probably in full proportion to the greater cheapness of food. If the effect is not produced in this mode, it will be produced by earlier and more numerous marriages, or by an increased number of births to a marriage. According to all experience, a great increase invariably takes place in the number of marriages, in seasons of cheap food and full employment. I cannot, therefore, agree in the importance so often attached to the repeal of the corn laws, considered merely as a laborer's question, or to any of the schemes, of which some one or other is at all times in vogue, for making the laborers a very little better off. Things which only affect them a very little, make no permanent impression upon their habits and requirements, and they soon slide back into their former state. To produce permanent advantage, the temporary cause operating upon them must be sufficient to make a great change in their condition—a change such as will be felt for many years, notwithstanding any stimulus which it may give during one generation to the increase of people. When, indeed, the improvement is of this signal character, and a generation grows up which has always been used to an improved scale of comfort, the habits of this new generation in respect to population become formed upon a higher minimum, and the im-

[1] See the historical sketch of the condition of the English peasantry, prepared from the best authorities by Mr. William Thornton, in his work entitled "Over-Population and Its Remedy": a work honorably distinguished from most others which have been published in the present generation, by its rational treatment of questions affecting the economical condition of the laboring classes.

provement in their condition becomes permanent. Of cases in point, the most remarkable is France after the Revolution. The majority of the population being suddenly raised from misery, to independence and comparative comfort; the immediate effect was that population, notwithstanding the destructive wars of the period, started forward with unexampled rapidity, partly because improved circumstances enabled many children to be reared who would otherwise have died, and partly from increase of births. The succeeding generation however grew up with habits considerably altered; and though the country was never before in so prosperous a state, the annual number of births is now nearly stationary, and the increase of population extremely slow.[2]

§ 3. Wages depend, then, on the proportion between the number of the laboring population, and the capital or other funds devoted to the purchase of labor; we will say, for shortness, the capital. If wages are higher at one time or place than at another, if the subsistence and comfort of the class of hired laborers are more ample, it is for no other reason than because capital bears a greater proportion to population. It is not the absolute amount of accumulation or of production, that is of importance to the laboring class; it is not the amount even of the funds destined for distribution among the laborers: it is the proportion between those funds and the numbers among whom they are shared. The condition of the class can be bettered in no other way than by altering that proportion to their advantage: and every scheme for their benefit, which does not proceed on this as its foundation, is, for all permanent purposes, a delusion.

In countries like North America and the Australian colonies, where the knowledge and arts of civilized life, and a high effective desire of accumulation, co-exist with a boundless extent of unoccupied land; the growth of capital easily keeps pace with the utmost possible increase of population, and is chiefly retarded by the impracticability of obtaining laborers enough.

---

[2] A similar, though not an equal improvement in the standard of living took place among the laborers of England during the remarkable fifty years from 1715 to 1765, which were distinguished by such an extraordinary succession of fine harvests (the years of decided deficiency not exceeding five in all that period) that the average price of wheat during those years was much lower than during the previous half century. Mr. Malthus computes that on the average of sixty years preceding 1720, the laborer could purchase with a day's earnings only two-thirds of a peck of wheat, while from 1720 to 1750 he could purchase a whole peck. The average price of wheat according to the Eton tables, for fifty years ending with 1715, 41s. 7¾d. the quarter, and for the last twenty-three of these, 45s. 8d., while for the fifty years following, it was no more than 34s. 11d. So considerable an improvement in the condition of the laboring class, though arising from the accidents of seasons, yet continuing for more than a generation, had time to work a change in the habitual requirements of the laboring class; and this period is always noted as the date of "a marked improvement of the quality of the food consumed, and a decided elevation in the standard of their comforts and conveniences." (Malthus, *Principles of Political Economy*, p. 225.) For the character of the period, see Mr. Tooke's excellent *History of Prices*, Vol. I, pp. 38 to 61, and for the prices of corn, the Appendix to that work.

All, therefore, who can possibly be born, can find employment without overstocking the market: every laboring family enjoys in abundance the necessaries, many of the comforts, and some of the luxuries of life; and, unless in case of individual misconduct, or actual inability to work, poverty does not, and dependence needs not, exist. A similar advantage, though in a less degree, is occasionally enjoyed by some special class of laborers in old countries, from an extraordinarily rapid growth, not of capital generally, but of the capital employed in a particular occupation. So gigantic has been the progress of the cotton manufacture since the inventions of Watt and Arkwright, that the capital engaged in it has probably quadrupled in the time which population requires for doubling. While, therefore, it has attracted from other employments nearly all the hands which geographical circumstances and the habits or inclinations of the people rendered available; and while the demand it created for infant labor has enlisted the immediate pecuniary interest of the operatives in favor of promoting, instead of restraining, the increase of population; nevertheless wages in the great seats of the manufacture are generally so high, that the collective earnings of a family amount, on an average of years, to a very satisfactory sum; and there is, as yet, no sign of permanent decrease, while the effect has also been felt in raising the general standard of agricultural wages in the counties adjoining.

But those circumstances of a country, or of an occupation, in which population can with impunity increase at its utmost rate, are rare, and transitory. Very few are the countries presenting the needful union of conditions. Either the industrial arts are backward and stationary, and capital therefore increases slowly; or the effective desire of accumulation being low, the increase soon reaches its limit; or, even though both these elements are at their highest known degree, the increase of capital is checked, because there is not fresh land to be resorted to, of as good quality as that already occupied. Though capital should for a time double itself simultaneously with population, if all this capital and population are to find employment on the same land, they cannot without an unexampled succession of agricultural inventions continue doubling the produce; therefore, if wages do not fall, profits must; and when profits fall, increase of capital is slackened. Besides, even if wages did not fall, the price of food (as will be shown more fully hereafter) would in these circumstances necessarily rise; which is equivalent to a fall of wages.

Except, therefore, in the very peculiar cases which I have just noticed, of which the only one of any practical importance is that of a new colony, or a country in circumstances equivalent to it; it is impossible that population should increase at its utmost rate without lowering wages. Nor will the fall be stopped at any point, short of that which either by its physical or its moral operation, checks the increase of population. In no old country, therefore, does population increase at anything like its utmost rate; in most, at a very moderate rate: in some countries not at all. These facts are only to be accounted for in two ways. Either the whole number of births which nature admits of, and which happen in some circumstances, do not take place; or if they do, a large proportion of those who are born, die. The retardation of increase results either from mortality or prudence; from Mr. Malthus's positive, or from his preventive check: and one or the other of these must and does exist, and very powerfully too, in all old societies. Wherever population is not kept down by the prudence either of individuals or of the state, it is kept down by starvation or disease.

Mr. Malthus has taken great pains to ascertain, for almost every country in the world, which of these checks it is that operates: and the evidence which he collected on the subject, in his Essay on Population, may even now be read with advantage. Throughout Asia, and formerly in most European countries in which the laboring classes were not in personal bondage, there is, or was, no restrainer of population but death. The mortality was not always the result of poverty: much of it proceeded from unskilful and careless management of children, from uncleanly and otherwise unhealthy habits of life among the adult population, and from the almost periodical occurrence of destructive epidemics. Throughout Europe these causes of shortened life have much diminished, but they have not ceased to exist. Until a period not very remote, hardly any of our large towns kept up its population, independently of the stream always flowing into them from the rural districts: this was still true of Liverpool until very recently; and even in London, the mortality is larger, and the average duration of life shorter, than in rural districts where there is much greater poverty. In Ireland, epidemic fevers, and deaths from the exhaustion of the constitution by insufficient nutriment, have always accompanied even the most moderate deficiency of the potato crop. Nevertheless, it cannot now be said that in any part of Europe, population is principally kept down by disease, still less by starvation, either in a direct or in an indirect form. The agency by which it is limited is chiefly preventive, not (in the language of Mr. Malthus) positive. But the preventive remedy seldom, I believe, consists in the unaided operation of prudential motives on a class wholly or mainly composed of laborers for hire, and looking forward to no other lot. In England, for example, I much doubt if the generality of agricultural laborers practise any prudential restraint whatever. They generally marry as early, and have as many children to a marriage, as they would or could do if they were settlers in the United States. During the generation which preceded the enactment of the present Poor Law, they received the most direct encouragement to this sort of improvidence: being not only assured of support, on easy terms, whenever out of employment, but even when in employment, very commonly receiving from the parish a weekly allowance proportioned to their number of children; and the married with large families being always, from a short-sighted economy, employed in preference to the unmarried; which last premium on population still exists. Under such prompting, the rural laborers acquired habits of recklessness, which are so congenial to the uncultivated mind, that in whatever manner produced, they in general long survive their immediate causes. There are so many new elements at work in society, even in those deeper *strata* which are inaccessible to the mere movements on the surface, that it is hazardous to affirm anything positive on the mental state or practical impulses of classes and bodies of men, when the same assertion may be true to-day, and may require great modification in a few years' time. It does, however, seem, that if the rate of increase of population depended solely on the agricultural laborers, it would, as far as dependent on births, and unless repressed by deaths, be as rapid in the southern counties of England as in America. The restraining principle lies in the very great proportion of the population composed of the middle classes and the skilled artisans, who in this country almost equal in number the common laborers, and on whom prudential motives do, in a considerable degree, operate.

. . .

Chapter 15: OF PROFITS

§ 1. Having treated of the laborer's share of the produce, we next proceed to the share of the capitalist; the profits of capital or stock; the gains of the person who advances the expenses of production—who, from funds in his possession, pays the wages of the laborers, or supports them during the work; who supplies the requisite buildings, materials, and tools or machinery; and to whom, by the usual terms of the contract, the produce belongs, to be disposed of at his pleasure. After indemnifying him for his outlay, there commonly remains a surplus, which is his profit; the net income from his capital: the amount which he can afford to expend in necessaries or pleasures, or from which by further saving he can add to his wealth.

As the wages of the laborer are the remuneration of labor, so the profits of the capitalist are properly, according to Mr. Senior's well-chosen expression, the remuneration of abstinence. They are what he gains by forbearing to consume his capital for his own uses, and allowing it to be consumed by productive laborers for their uses. For this forbearance he requires a recompense. Very often in personal enjoyment he would be a gainer by squandering his capital, the capital amounting to more than the sum of the profits which it will yield during the years he can expect to live. But while he retains it undiminished, he has always the power of consuming it if he wishes or needs; he can bestow it upon others at his death; and in the meantime he derives from it an income, which he can without impoverishment apply to the satisfaction of his own wants or inclinations.

Of the gains, however, which the possession of a capital enables a person to make, a part only is properly an equivalent for the use of the capital itself; namely, as much as a solvent person would be willing to pay for the loan of it. This, which as everybody knows is called interest, is all that a person is enabled to get by merely abstaining from the immediate consumption of his capital, and allowing it to be used for productive purposes by others. The remuneration which is obtained in any country for mere abstinence, is measured by the current rate of interest on the best security; such security as precludes any appreciable chance of losing the principal. What a person expects to gain, who superintends the employment of his own capital, is always more, and generally much more, than this. The rate of profit greatly exceeds the rate of interest. The surplus is partly compensation for risk. By lending his capital, on unexceptionable security, he runs little or no risk. But if he embarks in business on his own account, he always exposes his capital to some, and in many cases to very great, danger of partial or total loss. For this danger he must be compensated, otherwise he will not incur it. He must likewise be remunerated for the devotion of his time and labor. The control of the operations of industry usually belongs to the person who supplies the whole or the greatest part of the funds by which they are carried on, and who, according to the ordinary arrangement, is either alone interested, or is the person most interested (at least directly), in the result. To exercise this control with efficiency, if the concern is large and complicated, requires great assiduity, and often no ordinary skill. This assiduity and skill must be remunerated.

The gross profits from capital, the gains returned to those who supply the funds for production, must suffice for these three purposes. They must afford a sufficient equivalent for abstinence, indemnity for risk, and remuneration for the labor and skill required for superintendence. These different compensations may be either paid to the same, or to different persons. The capital, or some part of it, may be borrowed: may belong to someone who does not undertake the risks or the trouble of business. In that case, the lender, or owner, is the person who practices the abstinence; and is remunerated for it by the interest paid to him, while the difference between the interest and the gross profit remunerates the exertions and risks of the undertaker.[1] Sometimes, again, the capital, or a part of it, is supplied by what is called a sleeping partner; who shares the risks of the employment, but not the trouble, and who, in consideration of those risks, receives not a mere interest, but a stipulated share of the gross profits. Sometimes the capital is supplied and the risk incurred by one person, and the business carried on exclusively in his name, while the trouble of management is made over to another, who is engaged for that purpose at a fixed salary.

[1] It is to be regretted that this word, in this sense, is not familiar to an English ear. French political economists enjoy a great advantage in being able to speak currently of *les profits de l'entrepreneur.*

Management, however, by hired servants, who have no interest in the result but that of preserving their salaries, is proverbially inefficient, unless they act under the inspecting eye, if not the controlling hand, of the person chiefly interested: and prudence almost always recommends giving to a manager not thus controlled, a remuneration partly dependent on the profits; which virtually reduces the case to that of a sleeping partner. Or finally, the same person may own the capital; and conduct the business; adding, if he will and can, to the management of his own capital, that of as much more as the owners may be willing to trust him with. But under any and all of these arrangements, the same three things require their remuneration, and must obtain it from the gross profit: abstinence, risk, exertion. And the three parts into which profit may be considered as resolving itself, may be described respectively as interest, insurance, and wages of superintendence.

§ 2. The lowest rate of profit which can permanently exist, is that which is barely adequate, at the given place and time, to afford an equivalent for the abstinence, risk, and exertion implied in the employment of capital. From the gross profit, has first to be deducted as much as will form a fund sufficient on the average to cover all losses incident to the employment. Next, it must afford such an equivalent to the owner of the capital for forbearing to consume it, as is then and there a sufficient motive to him to persist in his abstinence. How much will be required to form this equivalent, depends on the comparative value placed, in the given society, upon the present and the future: (in the words formerly used) on the strength of the effective desire of accumulation. Further, after covering all losses, and remunerating the owner for forbearing to consume, there must be something left to recompense the labor and skill of the person who devotes his time to the business. This recompense too must be sufficient to enable at least the owners of the larger capitals to receive for their trouble, or to pay to some manager for his, what to them or him will be a sufficient inducement for undergoing it. If the surplus is no more than this, none but large masses of capital will be employed productively, and if it did not even amount to this, capital would be withdrawn from production, and unproductively consumed, until, by an indirect consequence of its diminished amount, to be explained hereafter, the rate of profit was raised.

Such, then, is the minimum of profits: but that minimum is exceedingly variable, and at some times and places extremely low; on account of the great variableness of two out of its three elements. That the rate of necessary remuneration for abstinence, or in other words the effective desire of accumulation, differs widely in different states of society and civilization, has been seen in a former chapter. There is a still wider difference in the element which consists in compensation for risk. . . .

. . .

§ 4. After due allowance is made for these various causes of inequality, namely, differences in the risk or agreeableness of different employments, and natural or artificial monopolies; the rate of profit on capital in all employments tends to an equality. Such is the proposition usually laid down by political economists, and under proper explanations it is true.

That portion of profit which is properly interest, and which forms the real remuneration for abstinence, is strictly the same, at the same time and place, whatever be the employment. The rate of interest on equally good security, does not vary according to the destination of the principal, though it does vary from time to time very much, according to the circumstances of the market. There is no employment in which, in the present state of industry, competition is so active and incessant as in the lending and borrowing of money. All persons in business are occasionally, and most of them constantly, borrowers: while all persons not in business, who possess moneyed property, are lenders. Between these two great bodies there is a numerous, keen, and intelligent class of middlemen, composed of bankers, stockbrokers, discount brokers, and others, alive to the slightest breath of probable gain. The smallest circumstance, or the most transient impression on the public mind, which tends to an increase or diminution of the demand for loan, either at the time or prospectively, operates immediately on the rate of interest: and circumstances in the general state of trade, really tending to cause this difference of demand, are continually occurring, sometimes to such an extent, that the rate of interest on the best mercantile bills has been known to vary in little more than a year (even without the occurrence of the great derangement called a commercial crisis) from four or less, to eight or nine per cent. But, at the same time and place, the rate of interest is the same, to all who can give equally good security. The market rate of interest is at all times a known and definite thing.

It is far otherwise with gross profit; which, though (as will presently be seen) it does not vary much from employment to employment, varies very greatly from individual to individual, and can scarcely be in any two cases the same. It depends on the knowledge, talents, economy, and energy of the capitalist himself, or of the agents whom he employs; on the accidents of personal connection; and even on chance. Hardly any two dealers in the same trade, even if their commodities are equally good and equally cheap, carry on their business at the same expense, or turn over their capital in the same time. That equal capitals give equal profits, as a general maxim of trade, would be as false as that equal age or size gives equal bodily strength, or that equal reading or experience gives equal knowledge. The effect depends as much upon twenty other things, as upon the single cause specified.

But though profits thus vary, the parity, on the whole, of different modes of employing capital (in the absence of any natural or artificial monopoly) is in a certain, and a very important sense, maintained. On an average (whatever may be the occasional fluctuations) the various employ-ments of capital are on such a footing, as to hold out, not equal profits, but equal expectations of profit, to persons of average abilities and advantages. By equal, I mean after making compensation for any inferiority in the agreeableness or safety of an employment. . . .

It must not however be forgotten, that even in the countries of most active competition, custom also has a considerable share in determining the profits of trade. There is sometimes an idea afloat as to what the profit of an employment should be, which though not adhered to by all the dealers, nor perhaps rigidly by any, still exercises a certain influence over their operations. . . .

§ 5. The preceding remarks have, I hope, sufficiently elucidated what is meant by the common phrase, "the ordinary rate of profit;" and the sense in which, and the limitations under which, this ordinary rate has a real existence. It now remains to consider, what causes determine its amount.

To popular apprehension it seems as if the profits of business depended upon prices. A producer or dealer seems to obtain his profits by selling his commodity for more than it cost him.

. . .

§ 7. It thus appears that the two elements on which, and which alone, the gains of the capitalists depend, are, first, the magnitude of the produce, in other words, the productive power of labor; and secondly, the propor-tion of that produce obtained by the laborers themselves; the ratio which the remuneration of the laborers bears to the amount they produce. These two things form the data for determining the gross amount divided as profit among all the capitalists of the country; but the rate of profit, the percentage on the capital, depends only on the second of the two elements, the laborer's proportional share, and not on the amount to be shared. If the produce of labor were doubled, and the laborers obtained the same proportional share as before, that is, if their remuneration was also doubled, the capitalists, it is true, would gain twice as much; but as they would also have had to advance twice as much, the rate of their profit would be only the same as before.

We thus arrive at the conclusion of Ricardo and others, that the rate of profits depends on wages; rising as wages fall, and falling as wages rise. In adopting, however, this doctrine, I must insist upon making a most necessary alteration in its wording. Instead of saying that profits depend on wages, let us say (what Ricardo really meant) that they depend on the *cost of labor*.

Wages, and the cost of labor; what labor brings in to the laborer, and what it costs to the capitalist; are ideas quite distinct, and which it is of the utmost importance to keep so. For this purpose it is essential not to designate them, as is almost always done, by the same name. Wages, in public discussions, both oral and printed, being looked upon from the point of view of the payers, much often than from that of the receivers, nothing is more common than to say that wages are high or low, meaning only that the cost of labor is high or low. The reverse of this would be often the truth: the cost of labor is frequently at its highest where wages are lowest. This may arise from two causes. In the first place, the labor, though cheap, may be inefficient. In no European country are wages so low as they are (or at least were) in Ireland; the remuneration of an agricultural laborer in the west of Ireland not being more than half the wages of even the lowest-paid Englishman, the Dorsetshire laborer. But if, from inferior skill and industry, two days' labor of an Irishman accomplished no more work than an English laborer performed in one, the Irishman's labor cost as much as the Englishman's, though it brought in so much less to himself. The capitalist's profit is determined by the former of these two things, not by the latter. That a difference to this extent really existed in the efficiency of the labor, is proved not only by abundant testimony, but by the fact, that notwithstanding the lowness of wages, profits of capital are not understood to have been higher in Ireland than in England.

The other cause which renders wages, and the cost of labor, no real *criteria* of one another, is the varying costliness of the articles which the laborer consumes. If these are cheap, wages, in the sense which is of importance to the laborer, may be high, and yet the cost of labor may be low; if dear, the laborer may be wretchedly off, though his labor may cost much to the capitalist. This last is the condition of a country over-peopled in relation to its land; in which, food being dear, the poorness of the laborer's real reward does not prevent labor from costing much to the purchaser, and low wages and low profits co-exist. The opposite case is exemplified in the United States of America. The laborer there enjoys a greater abundance of comforts than in any other country of the world, except some of the newest colonies; but, owing to the cheap price at which these comforts can be obtained (combined with the great efficiency of the labor,) the cost of labor is at least not higher, nor the rate of profit lower, than in Europe.

The cost of labor, then, is, in the language of mathematics, a function of three variables: the efficiency of labor; the wages of labor (meaning thereby the real reward of the laborer); and the greater or less cost at which the articles composing that real reward can be produced or procured. It is plain that the cost of labor to the capitalist must be influenced by each of these three circumstances, and by no others. These, therefore, are also the circumstances which determine the rate of profit; and it cannot be in any way affected except through one or other of them. If labor generally became more efficient, without being more highly rewarded; if, without its becoming less efficient, its remuneration fell, no increase taking place in the cost of the articles composing that remuneration; or if those articles became less costly without the laborer's obtaining more of them; in any one of these three cases, profits would rise. If, on the contrary, labor became less efficient (as it might do from diminished bodily vigor in the people, destruction of fixed capital, or deteriorated education); or if the laborer obtained a higher remuneration, without any increased cheapness in the things composing it; or if, without his obtaining more, that which he did obtain became more costly; profits, in all these cases, would suffer a diminution. And there is no other combination of circumstances, in which the general rate of profit of a country, in all employments indifferently, can either fall or rise.

The evidence of these propositions can only be stated generally, though, it is hoped, conclusively, in this stage of our subject. It will come out in greater fulness and force when, having taken into consideration the theory of Value and Price, we shall be enabled to exhibit the law of profits in the concrete—in the complex entanglement of circumstances in which it actually works. This can only be done in the ensuing Book. One topic still remains to be discussed in the present one, so far as it admits of being treated independently of considerations of Value: the subject of Rent; to which we now proceed.

BOOK III / Exchange

Chapter 1: OF VALUE

The subject on which we are now about to enter fills so important and conspicuous a position in political economy, that in the apprehension of some thinkers its boundaries confound themselves with those of the science itself. One eminent writer has proposed as a name for Political Economy, "Catallactics," or the science of exchanges: by others it has been called the Science of Values. If these denominations had appeared to me logically correct, I must have placed the discussion of the elementary laws of value at the commencement of our inquiry, instead of postponing it to the Third Part; and the possibility of so long deferring it is alone a sufficient proof that this view of the nature of Political Economy is too confined. It is true that in the preceding Books we have not escaped the necessity of anticipating some small portion of the theory of Value, especially as to the value of labor and of land. It is nevertheless evident, that of the two great departments of Political Economy, the production of wealth and its distribution, the consideration of Value has to do with the latter alone; and with that only so far as competition, and not usage or custom, is the distributing agency. The conditions and laws of Production would be the same as they are, if the arrangements of society did not depend on exchange, or did not admit of it. Even in the present system of industrial life, in which employments are minutely subdivided, and all concerned in production depend for their remuneration on the price of a particular commodity, exchange is not the fundamental law of the distribution of the produce, no more than roads and carriages are the essential laws of motion, but merely a part of the machinery for effecting it. To confound these ideas, seems to me not only a logical, but a practical blunder. It is a case of the error too common in political economy, of not distinguishing between necessities arising from the nature of things, and those created by social arrangements: an error, which appears to me to be at all times producing two opposite mischiefs; on the one hand, causing political economists to class the merely temporary truths of their subject among its permanent and universal laws; and on the other, leading many persons to mistake the permanent laws of Production (such as those on which the necessity is grounded of restraining population) for temporary accidents arising from the existing constitution of society—which those who would frame a new system of social arrangements, are at liberty to disregard.

In a state of society, however, in which the industrial system is entirely founded on purchase and sale, each individual, for the most part, living not on things in the production of which he himself bears a part, but on things obtained by a double exchange, a sale followed by a purchase—the question of Value is fundamental. Almost every speculation respecting the economical interests of a society thus constituted, implies some theory of Value: the smallest error on that subject infects with corresponding error all our other conclusions; and anything vague or misty in our conception of it, creates confusion and uncertainty in everything else. Happily, there is nothing in the laws of Value which remains for the present or any future writer to clear up; the theory of the subject is complete: the only difficulty to be overcome is that of so stating it as to solve by anticipation the chief perplexities which occur in applying it: and to do this, some minuteness of exposition, and considerable demands on the patience of the reader, are unavoidable. He will be amply repaid, however (if a stranger to these inquiries), by the ease and rapidity with which a thorough understanding of this subject will enable him to fathom most of the remaining questions of political economy.

§ 2. We must begin by settling our phraseology. Adam Smith, in a passage often quoted, has touched upon the most obvious ambiguity of the word value; which, in one of its senses, signifies usefulness, in another, power of purchasing; in his own language, value in use, and value in exchange. But (as Mr. De Quincey has remarked) in illustrating this double meaning, Adam Smith has himself fallen into another ambiguity. Things (he says) which have the greatest value in use have often little or no value in exchange; which is true, since that which can be obtained without labor or sacrifice will command no price, however useful or needful it may be. But he proceeds to add, that things which have the greatest value in exchange, as a diamond for example, may have little or no value in use. This is employing the word use, not in the sense in which political economy is concerned with it, but in that other sense in which use is opposed to pleasure. Political economy has nothing to do with the comparative estimation of different uses in the judgment of a philosopher or of a moralist. The use of a thing, in political economy, means its capacity to satisfy a desire, or serve a purpose. Diamonds have this capacity in a high degree, and unless they had it, would not bear any price. Value in use, or as Mr. De Quincey calls it, *teleologic* value, is the extreme limit of value in exchange. The exchange value of a thing may fall short, to any amount, of its value in use; but that it can ever exceed the value in use, implies a contradiction; it supposes that persons will give, to possess a thing, more than the utmost value which they themselves put upon it, as a means of gratifying their inclinations.

The word Value, when used without adjunct, always means, in political economy, value in exchange; or as it has been called by Adam Smith and his successors, exchangeable value, a phrase which no amount of authority that can be quoted for it can make other than bad English. Mr. De Quincey substitutes the term Exchange Value, which is unexceptionable.

Exchange value requires to be distinguished from Price. The words Value and Price were used as synonymous by the early political economists, and are not always discriminated even by Ricardo. But the most accurate modern writers, to avoid the wasteful expenditure of two good scientific terms on a single idea, have employed Price to express the value of a thing in relation to money; the quantity of money for which it will exchange. By the price of a thing, therefore, we shall henceforth understand its value in money; by the value, or exchange value of a thing, its general power of purchasing; the command which its possession gives over purchasable commodities in general.

.   .   .

§ 5. Before commencing the inquiry into the laws of value and price, I have one further observation to make. I must give warning, once for all, that the cases I contemplate are those in which values and prices are determined by competition alone. In so far only as they are thus determined, can they be reduced to any assignable law. The buyers must be supposed as studious to buy cheap, as the sellers to sell dear. The values and prices, therefore, to which our conclusions apply, are mercantile values and prices; such prices as are quoted in price-currents; prices in the wholesale markets, in which buying as well as selling is a matter of business; in which the buyers take pains to know, and generally do know, the lowest price at which an article of a given quality can be obtained; and in which, therefore, the axiom is true, that there cannot be for the same article, of the same quality, two prices in the same market. Our propositions will be true in a much more qualified sense, of retail prices; the prices paid in shops for articles of personal consumption. For such things there often are not merely two, but many prices, in different shops, or even in the same shop; habit and accident having as much to do in the matter as general causes. Purchases for private use, even by people in business, are not always made on business principles: the feelings which come into play in the operation of getting, and in that of spending their income, are often extremely different. Either from indolence, or carelessness, or because people think it fine to pay and ask no questions, three-fourths of those who can afford it give much higher prices than necessary for the things they consume; while the poor often do the same from ignorance and defect of judgment, want of time for searching and making inquiry, and not unfrequently from coercion, open or disguised. For these reasons, retail prices do not follow with all the regularity which might be expected, the action of the causes which determine wholesale prices. The influence of those causes is ultimately felt in the retail markets, and is the real source of such variations in retail prices as are of a general and permanent character. But there is no regular or exact correspondence. Shoes of equally good quality are sold in different shops at prices which differ considerably; and the price of leather may fall without causing the richer class of buyers to pay less for shoes. Nevertheless, shoes do sometimes fall in price; and when they do, the cause is always some such general circumstance as the cheapening of leather: and when leather is cheapened, even if no difference shows itself in shops frequented by rich people, the artisan and the laborer generally get their shoes cheaper, and there is a visible diminution in the contract prices at which shoes are delivered for the supply of a workhouse or of a regiment. In all reasoning about prices, the proviso must be understood, "supposing all parties to take care of their own interest." Inattention to these distinctions has led to improper applications of the abstract principles of political economy, and still oftener to an undue discrediting of those principles, through their being compared with a different sort of facts from those which they contemplate, or which can fairly be expected to accord with them.

Chapter 2: OF DEMAND AND SUPPLY, IN THEIR RELATION TO
           VALUE

§ 1. That a thing may have any value in exchange, two conditions are necessary. It must be of some use; that is (as already explained) it must conduce to some purpose, satisfy some desire. No one will pay a price, or part with anything which serves some of his purposes, to obtain a thing

which serves none of them. But, secondly, the thing must not only have
some utility, there must also be some difficulty in its attainment. "Any
article whatever," says Mr. De Quincey, "to obtain that artificial sort of
value which is meant by exchange value, must begin by offering itself as a
means to some desirable purpose; and secondly, even though possessing
incontestably this preliminary advantage, it will never ascend to an
exchange value in cases where it can be obtained gratuitously and without
effort; of which last terms both are necessary as limitations. For often it
will happen that some desirable object may be obtained gratuitously; stoop,
and you gather it at your feet; but still, because the continued iteration of
this stooping exacts a laborious effort, very soon it is found, that to gather
for yourself virtually is not gratuitous. In the vast forests of the Canadas, at
intervals, wild strawberries may be gratuitously gathered by shiploads: yet
such is the exhaustion of a stooping posture, and of a labor so monotonous,
that everybody is soon glad to resign the service into mercenary hands."

As was pointed out in the last chapter, the utility of a thing in the
estimation of a purchaser, is the extreme limit of its exchange value: higher
the value cannot ascend; peculiar circumstances are required to raise it so
high. This topic is happily illustrated by Mr. De Quincey. "Walk into
almost any possible shop, buy the first article you see: what will determine
its price? In the ninety-nine cases out of a hundred, simply the element D
—difficulty of attainment. The other element U, or intrinsic utility, will
be perfectly inoperative. Let the thing (measured by its uses) be, for your
purposes, worth ten guineas, so that you would rather give ten guineas
than lose it; yet, if the difficulty of producing it be only worth one guinea,
one guinea is the price which it will bear. But still not the less, though U is
inoperative, can U be supposed absent? By no possibility; for, if it had been
absent, assuredly you would not have bought the article even at the lowest
price. U acts upon you, though it does not act upon the price. On the other
hand, in the hundredth case, we will suppose the circumstances reversed;
you are on Lake Superior in a steamboat, making your way to an unsettled
region 800 miles ahead of civilization, and consciously with no chance at
all of purchasing any luxury whatsoever, little luxury or big luxury, for the
space of ten years to come. One fellow-passenger, whom you will part with
before sunset, has a powerful musical snuff-box; knowing by experience the
power of such a toy over your own feelings, the magic with which at times
it lulls your agitations of mind, you are vehemently desirous to purchase it.
In the hour of leaving London you had forgot to do so; here is a final
chance. But the owner, aware of your situation not less than yourself, is
determined to operate by a strain pushed to the very uttermost upon U,
upon the intrinsic worth of the article in your individual estimate for your
individual purposes. He will not hear of D as any controlling power or
mitigating agency in the case; and finally, although at six guineas apiece
in London or Paris you might have loaded a wagon with such boxes,

you pay sixty rather than lose it when the last knell of the clock has sounded, which summons you to buy now or to forfeit forever. Here, as before, only one element is operative: before it was D, now it is U. But after all, D was not absent, though inoperative. The inertness of D allowed U to put forth its total effect. The practical compression of D being withdrawn, U springs up like water in a pump when released from the pressure of air. Yet still that D was present to your thoughts, though the price was otherwise regulated, is evident; both because U and D must coexist in order to found any case of exchange value whatever, and because undeniably you take into very particular consideration this D, the extreme difficulty of attainment (which here is the greatest possible, viz. an impossibility) before you consent to have the price racked up to U. The special D has vanished; but it is replaced in your thoughts by an unlimited D. Undoubtedly you have submitted to U in extremity as the regulating force of the price; but it was under a sense of D's latent presence. Yet D is so far from exerting any positive force, that the retirement of D from all agency whatever on the price—this it is which creates as it were a perfect vacuum, and through that vacuum U rushes up to its highest and ultimate gradation."

This case, in which the value is wholly regulated by the necessities or desires of the purchaser, is the case of strict and absolute monopoly; in which, the article desired being only obtainable from one person, he can exact any equivalent, short of the point at which no purchaser could be found. But it is not a necessary consequence, even of complete monopoly, that the value should be forced up to this ultimate limit: as will be seen when we have considered the law of value in so far as depending on the other element, difficulty of attainment.

§ 2. The difficulty of attainment which determines value, is not always the same kind of difficulty. It sometimes consists in an absolute limitation of the supply. There are things of which it is physically impossible to increase the quantity beyond certain narrow limits. Such are those wines which can be grown only in peculiar circumstances of soil, climate, and exposure. Such also are ancient sculptures; pictures by old masters; rare books or coins, or other articles of antiquarian curiosity. Among such may also be reckoned houses and building-ground, in a town of definite extent (such as Venice, or any fortified town where fortifications are necessary to security); the most desirable sites in any town whatever; houses and parks peculiarly favored by natural beauty, in places where that advantage is uncommon. Potentially, all land whatever is a commodity of this class; and might be practically so, in countries fully occupied and cultivated.

But there is another category (embracing the majority of all things that are bought and sold), in which the obstacle to attainment consists only in the labor and expense requisite to produce the commodity. Without a certain labor and expense it cannot be had: but when any one is willing to incur these, there needs be no limit to the multiplication of the product. If there were laborers enough and machinery enough, cottons, woollens, or linens might be produced by thousands of yards for every single yard now manufactured. There would be a point, no doubt, where further increase would be stopped by the incapacity of the earth to afford more of the material. But there is no need, for any purpose of political economy, to contemplate a time when this ideal limit could become a practical one.

There is a third case, intermediate between the two preceding, and rather more complex, which I shall at present merely indicate, but the importance of which in political economy is extremely great. There are commodities which can be multiplied to an indefinite extent by labor and expenditure, but not by a fixed amount of labor and expenditure. Only a limited quantity can be produced at a given cost; if more is wanted, it must be produced at a greater cost. To this class, as has been often repeated, agricultural produce belongs; and generally all the rude produce of the earth; and this peculiarity is a source of very important consequences; one of which is the necessity of a limit to population; and another, the payment of rent.

§ 3. These being the three classes, in one or other of which all things that are bought and sold must take their place, we shall consider them in their order. And first, of things absolutely limited in quantity, such as ancient sculptures or pictures.

Of such things it is commonly said, that their value depends upon their scarcity: but the expression is not sufficiently definite to serve our purpose. Others say, with somewhat greater precision, that the value depends on the demand and the supply. But even this statement requires much explanation, to make it a clear exponent of the relation between the value of a thing, and the causes of which that value is an effect.

The supply of a commodity is an intelligible expression: it means the quantity offered for sale; the quantity that is to be had, at a given time and place, by those who wish to purchase it. But what is meant by the demand? Not the mere desire for the commodity. A beggar may desire a diamond; but his desire, however great, will have no influence on the price. Writers have therefore given a more limited sense to demand, and have defined it, the wish to possess, combined with the power of purchasing. To distinguish demand in this technical sense, from the demand which is synonymous with desire, they call the former *effectual* demand.[1] After this explanation, it is usually supposed that there remains no further difficulty, and that the value depends upon the ratio between the effectual demand, as thus defined, and the supply.

These phrases, however, fail to satisfy anyone who requires clear ideas,

[1] Adam Smith, who introduced the expression "effectual demand," employed it to denote the demand of those who are willing and able to give for the commodity what he call its natural price, that is, the price which will enable it to be permanently produced and brought to market.—See his chapter on "Natural and Market Price" in *Wealth of Nations*, Book I, Chap. 7.

and a perfectly precise expression of them. Some confusion must always attach to a phrase so inappropriate as that of a ratio between two things not of the same denomination. What ratio can there be between a quantity and a desire, or even a desire combined with a power? A ratio between demand and supply is only intelligible if by demand we mean the quantity demanded, and if the ratio intended is that between the quantity demanded and the quantity supplied. But again, the quantity demanded is not a fixed quantity, even at the same time and place; it varies according to the value: if the thing is cheap, there is usually a demand for more of it than when it is dear. The demand, therefore, partly depends on the value. But it was before laid down that the value depends on the demand. From this contradiction how shall we extricate ourselves? How solve the paradox, of two things, each depending upon the other?

Though the solution of these difficulties is obvious enough, the difficulties themselves are not fanciful; and I bring them forward thus prominently, because I am certain that they obscurely haunt every inquirer into the subject who has not openly faced and distinctly realized them. Undoubtedly the true solution must have been frequently given, though I cannot call to mind anyone who had given it before myself, except the eminently clear thinker and skilful expositor, J. B. Say. I should have imagined, however, that it must be familiar to all political economists, if the writings of several did not give evidence of some want of clearness on the point, and if the instance of Mr. De Quincey did not prove that the complete non-recognition and implied denial of it are compatible with great intellectual ingenuity, and close intimacy with the subject matter.

§ 4. Meaning, by the word demand, the quantity demanded, and remembering that this is not a fixed quantity, but in general varies according to the value, let us suppose that the demand at some particular time exceeds the supply, that is, there are persons ready to buy, at the market value, a greater quantity than is offered for sale. Competition takes place on the side of the buyers, and the value rises: but how much? In the ratio (some may suppose) of the deficiency: if the demand exceeds the supply by one-third, the value rises one-third. By no means: for when the value has risen one-third, the demand may still exceed the supply; there may, even at that higher value, be a greater quantity wanted than is to be had; and the competition of buyers may still continue. If the article is a necessary of life, which, rather than resign, people are willing to pay for at any price, a deficiency of one-third may raise the price to double, triple, or quadruple.[2]

---

2 "The price of corn in this country has risen from 100 to 200 per cent. and upwards, when the utmost computed deficiency of the crops has not been more than between one-sixth and one-third below an average, and when that deficiency has been relieved by foreign supplies. If there should be a deficiency of the crops amounting to one-third, without any surplus from a former year, and without any chance of relief by importation, the price might rise five, six, or even tenfold." Tooke's *History of Prices*, Vol. I, pp. 13–15.

Or, on the contrary, the competition may cease before the value has risen in even the proportion of the deficiency. A rise, short of one-third, may place the article beyond the means or beyond the inclinations, of purchasers to the full amount. At what point, then, will the rise be arrested? At the point, whatever it be, which equalizes the demand and the supply: at the price which cuts off the extra third from the demand or brings forward additional sellers sufficient to supply it. When, in either of these ways, or by a combination of both, the demand becomes equal and no more than equal to the supply, the rise of value will stop.

The converse case is equally simple. Instead of a demand beyond the supply, let us suppose a supply exceeding the demand. The competition will now be on the side of the sellers: the extra quantity can only find a market by calling forth an additional demand equal to itself. This is accomplished by means of cheapness; the value falls, and brings the article within the reach of more numerous customers, or induces those who were already consumers to make increased purchases. The fall of value required to re-establish equality, is different in different cases. The kinds of things in which it is commonly greatest are at the two extremities of the scale; absolute necessaries, or those peculiar luxuries, the taste for which is confined to a small class. In the case of food, as those who have already enough do not require more on account of its cheapness, but rather expend in other things what they save in food, the increased consumption occasioned by cheapness, carries off, as experience shows, only a small part of the extra supply caused by an abundant harvest; and the fall is practically arrested only when the farmers withdraw their corn, and hold it back in hopes of a higher price; or by the operations of speculators who buy corn when it is cheap, and store it up to be brought out when more urgently wanted. Whether the demand and supply are equalized by an increased demand, the result of cheapness, or by withdrawing a part of the supply, equalized they are in either case.

Thus we see that the idea of a ratio, as between demand and supply, is out of place, and has no concern in the matter: the proper mathematical analogy is that of an equation. Demand and supply, the quantity demanded and the quantity supplied, will be made equal. If unequal at any moment, competition equalizes them, and the manner in which this is done is by an adjustment of the value. If the demand increases, the value rises; if the demand diminishes, the value falls: again, if the supply falls off, the value rises; and falls, if the supply is increased. The rise or the fall continues until the demand and supply are again equal to one another: and the value which a commodity will bring in any market, is no other than the value which, in that market, gives a demand just sufficient to carry off the existing or expected supply.

This, then, is the Law of Value, with respect to all commodities not susceptible of being multiplied at pleasure. Such commodities, no doubt, are exceptions. There is another law for that much larger class of things, which admit of indefinite multiplication. But it is not the less necessary to conceive distinctly and grasp firmly the theory of this exceptional case. In the first place, it will be found to be of great assistance in rendering the more common case intelligible. And in the next place, the principle of the exception stretches wider, and embraces more cases, than might at first be supposed.

§ 5. There are but few commodities which are naturally and necessarily limited in supply. But any commodity whatever may be artificially so. Any commodity may be the subject of a monopoly: like tea, in this country, up to 1834; tobacco in France, opium in British India, at present. The price of a monopolized commodity is commonly supposed to be arbitrary; depending on the will of the monopolist, and limited only (as in Mr. De Quincey's case of the musical box in the wilds of America) by the buyer's extreme estimate of its worth to himself. This is in one sense true, but forms no exception, nevertheless, to the dependence of the value on supply and demand. The monopolist can fix the value as high as he pleases, short of what the consumer either could not or would not pay; but he can only do so by limiting the supply. The Dutch East India Company obtained a monopoly price for the produce of the Spice Islands, but to do so they were obliged, in good seasons, to destroy a portion of the crop. Had they persisted in selling all that they produced, they must have forced a market by reducing the price, so low, perhaps, that they would have received for the larger quantity a less total return than for the smaller: at least they showed that such was their opinion by destroying the surplus. Even on Lake Superior, Mr. De Quincey's huckster could not have sold his box for sixty guineas, if he had possessed two musical boxes and desired to sell them both. Supposing the cost price of each to be six guineas, he would have taken seventy for the two in preference to sixty for one; that is, although his monopoly was the closest possible, he would have sold the boxes at thirty-five guineas each, notwithstanding that sixty was not beyond the buyer's estimate of the article for his purposes. Monopoly value, therefore, does not depend on any peculiar principle, but is a mere variety of the ordinary case of demand and supply.

Again, though there are few commodities which are at all times and for-ever unsusceptible of increase of supply, any commodity whatever may be temporarily so; and with some commodities this is habitually the case. Agricultural produce, for example, cannot be increased in quantity before the next harvest; the quantity of corn already existing in the world, is all that can be had for sometimes a year to come. During that interval, corn is practically assimilated to things of which the quantity cannot be increased. In the case of most commodities, it requires a certain time to increase their quantity; and if the demand increases, then until a corresponding supply can be brought forward, that is, until the supply can accommodate itself to the demand, the value will so rise as to accommodate the demand to the supply.

There is another case, the exact converse of this. There are some articles of which the supply may be indefinitely increased, but cannot be rapidly diminished. There are things so durable that the quantity in existence is at all times very great in comparison with the annual produce. Gold, and the more durable metals, are things of this sort; and also houses. The supply of such things might be at once diminished by destroying them; but to do this could only be the interest of the possessor if he had a monopoly of the article, and could repay himself for the destruction of a part by the increased value of the remainder. The value, therefore, of such things may continue for a long time so low, either from excess of supply or falling off in the demand, as to put a complete stop to further production: the diminution of supply by wearing out being so slow a process, that a long time is requisite, even under a total suspension of production, to restore the original value. During that interval the value will be regulated solely by supply and demand, and will rise very gradually as the existing stock wears out, until there is again a remunerating value, and production resumes its course.

Finally, there are commodities of which, though capable of being increased or diminished to a great, and even an unlimited extent, the value never depends upon anything but demand and supply. This is the case, in particular, with the commodity Labor: of the value of which we have treated copiously in the preceding Book: and there are many cases besides, in which we shall find it necessary to call in this principle to solve difficult questions of exchange value. This will be particularly exemplified when we treat of International Values; that is, of the terms of interchange between things produced in different countries, or, to speak more generally, in distant places. But into these questions we cannot enter until we shall have examined the case of commodities which can be increased in quantity indefinitely and at pleasure; and shall have determined by what law other than that of Demand and Supply the permanent or average values of such commodities are regulated. This we shall do in the next chapter.

Chapter 3: OF COST OF PRODUCTION, IN ITS RELATION TO VALUE

§ 1. When the production of a commodity is the effect of labor and expenditure, whether the commodity is susceptible of unlimited multiplication or not, there is a minimum value which is the essential condition of its being permanently produced. The value at any particular time is the result of supply and demand; and is always that which is necessary to create a market for the existing supply. But unless that value is sufficient to repay the Cost of Production, and to afford, besides, the ordinary expectation of profit, the commodity will not continue to be produced. Capitalists will not go on permanently producing at a loss. They will not even go on producing at a profit less than they can live upon. Persons whose capital is already embarked, and cannot be easily extricated, will persevere for a considerable time without profit, and have been known to persevere even at a loss, in hope of better times. But they will not do so indefinitely, or when there is nothing to indicate that times are likely to improve. No new capital will be invested in an employment, unless there be an expectation not only of some profit, but of a profit as great (regard being had to the degree of eligibility of the employment in other respects), as can be hoped for in any other occupation at that time and place. When such profit is evidently not to be had, if people do not actually withdraw their capital, they at least abstain from replacing it when consumed. The cost of production, together with the ordinary profit, may, therefore be called the *necessary* price or value, of all things made by labor and capital. Nobody willingly produces in the prospect of loss. Whoever does so, does it under a miscalculation, which he corrects as fast as he is able.

When a commodity is not only made by labor and capital, but can be made by them in indefinite quantity, this Necessary Value, the minimum with which the producers will be content, is also, if competition is free and active, the maximum which they can expect. If the value of a commodity is such that it repays the cost of production not only with the customary, but with a higher rate of profit, capital rushes to share in this extra gain, and by increasing the supply of the article, reduces its value. This is not a mere supposition or surmise, but a fact familiar to those conversant with commercial operations. Whenever a new line of business presents itself, offering a hope of unusual profits, and whenever any established trade or manufacture is believed to be yielding a greater profit than customary, there is sure to be in a short time so large a production or importation of the commodity, as not only destroys the extra profit, but generally goes beyond the mark, and sinks the value as much too low as it had before been raised too high; until the over-supply is corrected by a total or partial suspension of further production. As already intimated, these variations in the quantity produced do not presuppose or require that any person should change his employment. Those whose business is thriving, increase their produce by availing themselves more largely of their credit, while those who are not making the ordinary profit, restrict their operations, and (in manufacturing phrase) work short time. In this mode is surely and speedily effected the equalization, not of profits perhaps, but of the expectations of profit, in different occupations.

As a general rule, then, things tend to exchange for one another at such values as will enable each producer to be repaid the cost of production with

the ordinary profit; in other words, such as will give to all producers the
same rate of profit on their outlay. But in order that the profit may be equal
where the outlay, that is, the cost of production, is equal, things must on
the average exchange for one another in the ratio of their cost of production; things of which the cost of production is the same, must be of the
same value. For only thus will an equal outlay yield an equal return. If a
farmer with a capital equal to 1,000 quarters of corn, can produce 1,200
quarters, yielding him a profit of twenty per cent.; whatever else can be produced in the same time by a capital of 1,000 quarters, must be worth, that
is, must exchange for, 1,200 quarters, otherwise the producer would gain
either more or less than twenty per cent.

Adam Smith and Ricardo have called that value of a thing which is proportional to its cost of production, its Natural Value (or its Natural Price).
They meant by this, the point about which the value oscillates, and to
which it always tends to return; the centre value, towards which, as Adam
Smith expresses it, the market value of a thing is constantly gravitating;
and any deviation from which is but a temporary irregularity, which, the
moment it exists, sets forces in motion tending to correct it. On an average
of years sufficient to enable the oscillations on one side of the central line
to be compensated by those on the other, the market value agrees with the
natural value; but it very seldom coincides exactly with it at any particular
time. The sea everywhere tends to a level; but it never is at an exact level;
its surface is always ruffled by waves, and often agitated by storms. It is
enough that no point, at least in the open sea, is permanently higher than
another. Each place is alternately elevated and depressed; but the ocean
preserves its level.

. . .

It is, therefore, strictly correct to say, that the value of things which can
be increased in quantity at pleasure, does not depend (except accidentally,
and during the time necessary for production to adjust itself), upon demand and supply; on the contrary, demand and supply depend upon it.
There is a demand for a certain quantity of the commodity at its natural
or cost value, and to that the supply in the long run endeavors to conform.
When at any time it fails of so conforming, it is either from miscalculation,
or from a change in some of the elements of the problem: either in the
natural value, that is, in the cost of production; or in the demand, from an
alteration in public taste or in the number or wealth of the consumers.
These causes of disturbance are very liable to occur, and when any one of
them does occur, the market value of the article ceases to agree with the
natural value. The real law of demand and supply, the equation between
them, holds good in all cases: if a value different from the natural value be
necessary to make the demand equal to the supply, the market value will

deviate from the natural value; but only for a time; for the permanent tendency of supply is to conform itself to the demand which is found by experience to exist for the commodity when selling at its natural value. If the supply is either more or less than this, it is so accidentally, and affords either more or less than the ordinary rate of profit; which, under free and active competition, cannot long continue to be the case.

To recapitulate: demand and supply govern the value of all things which cannot be indefinitely increased; except that even for them, when produced by industry, there is a minimum value, determined by the cost of production. But in all things which admit of indefinite multiplication, demand and supply only determine the perturbations of value, during a period which cannot exceed the length of time necessary for altering the supply. While thus ruling the oscillations of value, they themselves obey a superior force, which makes value gravitate towards Cost of Production, and which would settle it and keep it there, if fresh disturbing influences were not continually arising to make it again deviate. To pursue the same strain of metaphor, demand and supply always rush to an equilibrium, but the condition of stable equilibrium is when things exchange for each other according to their cost of production, or, in the expression we have used, when things are at their Natural Value.

Chapter 4: ULTIMATE ANALYSIS OF COST OF PRODUCTION

. . .

§ 2. It will have been observed that Ricardo expresses himself as if the *quantity* of labor which it costs to produce a commodity and bring it to market, were the only thing on which its value depended. But since the cost of production to the capitalist is not labor but wages, and since wages may be either greater or less, the quantity of labor being the same; it would seem that the value of the product cannot be determined solely by the quantity of labor, but by the quantity together with the remuneration; and that values must partly depend on wages.

In order to decide this point, it must be considered, that value is a relative term; that the value of a commodity is not a name for an inherent and substantive quality of the thing itself, but means the quantity of other things which can be obtained in exchange for it. The value of one thing, must always be understood relatively to some other thing, or to things in general. Now the relation of one thing to another cannot be altered by any cause which affects them both alike. A rise or fall of general wages is a fact which affects all commodities in the same manner, and therefore affords no reason why they should exchange for each other in one rather than in another proportion. To suppose that high wages make high values, is to suppose that there can be such a thing as general high values. But this is a contradiction in terms: the high value of some things is synonymous with the low value of others. The mistake arises from not attending to values, but only to prices. Though there is no such thing as a general rise of values, there is such a thing as a general rise of prices. As soon as we form distinctly the idea of values, we see that high or low wages can have nothing to do with them: but that high wages make high prices, is a popular and wide-spread opinion. The whole amount of error involved in this proposition can only be seen thoroughly when we come to the theory of money; at present we need only say that if it be true, there can be no such thing as a real rise of wages; for if wages could not rise without a proportional rise of the price of everything, they could not, for any substantial purpose, rise at all. This surely is a sufficient *reductio ad absurdum*, and shows the amazing folly of the propositions which may and do become, and long remain, accredited doctrines of popular political economy. It must be remembered, too, that general high prices, even supposing them to exist, can be of no use to a producer or dealer, considered as such; for if they increase his money returns, they increase in the same degree all his expenses. There is no mode in which capitalists can compensate themselves for a high cost of labor, through any action on values or prices. It cannot be prevented from taking its effect in low profits. If the laborers really get more, that is, get the produce of more labor, a smaller percentage must remain for profit. From this Law of Distribution, resting as it does on a law of arithmetic, there is no escape. The mechanism of Exchange and Price may hide it from us, but is quite powerless to alter it.

§ 3. Although, however, general wages, whether high or low, do not affect values, yet if wages are higher in one employment than another, or if they rise or fall permanently in one employment without doing so in others, these inequalities do really operate upon values. The causes which make wages vary from one employment to another, have been considered in a former chapter. When the wages of an employment permanently exceed the average rate, the value of the thing produced will, in the same degree, exceed the standard determined by mere quantity of labor. Things, for example, which are made by skilled labor, exchange for the produce of a much greater quantity of unskilled labor; for no reason but because the labor is more highly paid. If, through the extension of education, the laborers competent to skilled employments were so increased in number as to diminish the difference between their wages and those of common labor, all things produced by labor of the superior kind would fall in value, compared with things produced by common labor, and these might be said therefore to rise in value. We have before remarked that the difficulty of passing from one class of employments to a class greatly superior, has hitherto caused the wages of all those classes of laborers who are separated from one another by any very marked barrier, to depend more than might be supposed upon the increase of the population of each class, considered separately; and that the inequalities in the remuneration of labor are much greater than could exist if the competition of the laboring people generally, could be brought practically to bear on each particular employment. It follows from this, that wages in different employments do not rise or fall simultaneously, but are, for short and sometimes even for long periods, nearly independent of one another. All such disparities evidently alter the relative cost of production of different commodities, and will therefore be completely represented in their natural or average value.

It thus appears that the maxim laid down by some of the best political economists, that wages do not enter into value, is expressed with greater latitude than the truth warrants, or than accords with their own meaning. Wages do enter into value. The relative wages of the labor necessary for producing different commodities, affect their value just as much as the relative quantities of labor. It is true, the absolute wages paid have no effect upon values; but neither has the absolute quantity of labor. If that were to vary simultaneously and equally in all commodities, values would not be affected. If, for instance, the general efficiency of all labor were increased, so that all things without exception could be produced in the same quantity as before with a smaller amount of labor, no trace of this general diminution of cost of production would show itself in the values of commodities. Any change which might take place in them would only represent the unequal degrees in which the improvement affected different things; and would consist in cheapening those in which the saving of labor had been the greatest, while those in which there had been some, but a less saving of labor, would actually rise in value. In strictness, therefore, wages of labor have as much to do with value as quantity of labor: and neither Ricardo nor any one else has denied the fact. In considering, however, the causes of variations in value, quantity of labor is the thing of chief importance; for when that varies, it is generally in one or a few commodities at a time, but the variations of wages (except passing fluctuations) are usually general, and have no considerable effect on value.

§ 4. Thus far of labor, or wages, as an element in cost of production. But in our analysis, in the First Book, of the requisites of production, we found that there is another necessary element in it besides labor. There is also capital; and this being the result of abstinence, the produce, or its value, must be sufficient to remunerate, not only all the labor required, but the abstinence of all the persons by whom the remuneration of the different classes of laborers was advanced. The return for abstinence is Profit. And profit, we have also seen, is not exclusively the surplus remaining to the capitalist after he has been compensated for his outlay, but forms, in most cases, no unimportant part of the outlay itself. The flax-spinner, part of whose expenses consists of the purchase of flax and of machinery, has had to pay, in their price, not only the wages of the labor by which the flax was grown and the machinery made, but the profits of the grower, the flax-dresser, the miner, the iron-founder, and the machine-maker. All these profits, together with those of the spinner himself, were again advanced by the weaver, in the price of his material, linen yarn: and along with them the profits of a fresh set of machine-makers, and of the miners and iron-workers who supplied them with their metallic material. All these advances form part of the cost of production of linen. Profits, therefore, as well as wages, enter into the cost of production which determines the value of the produce.

Value, however, being purely relative, cannot depend upon absolute profits, no more than upon absolute wages, but upon relative profits only. High general profits cannot, any more than high general wages, be a cause of high values, because high general values are an absurdity and a contradiction. In so far as profits enter into the cost of production of all things, they cannot affect the value of any. It is only by entering in a greater degree into the cost of production of some things than of others, that they can have any influence on value.

For example, we have seen that there are causes which necessitate a permanently higher rate of profit in certain employments than in others. There must be a compensation for superior risk, trouble, and disagreeableness. This can only be obtained by selling the commodity at a value above that which is due to the quantity of labor necessary for its production. If gunpowder exchanged for other things in no higher ratio than that of the labor required from first to last for producing it, no one would set up a powder-mill. Butchers are certainly a more prosperous class than bakers, and do not seem to be exposed to greater risks, since it is not remarked that they are oftener bankrupts. They seem, therefore, to obtain higher profits, which can only arise from the more limited competition caused by the unpleasantness, and to a certain degree, the unpopularity of their trade. But this higher profit implies that they sell their commodity at a higher value than that due to their labor and outlay. All inequalities of profit which are necessary and permanent, are represented in the relative values of the commodities.

§ 5. Profits, however, may enter more largely into the conditions of production of one commodity than of another, even though there be no difference in the rate of profit between the two employments. The one commodity may be called upon to yield profit during a longer period of time than the other. The example by which this case is usually illustrated is that of wine. Suppose a quantity of wine, and a quantity of cloth, made by equal amounts of labor, and that labor paid at the same rate. The cloth does not improve by keeping; the wine does. Suppose that, to attain the desired quality, the wine requires to be kept five years. The producer or dealer will not keep it, unless at the end of five years he can sell it for as much more than the cloth, as amounts to five years' profit, accumulated at compound interest. The wine and the cloth were made by the same original outlay. Here then is a case in which the natural values, relatively to one another, of two commodities, do not conform to their cost of production alone, but to their cost of production plus something else. Unless, indeed, for the sake of generality in the expression, we include the profit which the wine-merchant foregoes during the five years, in the cost of production of the wine: looking upon it as a kind of additional outlay, over and above his other advances, for which outlay he must be indemnified at last. . . .

. . .

From the unequal proportion in which, in different employments, profits enter into the advances of the capitalist, and therefore into the returns required by him, two consequences follow in regard to value. One is, that commodities do not exchange in the ratio simply of the quantities of labor required to produce them; not even if we allow for the unequal rates at which different kinds of labor are permanently remunerated. We have already illustrated this by the example of wine: we shall now further exemplify it by the case of commodities made by machinery. Suppose, as before, an article A, made by a thousand pounds' worth of immediate labor. But instead of B, made by £500 worth of immediate labor and a machine worth £500, let us suppose C, made by £500 worth of immediate labor with the aid of a machine which has been produced by another £500 worth of immediate labor: the machine requiring a year for making, and worn out by a year's use; profits being as before twenty per cent. A and C are made by equal quantities of labor, paid at the same rate: A costs £1,000 worth of direct labor; C, only £500 worth, which however is made up to £1,000 by the labor expended in the construction of the machine. If labor, or its remuneration, were the sole ingredient of cost of production, these two things would exchange for one another. But will they do so? Certainly not. The machine having been made in a year by an outlay of £500, and profits being twenty per cent., the natural price of the machine is £600: making an additional £100 which must be advanced, over and above his other expenses, by the manufacturer of C, and repaid to him with a profit of twenty per cent. While, therefore, the commodity A is sold for £1,200, C cannot be permanently sold for less than £1,320.

A second consequence is, that every rise or fall of general profits will have an effect on values. Not indeed by raising or lowering them generally (which, as we have so often said, is a contradiction and an impossibility): but by altering the proportion in which the values of things are affected by the unequal lengths of time for which profit is due. When two things, though made by equal labor, are of unequal value because the one is called upon to yield profit for a greater number of years or months than the other; this difference of value will be greater when profits are greater, and less when they are less. The wine which has to yield five years' profit more than the cloth, will surpass it in value much more if profits are forty per cent. than if they are only twenty. The commodities A and C, which, though made by equal quantities of labor, were sold for £1,200 and £1,320, a difference of ten per cent., would, if profits had been only half as much, have been sold for £1,100 and £1,155, a difference of only five per cent.

It follows from this, that even a general rise of wages, when it involves a real increase in the cost of labor, does in some degree influence values. It does not affect them in the manner vulgarly supposed, by raising them universally. But an increase in the cost of labor, lowers profits; and therefore lowers in natural value the things into which profits enter in a greater proportion than the average, and raises those into which they enter in a less proportion than the average. All commodities in the production of which machinery bears a large part, especially if the machinery is very durable, are lowered in their relative value when profits fall; or, what is equivalent, other things are raised in value relatively to them. This truth is sometimes expressed in a phraseology more plausible than sound, by saying that a rise of wages raises the value of things made by labor, in comparison with those made by machinery. But things made by machinery, just as much as any other things, are made by labor, namely the labor which made the machinery itself: the only difference being that profits enter somewhat more largely into the production of things for which machinery is used, though the principal item of the outlay is still labor. It is better, therefore, to associate the effect with fall of profits than with rise of wages; especially as this last expression is extremely ambiguous, suggesting the idea of an increase of the laborer's real remuneration, rather than of what is alone to the purpose here, namely the cost of labor to its employer.

. . .

A natural agent being a possession in perpetuity, and being only serviceable by the products resulting from its continued employment, the ordinary mode of deriving benefit from its ownership is by an annual equivalent, paid by the person who uses it, from the proceeds of its use. This equivalent always might be, and generally is, termed rent. The question therefore, respecting the influence which the appropriation of natural agents produces on values, is often stated in this form: Does Rent enter into Cost of Production? and the answer of the best political economists is in the negative. The temptation is strong to the adoption of these sweeping expressions, even by those who are aware of the restrictions with which they must be taken; for there is no denying that they stamp a general principle more firmly on the mind, than if it were hedged round in theory with all its practical limitations. But they also puzzle and mislead, and create· an impression unfavorable to political economy, as if it disregarded the evidence of facts. No one can deny that rent sometimes enters into cost of production. If I buy or rent a piece of ground, and build a cloth manufactory on it, the ground-rent forms legitimately a part of my expenses of production, which must be repaid by the product. And since all factories are built on ground, and most of them in places where ground is peculiarly valuable, the rent paid for it must, on the average, be compensated in the values of all things made in factories. In what sense it is true that rent does not enter into the cost of production or affect the value of agricultural produce, will be shown in the succeeding chapter.

Chapter 5: OF RENT, IN ITS RELATION TO VALUE

. . .

§ 2. If the portion of produce raised in the most unfavorable circumstances, obtains a value proportioned to its cost of production; all the portions raised in more favorable circumstances, selling as they must do at the same value, obtain a value more than proportioned to their cost of production. Their value is not, correctly speaking, a scarcity value, for it is determined by the circumstances of the production of the commodity, and not by the degree of dearness necessary for keeping down the demand to the level of a limited supply. The owners, however, of those portions of the produce enjoy a privilege; they obtain a value which yields them more than the ordinary profit. If this advantage depends upon any special exemption, such as being free from a tax, or upon any personal advantages, physical or mental, or any peculiar process only known to themselves, or upon the possession of a greater capital than other people, or upon various other things which might be enumerated, they retain it to themselves as an extra gain, over and above the general profits of capital, of the nature, in some sort, of a monopoly profit. But when, as in the case which we are more particularly considering, the advantage depends on the possession of a natural agent of peculiar quality, as, for instance, of more fertile land than that which determines the general value of the commodity; and when this natural agent is not owned by themselves; the person who does own it, is able to exact from them, in the form of rent, the whole extra gain derived from its use. We are thus brought by another road to the Law of Rent, investigated in the concluding chapter of the Second Book. Rent, we again see, is the difference between the unequal returns to different parts of the capital employed on the soil. Whatever surplus any portion of agricultural capital produces, beyond what is produced by the same amount of capital on the worst soil, or under the most expensive mode of cultivation, which the existing demands of society compel a recourse to; that surplus will naturally be paid as rent from that capital, to the owner of the land on which it is employed.

It was long thought by political economists, among the rest even by Adam Smith, that the produce of land is always at a monopoly value, because (they said) in addition to the ordinary rate of profit, it always yields something further for rent. This we now see to be erroneous. A thing cannot be at a monopoly value, when its supply can be increased to an indefinite extent if we are only willing to incur the cost. If no more corn than the existing quantity is grown, it is because the value has not risen high enough to remunerate any one for growing it. Any land (not reserved for other uses, or for pleasure) which at the existing price, and by the existing processes, will yield the ordinary profit, is tolerably certain, unless some artificial hindrance intervenes, to be cultivated, although nothing may be left for rent. As long as there is any land fit for cultivation, which at the existing price cannot be profitably cultivated at all, there must be some land a little better, which will yield the ordinary profit, but allow nothing for rent: and that land, if within the boundary of a farm, will be cultivated by the farmer; if not so, probably by the proprietor, or by some other person on sufferance. Some such land at least, under cultivation, there can scarcely fail to be.

Rent, therefore, forms no part of the cost of production which determines the value of agricultural produce. Circumstances no doubt may be conceived in which it might do so, and very largely too. We can imagine a country so fully peopled, and with all its cultivable soil so completely occupied, that to produce any additional quantity would require more labor than the produce would feed: and if we suppose this to be the condition of the whole world, or of a country debarred from foreign supply, then, if population continued increasing, both the land and its produce would really rise to a monopoly or scarcity price. But this state of things never can have really existed anywhere, unless possibly in some small island cut off from the rest of the world; nor is there any danger whatever that it should exist. It certainly exists in no known region at present. Monopoly, we have seen, can take effect on value, only through limitation of supply. In all countries of any extent there is more cultivable land than is yet cultivated: and while there is any such surplus, it is the same thing, so far as that quality of land is concerned, as if there were an indefinite quantity. What is practically limited in supply is only the better qualities; and even for those, so much rent cannot be demanded as would bring in the competition of the lands not yet in cultivation; the rent of a piece of land must be somewhat less than the whole excess of its productiveness over that of the best land which it is not yet profitable to cultivate; that is, it must be about equal to the excess above the worst land which it is profitable to cultivate. The land or the capital most unfavorably circumstanced among those actually employed, pays no rent; and that land or capital determines the cost of production which regulates the value of the whole produce. Thus rent is, as we have already seen, no cause of value, but the price of the privilege which the inequality of the returns to different portions of agricultural produce confers on all except the least favored portion.

Rent, in short, merely equalizes the profits of different farming capitals, by enabling the landlord to appropriate all extra gains occasioned by superiority of natural advantages. If all landlords were unanimously to forego their rent, they would but transfer it to the farmers, without benefiting the consumer; for the existing price of corn would still be an indispensable condition of the production of part of the existing supply, and if a part obtained that price the whole would obtain it. Rent, therefore, unless artificially increased by restrictive laws, is no burden on the consumer; it does not raise the price of corn, and is not otherwise a detriment to the public, than inasmuch as if the state had retained it, or imposed an equivalent in the shape of a land-tax, it would then have been a fund applicable to general instead of private advantage.

§ 3. Agricultural productions are not the only commodities which have several different costs of production at once, and which, in consequence of that difference, and in proportion to it, afford a rent. Mines are also an instance. Almost all kinds of raw material extracted from the interior of the earth—metals, coals, precious stones, etc., are obtained from mines differing considerably in fertility, that is, yielding very different quantities of the product to the same quantity of labor and capital. This being the case, it is an obvious question, why are not the most fertile mines so worked as to supply the whole market? No such question can arise as to land; it being self-evident, that the most fertile lands could not possibly be made to supply the whole demand of a fully-peopled country; and even of what they do yield, a part is extorted from them by a labor and outlay as great as that required to grow the same amount on worse land. But it is not so with mines; at least, not universally. There are, perhaps, cases in which it is impossible to extract from a particular vein, in a given time, more than a certain quantity of ore, because there is only a limited surface of the vein exposed, on which more than a certain number of laborers cannot be simultaneously employed. But this is not true of all mines. In collieries, for example, some other cause of limitation must be sought for. In some instances the owners limit the quantity raised, in order not too rapidly to exhaust the mine: in others there are said to be combinations of owners, to keep up a monopoly price by limiting the production. Whatever be the causes, it is a fact that mines of different degrees of richness are in operation, and since the value of the produce must be proportional to the cost of production at the worst time (fertility and situation taken together), it is more than proportional to that of the best. All mines superior in produce to the worst actually worked, will yield, therefore, a rent equal to the excess. They may yield more; and the worst mine may itself yield a rent. Mines being comparatively few, their qualities do not graduate gently into one another, as the qualities of land do; and the demand may be such as to keep the value of the product considerably above the cost of production at the worst mine now worked, without being sufficient to bring into operation a still worse. During the interval, the produce is really at a scarcity value.

. . .

§ 4. Cases of extra profit analogous to rent, are more frequent in the transactions of industry than is sometimes supposed. Take the case, for example, of a patent, or exclusive privilege for the use of a process by which cost of production is lessened. If the value of the product continues to be regulated by what it costs to those who are obliged to persist in the old process, the patentee will make an extra profit equal to the advantage which his process possesses over theirs. This extra profit is essentially similar to rent, and sometimes even assumes the form of it; the patentee allowing to other producers the use of his privilege, in consideration of an annual payment. So long as he, and those whom he associates in the privilege, do not produce enough to supply the whole market, so long the original cost of production, being the necessary condition of producing a part, will regulate the value of the whole; and the patentee will be enabled to keep up his rent to a full equivalent for the advantage which his process gives him. In the commencement indeed he will probably forego a part of this advantage for the sake of underselling others: the increased supply which he brings forward will lower the value, and make the trade a bad one for those who do not share in the privilege: many of whom therefore will gradually retire, or restrict their operations, or enter into arrangements with the patentee. As his supply increases theirs will diminish, the value meanwhile continuing slightly depressed. But if he stops short in his operations before the market is wholly supplied by the new process, things will again adjust themselves to what was the natural value before the invention was made, and the benefit of the improvement will accrue solely to the patentee.

The extra gains which any producer or dealer obtains through superior talents for business, or superior business arrangements, are very much of a similar kind. If all his competitors had the same advantages, and used them, the benefit would be transferred to their customers, through the diminished value of the article: he only retains it for himself because he is able to bring his commodity to market at a lower cost, while its value is determined by a higher. All advantages, in fact, which one competitor has over another, whether natural or acquired, whether personal or the result of social arrangements, bring the commodity, so far, into the Third Class, and assimilate the possessor of the advantage to a receiver of rent. Wages and profits represent the universal elements in production, while rent may be taken to represent the differential and peculiar: any difference in favor of certain producers, or in favor of production in certain circumstances, being the source of a gain, which, though not called rent unless paid periodically by one person to another, is governed by laws entirely the same with it. The price paid for a differential advantage in producing a commodity, cannot enter into the general cost of production of the commodity.

A commodity may, no doubt, in some contingencies, yield a rent even under the most disadvantageous circumstances of its production; but only when it is, for the first time, in the condition of those commodities which are absolutely limited in supply, and is therefore selling at a scarcity value; which never is, nor has been, nor can be, a permanent condition of any of the great rent-yielding commodities: unless through their approaching exhaustion, if they are mineral products (coal, for example), or through an increase of population, continuing after a further increase of production becomes impossible; a contingency which the almost inevitable progress of human culture and improvement, in the long interval which has first to elapse, forbids us to consider as probable.

KARL MARX

(1 8 1 8 – 1 8 8 3)

At first glance Karl Marx may be a peculiar choice to include with the other economists who have gone before and those who are to follow. After all, Marx was not a native-born Englishman, but came to England following his expulsion first from the land of his birth, Germany, and later from France, for his radical writings. Furthermore, his view of capitalism is a far cry from that of the writers whom we have previously encountered. While the labor theory of value as set forth by Smith and Ricardo may have set the stage for Marx's concepts of value, surplus value, and exploitation, had either of the two gentlemen ever dreamed that such would be the case, the dream would have turned into a hideous nightmare.

There is, however, ample justification for Marx's inclusion in this volume. Following his expulsion from France, he spent the rest of his adult life, with the exception of a few brief visits abroad, in his adopted country. There, as he put it, the British Museum supplied him with the "bricks and mortar" with which to complete his study of the workings of capitalism. While Marx's views of the injustices evoked by capitalism and its eventual fate differed markedly from the Classical writers, even including someone as interested in social reform as John Stuart Mill, it is also true that much of Marx's analysis was based upon the economic principles laid down by those early economists. Marx probably did this deliberately as a means of strengthening his own case by being willing to oppose his opponents on their own ground.

Most students who know anything at all of Marx's writings are most familiar with his Communist Manifesto, coauthored with Frederick Engels. In this work, Marx developed his celebrated doctrine of economic history written in terms of class struggle, with each stage of history (his thesis) containing within it the seeds of its own destruction (the antithesis). From a blending of the two (thesis and antithesis), arose a synthesis which in turn became the new thesis. The process, Marx said, would continue to repeat itself until the final stage of communism was reached, when all classes save the proletariat would have been eliminated and all further class struggle thereby ended. Predictions as to the growing concentration of wealth, the increasing severity of the business cycle, and the spreading of misery of the proletariat are also familiar features of the Marx-Engels' view of capitalism.

The Communist Manifesto was long on sociological prophesying and short on economic theory—a defect which Marx tried to remedy in his Das Kapital. This latter book, only the first volume of which was to appear in print before Marx's death, was an attempt by Marx to justify his earlier predictions by rigorous economic analysis. As such, much of the verve and challenge of the Communist Manifesto was lost. Although some of the chapters on working conditions in English factories were designed to strike a responsive chord in the hearts of those sympathetic to the working classes, much of Das Kapital leaves the heart untouched, while exerting a considerable strain upon the reader's mental faculties.

In the passages that follow, Marx develops the point that the capitalist must inevitably be able to gain money in the process of exchange; otherwise he would not find it worthwhile. But from where is this profit to come? Alternatively, Marx rejects machinery, nature, and the services of the businessman as possible sources and by the process of elimination comes to labor. Because the capitalist by reason of his superior bargaining power can buy labor at a price necessary for its subsistence but below the value it can create for its employer, the capitalist is able to extort a surplus value from the employment of labor. If labor is the sole source of value, reasoned Marx, it follows that unless the laborer is paid the full value of the product rather than the cost of his maintenance, he is being exploited. By lengthening the working day, by driving workers ever harder, and by reducing the amount needed to enable the worker to subsist, the capitalist is able to increase the amount of surplus he can receive.

By the first two techniques, the capitalist was able to increase the amount of absolute surplus value. By reducing the cost of subsistence and thereby the amount necessarily paid workers for their subsistence, capitalists were able to increase the relative surplus value. In either case the worker wound up the same way—exploited still more!

Although Marx embraced the Ricardian labor theory of value, it was a different kind of labor that measured the value of the product. Ricardo had written of labor applied at the margin under the most difficult circumstances necessary as that labor which determined the value of a product. For Marx, however, it was the amount of socially necessary labor which was important (see p. 194). Nor did any of the qualifications to a labor theory of value which Ricardo felt it necessary to make, play any part in Marx's system.

Marx's dichotomy between variable capital (the amount available for the employment of labor) and constant capital (all the rest) forced him to two conclusions. The first was that the competition drove the capitalist to introduce more and more machinery. The capitalists who first introduced machinery would secure a temporary gain since they could produce the product with less than the socially necessary labor, thereby securing for them a greater surplus value. But in the long run machinery was as damaging to the capitalist as it was to the workers whom it displaced. Since variable capital (which employed labor) was the sole source of surplus value, increases in the proportion of constant capital would reduce the rate of profit on the total capital investment, that is, the sum of variable capital plus the constant capital.

The second implication of the distinction between variable and constant capital was recognized by Marx himself and emphasized by his critics. If surplus value and hence profit were obtained from variable capital alone, why were the rates of profits the same for firms with widely varying proportions of variable to constant capital? Marx gave scant recognition to this apparent inconsistency in the first volume of Kapital and, until Engels had edited the third volume years after Marx's death, the world waited for a solution. When it was finally revealed, it failed to stifle the criticism by Marx's opponents. An extended review of Marx's solution is beyond the scope of this book. Basically what he suggested was that while each capitalist was free to try to maximize surplus value in his own factory, the end result of his and his fellow capitalists' efforts was to create a stockpile of total capital in the economy from which he drew only that share appropriate to him in terms of the amount of capital he had invested. True to the Classical doctrine, the rate of profit was set by the force of competition preventing the existence of different rates in different firms.

One final word about Marx's treatment of capital is in order. In the closing section of the first volume, Marx spoke of the process of capital accumulation. In early times, Marx said, capital was accumulated by the simple means of direct expropriation. Thereafter the surplus value earned in the process of production was reinvested in hiring more workers—a process which led to the accumulation of additional amounts of surplus value.

Born into an upper middle-class family, Marx spent much of his life in abject poverty. His appeal on behalf of the rights of the poor were laudable, but his effort to justify the "expropriation of the expropriators" by the use of rigorous economic analysis satisfied few of his fellow economists. Marx as a sociologist preaching of the dangers of poverty and the danger of workers becoming alienated from their work provided a more constructive message than did Marx as an economist attempting to unravel the nature of value and surplus value.

DAS KAPITAL

BOOK I / Capitalist Production

Part I: Commodities and Money

Chapter 1: COMMODITIES

§ Section 1. The Two Factors of a Commodity: Use-Value and Value
(The Substance of Value and the Magnitude of Value)

The wealth of these societies in which the capitalist mode of production prevails, presents itself as "an immense accumulation of commodities,"[1] its unit being a single commodity. Our investigation must therefore begin with the analysis of a commodity.

A commodity is, in the first place, an object outside us, a thing that by its properties satisfies human wants of some sort or another. The nature of such wants, whether, for instance, they spring from the stomach or from fancy, makes no difference.[2] Neither are we here concerned to know how the object satisfies these wants, whether directly as means of subsistence, or indirectly as means of production.

Every useful thing, as iron, paper, &c., may be looked at from the two points of view of quality and quantity. It is an assemblage of many properties, and may therefore be of use in various ways. To discover the various use of things is the work of history.[3] So also is the establishment of socially-

[1] Karl Marx, *A Contribution to the Critique of Political Economy*, London, 1859, p. 19.

[2] "Desire implies want; it is the appetite of the mind, and as natural as hunger to the body. . . . The greatest number (of things) have their value from supplying the wants of the mind." Nicolas Barbon: *A Discourse on Coining the New Money Lighter, in Answer to Mr. Locke's Considerations*, &c. London, 1696, pp. 2, 3.

[3] "Things have an intrinsick virtue" (this is Barbon's special term for value in use) "which in all places have the same virtue; as the loadstone to attract iron." The property which the magnet possesses of attracting iron, became of use only after by means of that property the polarity of the magnet had been discovered.

recognised standards of measure for the quantities of these useful objects. The diversity of these measures has its origin partly in the diverse nature of the objects to be measured, partly in convention.

The utility of a thing makes it a use-value.[4] But this utility is not a thing of air. Being limited by the physical properties of the commodity, it has no existence apart from that commodity. A commodity, such as iron, corn, or a diamond, is therefore, so far as it is a material thing, a use-value, something useful. This property of a commodity is independent of the amount of labour required to appropriate its useful qualities. When treating of use-value, we always assume to be dealing with definite quantities, such as dozens of watches, yards of linen, or tons of iron. The use-values of commodities furnish the material for a special study, that of the commercial knowledge of commodities.[5] Use-values become a reality only by use or consumption: they also constitute the substance of all wealth, whatever may be the social form of that wealth. In the form of society we are about to consider, they are, in addition, the material depositories of exchange value.

Exchange value, at first sight, presents itself as a quantitative relation, as the proportion in which values in use of one sort are exchanged for those of another sort, a relation constantly changing with time and place. Hence exchange value appears to be something accidental and purely relative, and consequently an intrinsic value, i.e., an exchange value that is inseparably connected with, inherent in commodities, seems a contradiction in terms.[6] Let us consider the matter a little more closely.

A given commodity, e.g., a quarter of wheat is exchanged for x blacking, y silk, or z gold, &c.—in short, for other commodities in the most different proportions. Instead of one exchange value, the wheat has, therefore, a great many. But since x blacking, y silk, or z gold, &c., each represent the exchange value of one quarter of wheat, x blacking, y silk, z gold, &c., must as exchange values be replaceable by each other, or equal to each other. Therefore, first: the valid exchange values of a given commodity express something equal; secondly, exchange value, generally, is only the mode of expression, the phenomenal form, of something contained in it, yet distinguishable from it.

Let us take two commodities, e.g., corn and iron. The proportions in

[4] "The natural worth of anything consists in its fitness to supply the necessities, or serve the conveniences of human life." (John Locke, *Some Considerations on the Consequences of the Lowering of Interest*, 1691, in Works Edit., London, 1777, Vol. II, p. 28.) In English writers of the 17th century we frequently find "worth" in the sense of value in use, and "value" in the sense of exchange value. This is quite in accordance with the spirit of a language that likes to use a Teutonic word for the actual thing, and a Romance word for its reflexion.

[5] In bourgeois societies the economical fictio juris prevails, that every one, as a buyer, possesses an encyclopædic knowledge of commodities.

[6] "Nothing can have an intrinsick value." (N. Barbon); or as Butler says—"The value of a thing/Is just as much as it will bring."

which they are exchangeable, whatever those proportions may be, can always be represented by an equation in which a given quantity of corn is equated to some quantity of iron: *e.g.*, 1 quarter corn = x cwt. iron. What does this equation tell us? It tells us that in two different things—in 1 quarter of corn and x cwt. of iron, there exists in equal quantities something common to both. The two things must therefore be equal to a third, which in itself is neither the one nor the other. Each of them, so far as it is exchange value, must therefore be reducible to this third.

A simple geometrical illustration will make this clear. In order to calculate and compare the areas of rectilinear figures, we decompose them into triangles. But the area of the triangle itself is expressed by something totally different from its visible figure, namely, by half the product of the base into the altitude. In the same way the exchange values of commodities must be capable of being expressed in terms of something common to them all, of which thing they represent a greater or less quantity.

This common "something" cannot be either a geometrical, a chemical, or any other natural property of commodities. Such properties claim our attention only in so far as they affect the utility of those commodities, make them use-values. But the exchange of commodities is evidently an act characterised by a total abstraction from use-value. Then one use-value is just as good as another, provided only it be present in sufficient quantity. Or, as old Barbon says, "one sort of wares are as good as another, if the values be equal. There is no difference or distinction in things of equal value. . . . An hundred pounds' worth of lead or iron, is of as great value as one hundred pounds' worth of silver or gold." As use-values, commodities are, above all, of different qualities, but as exchange values they are merely different quantities, and consequently do not contain an atom of use-value.

If then we leave out of consideration the use-value of commodities, they have only one common property left, that of being products of labour. But even the product of labour itself has undergone a change in our hands. If we make abstraction from its use-value, we make abstraction at the same time from the material elements and shapes that make the product a use-value; we see in it no longer a table, a house, yarn, or any other useful thing. Its existence as a material thing is put out of sight. Neither can it any longer be regarded as the product of the labour of the joiner, the mason, the spinner, or of any other definite kind of productive labour. Along with the useful qualities of the products themselves, we put out of sight both the useful character of the various kinds of labour embodied in them, and the concrete forms of that labour; there is nothing left but what is common to them all; all are reduced to one and the same sort of labour, human labour in the abstract.

Let us now consider the residue of each of these products; it consists of the same unsubstantial reality in each, a mere congelation of homogeneous human labour, of labour-power expended without regard to the mode of its expenditure. All that these things now tell us is, that human labour-power has been expended in their production, that human labor is embodied in them. When looked at as crystals of this social substance, common to them all, they are—Values.

We have seen that when commodities are exchanged, their exchange value manifests itself as something totally independent of their use-value. But if we abstract from their use-value, there remains their Value as defined above. Therefore, the common substance that manifests itself in the exchange value of commodities, whenever they are exchanged, is their value. The progress of our investigation will show that exchange value is the only form in which the value of commodities can manifest itself or be expressed. For the present, however, we have to consider the nature of value independently of this, its form.

A use-value, or useful article, therefore, has value only because human labour in the abstract has been embodied or materialised in it. How, then, is the magnitude of this value to be measured? Plainly, by the quantity of the value-creating substance, the labour, contained in the article. The quantity of labour, however, is measured by its duration, and labour-time in its turn finds its standard in weeks, days, and hours.

Some people might think that if the value of a commodity is determined by the quantity of labour spent on it, the more idle and unskilful the labourer, the more valuable would his commodity be, because more time would be required in its production. The labour, however, that forms the substance of value, is homogeneous human labour, expenditure of one uniform labour-power. The total labour-power of society, which is embodied in the sum total of the values of all commodities produced by that society, counts here as one homogeneous mass of human labour-power, composed though it be of innumerable individual units. Each of these units is the same as any other, so far as it has the character of the average labour-power of society, and takes effect as such; that is, so far as it requires for producing a commodity, no more time than is needed on an average, no more than is socially necessary. The labour-time socially necessary is that required to produce an article under the normal conditions of production, and with the average degree of skill and intensity prevalent at the time. The introduction of power looms into England probably reduced by one-half the labour required to weave a given quantity of yarn into cloth. The hand-loom weavers, as a matter of fact, continued to require the same time as before; but for all that, the product of one hour of their labour represented after the change only half an hour's social labour, and consequently fell to one-half its former value.

We see then that that which determines the magnitude of the value of any article is the amount of labour socially necessary, or the labour-time socially necessary for its production.[7] Each individual commodity, in this connexion, is to be considered as an average sample of its class. Commodities, therefore, in which equal quantities of labour are embodied, or which can be produced in the same time, have the same value. The value of one commodity is to the value of any other, as the labour-time necessary for the production of the one is to that necessary for the production of the other. "As values, all commodities are only definite masses of congealed labour-time."

The value of a commodity would therefore remain constant if the labour-time required for its production also remained constant. But the latter changes with every variation in the productiveness of labour. This productiveness is determined by various circumstances, amongst others, by the average amount of skill of the workmen, the state of science, and the degree of its practical application, the social organisation of production, the extent and capabilities of the means of production, and by physical conditions. For example, the same amount of labour in favourable seasons is embodied in 8 bushels of corn, and in unfavourable, only in four. The same labour extracts from rich mines more metal than from poor mines. Diamonds are of very rare occurrence on the earth's surface, and hence their discovery costs, on an average, a great deal of labour-time. Consequently much labour is represented in a small compass. Jacob doubts whether gold has ever been paid for at its full value. This applies still more to diamonds. According to Eschwege, the total produce of the Brazilian diamond mines for the eighty years, ending in 1823, had not realised the price of one-and-a-half years' average produce of the sugar and coffee plantations of the same country, although the diamonds cost much more labour, and therefore represented more value. With richer mines, the same quantity of labour would embody itself in more diamonds and their value would fall. If we could succeed at a small expenditure of labour, in converting carbon into diamonds, their value might fall below that of bricks. In general, the greater the productiveness of labour, the less is the labour-time required for the production of an article, the less is the amount of labour crystallised in that article, and the less is its value; and *vise versâ*, the less the productiveness of labour, the greater is the labour-time required for the production of an article, and the greater is its value. The value of a commodity, therefore, varies directly as the quantity, and inversely as the productiveness, of the labour incorporated in it.

A thing can be a use-value, without having value. This is the case when-

7 The value of them (the necessaries of life), when they are exchanged the one for another, is regulated by the quantity of labour necessarily required, and commonly taken in producing them." (*Some Thoughts on the Interest of Money in General, and Particularly in the Publick Funds, &c.*, Lond., p. 36.) This remarkable anonymous work, written in the last century, bears no date. It is clear, however, from internal evidence, that it appeared in the reign of George II, about 1739 or 1740.

ever its utility to man is not due to labour. Such are air, virgin soil, natural meadows, &c. A thing can be useful, and the product of human labour, without being a commodity. Whoever directly satisfies his wants with the produce of his own labour, creates, indeed, use-values, but not commodities. In order to produce the latter, he must not only produce use-values, but use-values for others, social use-values. Lastly, nothing can have value, without being an object of utility. If the thing is useless, so is the labour contained in it; the labour does not count as labour, and therefore creates no value.

§ Section 2. The Twofold Character of the Labour Embodied in Commodities

. . .

To resume, then: In the use-value of each commodity there is contained useful labour, *i.e.*, productive activity of a definite kind and exercised with a definite aim. Use-values cannot confront each other as commodities, unless the useful labour embodied in them is qualitatively different in each of them. In a community, the produce of which in general takes the form of commodities, *i.e.*, in a community of commodity producers, this qualitative difference between the useful forms of labour that are carried on independently by individual producers, each on their own account, develops into a complex system, a social division of labour.

Anyhow, whether the coat be worn by the tailor or by his customer, in either case it operates as a use-value. Nor is the relation between the coat and the labour that produced it altered by the circumstance that tailoring may have become a special trade, an independent branch of the social division of labour. Wherever the want of clothing forced them to it, the human race made clothes for thousands of years, without a single man becoming a tailor. But coats and linen, like every other element of material wealth that is not the spontaneous produce of nature, must invariably owe their existence to a special productive activity, exercised with a definite aim, an activity that appropriates particular nature-given materials to particular human wants. So far therefore as labour is a creator of use-value, is useful labour, it is a necessary condition, independent of all forms of society, for the existence of the human race; it is an eternal nature-imposed necessity, without which there can be no material exchanges between man and Nature, and therefore no life.

The use-values, coat, linen, &c., *i.e.*, the bodies of commodities, are combinations of two elements—matter and labour. If we take away the useful labour expended upon them, a material substratum is always left, which is furnished by Nature without the help of man. The latter can work only as Nature does, that is by changing the form of matter. Nay more, in this work of changing the form he is constantly helped by natural forces. We see, then, that labour is not the only source of material wealth, of use-values produced by labour. As William Petty puts it, labour is its father and the earth its mother.

Let us now pass from the commodity considered as a use-value to the value of commodities.

By our assumption, the coat is worth twice as much as the linen. But this is a mere quantitative difference, which for the present does not concern us. We bear in mind, however, that if the value of the coat is double that of 10 yds. of linen, 20 yds. of linen must have the same value as one coat. So far as they are values, the coat and the linen are things of a like substance, objective expressions of essentially identical labour. But tailoring and weaving are, qualitatively, different kinds of labour. There are, however, states of society in which one and the same man does tailoring and weaving alternately, in which case these two forms of labour are mere modifications of the labour of the same individual, and not special and fixed functions of different persons; just as the coat which our tailor makes one day, and the trousers which he makes another day, imply only a variation in the labour of one and the same individual. Moreover, we see at a glance that, in our capitalist society, a given portion of human labour is, in accordance with the varying demand, at one time supplied in the form of tailoring, at another in the form of weaving. This change may possibly not take place without friction, but take place it must.

Productive activity, if we leave out of sight its special form, viz., the useful character of the labour, is nothing but the expenditure of human labour-power. Tailoring and weaving, though qualitatively different productive activities, are each a productive expenditure of human brains, nerves, and muscles, and in this sense are human labour. They are but two different modes of expending human labour-power. Of course, this labour-power, which remains the same under all its modifications, must have attained a certain pitch of development before it can be expended in a multiplicity of modes. But the value of a commodity represents human labour in the abstract, the expenditure of human labour in general. And just as in society, a general or a banker plays a great part, but mere man, on the other hand, a very shabby part, so here with mere human labour. It is the expenditure of simple labour-power, i.e., of the labour-power which, on an average, apart from any special development, exists in the organism of every ordinary individual. Simple average labour, it is true, varies in character in different countries and at different times, but in a particular society it is given. Skilled labour counts only as simple labour intensified, or rather, as multiplied simple labour, a given quantity of skilled being considered equal to a greater quantity of simple labour. Experience shows that this reduction is constantly being made. A commodity may be the product of the most skilled labour, but its value, by equating it to the product of simple unskilled labour, represents a definite quantity of the latter labour alone.[8] The different proportions in which different sorts of labour are reduced to unskilled labour as their standard, are established by a social process that goes on behind the backs of the producers, and, consequently, appear to be fixed by custom. For simplicity's sake we shall henceforth account every kind of labour to be unskilled, simple labour; by this we do no more than save ourselves the trouble of making the reduction.

Just as, therefore, in viewing the coat and linen as values, we abstract from their different use-values, so it is with the labour represented by those values: we disregard the difference between its useful forms, weaving and tailoring. As the use-values, coat and linen, are combinations of special productive activities with cloth and yarn, while the values, coat and linen, are, on the other hand, mere homogeneous congelations of indifferentiated labour, so the labour embodied in these latter values does not count by virtue of its productive relation to cloth and yarn, but only as being expenditure of human labour-power. Tailoring and weaving are necessary factors in the creation of the use-values, coat and linen, precisely because these two kinds of labour are of different qualities; but only in so far as abstraction is made from their special qualities, only in so far as both possess the same quality of being human labour, do tailoring and weaving form the substance of the values of the same articles.

Coats and linen, however, are not merely values, but values of definite magnitude, and according to our assumption, the coat is worth twice as much as the ten yards of linen. Whence this difference in their values? It is owing to the fact that the linen contains only half as much labour as the coat, and consequently, that in the production of the latter, labour-power must have been expended during twice the time necessary for the production of the former.

While, therefore, with reference to use-value, the labour contained in a commodity counts only qualitatively, with reference to value it counts only quantitatively, and must first be reduced to human labour pure and simple. In the former case, it is a question of How and What, in the latter of How much? How long a time? Since the magnitude of the value of a commodity represents only the quantity of labour embodied in it, it follows that all commodities, when taken in certain proportions, must be equal in value.

---

[8] The reader must note that we are not speaking here of the wages or value that the labourer gets for a given labour time, but of the value of the commodity in which that labour time is materialised. Wages is a category that, as yet, has no existence at the present stage of our investigation.

§ Section 3. The Form of Value or Exchange-Value

. . .

1. *The two poles of the expression of value: relative form and equivalent
form.* The whole mystery of the form of value lies hidden in this elementary
form. Its analysis, therefore, is our real difficulty.

Here two different kinds of commodities (in our example the linen and
the coat), evidently play two different parts. The linen expresses its value
in the coat; the coat serves as the material in which that value is expressed.
The former plays an active, the latter a passive, part. The value of the linen
is represented as relative value, or appears in relative form. The coat offi-
ciates as equivalent, or appears in equivalent form.

The relative form and the equivalent form are two intimately connected,
mutually dependent and inseparable elements of the expression of value;
but, at the same time, are mutually exclusive, antagonistic extremes—*i.e.*,
poles of the same expression. They are allotted respectively to the two
different commodities brought into relation by that expression. It is not
possible to express the value of linen in linen. 20 yards of linen = 20 yards
of linen is no expression of value. On the contrary, such an equation merely
says that 20 yards of linen are nothing else than 20 yards of linen, a definite
quantity of the use-value linen. The value of the linen can therefore be
expressed only relatively—*i.e.*, in some other commodity. The relative form
of the value of the linen pre-supposes, therefore, the presence of some
other commodity—here the coat—under the form of an equivalent. On
the other hand, the commodity that figures as the equivalent cannot at the
same time assume the relative form. That second commodity is not the
one whose value is expressed. Its function is merely to serve as the material
in which the value of the first commodity is expressed.

No doubt, the expression 20 yards of linen = 1 coat, or 20 yards of linen
are worth 1 coat, implies the opposite relation: 1 coat = 20 yards of linen,
or 1 coat is worth 20 yards of linen. But, in that case, I must reverse the
equation, in order to express the value of the coat relatively; and, so soon as
I do that, the linen becomes the equivalent instead of the coat. A single
commodity cannot, therefore, simultaneously assume, in the same expression of value, both forms. The very polarity of these forms makes them
mutually exclusive.

Whether, then, a commodity assumes the relative form, or the opposite
equivalent form, depends entirely upon its accidental position in the
expression of value—that is, upon whether it is the commodity whose
value is being expressed or the commodity in which value is being
expressed.

. . .

4. *The elementary form of value considered as a whole.* The elementary form of value of a commodity is contained in the equation, expressing its value relation to another commodity of a different kind, or in its exchange relation to the same. The value of commodity A is qualitatively expressed by the fact that commodity B is directly exchangeable with it. Its value is quantitatively expressed by the fact, that a definite quantity of B is exchangeable with a definite quantity of A. In other words, the value of a commodity obtains independent and definite expression, by taking the form of exchange value. When, at the beginning of this chapter, we said, in common parlance, that a commodity is both a use-value and an exchange value, we were, accurately speaking, wrong. A commodity is a use-value or object of utility, and a value. It manifests itself as this two-fold thing, that it is, as soon as its value assumes an independent form—viz., the form exchange value. It never assumes this form when isolated, but only when placed in a value or exchange relation with another commodity of a different kind. When once we know this, such a mode of expression does no harm; it simply serves as an abbreviation.

Our analysis has shown, that the form or expression of the value of a commodity originates in the nature of value, and not that value and its magnitude originate in the mode of their expression as exchange value. This, however, is the delusion as well of the mercantilists and their recent revivors, Ferrier, Ganilh, and others, as also of their antipodes, the modern bagmen of Free Trade, such as Bastiat. The mercantilists lay special stress on the qualitative aspect of the expression of value, and consequently on the equivalent form of commodities, which attains its full perfection in money. The modern hawkers of Free Trade, who must get rid of their article at any price, on the other hand, lay most stress on the quantitative aspect of the relative form of value. For them there consequently exists neither value, nor magnitude of value, anywhere except in its expression by means of the exchange relation of commodities, that is, in the daily list of prices current. MacLeod, who has taken upon himself to dress up the confused ideas of Lombard Street in the most learned finery, is a successful cross between the superstitious mercantilists, and the enlightened Free Trade bagmen.

A close scrutiny of the expression of the value of A in terms of B, contained in the equation expressing the value relation of A to B, has shown us that, within that relation, the bodily form of A figures only as a use-value, the bodily form of B only as the form or aspect of value. The opposition or contrast existing internally in each commodity between use-value and value, is, therefore, made evident externally by two commodities being placed in such relation to each other, that the commodity whose value it is sought to express, figures directly as a mere use-value, while the commodity in which that value is to be expressed, figures directly as mere exchange value. Hence the elementary form of value of a commodity is the elementary form in which the contrast contained in that commodity, between use-value and value, becomes apparent.

Every product of labour is, in all states of society, a use-value; but it is only at a definite historical epoch in a society's development that such product becomes a commodity, viz., at the epoch when the labour spent on the production of a useful article becomes expressed as one of the objective qualities of that article, *i.e.*, as its value. It therefore follows that the elementary value-form is also the primitive form under which a product of labour appears historically as a commodity, and that the gradual trans-formation of such products into commodities, proceeds *pari passu* with the development of the value-form.

We perceive, at first sight, the deficiencies of the elementary form of value: it is a mere germ, which must undergo a series of metamorphoses before it can ripen into the Price-form.

The expression of the value of commodity A in terms of any other commodity B, merely distinguishes the value from the use-value of A, and therefore places A merely in a relation of exchange with a single different commodity, B; but it is still far from expressing A's qualitative equality, and quantitative proportionality, to all commodities. To the elementary relative value-form of a commodity, there corresponds the single equivalent form of one other commodity. Thus, in the relative expression of value of the linen, the coat assumes the form of equivalent, or of being directly exchangeable, only in relation to a single commodity, the linen.

Nevertheless, the elementary form of value passes by an easy transition into a more complete form. It is true that by means of the elementary form, the value of a commodity A, becomes expressed in terms of one, and only one, other commodity. But that one may be a commodity of any kind, coat, iron, corn, or anything else. Therefore, according as A is placed in relation with one or the other, we get for one and the same commodity, different elementary expressions of value. The number of such possible expressions is limited only by the number of the different kinds of com-modities distinct from it. The isolated expression of A's value, is therefore convertible into a series, prolonged to any length, of the different elemen-tary expressions of that value.

.   .   .

Chapter 6: THE BUYING AND SELLING OF LABOUR-POWER

The change of value that occurs in the case of money intended to be converted into capital, cannot take place in the money itself, since in its function of means of purchase and of payment, it does no more than realise the price of the commodity it buys or pays for; and, as hard cash, it is value petrified, never varying.[1] Just as little can it originate in the second act of circulation, the re-sale of the commodity, which does no more than transform the article from its bodily form back again into its money-form. The change must, therefore, take place in the commodity bought by the first act, M—C, but not in its value, for equivalents are exchanged, and the commodity is paid for at its full value. We are, therefore, forced to the conclusion that the change originates in the use-value, as such, of the commodity, i.e., in its consumption. In order to be able to extract value from the consumption of a commodity, our friend, Moneybags, must be so lucky as to find, within the sphere of circulation, in the market, a commodity, whose use-value possesses the peculiar property of being a source of value, whose actual consumption, therefore, is itself an embodiment of labour, and, consequently, a creation of value. The possessor of money does find on the market such a special commodity in capacity for labour or labour-power.

By labour-power or capacity for labour is to be understood the aggregate of those mental and physical capabilities existing in a human being, which he exercises whenever he produces a use-value of any description.

But in order that our owner of money may be able to find labour-power offered for sale as a commodity, various conditions must first be fulfilled. The exchange of commodities of itself implies no other relations of dependence than those which result from its own nature. On this assumption, labour-power can appear upon the market as a commodity only if, and so far as, its possessor, the individual whose labour-power it is, offers it for sale, or sells it, as a commodity. In order that he may be able to do this, he must have it at his disposal, must be the untrammelled owner of his capacity for labour, i.e., of his person.[2] He and the owner of money meet in the market, and deal with each other as on the basis of equal rights, with this difference alone, that one is buyer, the other seller; both, therefore, equal in the eyes of the law. The continuance of this relation demands that the owner of the labour-power should sell it only for a definite period, for if he were to sell it rump and stump, once for all, he would be selling himself, converting himself from a free man into a slave, from an owner of a commodity into a commodity. He must constantly look upon his labour-power as his own property, his own commodity, and this he can only do by placing it at the disposal of the buyer temporarily, for a definite period of time. By this means alone can he avoid renouncing his rights of ownership over it.[3]

[1] In the form of money . . . capital is productive of no profit." Ricardo, *Principles of Political Economy*, p. 267.

[2] In encyclopædias of classical antiquities we find such nonsense as this—that in the ancient world capital was fully developed, "except that the free labourer and a system of credit was wanting." Mommsen also, in his *History of Rome*, commits, in this respect, one blunder after another.

[3] Hence legislation in various countries fixes a maximum for labour-contracts. Wherever free labour is the rule, the laws regulate the mode of terminating this contract. In

The second essential condition to the owner of money finding labour-power in the market as a commodity is this—that the labourer instead of being in the position to sell commodities in which his labour is incorporated, must be obliged to offer for sale as a commodity that very labour-power, which exists only in his living self.

In order that a man may be able to sell commodities other than labour-power, he must of course have the means of production, as raw material, implements, &c. No boots can be made without leather. He requires also the means of subsistence. Nobody—not even "a musician of the future"—can live upon future products, or upon use-values in an unfinished state; and ever since the first moment of his appearance on the world's stage, man always has been, and must still be a consumer, both before and while he is producing. In a society where all products assume the form of commodities, these commodities must be sold after they have been produced; it is only after their sale that they can serve in satisfying the requirements of their producer. The time necessary for their sale is superadded to that necessary for their production.

For the conversion of his money into capital, therefore, the owner of money must meet in the market with the free labourer, free in the double sense, that as a free man he can dispose of his labour-power as his own commodity, and that on the other hand he has no other commodity for sale, is short of everything necessary for the realisation of his labour-power.

The question why this free labourer confronts him in the market, has no interest for the owner of money, who regards the labour market as a branch of the general market for commodities. And for the present it interests us just as little. We cling to the fact theoretically, as he does practically. One thing, however, is clear—nature does not produce on the one side owners of money or commodities, and on the other men possessing nothing but their own labour-power. This relation has no natural basis, neither is its social basis one that is common to all historical periods. It is clearly the result of a past historical development, the product of many economical revolutions, of the extinction of a whole series of older forms of social production.

---

some States, particularly in Mexico (before the American Civil War, also in the territories taken from Mexico, and also as a matter of fact, in the Danubian provinces till the revolution affected by Kusa), slavery is hidden under the form of *peonage*. By means of advances, repayable in labour, which are handed down from generation to generation, not only the individual labourer, but his family, become, *de facto*, the property of other persons and their families. Juarez abolished *peonage*. The so-called Emperor Maximilian re-established it by a decree, which, in the House of Representatives at Washington, was aptly denounced as a decree for the re-introduction of slavery into Mexico. "I may make over to another the use, for a limited time, of my particular bodily and mental aptitudes and capabilities; because, in consequence of this restriction, they are impressed with a character of alienation with regard to me as a whole. But by the alienation of all my labour-time and the whole of my work, I should be converting the substance itself, in other words, my general activity and reality, my person, into the property of another." Hegel, *Philosophie des Rechts*, Berlin, 1840, p. 104, § 67.

So, too, the economical categories, already discussed by us, bear the stamp of history. Definite historical conditions are necessary that a product may become a commodity. It must not be produced as the immediate means of subsistence of the producer himself. Had we gone further, and inquired under what circumstances all, or even the majority of products take the form of commodities, we should have found that this can only happen with production of a very specific kind, capitalist production. Such an inquiry, however, would have been foreign to the analysis of commodities. Production and circulation of commodities can take place, although the great mass of the objects produced are intended for the immediate requirements of their producers, are not turned into commodities, and consequently social production is not yet by a long way dominated in its length and breadth by exchange-value, the appearance of products as commodities presupposed such a development of the social division of labour, that the separation of use-value from exchange-value, a separation which first begins with barter, must already have been completed. But such a degree of development is common to many forms of society, which in other respects present the most varying historical features. On the other hand, if we consider money, its existence implies a definite stage in the exchange of commodities. The particular functions of money which it performs, either as the mere equivalent of commodities, or as means of circulation, or means of payment, as hoard or as universal money, point, according to the extent and relative preponderance of the one function or the other, to very different stages in the process of social production. Yet we know by experience that a circulation of commodities relatively primitive, suffices for the production of all these forms. Otherwise with capital. The historical conditions of its existence are by no means given with the mere circulation of money and commodities. It can spring into life, only when the owner of the means of production and subsistence meets in the market with the free labourer selling his labour-power. And this one historical condition comprises a world's history. Capital therefore, announces from its first appearance a new epoch in the process of social production.[4]

We must now examine more closely this peculiar commodity, labour-power. Like all others it has a value.[5] How is that value determined?

The value of labour-power is determined, as in the case of every other commodity, by the labour-time necessary for the production, and consequently also the reproduction, of this special article. So far as it has value, it represents no more than a definite quantity of the average labour of

---

[4] The capitalist epoch is therefore characterised by this, that labour-power takes in the eyes of the labourer himself the form of a commodity which is his property; his labour consequently becomes wage labour. On the other hand, it is only from this moment that the produce of labour universally becomes a commodity.

[5] "The value or worth of a man, is as of all other things his price—that is to say, so much as would be given for the use of his power." Thomas Hobbes, *Leviathan*, in Works, Ed. Molesworth, London, 1839–1844, Vol. III, p. 76.

society incorporated in it. Labour-power exists only as a capacity, or power of the living individual. Its production consequently presupposes his existence. Given the individual, the production of labour-power consists in his reproduction of himself or his maintenance. For his maintenance he requires a given quantity of the means of subsistence. Therefore the labour-time requisite for the production of labour-power reduces itself to that necessary for the production of those means of subsistence; in other words, the value of labour-power is the value of the means of subsistence necessary for the maintenance of the labourer. Labour-power, however, becomes a reality only by its exercise; it sets itself in action only by working. But thereby a definite quantity of human muscle, nerve, brain, &c., is wasted, and these require to be restored. This increased expenditure demands a larger income.[6] If the owner of labour-power works to-day, to-morrow he must again be able to repeat the same process in the same conditions as regards health and strength. His means of subsistence must therefore be sufficient to maintain him in his normal state as a labouring individual. His natural wants, such as food, clothing, fuel, and housing, vary according to the climatic and other physical conditions of his country. On the other hand, the number and extent of his so-called necessary wants, as also the modes of satisfying them, are themselves the product of historical development, and depend therefore to a great extent on the degree of civilisation of a country, more particularly on the conditions under which, and consequently on the habits and degree of comfort in which, the class of free labourers has been formed.[7] In contradistinction therefore to the case of other commodities, there enters into the determination of the value of labour-power a historical and moral element. Nevertheless, in a given country, at a given period, the average quantity of the means of subsistence necessary for the labourer is practically known.

The owner of labour-power is mortal. If then his appearance in the market is to be continuous, and the continuous conversion of money into capital assumes this, the seller of labour-power must perpetuate himself, "in the way that every living individual perpetuates himself, by procreation." The labour-power withdrawn from the market by wear and tear and death, must be continually replaced by, at the very least, an equal amount of fresh labour-power. Hence the sum of the means of subsistence necessary for the production of labour-power must include the means necessary for the labourer's substitutes, i.e., his children, in order that this race of peculiar commodity-owners may perpetuate its appearance in the market.[8]

[6] Hence the Roman Villicus, as overlooker of the agricultural slaves, received "more meagre fare than working slaves, because his work was lighter." Thomas Mommsen, Römische Geschichte, 1856, p. 810.
[7] Compare W. H. Thornton, Overpopulation and its Remedy, London, 1846.
[8] Its (labour's) natural price . . . consists in such a quantity of necessaries and comforts of life, as, from the nature of the climate, and the habits of the country, are necessary to support the labourer, and to enable him to rear such a family as may preserve,

In order to modify the human organism, so that it may acquire skill and handiness in a given branch of industry, and become labour-power of a special kind, a special education or training is requisite, and this, on its part, costs an equivalent in commodities of a greater or less amount. This amount varies according to the more or less complicated character of the labour-power. The expenses of this education (excessively small in the case of ordinary labour-power), enter pro tanto into the total value spent in its production.

The value of labour-power resolves itself into the value of a definite quantity of the means of subsistence. It therefore varies with the value of these means or with the quantity of labour requisite for their production.

Some of the means of subsistence, such as food and fuel, are consumed daily, and a fresh supply must be provided daily. Others such as clothes and furniture last for longer periods and require to be replaced only at longer intervals. One article must be bought or paid for daily, another weekly, another quarterly, and so on. But in whatever way the sum total of these outlays may be spread over the year, they must be covered by the average income, taking one day with another. If the total of the commodities required daily for the production of labour-power = A, and those required weekly = B, and those required quarterly = C, and so on, the daily average of these commodities =

$$\frac{365A + 52B + 4C + \&c}{365}.$$

Suppose that in this mass of commodities requisite for the average day there are embodied 6 hours of social labour, then there is incorporated daily in labour-power half a day's average social labour, in other words, half a day's labour is requisite for the daily production of labour-power. This quantity of labour forms the value of a day's labour-power or the value of the labour-power daily reproduced. If half a day's average social labour is incorporated in three shillings, then three shillings is the price corresponding to the value of a day's labour-power. If its owner therefore offers it for sale at three shillings a day, its selling price is equal to its value, and according to our supposition, our friend Moneybags, who is intent upon converting his three shillings into capital, pays this value.

The minimum limit of the value of labour-power is determined by the value of the commodities, without the daily supply of which the labourer cannot renew his vital energy, consequently by the value of those means of subsistence that are physically indispensable. If the price of labour-power falls to this minimum, it falls below its value, since under such circum-

---

in the market, an undiminished supply of labour." R. Torrens, *An Essay on the External Corn Trade*, London, 1815, p. 62. The word labour is here used incorrectly for labour-power.

stances it can be maintained and developed only in a crippled state. But the value of every commodity is determined by the labour-time requisite to turn it out so as to be of normal quality.

. . .

Part III: The Production of Absolute Surplus-Value

Chapter 7: THE LABOUR-PROCESS AND THE PROCESS OF PRODUCING SURPLUS-VALUE

. . .

The labour-process, turned into the process by which the capitalist consumes labour-power, exhibits two characteristic phenomena. First, the labourer works under the control of the capitalist to whom his labour belongs; the capitalist taking good care that the work is done in a proper manner, and that the means of production are used with intelligence, so that there is no unnecessary waste of raw material, and no wear and tear of the implements beyond what is necessarily caused by the work.

Secondly, the product is the property of the capitalist and not that of the labourer, its immediate producer. Suppose that a capitalist pays for a day's labour-power at its value; then the right to use that power for a day belongs to him, just as much as the right to use any other commodity, such as a horse that he has hired for the day. To the purchaser of a commodity belongs its use, and the seller of labour-power, by giving his labour, does no more, in reality, than part with the use-value that he has sold. From the instant he steps into the workshop, the use-value of his labour-power, and therefore also its use, which is labour, belongs to the capitalist. By the purchase of labour-power, the capitalist incorporates labour, as a living ferment, with the lifeless constituents of the product. From his point of view, the labour-process is nothing more than the consumption of the commodity purchased, i.e., of labour-power; but this consumption cannot be effected except by supplying the labour-power with the means of production. The labour-process is a process between things that the capitalist has purchased, things that have become his property. The product of this process also belongs, therefore, to him, just as much as does the wine which is the product of a process of fermentation completed in his cellar.[1]

1 "Products are appropriated before they are converted into capital; this conversion does not secure them from such appropriation." Cherbuliez, *Riche ou Pauvre*, edit. Paris, 1841, pp. 53, 54. "The Proletarian, by selling his labour for a definite quantity of the necessaries of life, renounces all claim to a share in the product. The mode of appropriation of the products remains the same as before; it is no way altered by the bargain we have mentioned. The product belongs exclusively to the capitalist, who supplied the raw

208 DAS KAPITAL

§ Section 2. The Production of Surplus-Value

The product appropriated by the capitalist is a use-value, as yarn, for example, or boots. But, although boots are, in one sense, the basis of all social progress, and our capitalist is a decided "progressist," yet he does not manufacture boots for their own sake. Use-value is, by no means, the thing "qu'on aime pour lui-même" in the production of commodities. Use-values are only produced by capitalists, because, and in so far as, they are the material substratum, the depositaries of exchange-value. Our capitalist has two objects in view: in the first place, he wants to produce a use-value that has a value in exchange, that is to say, an article destined to be sold, a commodity; and secondly, he desires to produce a commodity whose value shall be greater than the sum of the values of the commodities used in its production, that is, of the means of production and the labour-power, that he purchased with his good money in the open market. His aim is to produce not only a use-value, but a commodity also; not only use-value, but value; not only value, but at the same time surplus-value.

It must be borne in mind, that we are now dealing with the production of commodities, and that, up to this point, we have only considered one aspect of the process. Just as commodities are, at the same time, use-values and values, so the process of producing them must be a labour-process, and at the same time, a process of creating value.[2]

Let us now examine production as a creation of value.

We know that the value of each commodity is determined by the quantity of labour expended on and materialised in it, by the working-time necessary, under given social conditions, for its production. This rule also holds good in the case of the product that accrued to our capitalist, as the result of the labour-process carried on for him. Assuming this product to be 10 lbs. of yarn, our first step is to calculate the quantity of labour realised in it.

For spinning the yarn, raw material is required; suppose in this case 10 lbs. of cotton. We have no need at present to investigate the value of this

---

material and the necessaries of life; and this is a rigorous consequence of the law of appropriation, a law whose fundamental principle was the very opposite, namely, that every labourer has an exclusive right to the ownership of what he produces." "When the labourers receive wages for their labour . . . the capitalist is then the owner not of the capital only" (he means the means of production) "but of the labour also. If what is paid as wages is included, as it commonly is, in the term capital, it is absurd to talk of labour separately from capital. The word capital as thus employed includes labour and capital both." James Mill, *Elements of Political Economy*, &c., ed. 1821, pp. 70, 71.

2 As has been stated in a previous note, the English language has two different expressions for these two different aspects of labour; in the Simple Labour-process, the process of producing Use-Values, it is Work; in the process of creation of Value, it is *Labour*, taking the term in its strictly economical sense. *Ed.*

cotton, for our capitalist has, we will assume, bought it at its full value, say of ten shillings. In this price the labour required for the production of the cotton is already expressed in terms of the average labour of society. We will further assume that the wear and tear of the spindle, which, for our present purpose, may represent all other instruments of labour employed, amounts to the value of 2s. If, then, twenty-four hours' labour, or two working days, are required to produce the quantity of gold represented by twelve shillings, we have here, to begin with, two days' labour already incorporated in the yarn.

We must not let ourselves be misled by the circumstance that the cotton has taken a new shape while the substance of the spindle has to a certain extent been used up. By the general law of value, if the value of 40 lbs. of yarn = the value of 40 lbs. of cotton + the value of a whole spindle, *i.e.*, if the same working time is required to produce the commodities on either side of this equation, then 10 lbs. of yarn are an equivalent for 10 lbs. of cotton, together with one-fourth of a spindle. In the case we are considering the same working time is materialised in the 10 lbs. of yarn on the one hand, and in the 10 lbs. of cotton and the fraction of a spindle on the other. Therefore, whether value appears in cotton, in a spindle, or in yarn, makes no difference in the amount of that value. The spindle and cotton, instead of resting quietly side by side, join together in the process, their forms are altered, and they are turned into yarn; but their value is no more affected by this fact than it would be if they had been simply exchanged for their equivalent in yarn.

The labour required for the production of the cotton, the raw material of the yarn, is part of the labour necessary to produce the yarn, and is therefore contained in the yarn. The same applies to the labour embodied in the spindle, without whose wear and tear the cotton could not be spun.

Hence, in determining the value of the yarn, or the labour-time required for its production, all the special processes carried on at various times and in different places, which were necessary, first to produce the cotton and the wasted portion of the spindle, and then with the cotton and spindle to spin the yarn, may together be looked on as different and successive phases of one and the same process. The whole of the labour in the yarn is past labour; and it is a matter of no importance that the operations necessary for the production of its constituent elements were carried on at times which, referred to the present, are more remote than the final operation of spinning. If a definite quantity of labour, say thirty days, is requisite to build a house, the total amount of labour incorporated in it is not altered by the fact that the work of the last day is done twenty-nine days later than that of the first. Therefore the labour contained in the raw material and the instruments of labour can be treated just as if it were labour expended in an earlier stage of the spinning process, before the labour of actual spinning commenced.

The values of the means of production, *i.e.*, the cotton and the spindle, which values are expressed in the price of twelve shillings, are therefore constituent parts of the value of the yarn, or, in other words, of the value of the product.

Two conditions must nevertheless be fulfilled. First, the cotton and spindle must concur in the production of a use-value; they must in the present case become yarn. Value is independent of the particular use-value by which it is borne, but it must be embodied in a use-value of some kind. Secondly, the time occupied in the labor of production must not exceed the time really necessary under the given social conditions of the case. Therefore, if no more than 1 lb. of cotton be requisite to spin 1 lb. of yarn, care must be taken that no more than this weight of cotton is consumed in the production of 1 lb. of yarn; and similarly with regard to the spindle. Though the capitalist have a hobby, and use a gold instead of a steel spindle, yet the only labour that counts for anything in the value of the yarn is that which would be required to produce a steel spindle, because no more is necessary under the given social conditions.

We now know what portion of the value of the yarn is owing to the cotton and the spindle. It amounts to twelve shillings or the value of two days' work. The next point for our consideration is, what portion of the value of the yarn is added to the cotton by the labour of the spinner.

We have now to consider this labour under a very different aspect from that which it had during the labour-process; there, we viewed it solely as that particular kind of human activity which changes cotton into yarn; there, the more the labour was suited to the work, the better the yarn, other circumstances remaining the same. The labour of the spinner was then viewed as specifically different from other kinds of productive labour, different on the one hand in its special aim, viz., spinning, different, on the other hand, in the special character of its operations, in the special nature of its means of production and in the special use-value of its product. For the operation of spinning, cotton and spindles are a necessity, but for making rifled cannon they would be of no use whatever. Here, on the contrary, where we consider the labour of the spinner only so far as it is value-creating, *i.e.*, a source of value, his labour differs in no respect from the labour of the man who bores cannon, or (what here more nearly concerns us), from the labour of the cotton-planter and spindle-maker incorporated in the means of production. It is solely by reason of this identity, that cotton planting, spindle making and spinning, are capable of forming the component parts, differing only quantitatively from each other, of one whole, namely, the value of the yarn. Here, we have nothing more to do with the quality, the nature and the specific character of the labour, but merely with its quantity. And this simply requires to be calculated. We proceed upon the assumption that spinning is simple, unskilled labour, the average labour of a given state of society. Hereafter we shall see that the contrary assumption would make no difference.

While the labourer is at work, his labour constantly undergoes a transformation: from being motion, it becomes an object without motion; from being the labourer working, it becomes the thing produced. At the end of one hour's spinning, that act is represented by a definite quantity of yarn; in other words, a definite quantity of labour, namely that of one hour, has become embodied in the cotton. We say labour, *i.e.*, the expenditure of his vital force by the spinner, and not spinning labour, because the special work of spinning counts here, only so far as it is the expenditure of labour-power in general, and not in so far as it is the specific work of the spinner.

In the process we are now considering it is of extreme importance, that no more time be consumed in the work of transforming the cotton into yarn than is necessary under the given social conditions. If under normal, *i.e.*, average social conditions of production, *a* pounds of cotton ought to be made into *b* pounds of yarn by one hour's labour, then a day's labour does not count as 12 hours' labour unless 12 *a* pounds of cotton have been made into 12 *b* pounds of yarn; for in the creation of value, the time that is socially necessary alone counts.

Not only the labour, but also the raw material and the product now appear in quite a new light, very different from that in which we viewed them in the labour-process pure and simple. The raw material serves now merely as an absorbent of a definite quantity of labour. By this absorption it is in fact changed into yarn, because it is spun, because labour-power in the form of spinning is added to it; but the product, the yarn, is now nothing more than a measure of the labour absorbed by the cotton. If in one hour 1⅔ lbs. of cotton can be spun into 1⅔ lbs. of yarn, then 10 lbs. of yarn indicate the absorption of 6 hours' labour. Definite quantities of product, these quantities being determined by experience, now represent nothing but definite quantities of labour, definite masses of crystallized labour-time. They are nothing more than the materialisation of so many hours or so many days of social labour.

We are here no more concerned about the facts, that the labour is the specific work of spinning, that its subject is cotton and its product yarn, than we are about the fact that the subject itself is already a product and therefore raw material. If the spinner, instead of spinning, were working in a coal mine, the subject of his labour, the coal, would be supplied by Nature; nevertheless, a definite quantity of extracted coal, a hundred weight, for example, would represent a definite quantity of absorbed labour.

We assumed, on the occasion of its sale, that the value of a day's labour-power is three shillings, and that six hours' labour are incorporated in that sum; and consequently that this amount of labour is requisite to produce the necessaries of life daily required on an average by the labourer. If now our spinner by working for one hour, can convert 1⅔ lbs. of cotton into 1⅔ lbs. of yarn,[3] it follows that in six hours he will convert 10 lbs. of cotton into 10 lbs. of yarn. Hence, during the spinning process, the cotton absorbs six hours' labour. The same quantity of labour is also embodied in a piece of gold of the value of three shillings. Consequently by the mere labour of spinning, a value of three shillings is added to the cotton.

Let us now consider the total value of the product, the 10 lbs. of yarn. Two and a half days' labour have been embodied in it, of which two days were contained in the cotton and in the substance of the spindle worn away, and half a day was absorbed during the process of spinning. This two and a half days' labour is also represented by a piece of gold of the value of fifteen shillings. Hence, fifteen shillings is an adequate price for the 10 lbs. of yarn, or the price of one pound is eighteen-pence.

Our capitalist stares in astonishment. The value of the product is exactly equal to the value of the capital advanced. The value so advanced has not expanded, no surplus-value has been created, and consequently money has not been converted into capital. The price of the yarn is fifteen shillings, and fifteen shillings were spent in the open market upon the constituent elements of the product, or, what amounts to the same thing, upon the factors of the labour-process; ten shillings were paid for the cotton, two shillings for the substance of the spindle worn away, and three shillings for the labour-power. The swollen value of the yarn is of no avail, for it is merely the sum of the values formerly existing in the cotton, the spindle, and the labour-power; out of such a simple addition of existing values, no surplus-value can possibly arise.[4] These separate values are now all concentrated in one thing; but so they were also in the sum of fifteen shillings, before it was split up into three parts, by the purchase of the commodities.

There is in reality nothing very strange in this result. The value of one pound of yarn being eighteen-pence, if our capitalist buys 10 lbs. of yarn in the market, he must pay fifteen shillings for them. It is clear that, whether a man buys his house ready built, or gets it built for him, in neither case will the mode of acquisition increase the amount of money laid out on the house.

Our capitalist, who is at home in his vulgar economy, exclaims: "Oh! but I advanced my money for the express purpose of making more money." The way to Hell is paved with good intentions, and he might just as easily have intended to make money, without producing at all.[5] He threatens all

[3] These figures are quite arbitrary.

[4] This is the fundamental proposition on which is based the doctrine ·of the Physiocrats as to the unproductiveness of all labour that is not agriculture: it is irrefutable for the orthodox economist.

[5] Thus from 1844–1847 he withdrew part of his capital from productive employment, in order to throw it away in railway speculations; and so also, during the American Civil

sorts of things. He won't be caught napping again. In future he will buy the commodities in the market, instead of manufacturing them himself. But if all his brother capitalists were to do the same, where would he find his commodities in the market? And his money he cannot eat. He tries persuasion. "Consider my abstinence; I might have played ducks and drakes with the 15 shillings; but instead of that I consumed it productively, and made yarn with it." Very well, and by way of reward he is now in possession of good yarn instead of a bad conscience; and as for playing the part of a miser, it would never do for him to relapse into such bad ways as that; we have seen before to what results such asceticism leads. Besides, where nothing is, the king has lost his rights: whatever may be the merit of his abstinence, there is nothing wherewith specially to remunerate it, because the value of the product is merely the sum of the values of the commodities that were thrown into the process of production. Let him therefore console himself with the reflection that virtue is its own reward. But no, he becomes importunate. He says: "The yarn is of no use to me: I produced it for sale." In that case let him sell it, or, still better, let him for the future produce only things for satisfying his personal wants, a remedy that his physician M'Culloch has already prescribed as infallible against an epidemic of over-production. He now gets obstinate. "Can the labourer," he asks, "merely with his arms and legs, produce commodities out of nothing? Did I not supply him with the materials, by means of which, and in which alone, his labour could be embodied? And as the greater part of society consists of such ne'er-do-weels, have I not rendered society incalculable service by my instruments of production, my cotton and my spindle, and not only society, but the labourer also, whom in addition I have provided with the necessaries of life? And am I to be allowed nothing in return for all this service?" Well, but has not the labourer rendered him the equivalent service of changing his cotton and spindle into yarn? Moreover, there is here no question of service.[6] A service is nothing more than the useful effect of a use-value, be it of a commodity, or be it

---

War, he closed his factory, and turned his work-people into the streets, in order to gamble on the Liverpool cotton exchange.

6 "Extol thyself, put on finery and adorn thyself . . . but whoever takes more or better than he gives, that is usury, and is not service, but wrong done to his neighbour, as when one steals and robs. All is not service and benefit to a neighbour that is called service and benefit. For an adulteress and adulterer do one another great service and pleasure. A horseman does an incendiary a great service, by helping him to rob on the highway, and pillage land and houses. The papists do ours a great service in that they don't drown, burn, murder all of them, or let them all rot in prison; but lest some live, and only drive them out, or take from them what they have. The devil himself does his servants inestimable service. . . . To sum up, the world is full of great, excellent, and daily service and benefit." Martin Luther, *An die Pfarherrn, wider den Wucher zu predigen*, Wittenberg, 1540.

of labour.[7] But here we are dealing with exchange-value. The capitalist paid to the labourer a value of 3 shillings, and the labourer gave him back an exact equivalent in the value of 3 shillings, added by him to the cotton: he gave him value for value. Our friend, up to this time so purse-proud, suddenly assumes the modest demeanour of his own workman, and exclaims: "Have I myself not worked? Have I not performed the labour of superintendence and of overlooking the spinner? And does not this labour, too, create value?" His overlooker and his manager try to hide their smiles. Meanwhile, after a hearty laugh, he re-assumes his usual mien. Though he chanted to us the whole creed of the economists, in reality, he says, he would not give a brass farthing for it. He leaves this and all such like subterfuges and juggling tricks to the professors of political economy, who are paid for it. He himself is a practical man; and though he does not always consider what he says outside his business, yet in his business he knows what he is about.

Let us examine the matter more closely. The value of a day's labour-power amounts to 3 shillings, because on our assumption half a day's labour is embodied in that quantity of labour-power, *i.e.*, because the means of subsistence that are daily required for the production of labour-power, cost half a day's labour. But the past labour that is embodied in the labour-power, and the living labour that it can call into action; the daily cost of maintaining it, and its daily expenditure in work, are two totally different things. The former determines the exchange-value of the labour-power, the latter is its use-value. The fact that half a day's labour is necessary to keep the labourer alive during 24 hours, does not in any way prevent him from working a whole day. Therefore, the value of labour-power, and the value which that labour-power creates in the labour process, are two entirely different magnitudes; and this difference of the two values was what the capitalist had in view, when he was purchasing the labour-power. The useful qualities that labour-power possesses, and by virtue of which it makes yarn or boots, were to him nothing more than a conditio sine qua non; for in order to create value, labour must be expended in a useful manner. What really influenced him was the specific use-value which this commodity possesses of being *a source not only of value, but of more value than it has itself.* This is the special service that the capitalist expects from labour-power, and in this transaction he acts in accordance with the "eternal laws" of the exchange of commodities. The seller of labour-power, like the seller of any other commodity, realises its exchange-value, and parts with its use-value. He cannot take the one without giving the other. The use-value of labour-power, or in other words, labour, belongs just as little to its seller, as the use-value of oil after it has been sold belongs to the dealer who has

[7] In *Critique of Political Economy*, p. 34, I make the following remark on this point— "It is not difficult to understand what 'service' the category 'service' must render to a class of economists like J. B. Say and F. Bastiat."

sold it. The owner of the money has paid the value of a day's labour-power; his, therefore, is the use of it for a day; a day's labour belongs to him. The circumstance, that on the one hand the daily sustenance of labour-power costs only half a day's labour, while on the other hand the very same labour-power can work during a whole day, that consequently the value which its use during one day creates, is double what he pays for that use, this circumstance is, without doubt, a piece of good luck for the buyer, but by no means an injury to the seller.

· · ·

Chapter 8: CONSTANT CAPITAL AND VARIABLE CAPITAL

The various factors of the labour-process play different parts in forming the value of the product.

The labourer adds fresh value to the subject of his labour by expending upon it a given amount of additional labour, no matter what the specific character and utility of that labour may be. On the other hand, the values of the means of production used up in the process are preserved, and present themselves afresh as constituent parts of the value of the product; the values of the cotton and the spindle, for instance, reappear again in the value of the yarn. The value of the means of production is therefore preserved, by being transferred to the product. This transfer takes place during the conversion of those means into a product, or in other words, during the labour-process. It is brought about by labour; but how?

The labourer does not perform two operations at once, one in order to add value to the cotton, the other in order to preserve the value of the means of production, or, in what amounts to the same thing, to transfer to the yarn, to the product, the value of the cotton on which he works, and part of the value of the spindle with which he works. But, by the very act of adding new value, he preserves their former values. Since, however, the addition of new value to the subject of his labour, and the preservation of its former value, are two entirely distinct results, produced simultaneously by the labourer, during one operation, it is plain that this twofold nature of the result can be explained only by the twofold nature of his labour; at one and the same time, it must in one character create value, and in another character preserve or transfer value.

Now, in what manner does every labourer add new labour and consequently new value? Evidently, only by labouring productively in a particular way; the spinner by spinning, the weaver by weaving, the smith by forging. But, while thus incorporating labour generally, that is value, it is by the particular form alone of the labour, by the spinning, the weaving and the forging respectively, that the means of production, the cotton and spindle, the yarn and loom, and the iron and anvil become constituent elements of the product, of a new use-value.[1] Each use-value disappears, but only to re-appear under a new form in a new use-value. Now, we saw, when we were considering the process of creating value, that, if a use-value be effectively consumed in the production of a new use-value, the quantity of labour expended in the production of the consumed article, forms a portion of the quantity of labour necessary to produce the new use-value; this portion is therefore labour transferred from the means of production to the new product. Hence, the labourer preserves the values of the consumed means of production, or transfers them as portions of its value to the product, not by virtue of his additional labour, abstractedly considered, but by virtue of the particular useful character of that labour, by virtue of its special productive form. In so far then as labour is such specific productive activity, in so far as it is spinning, weaving, or forging, it raises, by mere contact, the means of production from the dead, makes them living factors of the labour-process, and combines with them to form the new products.

If the special productive labour of the workman were not spinning, he could not convert the cotton into yarn, and therefore could not transfer the values of the cotton and spindle to the yarn. Suppose the same workman were to change his occupation to that of a joiner, he would still by a day's labour add value to the material he works upon. Consequently, we see, first, that the addition of new value takes place not by virtue of his labour being spinning in particular, or joinering in particular, but because it is labour in the abstract, a portion of the total labour of society; and we see next, that the value added is of a given definite amount, not because his labour has a special utility, but because it is exerted for a definite time. On the one hand, then, it is by virtue of its general character, as being expenditure of human labour-power in the abstract, that spinning adds new value to the values of the cotton and the spindle; and on the other hand, it is by virtue of its special character, as being a concrete, useful process, that the same labour of spinning both transfers the values of the means of production to the product, and preserves them in the product. Hence at one and the same time there is produced a twofold result.

By the simple addition of a certain quantity of labour, new value is added, and by the quality of this added labour, the original values of the means of production are preserved in the product. This twofold effect, resulting from the twofold character of labour, may be traced in various phenomena.

Let us assume, that some invention enables the spinner to spin as much cotton in 6 hours as he was able to spin before in 36 hours. His labour is now six times as effective as it was, for the purposes of useful production. The

[1] "Labour gives a new creation for one extinguished." *An Essay on the Political Economy of Nations*, London, 1821, p. 13.

product of 6 hours' work has increased sixfold, from 6 lbs. to 36 lbs. But now the 36 lbs. of cotton absorb only the same amount of labour as formerly did the 6 lbs. One-sixth as much new labour is absorbed by each pound of cotton, and consequently, the value added by the labour to each pound is only one-sixth of what it formerly was. On the other hand, in the product, in the 36 lbs. of yarn, the value transferred from the cotton is six times as great as before. By the 6 hours' spinning, the value of the raw material preserved and transferred to the product is six times as great as before, although the new value added by the labour of the spinner to each pound of the very same raw material is one-sixth what it was formerly. This shows that the two properties of labour, by virtue of which it is enabled in one case to preserve value, and in the other to create value, are essentially different. On the one hand, the longer the time necessary to spin a given weight of cotton into yarn, the greater is the new value added to the material; on the other hand, the greater the weight of the cotton spun in a given time, the greater is the value preserved, by being transferred from it to the product.

Let us now assume, that the productiveness of the spinner's labour, instead of varying, remains constant, that he therefore requires the same time as he formerly did, to convert one pound of cotton into yarn, but that the exchange value of the cotton varies, either by rising to six times its former value or falling to one-sixth of that value. In both these cases, the spinner puts the same quantity of labour into a pound of cotton, and therefore adds as much value, as he did before the change in the value: he also produces a given weight of yarn in the same time as he did before. Nevertheless, the value that he transfers from the cotton to the yarn is either one-sixth of what it was before the variation, or, as the case may be, six times as much as before. The same result occurs when the value of the instruments of labour rises or falls, while their useful efficacy in the process remains unaltered.

Again, if the technical conditions of the spinning process remain unchanged, and no change of value takes place in the means of production, the spinner continues to consume in equal working-time equal quantities of raw material, and equal quantities of machinery of unvarying value. The value that he preserves in the product is directly proportional to the new value that he adds to the product. In two weeks he incorporates twice as much labour, and therefore twice as much value, as in one week, and during the same time he consumes twice as much material, and wears out twice as much machinery, of double the value in each case; he therefore preserves, in the product of two weeks, twice as much value as in the product of one week. So long as the conditions of production remain the same, the more value the labourer adds by fresh labour, the more value he transfers and preserves; but he does so merely because this addition of new value takes place under conditions that have not varied and are independent of his own labour. Of course, it may be said in one sense, that the labourer preserves old value always in proportion to the quantity of new value that he adds. Whether the value of cotton rise from one shilling to two shillings, or fall to sixpence, the workman invariably preserves in the product of one hour only one half as much value as he preserves in two hours. In like manner, if the productiveness of his own labour varies by rising or falling, he will in one hour spin either more or less cotton, as the case may be, than he did before, and will consequently preserve in the product of one hour, more or less value of cotton; but, all the same, he will preserve by two hours' labour twice as much value as he will by one.

Value exists only in articles of utility, in objects: we leave out of consideration its purely symbolical representation by tokens. (Man himself, viewed as the impersonation of labour-power, is a natural object, a thing, although a living conscious thing, and labour is the manifestation of this power residing in him.) If therefore an article loses its utility, it also loses its value. The reason why means of production do not lose their value, at the same time that they lose their use-value, is this: they lose in the labour-process the original form of their use-value, only to assume in the product the form of a new use-value. But, however important it may be to value, that it should have some object of utility to embody itself in, yet it is a matter of complete indifference what particular object serves this purpose; this we saw when treating of the metamorphosis of commodities. Hence it follows that in the labour-process the means of production transfer their value to the product only so far as along with their use-value they lose also their exchange value. They give up to the product that value alone which they themselves lose as means of production. But in this respect the material factors of the labour-process do not all behave alike.

The coal burnt under the boiler vanishes without leaving a trace; so, too, the tallow with which the axles of wheels are greased. Dye stuffs and other auxiliary substances also vanish but re-appear as properties of the product. Raw material forms the substance of the product, but only after it has changed its form. Hence raw material and auxiliary substances lose the characteristic form with which they are clothed on entering the labour-process. It is otherwise with the instruments of labour. Tools, machines, workshops, and vessels, are of use in the labour-process, only so long as they retain their original shape, and are ready each morning to renew the process with their shape unchanged. And just as during their lifetime, that is to say, during the continued labour-process in which they serve, they retain their shape independent of the product, so, too, they do after their death. The corpses of machines, tools, workshops, &c., are always separate and distinct from the product they helped to turn out. If we now consider the case of any instrument of labour during the whole period of its service, from the day of its entry into the workshop, till the day of its banishment into the lumber room, we find that during this period its use-value has been completely consumed, and therefore its exchange value completely transferred to the product. For instance, if a spinning machine lasts for 10 years, it is plain that during that working period its total value is gradually transferred to the product of the 10 years. The lifetime of an instrument of labour, therefore, is spent in the repetition of a greater or less number of similar operations. Its life may be compared with that of a human being. Every day brings a man 24 hours nearer to his grave: but how many days he has still to travel on that road, no man can tell accurately by merely looking at him. This difficulty, however, does not prevent life insurance offices from drawing, by means of the theory of averages, very accurate, and at the same time very profitable conclusions. So it is with the instruments of labour. It is known by experience how long on the average a machine of a particular kind will last. Suppose its use-value in the labour-process to last only six days. Then, on the average, it loses each day one-sixth of its use-value, and therefore parts with one-sixth of its value to the daily product. The wear and tear of all instruments, their daily loss of use-value, and the corresponding quantity of value they part with to the product, are accordingly calculated upon this basis.

It is thus strikingly clear, that means of production never transfer more value to the product than they themselves lose during the labour-process by the destruction of their own use-value. If such an instrument has no value to lose, if, in other words, it is not the product of human labour, it transfers no value to the product. It helps to create use-value without contributing to the formation of exchange value. In this class are included all means of production supplied by Nature without human assistance, such as land, wind, water, metals in situ, and timber in virgin forests.

Yet another interesting phenomenon here presents itself. Suppose a machine to be worth £1000, and to wear out in 1000 days. Then one thousandth part of the value of the machine is daily transferred to the day's product. At the same time, though with diminishing vitality, the machine as a whole continues to take part in the labour-process. Thus it appears that one factor of the labour-process, a means of production, continually enters as a whole into that process, while it enters into the process of the formation of value by fractions only. The difference between the two processes is here reflected in their material factors, by the same instrument of production taking part as a whole in the labour-process, while at the same time as an element in the formation of value, it enters only by fractions.

. . .

We have seen that the means of production transfer value to the new product, so far only as during the labour-process they lose value in the shape of their old use-value. The maximum loss of value that they can suffer in the process, is plainly limited by the amount of the original value with which they came into the process, or in other words, by the labour-time necessary for their production. Therefore the means of production can never add more value to the product than they themselves possess independently of the process in which they assist. However ueseful a given kind of raw material, or a machine, or other means of production may be, though it may cost £150, or, say, 500 days' labour, yet it cannot, under any circumstances, add to the value of the product more than £150. Its value is determined not by the labour-process into which it enters as a means of production, but by that out of which it has issued as a product. In the labour-process it only serves as a mere use-value, a thing with useful properties and could not, therefore, transfer any value to the product, unless it possessed such value previously.[2]

While productive labour is changing the means of production into constituent elements of a new product, their value undergoes a metempsychosis. It deserts the consumed body, to occupy the newly created one. But this transmigration takes place, as it were, behind the back of the labourer. He is unable to add new labour, to create new value, without at the same time preserving old values, and this, because the labour he adds must be of a specific useful kind; and he cannot do work of a useful kind, without employing products as the means of production of a new product, and thereby transferring their value to the new product. The property therefore which labour-power in action, living labour, possesses of preserving value, at the same time that it adds it, is a gift of Nature which costs the labourer nothing, but which is very advantageous to the capitalist inasmuch as it preserves the existing value of his capital.[3] So long as trade is good, the

---

[2] From this we may judge of the absurdity of J. B. Say, who pretends to account for surplus-value (Interest, Profit, Rent), by the "services productifs" which the means of production, soil, instruments, and raw material, render in the labour-process by means of their use-values. Mr. Wm. Roscher who seldom loses an occasion of registering, in black and white, ingenious apologetic fancies, records the following specimen:—"J. B. Say (Treatise, t. 1. Chap. 4) very truly remarks: the value produced by an oil mill, after deduction of all costs, is something new, something quite different from the labour by which the oil mill itself was erected." (l. c., p. 82, note.) Very true, Mr. Professor! the oil produced by the oil mill is indeed something very different from the labour expended in constructing the mill! By value, Mr. Roscher understands such stuff as "oil," because oil has value, notwithstanding that "Nature" produces petroleum, though relatively "in small quantities," a fact to which he seems to refer in his further observation: "It (Nature) produces scarcely any exchange value." Mr. Roscher's "Nature" and the exchange value it produces are rather like the foolish virgin who admitted indeed that she had had a child, but "it was such a little one." This "savant sérieux" in continuation remarks: "Ricardo's school is in the habit of including capital as accumulated labour under the head of labour. This is unskilful work, because, indeed, the owner of capital, after all, does something more than the merely creating and preserving of the same: namely, the abstention from the enjoyment of it, for which he demands, e.g., interest." (l. c.) How very "skilful" is this "anatomico-physiological method" of political economy, which, "indeed," converts a mere desire "after all" into a source of value.

[3] "Of all the instruments of the farmers' trade, the labour of man . . . is that on which he is most to rely for the repayment of his capital. The other two . . . the working stock of the cattle and the . . . carts, ploughs, spades, and so forth, without a given portion of

capitalist is too much absorbed in money-grubbing to take notice of this gratuitous gift of labour. A violent interruption of the labour-process by a crisis, makes him sensitively aware of it.[4]

As regards the means of production, what is really consumed is their use-value, and the consumption of this use-value by labour results in the product. There is no consumption of their value,[5] and it would therefore be inaccurate to say that it is reproduced. It is rather preserved; not by reason of any operation it undergoes itself in the process; but because the article in which it originally exists, vanishes, it is true, but vanishes into some other article. Hence, in the value of the product, there is a re-appearance of the value of the means of production, but there is, strictly speaking, no reproduction of that value. That which is produced is a new use-value in which the old exchange-value re-appears.[6]

It is otherwise with the subjective factor of the labour-process, with labour-power in action. While the labourer, by virtue of his labour being of a specialised kind that has a special object, preserves and transfers to the product the value of the means of production, he at the same time, by the mere act of working, creates each instant an additional or new value. Sup-

---

the first, are nothing at all." Edmund Burke, *Thoughts and Details on Scarcity, originally presented to the Right Hon. W. Pitt, in the month of November 1795*, edit. London, 1800, p. 10.

[4] In "The Times" of 26th November, 1862, a manufacturer, whose mill employed 800 hands, and consumed, on the average, 150 bales of East Indian, or 130 bales of American cotton, complains, in doleful manner, of the standing expenses of his factory when not working. He estimates them at £6,000 a year. Among them are a number of items that do not concern us here, such as rent, rates, and taxes, insurance, salaries of the manager, book-keeper, engineer, and others. Then he reckons £150 for coal used to heat the mill occasionally, and run the engine now and then. Besides this, he includes the wages of the people employed at odd times to keep the machinery in working order. Lastly, he puts down £1,200 for depreciation of machinery, because "the weather and the natural principle of decay do not suspend their operations because the steam-engine ceases to revolve." He says, emphatically, he does not estimate his depreciation at more than the small sum of £1,200, because his machinery is already nearly worn out.

[5] "Productive consumption . . . where the consumption of a commodity is a part of the process of production. . . . In these instances there is no consumption of value." S. P. Newman.

[6] In an American compendium that has gone through, perhaps, 20 editions, this passage occurs: "It matters not in what form capital re-appears"; then after a lengthy enumeration of all the possible ingredients of production whose value re-appears in the product, the passage concludes thus: "The various kinds of food, clothing, and shelter, necessary for the existence and comfort of the human being, are also changed. They are consumed from time to time, and their value re-appears in that new vigour imparted to his body and mind, forming fresh capital, to be employed again in the work of production." F. Wayland. Without noticing any other oddities, it suffices to observe, that what re-appears in the fresh vigour, is not the bread's price, but its blood-forming substances. What, on the other hand, re-appears in the value of that vigour, is not the means of subsistence, but their value. The same necessaries of life, at half the price, would form just as much muscle and bone, just as much vigour, but not vigour of the same value. This confusion of "value" and "vigour" coupled with our author's pharisaical indefiniteness, mark an attempt, futile for all that, to thrash out an explanation of surplus-value from a mere re-appearance of pre-existing values.

pose the process of production to be stopped just when the workman has produced an equivalent for the value of his own labour-power, when, for example, by six hours' labour, he has added a value of three shillings. This value is the surplus, of the total value of the product, over the portion of its value that is due to the means of production. It is the only original bit of value formed during this process, the only portion of the value of the product created by this process. Of course, we do not forget that this new value only replaces the money advanced by the capitalist in the purchase of the labour-power, and spent by the labourer on the necessaries of life. With regard to the money spent, the new value is merely a reproduction; but, nevertheless, it is an actual, and not, as in the case of the value of the means of production, only an apparent, reproduction. The substitution of one value for another, is here effected by the creation of new value.

We know, however, from what has gone before, that the labour-process may continue beyond the time necessary to reproduce and incorporate in the product a mere equivalent for the value of the labour-power. Instead of the six hours that are sufficient for the latter purpose, the process may continue for twelve hours. The action of labour-power, therefore, not only reproduces its own value, but produces value over and above it. This surplus-value is the difference between the value of the product and the value of the elements consumed in the formation of that product, in other words, of the means of production and the labour-power.

By our explanation of the different parts played by the various factors of the labour-process in the formation of the product's value, we have, in fact, disclosed the characters of the different functions allotted to the different elements of capital in the process of expanding its own value. The surplus of the total value of the product, over the sum of the values of its constituent factors, is the surplus of the expanded capital over the capital originally advanced. The means of production on the one hand, labour-power on the other, are merely the different modes of existence which the value of the original capital assumed when from being money it was transformed into the various factors of the labour-process. That part of capital then, which is represented by the means of production, by the raw material, auxiliary material and the instruments of labour, does not, in the process of production, undergo any quantitative alteration of value. I therefore call it the constant part of capital, or, more shortly, *constant capital*.

On the other hand, that part of capital, represented by labour-power, does, in the process of production, undergo an alteration of value. It both reproduces the equivalent of its own value, and also produces an excess, a surplus-value, which may itself vary, may be more or less according to circumstances. This part of capital is continually being transformed from a constant into a variable magnitude. I therefore call it the variable part of capital, or, shortly, *variable capital*. The same elements of capital which, from the point of view of the labour-process, present themselves respectively as the objective and subjective factors, as means of production and labour-power, present themselves, from the point of view of the process of creating surplus-value, as the constant and variable capital.

. . .

Chapter 9: THE RATE OF SURPLUS-VALUE

§ Section 1. The Degree of Exploitation of Labour-Power

The surplus-value generated in the process of production by C, the capital advanced, or in other words, the self-expansion of the value of the capital C, presents itself for our consideration, in the first place, as a surplus, as the amount by which the value of the product exceeds the value of its constituent element.

The capital C is made up of two components, one, the sum of money c laid out upon the means of production, and the other, the sum of money v expended upon the labour-power; c represents the portion that has become constant capital, and v the portion that has become variable capital. At first then, C = c + v: for example, if £500 is the capital advanced, its components may be such that the £500 = £410 const. + £90 var. When the process of production is finished, we get a commodity whose value = (c + v) + s, where s is the surplus-value; or taking our former figures, the value of this commodity may be (£410 const. + £90 var.) + £90 surpl. The original capital has now changed from C to C', from £500 to £590. The difference is s or a surplus value of £90. Since the value of the constituent elements of the product is equal to the value of the advanced capital, it is mere tautology to say, that the excess of the value of the product over the value of its constituent elements, is equal to the expansion of the capital advanced or to the surplus-value produced.

Nevertheless, we must examine this tautology a little more closely. The two things compared are, the value of the product, and the value of its constituents consumed in the process of production. Now we have seen how that portion of the constant capital which consists of the instruments of labour, transfers to the product only a fraction of its value, while the remainder of that value continues to reside in those instruments. Since this remainder plays no part in the formation of value, we may at present leave it on one side. To introduce it into the calculation would make no difference. For instance, taking our former example, c = £410: suppose this sum to consist of £312 value of raw material, £44 value of auxiliary material, and £54 value of the machinery worn away in the process; and suppose that the total value of the machinery employed is £1,054. Out of this latter sum, then, we reckon as advanced for the purpose of turning out the product, the sum of £54 alone, which the machinery loses by wear and tear in the process; for this is all it parts with to the product. Now if we also reckon the remaining £1,000, which still continues in the machinery, as transferred to the product, we ought also to reckon it as part of the value advanced, and thus make it appear on both sides of our calculation.[1] We should, in this way, get £1,500 on one side and £1,590 on the other. The difference of these two sums, or the surplus-value, would still be £90. Throughout this Book therefore, by constant capital advanced for the production of value, we always mean, unless the context is repugnant thereto, the value of the means of production actually consumed in the process, and that value alone.

This being so, let us return to the formula $C = c + v$, which we saw transformed into $C' = (c + v) + s$, C becoming C'. We know that the value of the constant capital is transferred to, and merely re-appears in the product. The new value actually created in the process, the value produced, or value-product, is therefore not the same as the value of the product; it is not, as it would at first sight appear $(c + v) + s$ or £410 const. + £90 var. + £90 surpl.; but $v + s$ or £90 var.+ £90 surpl. not £590 but £180. If $c = 0$, or in other words, if there were branches of industry in which the capitalist could dispense with all means of production made by previous labour, whether they be raw material, auxiliary material, or instruments of labour, employing only labour-power and materials supplied by Nature, in that case, there would be no constant capital to transfer to the product. This component of the value of the product, i.e., the £410 in our example, would be eliminated, but the sum of £180, the amount of new value created, or the value produced, which contains £90 of surplus-value, would remain just as great as if c represented the highest value imaginable. We should have $C = (0 + v) = v$ or C' the expanded capital $= v + s$ and therefore $C' - C = s$ as before. On the other hand, if $s = 0$, or in other words, if the labour-power, whose value is advanced in the form of variable capital, were to produce only its equivalent, we should have $C = c + v$ or C' the value of the product $= (c + v) + 0$ or $C = C'$. The capital advanced would, in this case, not have expanded its value.

From what has gone before, we know that surplus-value is purely the result of a variation in the value of v, of that portion of the capital which is transformed into labour-power; consequently, $v + s = v + v'$ or v plus an increment of v. But the fact that it is v alone that varies, and the conditions of that variation, are obscured by the circumstance that in consequence of the increase in the variable component of the capital, there is also an increase in the sum total of the advanced capital. It was originally

1 "If we reckon the value of the fixed capital employed as a part of the advances, we must reckon the remaining value of such capital at the end of the year as a part of the annual returns." Malthus, *Principles of Political Economy*, 2nd ed., London, 1836, p. 269.

£500 and becomes £590. Thereupon in order that our investigation may lead to accurate results, we must make abstraction from that portion of the value of the product, in which constant capital alone appears, and consequently must equate the constant capital to zero or make c = o. This is merely an application of a mathematical rule, employed whenever we operate with constant and variable magnitudes, related to each other by the symbols of addition and subtraction only.

A further difficulty is caused by the original form of the variable capital. In our example, C′ = £410 const. + £90 var. + £90 surpl.; but £90 is a given and therefore a constant quantity; hence it appears absurd to treat it as variable. But in fact, the term £90 var. is here merely a symbol to show that this value undergoes a process. The portion of the capital invested in the purchase of labour-power is a definite quantity of materialised labour, a constant value like the value of the labour-power purchased. But in the process of production the place of the £90 is taken by the labour-power in action, dead labour is replaced by living labour, something stagnant by something flowing, a constant by a variable. The result is the reproduction of v plus an increment of v. From the point of view, then, of capitalist production, the whole process appears as the spontaneous variation of the originally constant value, which is transformed into labour-power. Both the process and its result, appear to be owing to this value. If, therefore, such expressions as "£90 variable capital," or "so much self-expanding value," appear contradictory, this is only because they bring to the surface a contradiction immanent in capitalist production.

At first sight it appears a strange proceeding, to equate the constant capital to zero. Yet it is what we do every day. If, for example, we wish to calculate the amount of England's profits from the cotton industry, we first of all deduct the sums paid for cotton to the United States, India, Egypt and other countries; in other words, the value of the capital that merely re-appears in the value of the product, is put = o.

Of course the ratio of surplus-value not only to that portion of the capital from which it immediately springs, and whose change of value it represents, but also to the sum total of the capital advanced is economically of very great importance. We shall, therefore, in the third book, treat of this ratio exhaustively. In order to enable one portion of a capital to expand its value by being converted into labour-power, it is necessary that another portion be converted into means of production. In order that variable capital may perform its function, constant capital must be advanced in proper proportion, a proportion given by the special technical conditions of each labour-process. The circumstances, however, that retorts and other vessels, are necessary to a chemical process, does not compel the chemist to notice them in the result of his analysis. If we look at the means of production, in their relation to the creation of value, and to the variation in the quantity of value, apart from anything else, they appear simply as the material in which labour-power, the value-creator, incorporates itself. Neither the nature, nor the value of this material is of any importance. The only requisite is that there be a sufficient supply to absorb the labour expended in the process of production. That supply once given, the material may rise or fall in value, or even be, as land and the sea, without any value in itself; but this will have no influence on the creation of value or on the variation in the quantity of value.[2]

In the first place then we equate the constant capital to zero. The capital advanced is consequently reduced from c + v to v, and instead of the value of the product (c + v) + s we have now the value produced (v + s). Given the new value produced = £180, which sum consequently represents the whole labour expended during the process, then subtracting from it £90, the value of the variable capital, we have remaining £90, the amount of the surplus-value. This sum of £90 or s expresses the absolute quantity of surplus-value produced. The relative quantity produced, or the increase per cent of the variable capital, is determined, it is plain, by the ratio of the surplus-value to the variable capital, or is expressed by s/v. In our example this ratio is $\frac{90}{90}$, which gives an increase of 100%. This relative increase in the value of the variable capital, or the relative magnitude of the surplus-value, I call, "The rate of surplus-value."[3]

We have seen that the labourer, during one portion of the labour-process, produces only the value of his labour-power, that is, the value of his means of subsistence. Now since his work forms part of a system, based on the social division of labour, he does not directly produce the actual necessaries which he himself consumes; he produces instead a particular commodity, yarn for example, whose value is equal to the value of those necessaries or of the money with which they can be bought. The portion of his day's labour devoted to this purpose, will be greater or less, in proportion to the value of the necessaries that he daily requires on an average, or, what amounts to the same thing, in proportion to the labour-time required on an average to produce them. If the value of those necessaries represents on an average the expenditure of six hours' labour, the workman must on an average work for six hours to produce that value. If instead of working for the capitalist, he worked independently on his own account, he would, other things being equal, still be obliged to labour for the same number of hours, in order to produce the value of his labour-power, and thereby to gain the means of subsistence necessary for his conservation or continued reproduction. But as we have seen, during that portion of his day's labour

---

[2] What Lucretius says is self-evident; "nil posse creari de nihilo," out of nothing, nothing can be created. Creation of value is transformation of labour-power into labour. Labour-power itself is energy transferred to a human organism by means of nourishing matter.

[3] In the same way that the English use the terms "rate of profit," "rate of interest." The rate of profit is no mystery, so soon as we know the laws of surplus-value. If we reverse the process, we cannot comprehend either the one or the other.

in which he produces the value of his labour-power, say three shillings, he produces only an equivalent for the value of his labour-power already advanced by the capitalist; the new value created only replaces the variable capital advanced. It is owing to this fact, that the production of the new value of three shillings takes the semblance of a mere reproduction. That portion of the working day, then, during which this reproduction takes place, I call "*necessary*" labour-time, and the labour expended during that time I call "*necessary*" labour.[4] Necessary, as regards the labourer, because independent of the particular social form of his labour; necessary, as regards capital, and the world of capitalists, because on the continued existence of the labourer depends their existence also.

During the second period of the labour-process, that in which his labour is no longer necessary labour, the workman, it is true, labours, expends labour-power; but his labour, being no longer necessary labour, he creates no value for himself. He creates surplus-value which, for the capitalist, has all the charms of a creation out of nothing. This portion of the working day, I name surplus labour-time, and to the labour expended during that time, I give the name of surplus-labour. It is every bit as important, for a correct understanding of surplus-value, to conceive it as a mere congelation of surplus-labour-time, as nothing but materialised surplus-labour, as it is, for a proper comprehension of value, to conceive it as a mere congelation of so many hours of labour, as nothing but materialised labour. The essential difference between the various economic forms of society, between, for instance, a society based on slave labour, and one based on wage labour, lies only in the mode in which this surplus-labour is in each case extracted from the actual producer, the labourer.[5]

Since, on the one hand, the values of the variable capital and of the labour-power purchased by that capital are equal, and the value of this labour-power determines the necessary portion of the working day; and since, on the other hand, the surplus-value is determined by the surplus portion of the working day, it follows that surplus-value bears the same

---

[4] In this work, we have, up to now, employed the term "necessary labour-time," to designate the time necessary under given social conditions for the production of any commodity. Henceforward we use it to designate also the time necessary for the production of the particular commodity labour-power. The use of one and the same technical term in different senses is inconvenient, but in no science can it be altogether avoided. Compare, for instance, the higher with the lower branches of mathematics.

[5] Herr Wilhelm Thucydides Roscher has found a mare's nest. He has made the important discovery that if, on the one hand, the formation of surplus-value, or surplus-produce, and the consequent accumulation of capital, is now-a-days due to the thrift of the capitalist, on the other hand, in the lowest stages of civilisation it is the strong who compel the weak to economise (l. c. p. 78). To economise what? Labour? Or superfluous wealth that does not exist? What is it that makes such men as Roscher account for the origin of surplus-value, by a mere rechauffé of the more or less plausible excuses by the capitalist, for his appropriation of surplus-value? It is, besides their real ignorance, their apologetic dread of a scientific analysis of value and surplus-value, and of obtaining a result, possibly not altogether palatable to the powers that be.

ratio to variable capital, that surplus-labour does to necessary labour, or in other words, the rate of surplus-value $s/v =$ surplus labor/necessary labor. Both ratios, s/v and surplus labor/necessary labor express the same thing in different ways; in the one case by reference to materialised, incorporated labour, in the other by reference to living, fluent labour.

The rate of surplus-value is therefore an exact expression for the degree of exploitation of labour-power by capital, or of the labourer by the capitalist.[6]

We assumed in our example, that the value of the product = £410 const. + £90 var. + £90 surpl., and that the capital advanced = £500. Since the surplus-value = £90, and the advanced capital = £500, we should, according to the usual way of reckoning, get as the rate of surplus-value (generally confounded with rate of profits) 18%, a rate so low as possibly to cause a pleasant surprise to Mr. Carey and other harmonisers. But in truth, the rate of surplus-value is not equal to s/C or $s/c + v$ but to s/v: thus it is not $90/500$ but $90/90$ or 100%, which is more than five times the apparent degree of exploitation. Although, in the case we have supposed, we are ignorant of the actual length of the working day, and of the duration in days or weeks of the labour-process, as also of the number of labourers employed, yet the rate of surplus-value s/v accurately discloses to us, by means of its equivalent expression, surplus labor/necessary labor, the relation between the two parts of the working day. This relation is here one of equality, the rate being 100%. Hence, it is plain, the labourer, in our example, works one half of the day for himself, the other half for the capitalist.

The method of calculating the rate of surplus-value is therefore, shortly, as follows. We take the total value of the product and put the constant capital which merely re-appears in it, equal to zero. What remains, is the only value that has, in the process of producing the commodity, been actually created. If the amount of surplus-value be given, we have only to deduct it from this remainder, to find the variable capital. And *vice versa*, if the latter be given, and we require to find the surplus-value. If both be given, we have only to perform the concluding operation, viz., to calculate s/v, the ratio of the surplus-value to the variable capital.

Though the method is so simple, yet it may not be amiss, by means of a few examples, to exercise the reader in the application of the novel principles underlying it.

First we will take the case of a spinning mill containing 10,000 mule spindles, spinning No. 32 yarn from American cotton, and producing 1 lb.

---

[6] Although the rate of surplus-value is an exact expression for the degree of exploitation of labour-power, it is, in no sense, an expression for the absolute amount of exploitation. For example, if the necessary labour = 5 hours and the surplus-labour = 5 hours, the degree of exploitation is 100%. The amount of exploitation is here measured by 5 hours. If, on the other hand, the necessary labour = 6 hours and the surplus-labour = 6 hours, the degree of exploitation remains, as before, 100%, while the actual amount of exploitation has increased 20%, namely from five hours to six.

of yarn weekly per spindle. We assume the waste to be 6%: under these circumstances 10,600 lbs. of cotton are consumed weekly, of which 600 lbs. go to waste. The price of the cotton in April, 1871, was 7¾d. per lb.; the raw material therefore costs in round numbers £342. The 10,000 spindles, including preparation-machinery, and motive power, cost, we will assume, £1 per spindle, amounting to a total of £10,000. The wear and tear we put at 10%, or £1000 yearly = £20 weekly. The rent of the building we suppose to be £300 a year or £6 a week. Coal consumed (for 100 horse-power indicated, at 4 lbs. of coal per horse-power per hour during 60 hours, and inclusive of that consumed in heating the mill), 11 tons a week at 8s. 6d. a ton, amounts to about £4½ a week: gas, £1 a week, oil, &c., £4½ a week. Total cost of the above auxiliary materials, £10 weekly. Therefore the constant portion of the value of the week's product is £378. Wages amount to £52 a week. The price of the yarn is 12¼d. per lb., which gives for the value of 10,000 lbs. the sum of £510. The surplus-value is therefore in this case £510 − £430 = £80. We put the constant part of the value of the product = 0, as it plays no part in the creation of value. There remains £132 as the weekly value created, which = £52 var. + £80 surpl. The rate of surplus-value is therefore $^{80}/_{52}$ = 153$^{11}/_{13}$%. In a working day of 10 hours with average labour the result is: necessary labour = 3$^{31}/_{33}$ hours and surplus-labour = 6$^{2}/_{33}$.[7] . . .

[7] The above data, which may be relied upon, were given me by a Manchester spinster. In England the horse-power of an engine was formerly calculated from the diameter of its cylinder, now the actual horse-power shown by the indicator is taken.

WILLIAM STANLEY JEVONS

(1 8 3 5 – 1 8 8 1)

In terms of the Classical School of English economic thought, Jevons was even more of a maverick than Marx. Whereas Marx found it possible to agree with many of the Classical tenets and to rest his case against capitalism on many of the same grounds upon which the earlier writers had founded their case, Jevons found himself in basic disagreement with the Classical version of a cost of production theory of value. It was while in Australia, where he was working because of straitened family finances, that Jevons worked out a major part of his theory of value—a discovery which left him with a deep distaste for all of the earlier theories.

Jevons' theory of marginal utility, which is found in the passages that follow, needs no further comment here save to mention that Jevons was aware of and treated many of the exceptions and qualifications that critics of marginal utility were later to present. We should note, however, the development of the same idea elsewhere in the world and the early reception it received in England. The concept of utility had not been completely neglected by earlier economists, but little or no stress had been placed on the role of marginality. After years of neglect, the idea suddenly was brought forth virtually simultaneously by three economists working in three different countries and unaware of each other's existence. One of these was Jevons; the other two were equally distinguished—Karl Menger, founder of the Austrian School, and Leon Walras, a Frenchman, who was one of the pioneers in mathematical economics. The approach to the question of marginality was somewhat different in each instance. Menger's analysis was devoid of all mathematical trimmings, while Walras' book was difficult reading even for those readers well versed in mathematics. Jevons' approach was also somewhat mathematical, but not unreasonably so, even for the uninitiated. Some of the more complicated mathematical passages have been omitted from the following selection.

Of the three, only Menger was accorded full recognition by his contemporaries. Jevons, who had won early notoriety by his application of the Malthusian Law of Population to the question of coal, found a deaf ear turned toward his views on value and was forced to subsidize the publication of much of his early writing. Jevons' attempts to gain a hearing in England were frustrated at every turn by the general acceptance of John Stuart Mill's brand of economics. For much of his life, Jevons remained a lonely and introspective man who never attained membership in the inner circles of economics scholars in England. He was a poor teacher—partly because he regarded teaching as a distasteful chore and partly because he was reluctant to teach his own ideas, but taught instead the theories of those earlier economists which were so little to his liking. As a result, he never developed a band of student followers to help propagate his ideas.

Although contemporary English economists never accorded Jevons full recognition for the originality of his value theory during his lifetime, he nevertheless preserved England's reputation for originality in economic thought. With Walras and Menger, he shares credit for founding the marginal utility approach to the question of value. An accident while swimming precluded Jevons from living to see the full fruits of his contribution.

THE THEORY OF
POLITICAL ECONOMY

Chapter 3: THEORY OF UTILITY

§ Definition of Terms

Pleasure and pain are undoubtedly the ultimate objects of the Calculus of Economy. To satisfy our wants to the utmost with the least effort—to procure the greatest amount of what is desirable at the expense of the least that is undesirable—in other words, to maximise comfort and pleasure, is the problem of Economy. But it is convenient to transfer our attention as soon as possible to the physical objects or actions which are the source to us of pleasures or pains. A very large part of the labour of any community is spent upon the production of the ordinary necessaries and conveniences of life, food, clothing, buildings, utensils, furniture, ornaments, &c.; and the aggregate of these objects constitute, therefore, the immediate object of our attention.

It will be convenient at once to introduce and define some terms which will facilitate the expression of the Principles of Economy. By a *commodity* we shall understand any object, or, it may be, any action or service, which can afford pleasure or ward off pain. The name was originally abstract, and denoted the quality of anything by which it was capable of serving man. Having acquired, by a common process of confusion, a concrete signification, it will be well to retain it entirely for that signification, and employ the word *utility* to denote the abstract quality whereby an object serves our purposes, and becomes entitled to rank as a commodity. Whatever can produce pleasure or prevent pain *may* possess utility. M. Say has correctly and briefly defined utility as 'la faculté qu'ont les choses de pouvoir servir à l'homme, de quelque manière que ce soit.' The food which prevents the pangs of hunger, the clothes which fend off the cold of winter, possess incontestable utility; but we must beware of restricting the meaning of the word by any moral considerations. Anything which an individual is found to desire and to labour for must be assumed to possess for him utility. In the science of Economy we treat men not as they ought to be, but as they are. Bentham, in establishing the foundation of Moral Science in his great 'Introduction to the Principles of Morals and Legislation', thus comprehensively defines the term in question:—'By utility is meant that property in any object, whereby it tends to produce benefit, advantage, pleasure, good, or happiness (all this, in the present case, comes to the same thing), or (what comes again to the same thing) to prevent the happening of mischief, pain, evil, or unhappiness to the party whose interest is considered.'

This perfectly expresses the meaning of the word in Economy, provided that the will or inclination of the person concerned is taken as the sole criterion, for the time, of what is good and desirable, or painful and evil.

§ Laws of Human Want the Basis of Economy

Political Economy must be founded upon a full and accurate investigation of the conditions of utility; and, to understand this element, we must necessarily examine the character of the wants and desires of man. We, first of all, need a theory of the consumption of wealth. Mr. J. S. Mill, indeed, has given an opinion inconsistent with this. 'Political Economy,' he says,[1] 'has nothing to do with the consumption of wealth, further than as the consideration of it is inseparable from that of production, or from that of distribution. We know not of any laws of the consumption of wealth, as the subject of a distinct science; they can be no other than the laws of human enjoyment.'

But it is surely obvious that Political Economy does rest upon the laws of human enjoyment; and that, if those laws are developed by no other science, they must be developed by economists. We labour to produce with the sole object of consuming, and the kinds and amounts of goods produced must be governed entirely by our requirements. Every manufacturer knows and feels how closely he must anticipate the tastes and needs of his customers: his whole success depends upon it; and, in like manner, the whole theory of Economy depends upon a correct theory of consumption. Many economists have had a clear perception of this truth. Lord Lauderdale distinctly states,[2] that 'the great and important step towards ascertaining the causes of the direction which industry takes in nations . . . seems to be the discovery of what dictates the proportion of demand for the

[1] *Essays on Some Unsettled Questions of Political Economy*, p. 132.
[2] *Inquiry into the Nature and Origin of Public Wealth*, 2nd ed., 1819, p. 306.

various articles which are produced.' Mr. Senior, in his admirable treatise, has also recognised this truth, and pointed out what he calls the *Law of Variety* in human requirements. The necessaries of life are so few and simple, that a man is soon satisfied in regard to these, and desires to extend his range of enjoyment. His first object is to vary his food; but there soon arises the desire of variety and elegance in dress; and to this succeeds the desire to build, to ornament, and to furnish—tastes which are absolutely insatiable where they exist, and seem to increase with every improvement in civilisation.[3]

Bastiat has also observed that human wants are the ultimate object of Economy; and in his *Harmonies of Political Economy* he says,[4] 'Wants Efforts, Satisfaction—this is the circle of Political Economy.'

In still later years, M. Courcelle-Seneuil actually commenced his treatise with a definition of *want*—'Le besoin économique est un désir qui a pour but la possession et la jouissance d'un objet matériel.'[5] And I conceive that he has given the best possible statement of the problem of Economy when he expresses its object as 'à satisfaire nos besoins avec la moindre somme de travail possible.'[6]

Professor Hearn also commences his excellent treatise, entitled *Plutology, or the Theory of Efforts to Supply Human Wants*, with a chapter in which he considers the nature of the wants impelling man to exertion.

The writer, however, who seems to me to have reached the deepest comprehension of the foundation of Economy, is Mr. T. E. Banfield. His course of Lectures delivered in the University of Cambridge in 1844, and published under the title of *The Organization of Labour*,' is highly interesting, but perhaps not always correct. In the following passage[7] he profoundly points out that the scientific basis of Economy is in a theory of consumption: I need make no excuses for quoting this passage at full length.

'The lower wants man experiences in common with brutes. The cravings of hunger and thirst, the effects of heat and cold, of drought and damp, he feels with more acuteness than the rest of the animal world. His sufferings are doubtless sharpened by the consciousness that he has no right to be subject to such inflictions. Experience, however, shows that privations of various kinds affect men differently in degree, according to the circumstances in which they are placed. For some men the privation of certain enjoyments is intolerable, whose loss is not even felt by others. Some, again, sacrifice all that others hold dear for the gratification of longings and aspirations that are incomprehensible to their neighbours. Upon this

---

[3] *Encyclopædia Metropolitana*, art, "Political Economy," p. 133. Fifth edition of Reprint, p. 11.

[4] *Harmonies of Political Economy*, trans. by P. J. Stirling, 1860, p. 65.

[5] *A Treatise Theoretical and Practical on Political Economy*, J. G. Courcelle-Seneuil, 2nd ed., Paris, 1867, Vol. I, p. 25.

[6] *Ibid.*, p. 33.

[7] 2nd ed., p. 11.

complex foundation of low wants and high aspirations the Political Economist has to build the theory of production and consumption.

'An examination of the nature and intensity of man's wants shows that this connection between them gives to Political Economy its scientific basis. The first proposition of the theory of consumption is, that *the satisfaction of every lower want in the scale creates a desire of a higher character*. If the higher desire existed previous to the satisfaction of the primary want, it becomes more intense when the latter is removed. The removal of a primary want commonly awakens the sense of more than one secondary privation: thus a full supply of ordinary food not only excites to delicacy in eating, but awakens attention to clothing. The highest grade in the scale of wants, that of pleasure derived from the beauties of nature and art, is usually confined to men who are exempted from all the lower privations. Thus the demand for, and the consumption of, objects of refined enjoyment has its lever in the facility with which the primary wants are satisfied. This, therefore, is the key to the true theory of value. Without relative values in the objects to the acquirement of which we direct our power, there would be no foundation for Political Economy as a science.'

§ Utility Not an Intrinsic Quality

My principal work now lies in tracing out the exact nature and conditions of utility. It seems strange indeed that economists have not bestowed more minute attention on a subject which doubtless furnishes the true key to the problem of Economy.

In the first place, utility, though a quality of things, is *no inherent quality*. It might be more accurately described, perhaps, as *a circumstance of things* arising out of their relation to man's requirements. As Mr. Senior most accurately says, 'Utility denotes no intrinsic quality in the things which we call useful; it merely expresses their relations to the pains and pleasures of mankind.' We can never, therefore, say absolutely that some objects have utility and others have not. The ore lying in the mine, the diamond escaping the eye of the searcher, the wheat lying unreaped, the fruit ungathered for want of consumers, have not utility at all. The most wholesome and necessary kinds of food are useless unless there are hands to collect and mouths to eat them. Nor, when we consider the matter closely, can we say that all portions of the same commodity possess equal utility. Water, for instance, may be roughly described as the most useful of all substances. A quart of water per day has the high utility of saving a person from dying in a most distressing manner. Several gallons a day may possess much utility for such purposes as cooking and washing; but after an adequate supply is secured for these uses, any additional quantity is a matter of indifference. All that we can say, then, is, that water, up to a certain quantity, is indispensable; that further quantities will have various degrees of utility; but that beyond a certain point the utility appears to cease.

Exactly the same considerations apply more or less clearly to every other article. A pound of bread per day supplied to a person saves him from starvation, and has the highest conceivable utility. A second pound per day has also no slight utility: it keeps him in a state of comparative plenty, though it be not altogether indispensable. A third pound would begin to be superfluous. It is clear, then, that *utility is not proportional to commodity:* the very same articles vary in utility according as we already possess more or less of the same article. The like may be said of other things. One suit of clothes per annum is necessary, a second convenient, a third desirable, a fourth not unacceptable; but we, sooner or later, reach a point at which further supplies are not desired with any perceptible force, unless it be for subsequent use.

§ Law of the Variation of Utility

Let us now investigate this subject a little more closely. Utility must be considered as measured by, or even as actually identical with, the addition made to a person's happiness. It is a convenient name for the aggregate of the favourable balance of feeling produced—the sum of the pleasure created and the pain prevented. We must now carefully discriminate between the *total utility* belonging to any commodity and the utility belonging to any particular portion of it. Thus the total utility of the food we eat consists in maintaining life, and may be considered as infinitely great; but if we were to subtract a tenth part from what we eat daily, our loss would be but slight. It might be doubtful whether we should suffer any harm at all. Let us imagine the whole quantity of food which a person consumes on an average during twenty-four hours to be divided into ten equal parts. If his food be reduced by the last part, he will suffer very little; if a second tenth part be deficient, he will feel the want distinctly; the subtraction of the third tenth part will be decidedly injurious; with every subsequent subtraction of a tenth part his sufferings will be more and more serious, until at length he will be upon the verge of starvation. Now, if we call each of the tenth parts *an increment,* the meaning of these facts is, that each increment of food is less necessary, or possesses less utility, than the previous one. To represent this variation of utility, we may make use of space-representations, which I have found it convenient to employ in illustrating the laws of Economy in my lectures during seven or eight years past.

Let the line *ox* be used as a measure of the quantity of food, and let it be divided into ten equal parts to correspond to the ten parts of food mentioned above. Upon these equal lines are constructed rectangles, and the

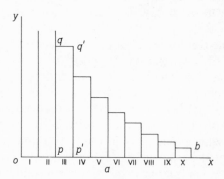

area of each rectangle may be assumed to represent the utility of the increment of food corresponding to its base. Thus the utility of the last increment is small, being proportional to the small rectangle on x. As we approach towards o, each increment bears a larger rectangle, that standing upon III being the largest complete rectangle. The utility of the next increment, II, as also that of I, is undefined, since these portions of food would be indispensable to life, and their utility, therefore, infinitely great.

We can now form a clear notion of the utility of the whole food, or of any part of it; for we have only to add together the proper rectangles. The utility of the first half of the food will be the sum of the rectangles standing on the line oa; that of the second half will be represented by the sum of the smaller rectangles between a and b. The total utility of the food will be the whole sum of the rectangles, and will be infinitely great.

The comparative degree of utility of the several portions is, however, the most important point to be considered. Utility is *a quantity of at least two dimensions*, one dimension consisting in the quantity of the commodity, and another in the intensity of the effect produced upon the consumer. Now, the quantity of the commodity is measured on the horizontal line ox, and the intensity of utility will be measured by the length of the upright lines, or *ordinates*, as they are commonly called by mathematicians. The intensity of utility of the third increment is measured either by pq, or $p'q'$, and its utility is the product of the units in pp' by those in pq.

But the division of the food into ten equal parts is an arbitrary supposition. If we had taken twenty or a hundred or more equal parts, the same general principle would hold true, namely, that each small portion would be less useful and necessary than the last. The law may be considered to hold true theoretically, however small the increments are made; and in this way we shall at last reach a figure which is undistinguishable from a continuous curve. The notion of infinitely small quantities of food may seem absurd as regards one individual; but, when we come to consider the consumption of nations as a whole, the consumption may well be conceived to increase or diminish by quantities which are, practically speaking, infinitely small compared with the whole consumption.

The law of the variation of the degree of utility of food may thus be represented by a continuous curve *pbq* (see figure below), and the perpendicular height of each point of the curve above the line *ox*, represents the degree of utility of the commodity when a certain amount has been consumed.

Thus, when the quantity *oa* has been consumed, the degree of utility corresponds to the length of the line *ab*; for if we take a very little more

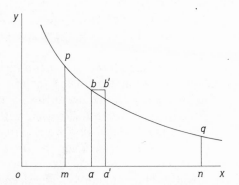

food, *aa'*, its utility will be the product of *aa'* and *ab* very nearly, and more nearly the less is the magnitude of *aa'*. The degree of utility is thus properly measured by the height of a very narrow rectangle corresponding to a very small quantity of food, which theoretically ought to be infinitely small.

§ Distinction Between Total Utility and Degree of Utility

We are now in a position fully to appreciate the difference between the *total utility* of any commodity and *the degree of utility* of the commodity at any point. These are, in fact, quantities of altogether different kinds, the first being represented by an area, and the second by a line. We must consider how we may express these notions in appropriate mathematical language.

Let *x* signify, as is usual in mathematical books, the quantity which varies independently,—in this case the quantity of commodity. Let *u* denote the *whole utility* proceeding from the consumption of *x*. Then *u* will be, as mathematicians say, *a function of x*; that is, it will vary in some continuous and regular, but probably unknown, manner, when *x* is made to vary. Our great object, however, is to express the *degree of utility*.

By prefixing the sign Δ to a quantity, mathematicians denote that a very small part of that quantity is taken into consideration. Thus Δ*x* means a very small part of x, the quantity of commodity; and $x + \Delta x$ therefore means a very little more commodity than x. Now the utility of $x + \Delta x$ will be more than that of x as a general rule. Let the whole utility of $x + \Delta x$ be denoted by $u + \Delta u$; then it is obvious that the increment of utility Δu belongs to the increment of commodity Δx; and if, for a moment, we suppose the degree of utility uniform over the whole of Δx, which is nearly true owing to its smallness, we shall find the corresponding degree of utility by dividing Δu by Δx.

We find these considerations fully illustrated in the figure on page 239, in which $oa = x$ and ab will be the degree of utility at the point a. Now, if we increase x by the small quantity aa', or Δx, the utility may be considered as increased by a small rectangle $abb'a'$, or Δu; and, since a rectangle is the product of its sides, we find that the line ab, the degree of utility, is represented by the fraction $\Delta u / \Delta x$.

The utility of a commodity may, however, be considered to vary with perfect continuity, so that we commit a small error in assuming it to be uniform over the whole increment Δx. To avoid this we must imagine Δx to be reduced to an infinitely small size, Δu decreasing with it. The smaller the quantities are the more nearly we shall have a correct expression for ab, the degree of utility at the point a. Thus the *limit* of this fraction $\Delta u / \Delta x$, or, as it is commonly expressed, du/dx, is the degree of utility corresponding to the quantity of commodity x. *The degree of utility is*, in mathematical language, *the differential coefficient of u considered as a function of x*, and will itself be another function of x.

We shall seldom need to consider the degree of utility except as regards the last increment which is consumed, and I shall therefore commonly use the expression *final degree of utility* meaning the degree of utility of the last addition, or the next possible addition of a very small, or infinitely small, quantity to the existing stock. In ordinary circumstances, too, the final degree of utility will not be great compared with what it might be. Only in famine or other extreme circumstances do we approach the higher degrees of utility. Accordingly, we can often treat the lower portions of the curve of variation (*pbq*, in the figure on page 239) which concern ordinary commercial transactions, while we leave out of sight the portions beyond p or q. It is also evident that we may know the degree of utility at any point while ignorant of the total utility, that is, the area of the whole curve.

§ The Final Degree of Utility and the Law of Its Variation

The final degree of utility is that function upon which the whole Theory of Economy will be found to turn. Political Economists, generally speaking, have failed to discriminate between this function and the total utility.

From this confusion has arisen much perplexity. Many of those commodities which are the most useful to us are esteemed and desired the least. We cannot live a day without water, and yet in ordinary circumstances we set no value on it. Why is this? Simply because we usually have so much of it that its final degree of utility is reduced nearly to zero. We enjoy, every day, the almost infinite utility of water, but then we do not need to consume more than we have. Let the supply run short by drought, and we begin to feel the higher degree of utility, of which we think but little at other times.

The variation of the function expressing the final degree of utility is the all-important point in all economical problems. We may state, as a general law, that *it varies with the quantity of commodity, and ultimately decreases as that quantity increases.* No commodity can be named which we continue to desire with the same force, whatever be the quantity already in use or possession. All our appetites are capable of *satisfaction* or *satiety* sooner or later, both these words meaning, etymologically, that we have had *enough*, so that more is of no use to us. It does not follow, indeed, that the degree of utility will always sink to zero. This may be the case with many things, especially the simple animal requirements, food, water, air, &c. But the more refined and intellectual our needs become, the less are they capable of satiety. To the desire for articles of taste, science, or curiosity, when once excited, there is hardly a limit.

This great principle of the ultimate decrease of the final degree of utility of any commodity is implied in the writings of many economists, though seldom distinctly stated. It is the real law which lies at the basis of Senior's so-called 'Law of Variety.' Indeed, Senior states the law itself. He says: 'It is obvious that our desires do not aim so much at quantity as at diversity. Not only are there limits to the pleasure which commodities of any given class can afford, but the pleasure diminishes in a rapidly increasing ratio long before those limits are reached. Two articles of the same kind will seldom afford twice the pleasure of one, and still less will ten give five times the pleasure of two. In proportion, therefore, as any article is abundant, the number of those who are provided with it, and do not wish, or wish but little, to increase their provision, is likely to be great; and, so far as they are concerned, the additional supply loses all, or nearly all, its utility. And, in proportion to its scarcity, the number of those who are in want of it, and the degree in which they want it, are likely to be increased; and its utility, or, in other words, the pleasure which the possession of a given quantity of it will afford, increases proportionally.'[8]

Banfield's 'Law of the Subordination of Wants' also rests upon the same basis. It cannot be said, with accuracy, that the satisfaction of a lower want *creates* a higher want; it merely permits the higher want to manifest

[8] *Encyclopædia Metropolitana*, p. 133. Reprint, p. 12.

itself. We distribute our labour and possessions in such a way as to satisfy the more pressing wants first. If food runs short, the all-absorbing question is, how to obtain more, because, at the moment, more pleasure or pain depends upon food than upon any other commodity. But, when food is moderately abundant, its final degree of utility falls very low, and wants of a much more complex and less satiable nature become comparatively prominent.

The writer, however, who appears to me to have most clearly appreciated the nature and importance of the law of utility, is Mr. Richard Jennings, who, in 1855, published a small book called *The Natural Elements of Political Economy*. This work treats of the physical groundwork of Economy, showing its dependence on physiological laws. It appears to me to display a great insight into the real basis of Economy; yet I am not aware that economists have bestowed the slightest attention on Mr. Jennings' views.[9] I take the liberty, therefore, of giving a full extract from his remarks on the nature of utility. It will thus be seen that the law, as I state it, is no novelty, and that it is only careful deduction from principles in our possession that is needed to give us a correct Theory of Economy.

'To turn from the relative effect of commodities, in producing sensations, to those which are absolute, or dependent only on the quantity of each commodity, it is but too well known to every condition of men, that the degree of each sensation which is produced, is by no means commensurate with the quantity of the commodity applied to the senses. . . . These effects require to be closely observed, because they are the foundation of the changes of money price, which valuable objects command in times of varied scarcity and abundance; we shall therefore direct our attention to them for the purpose of ascertaining the nature of the law according to which the sensations that attend on consumption vary in degree with changes in the quantity of the commodity consumed.

'We may gaze upon an object until we can no longer discern it, listen until we can no longer hear, smell until the sense of odour is exhausted, taste until the object becomes nauseous, and touch until it becomes painful; we may consume food until we are fully satisfied, and use stimulants until more would cause pain. On the other hand, the same object offered to the special senses for a moderate duration of time, and the same food or stimulants consumed when we are exhausted or weary, may convey much gratification. If the whole quantity of the commodity consumed during the interval of these two states of sensation, the state of satiety and the state of inanition, be conceived to be divided into a number of equal parts, each marked with its proper degrees of sensation, the question to be determined will be, what relation does the difference in the degrees of the sensation bear to the difference in the quantities of the commodity? First,

[9] Professor Cairnes is, however, an exception. See his *Lectures on the Character and Logical Method of Political Economy*, London, 1857, p. 81.

with respect to all commodities, our feelings show that the degrees of satisfaction do not proceed *pari passu* with the quantities consumed; they do not advance equally with each instalment of the commodity offered to the senses, and then suddenly stop; but diminish gradually, until they ultimately disappear, and further instalments can produce no further satisfaction. In this progressive scale the increments of sensation resulting from equal increments of the commodity are obviously less and less at each step,—each degree of sensation is less than the preceding degree. Placing ourselves at that middle point of sensation, the *juste milieu*, the *aurea mediocritas*, the ἄριστον μέτρον of sages, which is the most usual status of the mass of mankind, and which, therefore, is the best position that can be chosen for measuring deviations from the usual amount, we may say that the law which expresses the relation of degrees of sensation to quantities of commodities is of this character: if the average or temperate quantity of commodities be increased, the satisfaction derived is increased in a less degree, and ultimately ceases to be increased at all; if the average or temperate quantity be diminished, the loss of more and more satisfaction will continually ensue, and the detriment thence arising will ultimately become exceedingly great.'

§ Distribution of Commodity in Different Uses

The principles of utility may be illustrated by considering the mode in which we distribute a commodity when it is capable of several uses. There are articles which may be employed for many distinct purposes: thus, barley may be used either to make beer, spirits, bread, or to feed cattle; sugar may be used to eat, or for producing alcohol; timber may be used in construction, or as fuel; iron and other metals may be applied to many different purposes. Imagine, then, a community in the possession of a certain stock of barley; what principles will regulate their mode of consuming it? Or, as we have not yet reached the subject of exchange, imagine an isolated family, or even an individual, possessing an adequate stock, and using some in one way and some in another. The theory of utility gives, theoretically speaking, a complete solution of the question.

Let s be the whole stock of some commodity, and let it be capable of three distinct uses. Then we may represent the three quantities appropriated to these uses by x_1, y_1, and z_1, it being a necessary condition that $x_1 + y_1 + z_1 = s$. The person may be conceived as successively expending small quantities of the commodity; now it is the inevitable tendency of human nature to choose that course which offers the most apparent good at the moment. Hence, when the person remains satisfied with the distribution he has made, it follows that no alteration would yield him more pleasure; which amounts to saying that an increment of commodity would yield exactly as much utility in one use as in another. Let Δu_1, Δu_2, Δu_3, be the increments of utility arising from consuming one equal increment of commodity in three different ways. When the distribution is completed, we ought to have $\Delta u_1 = \Delta u_2 = \Delta u_3$; or at the limit we have the equations

$$\frac{du_1}{dx} = \frac{du_2}{dy} = \frac{du_3}{dz},$$

which are true when x, y, z, are respectively equal to x_1, y_1, z_1. We must, in other words, have the *final degrees of utility* in the three uses equal.

We might sometimes find these equations fail. Even when x is equal to $\frac{99}{100}$ of the stock, its degree of utility might still exceed the utility attaching to the remaining $\frac{1}{100}$ part in either of the other uses. This would mean that it was preferable to give the whole commodity to the first use. Such a case might perhaps be said to be not the exception but the rule; for, whenever a commodity is capable of only one use, the circumstance is theoretically represented by saying, that the final degree of utility in this employment always exceeds that in any other employment.

Under peculiar circumstances great changes may take place in the consumption of a commodity. In a time of scarcity the utility of barley as food might rise so high as to exceed altogether its utility, even as regards the smallest quantity, in producing alcoholic liquors; its consumption in the latter way would then cease. In a besieged town the employment of articles becomes revolutionised. Things of great utility in other respects are ruthlessly applied to strange purposes. In Paris a vast stock of horses were eaten, not so much because they were useless in other ways, as because they were needed more strongly as food. A certain stock of horses had, indeed, to be retained as a necessary aid to locomotion, so that the equation of the degrees of utility never wholly failed.

§ Duration of Utility

As utility corresponds to, and is measured by, pleasure produced, and as pleasure is a quantity of two dimensions, intensity and duration, so utility must be conceived as capable of duration. In a great many cases this is evidently true. Furniture, utensils, buildings, books, gems, ornaments, &c., may last a long time and possess more or less utility all the time. If the degree of utility of any such object be constant, the total amount of utility will be proportional to the duration. But the utility may be more or less independently of the time, so that in such cases utility is clearly a quantity of three dimensions. We have seen that utility has two dimensions depending upon the *quantity* of commodity enjoyed and the final degree of its utility. We must now add a third dimension depending upon the length of time during which the commodity can retain its useful qualities. We have more or less need of a thing; we may be more or less fully supplied with that thing; and can enjoy it a longer or shorter time.

§ Actual, Prospective, and Potential Utility

The difficulties of Political Economy are mainly the difficulties of conceiving clearly and fully the conditions of utility. Even at the risk of being tiresome, I will therefore more minutely point out how various are the senses in which a thing may be said to have utility.

It is quite usual, and perhaps correct, to call iron or water or timber a useful substance; but we may mean by these words at least three distinct facts. We may mean that a particular piece of iron is at the present moment actually useful to some person; or that, although not actually useful, it is expected to be useful at a future time; or we may only mean that it would be useful if it were in the possession of some person needing it. The iron rails of a railway, the iron which composes the Britannia Bridge, or an ocean steamer, is actually useful; the iron lying in a merchant's store is not useful at present, though it is expected soon to be so; but there is a vast quantity of iron existing in the bowels of the earth, which has all the physical properties of iron, and might be useful if extracted, though it never will be. These are instances of *actual, prospective, and potential utility*.

It will be apparent that *potential utility* does not really enter into the science of Political Economy, and when I speak of *utility* simply, I do not mean the term to include potential utility. It is a question of physical science whether a substance possesses qualities which might make it suitable to our needs if it were within our reach. Only when there arises some degree of probability, however slight, that a particular object will be needed, does it acquire *prospective utility* capable of rendering it a desirable possession. But a very large part in industry, and the science of industry, belongs to *prospective utility*. We can at any one moment use only a very small part of what we possess. By far the greater part of what we hold might be allowed to perish at any moment, without harm, if we could have it re-created with equal ease at a future moment, when need of it arises.

We might also distinguish, as is customary with French economists, between *direct* and *indirect utility*. Direct utility attaches to a thing like food which we can actually apply to satisfy our wants. But things which have no direct utility may be the means of procuring us such by exchange, and they may therefore be said to have indirect utility. To the latter form of utility I have elsewhere applied the name *acquired utility*. This distinction is not the same as that which is made in the Theory of Capital between *mediate* and *immediate utility*, the former being that of any implement, machine, or other means of procuring commodities possessing *immediate* and *direct utility*—that is, the power of satisfying want.

§ The Most Advantageous Distribution of a Commodity from Time to Time

We have seen that when a commodity is capable of being used for different purposes, definite principles regulate its application to those purposes. A similar question arises when a stock of commodity is in hand, and must be expended over a certain interval of time more or less definite. The science of Economy must point out the mode of consuming it to the greatest advantage—that is, with a maximum of utility. If we reckon all future pleasures and pains as if they were present, the solution will be exactly the same as in the case of different uses. If a commodity has to be distributed over n days' use, and v_1, v_2, &c. be the final degrees of utility on each day's consumption, then we ought clearly to have

$$v_1 = v_2 = v_3 = \ldots = v_n.$$

It may, however, be uncertain during how many days we may require the stock to last. The commodity might be of a perishable nature, so that if we keep some of it for ten days, it might become unserviceable, and its utility be sacrificed. Assuming that we can estimate more or less exactly the probability of its remaining good, let $p_1\ p_2\ p_3 \ldots p_{10}$ be these probabilities. Then, on the principle that a future pleasure or pain must be reduced in proportion to its want of certainty, we have the equations

$$v_1\ p_1 = v_2\ p_2 = \ldots = v_{10}\ p_{10}.$$

The general result is, that as the probability is less, the commodity assigned to each day is less, so that v will be greater.

So far we have taken no account of the varying influence of an event according to its propinquity or remoteness. The distribution of commodity described is that which should be made and would be made by a being of perfect good sense and foresight. To secure a maximum of benefit in life, all future events, all future pleasures or pains, should act upon us with the same force as if they were present, allowance being made for their uncertainty. The factor expressing the effect of remoteness should, in short, always be unity, so that time should have no effect. But no human mind is constituted in this perfect way: a future feeling is always less influential than a present one. To take this fact into account, let q_1, q_2, q_3, &c. be the undetermined fractions which express the ratios of the present pleasures or pains to those future ones from whose anticipation they arise. Having a stock of commodity in hand, our tendency will be to distribute it so that the following equations will hold true—

$$v_1 p_1 q_1 = v_2 p_2 q_2 = v_3 p_3 q_3 = \ldots = v_n p_n q_n.$$

It will be an obvious consequence of these equations that less commodity will be assigned to future days in some proportion to the intervening time.

An interesting problem, involving questions of prospective utility and probability, is found in the case of a vessel at sea, which is insufficiently victualled for the probable length of voyage to the nearest port. The actual length of the voyage depends on the winds, and must be uncertain; but we may suppose that it will almost certainly last ten days or more, but not more than thirty days. It is apparent that if the food were divided into thirty equal parts, partial famine and suffering would be certainly endured for the first ten days, to ward off later evils which may very probably not be encountered. To consume one-tenth part of the food on each of the first ten days would be still worse, as almost certainly entailing starvation on the following days. To determine the most beneficial distribution of the food, we should require to know the probability of each day between the tenth and thirtieth days forming part of the voyage, and also the law of variation of the degree of utility of food. The whole stock ought then to be divided into thirty portions, allotted to each of the thirty days, and of such magnitude that the final degrees of utility multiplied by the probabilities are all equal. Thus, let v_1, v_2, v_3, &c. be the final degrees of utility of the first, second, third, and other days supplied, and p_1, p_2, p_3, &c. the probabilities that the days in question will form part of the voyage; then we ought to have

$$p_1 v_1 = p_2 v_2 = p_3 v_3 = \ldots = p_{29} v_{29} = p_{30} v_{30}.$$

If these equations did not hold it would be beneficial to transfer a small portion from one lot to some other lot. As the voyage is supposed certainly to last the first ten days, we have

$$p_1 = p_2 = \ldots = p_{10} = 1;$$

hence we must have

$$v_1 = v_2 = \ldots = v_{10};$$

whence it will follow that the allotments to the first ten days should be equal. They should afterwards decrease according to some regular law; for, as the probability decreases, the final degree of utility should increase in inverse proportion.

Chapter 4: THEORY OF EXCHANGE

§ Ambiguity of the Term Value, and Proposed Introduction of the
Expression—Ratio of Exchange

I must, in the first place, point out the thoroughly ambiguous and un-
scientific character of the term *value*. Adam Smith noticed the extreme
difference of meaning between *value in use* and *value in exchange*; and it
is usual for the best writers on Economy to caution their readers against
the confusion to which they are liable. But I do not believe that either
writers or readers can avoid the confusion so long as they use the word.
In spite of the most acute feeling of the danger, I often detect myself using
the word improperly; nor do I think that the best authorities in Economy
escape the danger.

Let us turn to Mr. Mill's definition of Value,[1] and we at once see the
weakness of the term. He tells us—'Value is a relative term. The value of
a thing means the quantity of some other thing, or of things in general,
which it exchanges for.' Now, if there is any fact certain about value, it is,
that it means not an object at all, but a quality, attribute, or rather a circumstance of an object. Value implies, in fact, a relation; but if so, it
cannot possibly be *some other thing.* A student of Economy has no hope
of ever being clear and correct in his ideas of the science if he thinks of
value as at all a *thing* or *object,* or even as anything which lies in a thing
or object. Persons are thus led to speak of such a nonentity as *intrinsic
value.* There are, doubtless, qualities inherent in such a substance as gold
or iron which influence its value; but the word Value, so far as it can be
correctly used, merely expresses *the circumstance of its exchanging in a
certain ratio for some other substance.* If a ton of pig-iron exchanges in a
market for an ounce of standard gold, neither the iron is value, nor the
gold; nor is there value in the iron nor in the gold. The notion of value
is concerned only in the fact or circumstance of one exchanging for the
other. Thus it is scientifically incorrect to say that the value of the ton of
iron *is* the ounce of gold: we thus convert value into a concrete thing; and
it is, of course, equally incorrect to say that the value of the ounce of gold is
the ton of iron. The more correct and safe expression is, that *the value of
the ton of iron is equal to the value of the ounce of gold,* or that their
values are as one to one.

Value in exchange expresses nothing but a ratio, and the term should not
be used in any other sense. To speak simply of the value of an ounce of
gold is as absurd as to speak of the *ratio of the number seventeen.* What is
the ratio of the number seventeen? The question admits no answer, for
there must be another number named in order to make a ratio; and the

[1] *Principles of Political Economy*, Book III, Chap. 6.

ratio will differ according to the number suggested. What is the value of iron compared with that of gold?—is an intelligible question. The answer consists in stating the ratio of the quantities exchanged.

In the popular use of the word Value there is inextricable confusion with the notion of utility; and the conclusion to which I shall come, that exchange does depend entirely on degrees of utility, gives some countenance to the confusion. To avoid all difficulty, I shall discontinue the use of the word Value altogether, and substitute the unequivocal expression *Ratio of Exchange*. When we speak of the ratio of exchange of pig-iron and gold, there can be no possible doubt that we mean merely the quantity of one given for the other.

§ Definitions of Market and Trading Body

Before proceeding to the Theory of Exchange, it will be desirable to place beyond doubt the meanings of two other terms which I shall frequently employ.

By a *Market* I shall mean much what commercial men use it to express. Originally a market was a public place in a town where provisions and other objects were exposed for sale; but the word has been generalised, so as to mean any body of persons who are in intimate business relations and carry on extensive transactions in any commodity. A great city may contain as many markets as there are important branches of trade, and these markets may or may not be localised. The central point of a market is the public exchange,—mart or auction rooms, where the traders agree to meet and transact business. In London, the Stock Market, the Corn Market, the Coral Market, the Sugar Market, and many others, are distinctly localised; in Manchester, the Cotton Market, the Cotton Waste Market, and others. But this distinction of locality is not necessary. The traders may be spread over a whole town, or region of country, and yet make a market, if they are, by means of fairs, meetings, published price lists, the post office, or otherwise, in close communication with each other. Thus the common expression *Money Market* denotes no locality: it is applied to the aggregate of those bankers, capitalists, and other traders who lend or borrow money, and who constantly exchange information concerning the course of business.

In Political Economy we may usefully adopt this term with a clear and well-defined meaning. By a market I shall mean two or more persons dealing in two or more commodities, whose stocks of those commodities and intentions of exchanging are known to all. It is also essential that the ratio of exchange between any two persons should be known to all the others. It is only so far as this community of knowledge extends that the market extends. Any persons who are not acquainted at the moment with the prevailing ratio of exchange, and whose stocks are not available for want of communication, must not be considered part of the market. Secret or unknown stocks of a commodity must also be considered beyond reach of a market so long as they remain secret and unknown. Every individual must be considered as exchanging from a pure regard to his own requirements or private interests, and there must be perfectly free competition, so that any one will exchange with any one else upon the slightest advantage appearing. There must be no conspiracies for absorbing and holding supplies to produce unnatural ratios of exchange. Were a conspiracy of farmers to withhold all corn from market, the consumers might be driven, by starvation, to pay prices bearing no proper relation to the existing supplies, and the ordinary conditions of the market would be thus overthrown.

The theoretical conception of a perfect market is more or less completely carried out in practice. It is the work of brokers in any extensive market to organise the exchanges, so that every purchase shall be made with the most thorough acquaintance with the conditions of the trade. Each broker strives to have the best knowledge of the conditions of supply and demand, and the earliest intimation of any change. He is in communication with as many other traders as possible, in order to have the widest range of information, and the greatest chance of making suitable exchanges. It is only thus that a definite market price can be ascertained at every moment, and varied according to the frequent news capable of affecting buyers and sellers. By the mediation of a body of brokers a complete consensus is established, and the stocks of every seller or the demands of every buyer are brought into the market. It is of the very essence of trade to have wide and constant information. A market, then, is theoretically perfect only when all traders have perfect knowledge of the conditions of supply and demand, and the consequent ratio of exchange; and in such a market, as we shall now see, there can only be one ratio of exchange of one uniform commodity at any moment.

So essential is a knowledge of the real state of supply and demand to the smooth procedure of trade and the real good of the community, that I conceive it would be quite legitimate to compel the publication of any requisite statistics. Secrecy can only conduce to the profit of speculators who gain from great fluctuations of prices. Speculation is advantageous to the public only so far as it tends to equalise prices; and it is, therefore, against the public good to allow speculators to foster artificially the inequalities of prices by which they profit. The welfare of millions both of consumers and producers depends upon an accurate knowledge of the stocks of cotton and corn; and it would, therefore, be no unwarrantable interference with the liberty of the subject to require any information as to the stocks in hand. In Billingsgate fish market it has been a regulation that salesmen shall fix up in a conspicuous place every morning a statement of the kind and amount of their stock; and such a regulation, whenever it could be enforced on other markets, would always be to the advantage of every one except a few traders.

I find it necessary to adopt some expression for any number of people whose aggregate influence in a market, either in the way of supply or demand, we have to consider. By a *trading body* I mean, in the most general manner, any body either of buyers or sellers. The trading body may be a single individual in one case; it may be the whole inhabitants of a continent in another; it may be the individuals of a trade diffused through a country in a third. England and North America will be trading bodies if we are considering the corn we receive from America in exchange for iron and other goods. The continent of Europe is a trading body as purchasing coal from England. The farmers of England are a trading body when they sell corn to the millers, and the millers both when they buy corn from the farmers and sell flour to the bakers.

I use the expression with this very wide meaning, because the principles of exchange are the same in nature, however wide or narrow may be the market considered. Every trading body is either an individual or an aggregate of individuals, and the law, in the case of the aggregate, must depend upon the fulfilment of law in the individuals. We cannot usually observe any precise and continuous variation in the wants and deeds of an individual, because the action of extraneous motives, or what would seem to be caprice, overwhelms minute tendencies. As I have already remarked, a single individual does not vary his consumption of sugar, butter, or eggs from week to week by infinitesimal amounts, according to each small change in the price. He probably continues his ordinary consumption until accident directs his attention to a rise in price, and he then, perhaps, discontinues the use of the articles altogether for a time. But the aggregate, or what is the same, the average consumption of a large community will be found to vary continuously in a more or less rapid manner. The most minute tendencies make themselves apparent in a wide average. Thus, our laws of Economy will be theoretically true in the case of individuals, and practically true in the case of large aggregates; and the general principles will be the same, whatever the extent of the trading body considered. I am justified, then, in using the expression with the utmost generality.

At the same time, it would be an obvious error to suppose that the particular character of an economical law holding true of a great aggregate will be exactly the same as that of any individual. Only when the individuals are of perfectly uniform character will their average supply or demand for any commodity represent that of an individual. But every community is usually composed of individuals differing widely in powers, wants, habits, and possessions. An average will therefore partly depend upon the comparative numbers belonging to each class.

§ Of the Ratio of Exchange

When a commodity is perfectly uniform or homogeneous in quality, all portions may be indifferently used in place of equal portions: hence, in the same market, and at the same moment, all portions must be exchanged at the same ratio. There can be no reason why a person should treat exactly similar things differently, and the slightest excess in what is demanded for one over the other will cause him to take the latter instead of the former. In nicely-balanced exchanges it is a very minute scruple which will turn the scale and govern the choice. A minute difference of quality in a commodity may thus give rise to preference, and cause the ratio of exchange to differ. But where no difference exists at all, or where no difference is known to exist, there can be no ground for preference whatever. If, in selling a quantity of perfectly equal and uniform barrels of flour, a merchant arbitrarily fixed different prices on them, a purchaser would of course select the cheaper ones; and where there was absolutely no difference in the thing purchased, even a penny in the price might be a valid ground of choice. Hence follows what is undoubtedly true, with proper explanations, that *in the same open market, at any moment, there cannot be two prices for the same kind of article*. Such differences as may practically occur arise from extraneous circumstances, such as the defective credit of the purchasers, their imperfect knowledge of the market, and so on.

Though the price of the same commodity must be uniform at any one moment, it may vary from moment to moment, and must be conceived as in a state of continual change. Theoretically speaking, it may not be possible to buy two portions of the same commodity *successively* at the same ratio of exchange, because, no sooner has the first portion been bought, than the conditions of utility are altered. When exchanges are made on a large scale, this result will be verified in practice. If a wealthy person invested £100,000 in the funds in the morning, it is hardly likely that the operation could be repeated in the afternoon at the same price. In any market, if a person goes on buying largely, he will ultimately raise the price against himself. Thus it is apparent that extensive purchases would best be made gradually, so as to secure the advantage of a lower price upon the earlier portions. In theory this effect of exchange upon the ratio of exchange must be conceived to exist in some degree, however small may be the purchases made. Strictly speaking, the ratio of exchange at any moment is that of dy to dx, of an infinitely small quantity of one commodity to the infinitely small quantity of another which is given for it. The ratio of exchange is really a differential coefficient. The quantity of any article purchased is a function of the price with which it is purchased, and the ratio of exchange expresses the rate at which the quantity of the article increases compared with what is given for it.

We must carefully distinguish, at the same time, between the Statics and Dynamics of this subject. The real condition of industry is one of perpetual motion and change. Commodities are continually being manufactured and exchanged and consumed. If we wished to have a complete solution of the problem in all its natural complexity, we should have to treat it as a problem of dynamics. But it would surely be absurd to attempt the more difficult question when the more easy one is yet so imperfectly within our power. It is only as a purely statical problem that I can venture to treat the action of exchange. Holders of commodities will be regarded not as continuously passing on these commodities in streams of trade, but as possessing certain fixed amounts which they exchange until they come to equilibrium.

It is much more easy to determine the point at which a pendulum will come to rest than to calculate the velocity at which it will move when displaced from that point of rest. Just so, it is a far more easy task to lay down the conditions under which trade is completed and interchange ceases, than to attempt to ascertain at what rate trade will go on when equilibrium is not attained.

The difference will present itself in this form: dynamically we could not treat the ratio of exchange otherwise than as the ratio of dy and dx, infinitesimal quantities of commodity; but in the statical view of the question we can substitute the ratio of the finite quantities of y and x. Thus, from the self-evident principle that there cannot, in the same market, at the same moment, be two different prices for the same uniform commodity, it follows that *the last increments in an act of exchange must be exchanged in the same ratio as the whole quantities exchanged.* Suppose that two commodities are bartered in the ratio of x for y; then every m^{th} part of x is given for the mth part of y, and it does not matter for which of the mth parts. No part of the commodity can be treated differently to any other. We may carry this division to an indefinite extent by imagining m to be constantly increased, so that, at the limit, even an infinitely small part of x must be exchanged for an infinitely small part of y, in the same ratio as the whole quantities. This result we may express by stating that the increments concerned in the process of exchange must obey the quation

$$\frac{dy}{dx} = \frac{y}{x}.$$

The use which we shall make of this equation will be seen in the next section.

§ The Theory of Exchange

The keystone of the whole Theory of Exchange, and of the principal problems in Political Economy, lies in this proposition—*The ratio of ex-*

change of any two commodities will be inversely as the final degrees of utility of the quantities of commodity available for consumption after the exchange is effected. When the reader has reflected a little upon the meaning of this proposition, he will see, I think, that it is necessarily true, if the principles of human nature have been correctly represented in previous pages.

Imagine, for a moment, that there is one trading body possessing only corn, and another possessing only beef. It is certain that, under these circumstances, a portion of the corn may be given in exchange for a portion of the beef with a considerable increase of utility. How are we to determine at what point the exchange will cease to be beneficial? This question must involve both the ratio of exchange and the degrees of utility. Suppose, for a moment, that the ratio of exchange is approximately that of ten pounds of corn for one pound of beef: then, if to the trading body which possesses corn, ten pounds of corn are less useful than one of beef, that body will desire to carry the exchange further. Should the other body possessing beef find one pound less useful than ten pounds of corn, this body will also be desirous to continue the exchange. Exchange will thus go on till each party has obtained all the benefit that is possible, and loss of utility would result if more were exchanged. Both parties, then, rest in satisfaction and equilibrium, and the degrees of utility have come to their level, as it were.

This point of equilibrium will be known by the criterion, that an infinitely small amount of commodity exchanged in addition, at the same rate, will bring neither gain nor loss of utility. In other words, if increments of commodities be exchanged at the established ratio, their utilities will be equal for both parties. Thus, if ten pounds of corn were of exactly the same utility as one pound of beef, there would be neither harm nor good in further exchange at this ratio.

It would be hardly possible to represent this theory completely in a diagram, but the accompanying figure may, perhaps, render it clearer.

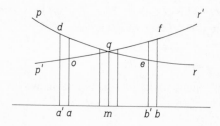

The line *pqr* is a small portion of the curve of utility of one commodity, while the broken line *p'qr'* is the like curve of another commodity which has been reversed and superposed on the other. Owing to this reversal, the quantities of the first commodity are measured along the base line from *a* towards *b*, whereas those of the second must be measured in the opposite direction. Let units of both commodities be represented by equal lengths: then the little line *a'a* indicates an increase of the first commodity, and a decrease of the second. Assume the ratio of exchange to be that of unit for unit, or 1 to 1: then, by receiving the commodity *a'a* the person will gain the utility *ad*, and lose the utility *a'c*; or he will make a net gain of the utility corresponding to the curvilinear figure *cd*. He will, therefore, wish to extend the exchange. If he were to go up to the point *b'*, and were still proceeding, he would, by the next small exchange, gain the utility *be*, and lose *b'f*; or he would have a net loss of *ef*. He would, therefore, have gone too far; and it is pretty obvious that the point of intersection, *q*, defines the place where he would stop with the greatest advantage. It is there that a net gain is converted into a net loss, or rather where, for an indefinitely small quantity, there is neither gain nor loss. To represent an indefinitely small quantity, or even an exceedingly small quantity, on a diagram is, of course, impossible; but on either side of the line *mq* I have represented the utilities of a small quantity of commodity more or less, and it is apparent that the net gain or loss upon the exchange of these quantities would be comparatively trifling.

. . .

§ On the Origin of Value

The preceding pages contain, if I am not mistaken, an explanation of the nature of value which will, for the most part, harmonise with previous views upon the subject. Ricardo has stated, like most other economists, that utility is absolutely essential to value; but that 'possessing utility, commodities derive their exchangeable value from two sources: from their scarcity, and from the quantity of labour required to obtain them.'[2] Senior, again, has admirably defined wealth, or objects possessing value, as 'those things, and those things only, which are transferable, are limited in supply, and are directly or indirectly productive of pleasure or preventive of pain.' Speaking only of things which are transferable, or capable of being passed from hand to hand, we find that the two clearest statements of the nature of value available, recognise *utility* and *scarcity* as the requisites. But the moment that we distinguish between the total utility of a mass of commodity and the degree of utility of different portions, we may say that the scarcity is that which prevents the fall in the final degree of utility. Bread has the almost infinite utility of maintaining life, and when it becomes a question of life or death, a small quantity of food exceeds in value all other things. But when we enjoy our ordinary supplies of food, a loaf

[2] *Principles of Political Economy and Taxation*, 3rd ed., p. 2.

of bread has little value, because the utility of an additional loaf is small, our appetite being satiated by our customary meals.

I have pointed out the excessive ambiguity of the word Value, and the apparent impossibility of safely using it. When used to express the mere fact of certain articles exchanging in a particular ratio, I have proposed to substitute the unequivocal expression—*ratio of exchange*. But I am inclined to believe that a ratio is not the meaning which most persons attach to the word Value. There is a certain sense of esteem, of desirableness, which we may have with regard to a thing apart from any distinct consciousness of the ratio in which it would exchange for other things. I may suggest that this distinct feeling of value is probably identical with the final degree of utility. While Adam Smith's often quoted *value in use* is the total utility of a commodity to us, the *value in exchange* is defined by the *terminal utility*, the remaining desire which we or others have for possessing more.

There remains the question of labour as an element of value. There have not been wanting economists who put forward labour as the *cause of value*, asserting that all objects derive their value from the fact that labour has been expended on them; and it is even implied, if not stated, that value will be exactly proportional to labour. This is a doctrine which cannot stand for a moment, being directly opposed to facts. Ricardo disposes of such an opinion when he says:[3] 'There are some commodities the value of which is determined by their scarcity alone. No labour can increase the quantity of such goods, and therefore their value cannot be lowered by an increased supply. Some rare statues and pictures, scarce books and coins, wines of a peculiar quality, which can only be made from grapes grown on a particular soil, of which there is a very limited quantity, are all of this description. Their value is wholly independent of the quantity of labour originally necessary to produce them, and varies with the varying wealth and inclinations of those who are desirous to possess them.'

The mere fact that there are many things, such as rare ancient books, coins, antiquities, which have high values, and which are absolutely incapable of production now, disperses the notion that value depends on labour. Even those things which are producible in any quantities by labour seldom exchange exactly at the corresponding values. The market price of corn, cotton, iron, and most other things is, in the prevalent theories of value, allowed to fluctuate above or below its natural or cost value. There may, again, be any discrepancy between the quantity of labour spent upon an object and the value ultimately attaching to it. A great undertaking like the Great Western Railway, or the Thames Tunnel, may embody a vast amount of labour, but its value depends entirely upon the number of persons who find it useful. If no use could be found for the Great Eastern steam ship, its value would be *nil*, except for the utility of some of its materials. On the other hand, a successful undertaking, which happens to pos-

3 *Ibid.*

sess great utility, may have a value for a time, at least, far exceeding what has been spent upon it, as in the case of the Atlantic cable. The fact is, that *labour once spent has no influence on the future value of any article*: it is gone and lost for ever. In commerce, by-gones are for ever by-gones; and we are always starting clear at each moment, judging the values of things with a view to future utility. Industry is essentially prospective, not retrospective; and seldom does the result of any undertaking exactly coincide with the first intentions of its founders.

But though labour is never the cause of value, it is in a large proportion of cases the determining circumstance, and in the following way:—Value depends solely on the final degree of utility. How can we vary this degree of utility?—By having more or less of the commodity to consume. And how shall we get more or less of it?—By spending more or less labour in obtaining a supply. According to this view, then, there are two steps between labour and value. Labour affects supply, and supply affects the degree of utility, which governs value, or the ratio of exchange.

But it is easy to go too far in considering labour as the regulator of value; it is equally to be remembered that labour is itself of unequal value. Ricardo, by a violent assumption, founded his theory of value on quantities of labour considered as one uniform thing. He was aware that labour differs infinitely in quality and efficiency, so that each kind is more or less scarce, and is consequently paid at a higher or lower rate of wages. He regarded these differences as disturbing circumstances which would have to be allowed for; but his theory rests on the assumed equality of labour. This theory rests on a wholly different ground. I hold labour to be *essentially variable*, so that *its value must be determined by the value of the produce, not the value of the produce by that of the labour*. I hold it to be impossible to compare *à priori* the productive powers of a navvy, a carpenter, an iron-puddler, a schoolmaster, and a barrister. Accordingly, it will be found that not one of my equations represents a comparison between one man's labour and another's. The equation, if there is one at all, is between the same person in two or more different occupations. The subject is one in which complicated action and re-action takes place, and which we must defer until after we have described, in the next chapter, the Theory of Labour.

ALFRED MARSHALL

(1842–1924)

Many of the continental economists judged Marshall to be something of a "Johnny-come-lately" because his procrastination in publishing his Principles meant that many of his ideas, particularly with respect to marginal utility, appeared dated. Despite this, he was, for over a quarter of a century, generally acknowledged in England to be that nation's leading economist.

Disregarding his father's urgings that he study for the ministry, Marshall began his university studies in mathematics. Later an interest in social reform led him to the study of economics. After a variety of fellowships and teaching positions, he was appointed to a chair as Professor of Political Economy at Cambridge in 1885 where he remained until his retirement in 1908. His marriage to Mary Paley, herself a competent economist, led to much productive collaboration in the field of economics, including The Economics of Industry.

Marshall's Principles is one of the most difficult books in this collection from which to make selections. Not only is it extremely long, running to nearly 900 pages, but the footnotes which often constitute fair game for an editor must in Marshall's case be retained in toto. In an attempt to appeal to the general reader, Marshall made his text deceptively easy to read, with many of his original contributions buried in footnotes or in the numerous appendices.

The passages which we have included herein represent the heart of Marshall's contribution to the theory of value. Here he develops his well-known notion of the Marshallian "scissors" of supply and demand which together work to determine the market price. From this point he leads the reader to an examination of what lies behind each blade—behind demand, the principle of marginal utility, and behind supply, the concept of a firm's cost with an explanation of prime (variable), supplementary (fixed), and marginal costs. The relationship between supply and demand is plotted over the range of a variety of time periods. Throughout his analysis Marshall deals with a nearly perfectly competitive economy; considerations of monopoly are permitted to enter in from time to time, but they always play a distinctly secondary role. In order to preserve the rationale of this competitive model, Marshall later developed the concept of the "representative firm." The "representative firm" was the average firm, neither too young and small nor too old and big. Firms were prevented from growing into monopolies by their age. Like the trees in the forest, they tended to die off as they grew older.

Limitations of space have prevented us from including any of Marshall's treatment of the topic of distribution, but Marshall accorded it lengthy study. In considering distribution, Marshall found that the tools of supply and demand again had a useful role to play. Gone was the emphasis on the role of classes that had characterized Mill and Ricardo. Distribution, Marshall declared, was an immensely complicated affair. Wages, rent, interest, and profits could be explained by means of the apparatus of supply and demand. Lying behind the demand for factors of production was the marginal productivity of the factors in question; elements affecting the supply schedule were also given careful attention by Marshall.

Although Marshall can thus be properly labeled a marginalist, he found the theories of Smith, Ricardo, and Mill far more to his liking than did the earlier marginalists. Whereas Jevons had seen both Ricardo and Mill as able but "wrongheaded," Marshall was disposed to treat them in a far more kindly fashion—emphasizing the strong features in their analyses and apologizing or glossing over the defects. The explanation for this is readily available—by seeking to supplement the role of costs rather than displace it by marginal utility, Marshall had reason to keep a foot in both camps.

Like Adam Smith before him, Marshall was an acute observer of the economic scene about him. Furthermore, like Smith, the landscape for Marshall was bathed in bright sunshine! Technological change lost most of its terrors, the Malthusian terrors could be offset by improvements in transportation and technology, and the business cycle represented at worst only temporary departures from an equilibrium of full employment. Imperfections in the economy were acknowledged, but their significance for the smooth functioning of the system was minimized.

The passages from the following selection do not make clear the fact that Marshall combined his optimism about the future with a spirit of reform dedicated to bringing about improvements in man's condition. Marshall was a much more cautious reformer than some of those who had gone before him; he believed that progress was best achieved by small but repeated steps forward.

PRINCIPLES OF ECONOMICS

BOOK III / Of Wants and Their Satisfaction

Chapter 3: GRADATIONS OF CONSUMERS' DEMAND

§ 1. When a trader or a manufacturer buys anything to be used in production, or to be sold again, his demand is based on his anticipations of the profits which he can derive from it. These profits depend at any time on speculative risks and on other causes, which will need to be considered later on. But in the long run the price which a trader or manufacturer can afford to pay for a thing depends on the prices which consumers will pay for it, or for the things made by aid of it. The ultimate regulator of all demand is therefore consumers' demand. And it is with that almost exclusively that we shall be concerned in the present Book.

Utility is taken to be correlative to Desire or Want. It has been already argued that desires cannot be measured directly, but only indirectly by the outward phenomena to which they give rise: and that in those cases with which economics is chiefly concerned the measure is found in the price which a person is willing to pay for the fulfilment or satisfaction of his desire. He may have desires and aspirations which are not consciously set for any satisfaction: but for the present we are concerned chiefly with those which do so aim; and we assume that the resulting satisfaction corresponds in general fairly well to that which was anticipated when the purchase was made.[1]

---

[1] It cannot be too much insisted that to measure directly, or *per se*, either desires or the satisfaction which results from their fulfilment is impossible, if not inconceivable. If we could, we should have two accounts to make up, one of desires, and the other of realized satisfactions. And the two might differ considerably. For, to say nothing of higher aspirations, some of those desires with which economics is chiefly concerned, and especially those connected with emulation, are impulsive; many result from the force of habit; some are morbid and lead only to hurt; and many are based on expectations that are never fulfilled. Of course many satisfactions are not common pleasures, but

There is an endless variety of wants, but there is a limit to each separate want. This familiar and fundamental tendency of human nature may be stated in the *law of satiable wants* or *of diminishing utility* thus:—The *total utility* of a thing to anyone (that is, the total pleasure or other benefit it yields him) increases with every increase in his stock of it, but not as fast as his stock increases. If his stock of it increases at a uniform rate the benefit derived from it increases at a diminishing rate. In other words, the additional benefit which a person derives from a given increase of his stock of a thing, diminishes with every increase in the stock that he already has.

That part of the thing which he is only just induced to purchase may be called his *marginal purchase*, because he is on the margin of doubt whether it is worth his while to incur the outlay required to obtain it. And the utility of his marginal purchase may be called the *marginal utility* of the thing to him. Or, if instead of buying it, he makes the thing himself, then its marginal utility is the utility of that part which he thinks it only just worth his while to make. And thus the law just given may be worded:—

The marginal utility of a thing to anyone diminishes with every increase in the amount of it he already has.[2]

There is however an implicit condition in this law which should be made clear. It is that we do not suppose time to be allowed for any alteration in the character or tastes of the man himself. It is therefore no exception to the law that the more good music a man hears, the stronger is his taste for it likely to become; that avarice and ambition are often insatiable; or that the virtue of cleanliness and the vice of drunkenness alike grow on what they feed upon. For in such cases our observations range over some period of time; and the man is not the same at the beginning as at the end of it. If we take a man as he is, without allowing time for any change in

---

belong to the development of a man's higher nature, or to use a good old word, to his *beatification;* and some may even partly result from self-abnegation. The two direct measurements then might differ. But as neither of them is possible, we fall back on the measurement which economics supplies, of the motive or moving force to action: and we make it serve, with all its faults, *both* for the desires which prompt activities and for the satisfactions that result from them. (Compare "Some Remarks on Utility" by Prof. Pigou in the *Economic Journal* for March, 1903.)

[2] This law holds a priority of position to the *law of diminishing return* from land; which however has the priority in time; since it was the first to be subjected to a rigid analysis of a semi-mathematical character. And if by anticipation we borrow some of its terms, we may say that the *return* of pleasure which a person gets from each additional *dose* of a commodity diminishes till at last a margin is reached at which it is no longer worth his while to acquire any more of it.

The term *marginal utility* (*Grenz-nutz*) was first used in this connection by the Austrian Wieser. It has been adopted by Prof. Wicksteed. It corresponds to the term *Final* used by Jevons, to whom Wieser makes his acknowledgments in the Preface (p. xxiii. of the English edition). His list of anticipators of his doctrine is headed by Gossen, 1854.

his character, the marginal utility of a thing to him diminishes steadily with every increase in his supply of it.[3]

§ 2. Now let us translate this law of diminishing utility into terms of price. Let us take an illustration from the case of a commodity such as tea, which is in constant demand and which can be purchased in small quantities. Suppose, for instance, that tea of a certain quality is to be had at 2s. per lb. A person might be willing to give 10s. for a single pound once a year rather than go without it altogether; while if he could have any amount of it for nothing he would perhaps not care to use more than 30 lbs. in the year. But as it is, he buys perhaps 10 lbs. in the year; that is to say, the difference between the satisfaction which he gets from buying 9 lbs. and 10 lbs. is enough for him to be willing to pay 2s. for it: while the fact that he does not buy an eleventh pound, shows that he does not think that it would be worth an extra 2s. to him. That is, 2s. a pound measures the utility to him of the tea which lies at the margin or terminus or end of his purchases; it measures the marginal utility to him. If the price which he is just willing to pay for any pound be called his *demand price*, then 2s. is his *marginal demand price*. And our law may be worded:—

The larger the amount of a thing that a person has the less, other things being equal (*i.e.* the purchasing power of money, and the amount of money at his command being equal), will be the price which he will pay for a little more of it: or in other words his marginal demand price for it diminishes.

His demand becomes *efficient*, only when the price which he is willing to offer reaches that at which others are willing to sell.

This last sentence reminds us that we have as yet taken no account of changes in the marginal utility of money, or general purchasing power. At one and the same time, a person's material resources being unchanged, the marginal utility of money to him is a fixed quantity, so that the prices he is just willing to pay for two commodities are to one another in the same ratio as the utility of those two commodities.

---

[3] It may be noticed here, though the fact is of but little practical importance, that a small quantity of a commodity may be insufficient to meet a certain special want; and then there will be a more than proportionate increase of pleasure when the consumer gets enough of it to enable him to attain the desired end. Thus, for instance, anyone would derive less pleasure in proportion from ten pieces of wall paper than from twelve, if the latter would, and the former would not, cover the whole of the walls of his room. Or again a very short concert or a holiday may fail of its purpose of soothing and re-creating: and one of double length might be of more than double total utility. This case corresponds to the fact, which we shall have to study in connection with the tendency to diminishing return, that the capital and labour already applied to any piece of land may be so inadequate for the development of its full powers, that some further expenditure on it even with the existing arts of agriculture would give a more than proportionate return; and in the fact that an improvement in the arts of agriculture may resist that tendency, we shall find an analogy to the condition just mentioned in the text as implied in the law of diminishing utility.

§ 3. A greater utility will be required to induce him to buy a thing if he is poor than if he is rich. We have seen how the clerk with £100 a year will walk to business in a heavier rain than the clerk with £300 a year. But although the utility, or the benefit, that is measured in the poorer man's mind by twopence is greater than that measured by it in the richer man's mind; yet if the richer man rides a hundred times in the year and the poorer man twenty times, then the utility of the hundredth ride which the richer man is only just induced to take is measured to him by twopence; and the utility of the twentieth ride which the poorer man is only just induced to take is measured to him by twopence. For each of them the marginal utility is measured by twopence; but this marginal utility is greater in the case of the poorer man than in that of the richer.

In other words, the richer a man becomes the less is the marginal utility of money to him; every increase in his resources increases the price which he is willing to pay for any given benefit. And in the same way every diminution of his resources increases the marginal utility of money to him, and diminishes the price that he is willing to pay for any benefit.

.   .   .

When we say that a person's demand for anything increases, we mean that he will buy more of it than he would before at the same price, and that he will buy as much of it as before at a higher price. A general increase in his demand is an increase throughout the whole list of prices at which he is willing to purchase different amounts of it, and not merely that he is willing to buy more of it at the current prices.

Chapter 4: THE ELASTICITY OF WANTS

§ 1. We have seen that the only universal law as to a person's desire for a commodity is that it diminishes, other things being equal, with every increase in his supply of that commodity. But this diminution may be slow or rapid. If it is slow the price that he will give for the commodity will not fall much in consequence of a considerable increase in his supply of it; and a small fall in price will cause a comparatively large increase in his purchases. But if it is rapid, a small fall in price will cause only a very small increase in his purchases. In the former case his willingness to purchase the thing stretches itself out a great deal under the action of a small inducement: the elasticity of his wants, we may say, is great. In the latter case the extra inducement given by the fall in price causes hardly any extension of his desire to purchase: the elasticity of his demand is small. If a fall in

price from say 16d. to 15d. per lb. of tea would much increase his purchases, then a rise in price from 15d. to 16d. would much diminish them.
That is, when the demand is elastic for a fall in price, it is elastic also for
a rise.

And as with the demand of one person so with that of a whole market.
And we may say generally:—The *elasticity* (or *responsiveness*) *of demand*
in a market is great or small according as the amount demanded increases
much or little for a given fall in price, and diminishes much or little for a
given rise in price.[1]

.   .   .

§ 3. There are some things the current prices of which in this country
are very low relatively even to the poorer classes; such are for instance salt,
and many kinds of savours and flavours, and also cheap medicines. It is
doubtful whether any fall in price would induce a considerable increase
in the consumption of these.

The current prices of meat, milk and butter, wool, tobacco, imported
fruits, and of ordinary medical attendance, are such that every variation
in price makes a great change in the consumption of them by the working
classes, and the lower half of the middle classes; but the rich would not
much increase their own personal consumption of them however cheaply
they were to be had. In other words, the direct demand for these commodities is very elastic on the part of the working and lower middle classes,

---

[1] We may say that the elasticity of demand is one, if a small fall in price will cause
an equal proportionate increase in the amount demanded:
or as we may say roughly, if a fall of one per cent. in price
will increase the sales by one per cent.; that it is two or a
half, if a fall of one per cent. in price makes an increase of
two or one half per cent. respectively in the amount demanded; and so on. (This statement is rough; because 98
does not bear exactly the same proportion to 100 that 100
does to 102.) The elasticity of demand can be best traced
in the demand curve with the aid of the following rule. Let
a straight line touching the curve at any point P meet Ox in
T and Oy in t, then *the measure of the elasticity at the
point P is the ratio of PT to Pt.*

If PT were twice Pt, a fall of 1 per cent. in price would cause an increase of 2 per
cent., in the amount demanded; the elasticity of demand would be two. If PT were one-
third of Pt, a fall of 1 per cent. in price would cause an increase of ⅓ per cent. in the
amount demanded; the elasticity of demand would be one-third; and so on. Another
way of looking at the same result is this:—the elasticity at the point P is measured by
the ratio of PT to Pt, that is of MT to MO (PM being drawn perpendicular to Om);
and therefore *the elasticity is equal to one when the angle TPM is equal to the angle
OPM; and it always increases when the angle TPM increases relatively to the angle
OPM, and vice versâ.*

though not on the part of the rich. But the working class is so numerous that their consumption of such things as are well within their reach is much greater than that of the rich; and therefore the aggregate demand for all things of the kind is very elastic. A little while ago sugar belonged to this group of commodities: but its price in England has now fallen so far as to be low relatively even to the working classes, and the demand for it is therefore not elastic.[2]

The current prices of wall-fruit, of the better kinds of fish, and other moderately expensive luxuries are such as to make the consumption of them by the middle class increase much with every fall in price; in other words, the middle class demand for them is very elastic: while the demand on the part of the rich and on the part of the working class is much less elastic, the former because it is already nearly satiated, the latter because the price is still too high.

The current prices of such things as rare wines, fruit out of season, highly skilled medical and legal assistance, are so high that there is but little demand for them except from the rich: but what demand there is, often has considerable elasticity. Part of the demand for the more expensive kinds of food is really a demand for the means of obtaining social distinction, and is almost insatiable.[3]

§ 4. The case of necessaries is exceptional. When the price of wheat is very high, and again when it is very low, the demand has very little elasticity: at all events if we assume that wheat, even when scarce, is the cheapest food for man; and that, even when most plentiful, it is not consumed in any other way. We know that a fall in the price of the quartern loaf from 6d. to 4d. has scarcely any effect in increasing the consumption of bread. With regard to the other end of the scale it is more difficult to speak with certainty, because there has been no approach to a scarcity in England since the repeal of the corn laws. But, availing ourselves of the experience of a less happy time, we may suppose that deficits in the supply of 1, 2, 3, 4, or 5 tenths would cause a rise in price of 3, 8, 16, 28, or 45 tenths re-

[2] We must however remember that the character of the demand schedule for any commodity depends in a great measure on whether the prices of its rivals are taken to be fixed or to alter with it. If we separated the demand for beef from that for mutton, and supposed the price of mutton to be held fixed while that for beef was raised, then the demand for beef would become extremely elastic. For any slight fall in the price of beef would cause it to be used largely in the place of mutton and thus lead to a very great increase of its consumption: while on the other hand even a small rise in price would cause many people to eat mutton to the almost entire exclusion of beef. But the demand schedule for all kinds of fresh meat taken together, their prices being supposed to retain always about the same relation to one another, and to be not very different from those now prevailing in England, shows only a moderate elasticity. And similar remarks apply to beet-root and cane-sugar.

[3] In April 1894, for instance, six plovers' eggs, the first of the season, were sold in London at 10s. 6d. each. The following day there were more, and the price fell to 5s.; the next day to 3s. each; and a week later to 4d.

spectively.[4] Much greater variations in prices indeed than this have not been uncommon. Thus wheat sold in London for ten shillings a bushel in 1335, but in the following year it sold for ten pence.[5]

There may be even more violent changes than this in the price of a thing which is not necessary, if it is perishable and the demand for it is inelastic: thus fish may be very dear one day, and sold for manure two or three days later.

Water is one of the few things the consumption of which we are able to observe at all prices, from the very highest down to nothing at all. At moderate prices the demand for it is very elastic. But the uses to which it can be put are capable of being completely filled: and as its price sinks towards zero the demand for it loses its elasticity. Nearly the same may be said of salt. Its price in England is so low that the demand for it as an article of food is very inelastic; but in India the price is comparatively high and the demand is comparatively elastic.

The price of house-room, on the other hand, has never fallen very low except when a locality is being deserted by its inhabitants. Where the condition of society is healthy, and there is no check to general prosperity, there seems always to be an elastic demand for house-room, on account both of the real conveniences and the social distinction which it affords. The desire for those kinds of clothing which are not used for the purpose of display, is satiable: when their price is low the demand for them has scarcely any elasticity.

The demand for things of a higher quality depends much on sensibility: some people care little for a refined flavour in their wine provided they can get plenty of it: others crave a high quality, but are easily satiated. In the ordinary working class districts the inferior and the better joints are sold at nearly the same price: but some well-paid artisans in the north of England have developed a liking for the best meat, and will pay for it nearly as high a price as can be got in the west end of London, where the price is

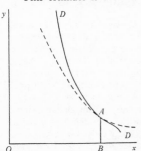

[4] This estimate is commonly attributed to Gregory King. Its bearing on the law of demand is admirably discussed by Lord Lauderdale (*Inquiry into the Nature and Origin of Public Wealth*, pp. 51–53). It is represented by the curve *DD'*, the point A corresponding to the ordinary price. If we take account of the fact that where the price of wheat is very low, it may be used, as it was for instance in 1834, for feeding cattle and sheep and pigs and for brewing and distilling, the lower part of the curve would take a shape somewhat like that of the dotted line in the figure. And if we assume that when the price is very high, cheaper substitutes can be got for it, the upper part of the curve would take a shape similar to that of the upper dotted line.

[5] *Chronicon Preciosum* (A.D. 1745) says that the price of wheat in London was as low as 2s. a quarter in 1336: and that at Leicester it sold at 40s. on a Saturday, and at 14s. on the following Friday.

kept artificially high by the necessity of sending the inferior joints away for sale elsewhere. Use also gives rise to acquired distastes as well as to acquired tastes. Illustrations which make a book attractive to many readers, will repel those whose familiarity with better work has rendered them fastidious. A person of high musical sensibility in a large town will avoid bad concerts: though he might go to them gladly if he lived in a small town, where no good concerts are to be heard, because there are not enough persons willing to pay the high price required to cover their expenses. The effective demand for first-rate music is elastic only in large towns; for second-rate music it is elastic both in large and small towns.

Generally speaking those things have the most elastic demand, which are capable of being applied to many different uses. Water for instance is needed first as food, then for cooking, then for washing of various kinds and so on. When there is no special drought, but water is sold by the pailful, the price may be low enough to enable even the poorer classes to drink as much of it as they are inclined, while for cooking they sometimes use the same water twice over, and they apply it very scantily in washing. The middle classes will perhaps not use any of it twice for cooking; but they will make a pail of water go a good deal further for washing purposes than if they had an unlimited supply at command. When water is supplied by pipes, and charged at a very low rate by meter, many people use as much of it even for washing as they feel at all inclined to do; and when the water is supplied not by meter but at a fixed annual charge, and is laid on in every place where it is wanted, the use of it for every purpose is carried to the full satiety limit.[6]

On the other hand, demand is, generally speaking, very inelastic, firstly, for absolute necessaries (as distinguished from conventional necessaries

· · ·

§ 6. Next, allowance must be made for changes in fashion, and taste and habit,[7] for the opening out of new uses of a commodity, for the dis-

---

[6] Thus the general demand of any one person for such a thing as water is the aggregate (or compound) of his demand for it for each use; in the same way as the demand of a group of people of different orders of wealth for a commodity, which is serviceable in only one use, is the aggregate of the demands of each member of the group. Again, just as the demand of the rich for peas is considerable even at a very high price, but loses all elasticity at a price that is still high relatively to the consumption of the poor; so the demand of the individual for water to drink is considerable even at a very high price, but loses all elasticity at a price that is still high relatively to his demand for it for the purpose of cleaning up the house. And as the aggregate of a number of demands on the part of different classes of people for peas retains elasticity over a larger range of price than will that of any one individual, so the demand of an individual for water for many uses retains elasticity over a larger range of prices than his demand for it for any one use. Compare an article by J. B. Clark on *A Universal Law of Economic Variation* in the *Harvard Journal of Economics*, Vol. VIII.

[7] For illustrations of the influence of fashion see articles by Miss Foley in the *Economic Journal*, Vol. III, and Miss Heather Bigg in the *Nineteenth Century*, Vol. XXIII.

and necessaries for efficiency); and secondly, for some of those luxuries of the rich which do not absorb much of their income.

covery or improvement or cheapening of other things that can be applied to the same uses with it. In all these cases there is great difficulty in allowing for the time that elapses between the economic cause and its effect. For time is required to enable a rise in the price of a commodity to exert its full influence on consumption. Time is required for consumers to become familiar with substitutes that can be used instead of it, and perhaps for producers to get into the habit of producing them in sufficient quantities. Time may be also wanted for the growth of habits of familiarity with the new commodities and the discovery of methods of economizing them.

For instance when wood and charcoal became dear in England, familiarity with coal as a fuel grew slowly, fireplaces were but slowly adapted to its use, and an organized traffic in it did not spring up quickly even to places to which it could be easily carried by water: the invention of processes by which it could be used as a substitute for charcoal in manufacture went even more slowly, and is indeed hardly yet complete. Again, when in recent years the price of coal became very high, a great stimulus was given to the invention of economies in its use, especially in the production of iron and steam; but few of these inventions bore much practical fruit till after the high price had passed away. Again, when a new tramway or suburban railway is opened, even those who live near the line do not get into the habit of making the most of its assistance at once; and a good deal more time elapses before many of those whose places of business are near one end of the line change their homes so as to live near the other end. Again, when petroleum first became plentiful few people were ready to use it freely; gradually petroleum and petroleum lamps have become familiar to all classes of society: too much influence would therefore be attributed to the fall in price which has occurred since then, if it were credited with all the increase of consumption.

Another difficulty of the same kind arises from the fact that there are many purchases which can easily be put off for a short time, but not for a long time. This is often the case with regard to clothes and other things which are worn out gradually, and which can be made to serve a little longer than usual under the pressure of high prices. For instance, at the beginning of the cotton famine the recorded consumption of cotton in England was very small. This was partly because retail dealers reduced their stock, but chiefly because people generally made shift to do as long as they could without buying new cotton goods. In 1864 however many found themselves unable to wait longer; and a good deal more cotton was entered for home consumption in that year, though the price was then much higher, than in either of the preceding years. For commodities of this kind then a sudden scarcity does not immediately raise the price fully up to the level, which properly corresponds to the reduced supply. Similarly after the great commercial depression in the United States in 1873 it was noticed that the boot trade revived before the general clothing trade; because there is a great deal of reserve wear in the coats and hats that are thrown aside in prosperous times as worn out, but not so much in the boots.

§ 7. The above difficulties are fundamental: but there are others which do not lie deeper than the more or less inevitable faults of our statistical returns.

We desire to obtain, if possible, a series of prices at which different amounts of a commodity can find purchasers during a given time in a market. A perfect market is a district, small or large, in which there are many buyers and many sellers all so keenly on the alert and so well acquainted with one another's affairs that the price of a commodity is always practically the same for the whole of the district. But independently of the fact that those who buy for their own consumption, and not for the purposes of trade, are not always on the look out for every change in the market, there is no means of ascertaining exactly what prices are paid in many transactions. Again, the geographical limits of a market are seldom clearly drawn, except when they are marked out by the sea or by custom-house barriers; and no country has accurate statistics of commodities produced in it for home consumption.

Again, there is generally some ambiguity even in such statistics as are to be had. They commonly show goods as entered for consumption as soon as they pass into the hands of dealers; and consequently an increase of dealers' stocks cannot easily be distinguished from an increase of consumption. But the two are governed by different causes. A rise of prices tends to check consumption; but if the rise is expected to continue, it will probably, as has already been noticed, lead dealers to increase their stocks.[8]

Next it is difficult to insure that the commodities referred to are always of the same quality. After a dry summer what wheat there is, is exceptionally good; and the prices for the next harvest year appear to be higher than they really are. It is possible to make allowance for this, particularly now that dry Californian wheat affords a standard. But it is almost impossible to allow properly for the changes in quality of many kinds of manufactured goods. This difficulty occurs even in the case of such a thing as tea: the substitution in recent years of the stronger Indian tea for the weaker Chinese tea has made the real increase of consumption greater than that which is shown by the statistics.

Chapter 6: VALUE AND UTILITY

§ 1. We may now turn to consider how far the price which is actually paid for a thing represents the benefit that arises from its possession. This

---

[8] In examining the effects of taxation, it is customary to compare the amounts entered for consumption just before and just after the imposition of the tax. But this is

is a wide subject on which economic science has very little to say, but that little is of some importance.

We have already seen that the price which a person pays for a thing can never exceed, and seldom comes up to that which he would be willing to pay rather than go without it: so that the satisfaction which he gets from its purchase generally exceeds that which he gives up in paying away its price; and he thus derives from the purchase a surplus of satisfaction. The excess of the price which he would be willing to pay rather than go without the thing, over that which he actually does pay, is the economic measure of this surplus satisfaction. It may be called *consumer's surplus.*

It is obvious that the consumer's surpluses derived from some commodities are much greater than from others. There are many comforts and luxuries of which the prices are very much below those which many people would pay rather than go entirely without them; and which therefore afford a very great consumer's surplus. Good instances are matches, salt, a penny newspaper, or a postage-stamp.

This benefit, which he gets from purchasing at a low price things for which he would rather pay a high price than go without them, may be called the benefit which he derives from his *opportunities,* or from his *environment;* or, to recur to a word that was in common use a few generations ago, from his *conjuncture.* Our aim in the present chapter is to apply the notion of consumer's surplus as an aid in estimating roughly some of the benefits which a person derives from his environment or his conjuncture.[1]

§ 2. In order to give definiteness to our notions, let us consider the case of tea purchased for domestic consumption. Let us take the case of a man, who, if the price of tea were 20s. a pound, would just be induced to buy one pound annually; who would just be induced to buy two pounds if the price were 14s., three pounds if the price were 10s., four pounds if the price were 6s., five pounds if the price were 4s., six pounds if the price were 3s., and who, the price being actually 2s., does purchase seven pounds. We have to

---

untrustworthy. For dealers anticipating the tax lay in large stocks just before it is imposed, and need to buy very little for some time afterwards. And *vice versâ* when a tax is lowered. Again, high taxes lead to false returns. For instance, the nominal importation of molasses into Boston increased fiftyfold in consequence of the tax being lowered by the Rockingham Ministry in 1766, from 6d. to 1d. per gallon. But this was chiefly due to the fact that with the tax at 1d., it was cheaper to pay the duty than to smuggle.

[1] This term is a familiar one in German economics, and meets a need which is much felt in English economics. For "opportunity" and "environment," the only available substitutes for it, are sometimes rather misleading. By *Conjunctur,* says Wagner (*Grundegung,* 3rd ed., p. 387), "we understand the sum total of the technical, economic, social and legal conditions; which, in a mode of national life (*Volkswirthschaft*) resting upon division of labour and private property,—especially private property in land and other material means of production—determine the demand for and supply of goods, and therefore their exchange value: this determination being as a rule, or at least in the main, *independent* of the will of the owner, of his activity and his remissness."

investigate the consumer's surplus which he derives from his power of purchasing tea at 2s. a pound.

The fact that he would just be induced to purchase one pound if the price were 20s., proves that the total enjoyment or satisfaction which he derives from that pound is as great as that which he could obtain by spending 20s. on other things. When the price falls to 14s., he could, if he chose, continue to buy only one pound. He would then get for 14s. what was worth to him at least 20s.; and he will obtain a surplus satisfaction worth to him at least 6s., or in other words a consumer's surplus of at least 6s. But in fact he buys a second pound of his own free choice, thus showing that he regards it as worth to him at least 14s., and that this represents the *additional* utility of the second pound to him. He obtains for 28s. what is worth to him at least 20s. + 14s.; *i.e.* 34s. His surplus satisfaction is at all events not diminished by buying it, but remains worth at least 6s. to him. The total utility of the two pounds is worth at least 34s., his consumer's surplus is at least 6s.[2] The fact that each additional purchase reacts upon

---

[2] Some further explanations may be given of this statement; though in fact they do little more than repeat in other words what has already been said. The significance of the condition in the text that he buys the second pound of his own free choice is shown by the consideration that if the price of 14s. had been offered to him on the condition that he took two pounds, he would then have to elect between taking one pound for 20s. or two pounds for 28s.: and then his taking two pounds would not have proved that he thought the second pound worth more than 8s. to him. But as it is, he takes a second pound paying 14s. unconditionally for it; and that proves that it is worth at least 14s. to him. (If he can get buns at a penny each, but seven for sixpence; and he elects to buy seven, we know that he is willing to give up his sixth penny for the sake of the sixth and the seventh buns: but we cannot tell how much he would pay rather than go without the seventh bun only.)

It is sometimes objected that as he increases his purchases, the urgency of his need for his earlier purchases is diminished, and their utility falls; therefore we ought to continually redraw the earlier parts of our list of demand prices at a lower level, as we pass along it towards lower prices (*i.e.* to redraw at a lower level our demand curve as we pass along it to the right). But this misconceives the plan on which the list of prices is made out. The objection would have been valid, if the demand price set against each number of pounds of tea represented the *average* utility of that number. For it is true that, if he would pay just 20s. for one pound, and just 14s. for a second, then he would pay just 34s. for the two; *i.e.* 17s. each on the average. And if our list had had reference to the *average* prices he would pay, and had set 17s. against the second pound; then no doubt we should have had to redraw the list as we passed on. For when he has bought a third pound the average utility to him of each of the three will be less than that of 17s.; being in fact 14s. 8d. if, as we go on to assume, he would pay just 10s. for a third pound. But this difficulty is entirely avoided on the plan of making out demand prices which is here adopted; according to which his second pound is credited, not with the 17s. which represents the average value per pound of the two pounds; but with the 14s., which represents the *additional* utility which a second pound has for him. For that remains unchanged when he has bought a third pound, of which the additional utility is measured by 10s.

The first pound was probably worth to him more than 20s. All that we know is that it was not worth less to him. He probably got some small surplus even on that. Again, the second pound was probably worth more than 14s. to him. All that we know is that it was worth at least 14s. and not worth 20s. to him. He would get therefore at this

the utility of the purchases which he had previously decided to make *has already been allowed for in making out the schedule and must not be counted a second time.*

When the price falls to 10s., he might, if he chose, continue to buy only two pounds; and obtain for 20s. what was worth to him at least 34s., and derive a surplus satisfaction worth at least 14s. But in fact he prefers to buy a third pound: and as he does this freely, we know that he does not diminish his surplus satisfaction by doing it. He now gets for 30s. three pounds; of which the first is worth to him at least 20s., the second at least 14s., and the third at least 10s. The total utility of the three is worth at least 44s., his consumer's surplus is at least 14s., and so on.

When at last the price has fallen to 2s. he buys seven pounds, which are severally worth to him not less than 20, 14, 10, 6, 4, 3, and 2s. or 59s. in all. This sum measures their total utility to him, and his consumer's surplus is (at least) the excess of this sum over the 14s. he actually does pay for them, *i.e.* 45s. This is the excess value of the satisfaction he gets from buying the tea over that which he could have got by spending the 14s. in extending a little his purchase of other commodities, of which he had just not thought it worth while to buy more at their current prices; and any further purchases of which at those prices would not yield him any consumer's surplus. In other words, he derives this 45s. worth of surplus enjoyment from his conjuncture, from the adaptation of the environment to his wants in the particular matter of tea. If that adaptation ceased, and tea could not be had at any price, he would have incurred a loss of satisfaction at least equal to that which he could have got by spending 45s. more on extra supplies of things that were worth to him only just what he paid for them.[3]

---

stage a surplus satisfaction of at least 6s., probably a little more. A ragged edge of this kind, as mathematicians are aware, always exists when we watch the effects of considerable changes, as that from 20s. to 14s. a pound. If we had begun with a very high price, had descended by practically infinitesimal changes of a farthing per pound, and watched infinitesimal variations in his consumption of a small fraction of a pound at a time, this ragged edge would have disappeared.

[3] Prof. Nicholson (*Principles of Political Economy*, Vol. I and *Economic Journal*, Vol. IV) has raised objections to the notion of consumers' surplus, which have been answered by Prof. Edgeworth in the same Journal. Prof. Nicholson says:—"Of what avail is it to say that the utility of an income of (say) £100 a year is worth (say) £1000 a year?" There would be no avail in saying that. But there might be use, when comparing life in Central Africa with life in England, in saying that, though the things which money will buy in Central Africa may on the average be as cheap there as here, yet there are so many things which cannot be bought there at all, that a person with a thousand a year there is not so well off as a person with three or four hundred a year here. If a man pays 1d. toll on a bridge, which saves him an additional drive that would cost a shilling, we do not say that the penny is worth a shilling, but that the penny together with the advantage offered him by the bridge (the part it plays in his conjuncture) is worth a shilling for that day. Were the bridge swept away on a day on which he needed it, he would be in at least as bad a position as if he had been deprived of eleven pence.

§ 3. In the same way if we were to neglect for the moment the fact that the same sum of money represents different amounts of pleasure to different people, we might measure the surplus satisfaction which the sale of tea affords, say, in the London market, by the aggregate of the sums by which the prices shown in a complete list of demand prices for tea exceeds its selling price.[4]

This analysis, with its new names and elaborate machinery, appears at first sight laboured and unreal. On closer study it will be found to intro-

[4] Let us then consider the demand curve DD' for tea in any large market.

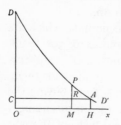

Let OH be the amount which is sold there at the price HA annually, a year being taken as our unit of time. Taking any point M in OH let us draw MP vertically upwards to meet the curve in P and cut a horizontal line through A in R. We will suppose the several lbs. numbered in the order of the eagerness of the several purchasers: the eagerness of the purchaser of any lb. being measured by the price he is just willing to pay for that lb. The figure informs us that OM can be sold at the price PM; but that at any higher price not quite so many lbs. can be sold. There must be then some individual who will buy more at the price PM, than he will at any higher price; and we are to regard the OMth lb. as sold to this individual. Suppose for instance that PM represents 4s., and that OM represents a million lbs. The purchaser described in the text is just willing to buy his fifth lb. of tea at the price 4s., and the OMth or millionth lb. may be said to be sold to him. If AH and therefore RM represent 2s., the consumers' surplus derived from the OMth lb. is the excess of PM or 4s. which the purchaser of that lb. would have been willing to pay for it over RM the 2s. which he actually does pay for it. Let us suppose that a very thin vertical parallelogram is drawn of which the height is PM and of which the base is the distance along Ox that measures the single unit or lb. of tea. It will be convenient henceforward to regard price as measured not by a mathematical straight line without thickness, as PM; but by a very thin parallelogram, or as it may be called a thick straight line, of which the breadth is in every case equal to the distance along Ox which measures a unit or lb. of tea. Thus we should say that the total satisfaction derived from the OMth lb. of tea is represented (or, on the assumption made in the last paragraph of the text is measured) by the thick straight line MP; that the price paid for this lb. is represented by the thick straight line MR and the consumers' surplus derived from this lb. by the thick straight line RP. Now let us suppose that such thin parallelograms, or thick straight lines, are drawn from all positions of M between O and H, one for each lb. of tea. The thick straight lines are drawn, as MP is, from Ox up to the demand curve will each represent the aggregate of the satisfaction derived from a lb. of tea; and taken together thus occupy and exactly fill up the whole area $DOHA$. Therefore we may say that the area $DOHA$ represents the aggregate of the satisfaction derived from the consumption of tea. Again, each of the straight lines drawn, as MR is, from Ox upwards as far as AC represents the price that actually is paid for a lb. of tea. These straight lines together make up the area $COHA$; and therefore this area represents the total price paid for tea. Finally each of the straight lines drawn as RP is from AC upwards as far as the demand curve, represents the consumers' surplus derived from the corresponding lb. of tea. These straight lines together make up the area DCA; and therefore this area represents the total consumers' surplus that is derived from tea when the price is AH. But it must be repeated that this geometrical measurement is only an aggregate of the measures of benefits which are not all measured on the same scale except on the assumption just made in the text. Unless that assumption is made the area only represents an aggregate of satisfactions, the several amounts of which are not exactly measured. On that assumption only, its area measures the volume of the total *net* satisfaction derived from the tea by its various purchasers.

duce no new difficulties and to make no new assumptions; but only to bring to light difficulties and assumptions that are latent in the common language of the market place. For in this, as in other cases, the apparent simplicity of popular phrases veils a real complexity, and it is the duty of science to bring out that latent complexity; to face it; and to reduce it as far as possible: so that in later stages we may handle firmly difficulties that could not be grasped with a good grip by the vague thought and language of ordinary life.

It is a common saying in ordinary life that the real worth of things to a man is not gauged by the price he pays for them: that, though he spends for instance much more on tea than on salt, yet salt is of greater real worth to him; and that this would be clearly seen if he were entirely deprived of it. This line of argument is but thrown into precise technical form when it is said that we cannot trust the marginal utility of a commodity to indicate its total utility. If some shipwrecked men, expecting to wait a year before they were rescued, had a few pounds of tea and the same number of pounds of salt to divide between them, the salt would be the more highly prized; because the marginal utility of an ounce of salt, when a person expects to get only a few of them in the year is greater than that of tea under like circumstances. But, under ordinary circumstances, the price of salt being low, every one buys so much of it that an additional pound would bring him little additional satisfaction: the total utility of salt to him is very great indeed, and yet its marginal utility is low. On the other hand, since tea is costly, most people use less of it and let the water stay on it rather longer than they would, if it could be got at nearly as low a price as salt can. Their desire for it is far from being satiated: its marginal utility remains high, and they may be willing to pay as much for an additional ounce of it as they would for an additional pound of salt. The common saying of ordinary life with which we began suggests all this: but not in an exact and definite form, such as is needed for a statement which will often be applied in later work. The use of technical terms at starting adds nothing to knowledge: but it puts familiar knowledge in a firm compact shape, ready to serve as the basis for further study.[5]

Or the real worth of a thing might be discussed with reference not to a single person but to people in general; and thus it would naturally be assumed that a shilling's worth of gratification to one Englishman might be

[5] Harris On Coins 1757, says "Things in general are valued, not according to their real uses in supplying the necessities of men; but rather in proportion to the land, labour and skill that are requisite to produce them. It is according to this proportion nearly, that things or commodities are exchanged one for another; and it is by the said scale, that the intrinsic values of most things are chiefly estimated. Water is of great use, and yet ordinarily of little or no value; because in most places, water flows spontaneously in such great plenty, as not to be withheld within the limits of private property; but all may have enough, without other expense than that of bringing or conducting it, when the case so requires. On the other hand, diamonds being very scarce, have upon that account a great value, though they are but little use."

taken as equivalent with a shilling's worth to another, "to start with," and "until cause to the contrary were shown." But everyone would know that this was a reasonable course only on the supposition that the consumers of tea and those of salt belonged to the same classes of people; and included people of every variety of temperament.[6]

This involves the consideration that a pound's worth of satisfaction to an ordinary poor man is a much greater thing than a pound's worth of satisfaction to an ordinary rich man: and if instead of comparing tea and salt, which are both used largely by all classes, we compared either of them with champagne or pineapples, the correction to be made on this account would be more than important: it would change the whole character of the estimate. In earlier generations many statesmen, and even some economists, neglected to make adequate allowance for considerations of this class, especially when constructing schemes of taxation; and their words or deeds seemed to imply a want of sympathy with the sufferings of the poor; though more often they were due simply to want of thought.

On the whole however it happens that by far the greater number of the events with which economics deals, affect in about equal proportions all the different classes of society; so that if the money measures of the happiness caused by two events are equal, there is not in general any very great difference between the amounts of the happiness in the two cases. And it is on account of this fact that the exact measurement of the consumers' surplus in a market has already much theoretical interest, and may become of high practical importance.

It will be noted however that the demand prices of each commodity, on which our estimates of its total utility and consumers' surplus are based, assume that *other things remain equal*, while its price rises to scarcity value: and when the total utilities of two commodities which contribute to the same purpose are calculated on this plan, we cannot say that the total utility of the two together is equal to the sum of the total utilities of each separately.[7]

[6] There might conceivably be persons of high sensibility who would suffer specially from the want of either salt or tea: or who were generally sensitive, and would suffer more from the loss of a certain part of their income than others in the same station of life. But it would be assumed that such differences between individuals might be neglected, since we were considering in either case the average of large numbers of people; though of course it might be necessary to consider whether there were some special reason for believing, say, that those who laid most store by tea were a specially sensitive class of people. If it could, then a separate allowance for this would have to be made before applying the results of economical analysis to practical problems of ethics or politics.

[7] Some ambiguous phrases in earlier editions appear to have suggested to some readers the opposite opinion. But the task of adding together the total utilities of all commodities, so as to obtain the aggregate of the total utility of all wealth, is beyond the range of any but the most elaborate mathematical formulæ. An attempt to treat it by them some years ago convinced the present writer that even if the task be theoretically feasible, the result would be encumbered by so many hypotheses as to be practically useless.

§ 4. The substance of our argument would not be affected if we took account of the fact that, the more a person spends on anything the less power he retains of purchasing more of it or of other things, and the greater is the value of money to him (in technical language every fresh expenditure increases the marginal value of money to him). But though its substance would not be altered, its form would be made more intricate without any corresponding gain; for there are very few practical problems, in which the corrections to be made under this head would be of any importance.[8]

There are however some exceptions. For instance, as Sir R. Giffen has pointed out, a rise in the price of bread makes so large a drain on the resources of the poorer labouring families and raises so much the marginal utility of money to them, that they are forced to curtail their consumption of meat and the more expensive farinaceous foods: and, bread being still the cheapest food which they can get and will take, they consume more, and not less of it. But such cases are rare; when they are met with, each must be treated on its own merits.

It has already been remarked that we cannot guess at all accurately how much of anything people would buy at prices very different from those which they are accustomed to pay for it: or in other words, what the demand prices for it would be for amounts very different from those which are commonly sold. Our list of demand prices is therefore highly con-

---

Attention has already been called to the fact that for some purposes such things as tea and coffee must be grouped together as one commodity: and it is obvious that, if tea were inaccessible, people would increase their consumption of coffee, and *vice versâ*. The loss that people would suffer from being deprived both of tea and coffee would be greater than the sum of their losses from being deprived of either alone: and therefore the total utility of tea and coffee is greater than the sum of the total utility of tea calculated on the supposition that people can have recourse to coffee, and that of coffee calculated on a like supposition as to tea. This difficulty can be theoretically evaded by grouping the two "rival" commodities together under a common demand schedule. On the other hand, if we have calculated the total utility of fuel with reference to the fact that without it we could not obtain hot water to obtain the beverage tea from tea leaves, we should count something twice over if we added to that utility the total utility of tea leaves, reckoned on a similar plan. Again the total utility of agricultural produce includes that of ploughs; and the two may not be added together; though the total utility of ploughs may be discussed in connection with one problem, and that of wheat in connection with another.

Prof. Patten has insisted on the latter of them in some able and suggestive writings. But his attempt to express the aggregate utility of all forms of wealth seems to overlook many difficulties.

[8] In mathematical language the neglected elements would generally belong to the second order of small quantities; and the legitimacy of the familiar scientific method by which they are neglected would have seemed beyond question, had not Prof. Nicholson challenged it. A short reply to him has been given by Prof. Edgeworth in the *Economic Journal* for March 1894; and a fuller reply by Prof. Barone in the *Giornale degli Economisti* for Sept. 1894; of which some account is given by Mr. Sanger in the *Economic Journal* for March 1895.

Formal account could be taken of changes in the marginal utility of money, if it were desired to do so. If we attempted to add together the total utilities of all commodities, we should be bound to do so: that task is however impracticable.

jectural except in the neighbourhood of the customary price; and the best estimates we can form of the whole amount of the utility of anything are liable to large error. But this difficulty is not important practically. For the chief applications of the doctrine of consumers' surplus are concerned with such changes in it as would accompany changes in the price of the commodity in question in the neighbourhood of the customary price: that is, they require us to use only that information with which we are fairly well supplied. These remarks apply with special force to necessaries.[9]

§ 5. There remains another class of considerations which are apt to be overlooked in estimating the dependence of well-being upon material wealth. Not only does a person's happiness often depend more on his own physical, mental and moral health than on his external conditions: but even among these conditions many that are of chief importance for his real happiness are apt to be omitted from an inventory of his wealth. Some are free gifts of nature; and these might indeed be neglected without great harm if they were always the same for everybody; but in fact they vary much from place to place. More of them however are elements of collective wealth which are often omitted from the reckoning of individual wealth; but which become important when we compare different parts of the modern civilized world, and even more important when we compare our own age with earlier times.

Collective action for the purposes of securing common well-being, as for instance in lighting and watering the streets, will occupy us much towards the end of our inquiries. Co-operative associations for the purchase of

[9] The notion of consumers' surplus may help us a little now; and, when our statistical knowledge is further advanced, it may help us a great deal to decide how much injury would be done to the public by an additional tax of 6d. a pound on tea, or by an addition of ten per cent. to the freight charges of a railway: and the value of the notion is but little diminished by the fact that it would not help us much to estimate the loss that would be caused by a tax of 30s. a pound on tea, or a tenfold rise in freight charges.

Reverting to our last diagram, we may express this by saying that, if A is the point on the curve corresponding to the amount that is wont to be sold in the market, data can be obtained sufficient for drawing the curve with tolerable correctness for some distance on either side of A; though the curve can seldom be drawn with any approach to accuracy right up to D. But this is practically unimportant, because in. the chief practical applications of the theory of value we should seldom make any use of a knowledge of the whole shape of the demand curve if we had it. We need just what we can get, that is, a fairly correct knowledge of its shape in the neighbourhood of A. We seldom require to ascertain the total area DCA; it is sufficient for most of our purposes to know the changes in this area that would be occasioned by moving A through small distances along the curve in either direction. Nevertheless it will save trouble to assume provisionally, as in pure theory we are at liberty to do, that the curve is completely drawn.

There is however a special difficulty in estimating the whole of the utility of commodities some supply of which is necessary for life. If any attempt is made to do it, the best plan is perhaps to take that necessary supply for granted, and estimate the total utility only of that part of the commodity which is in excess of this amount. But we must recollect that the desire for anything is much dependent on the difficulty of getting substitutes for it.

things for personal consumption have made more progress in England than elsewhere: but those for purchasing the things wanted for trade purposes by farmers and others, have until lately been backward in England. Both kinds are sometimes described as Consumers' associations; but they are really associations for economizing effort in certain branches of business, and belong to the subject of Production rather than Consumption.

. . .

BOOK V / General Relations of Demand, Supply and Value

Chapter 3: EQUILIBRIUM OF NORMAL DEMAND AND SUPPLY

§ 1. We have next to inquire what causes govern supply prices, that is prices which dealers are willing to accept for different amounts. In the last chapter we looked at the affairs of only a single day; and supposed the stocks offered for sale to be already in existence. But of course these stocks are dependent on the amount of wheat sown in the preceding year; and that, in its turn, was largely influenced by the farmers' guesses as to the price which they would get for it in this year. This is the point at which we have to work in the present chapter.

Even in the corn-exchange of a country town on a market-day the equilibrium price is affected by calculations of the future relations of production and consumption; while in the leading corn-markets of America and Europe dealings for future delivery already predominate and are rapidly weaving into one web all the leading threads of trade in corn throughout the whole world. Some of these dealings in "futures" are but incidents in speculative manœuvres; but in the main they are governed by calculations of the world's consumption on the one hand, and of the existing stocks and coming harvests in the Northern and Southern hemispheres on the other. Dealers take account of the areas sown with each kind of grain, of the forwardness and weight of the crops, of the supply of things which can be used as substitutes for grain, and of the things for which grain can be used as a substitute. Thus, when buying or selling barley, they take account of the supplies of such things as sugar, which can be used as substitutes for it in brewing, and again of all the various feeding stuffs, a scarcity of which might raise the value of barley for consumption on the farm. If it is thought that the growers of any kind of grain in any part of the world have been losing money, and are likely to sow a less area for a future harvest; it is argued that prices are likely to rise as soon as that harvest comes into sight, and its shortness is manifest to all. Anticipations of that rise exercise an influence on present sales for future delivery, and that in its turn influences cash prices; so that these prices are indirectly affected by estimates of the expenses of producing further supplies.

But in this and the following chapters we are specially concerned with movements of price ranging over still longer periods than those for which the most far-sighted dealers in futures generally make their reckoning: we have to consider the volume of production adjusting itself to the conditions of the market, and the normal price being thus determined at the position of stable equilibrium of normal demand and normal supply.

§ 2. In this discussion we shall have to make frequent use of the terms *cost* and *expenses* of production; and some provisional account of them must be given before proceeding further.

We may revert to the analogy between the supply price and the demand price of a commodity. Assuming for the moment that the efficiency of production depends solely upon the exertions of the workers, we saw that "the price required to call forth the exertion necessary for producing any given amount of a commodity may be called the supply price for that amount, with reference of course to a given unit of time." But now we have to take account of the fact that the production of a commodity generally requires many different kinds of labour and the use of capital in many forms. The exertions of all the different kinds of labour that are directly or indirectly involved in making it; together with the abstinences or rather the waitings required for saving the capital used in making it: all these efforts and sacrifices together will be called the *real cost of production* of the commodity. The sums of money that have to be paid for these efforts and sacrifices will be called either its *money cost of production*, or, for shortness, its *expenses of production*; they are the prices which have to be paid in order to call forth an adequate supply of the efforts and waitings that are required for making it; or, in other words, they are its supply price.[1]

The analysis of the expenses of production of a commodity might be carried backward to any length; but it is seldom worth while to go back

[1] Mill and some other economists have followed the practice of ordinary life in using the term Cost of production in two senses, sometimes to signify the difficulty of producing a thing, and sometimes to express the outlay of money that has to be incurred in order to induce people to overcome this difficulty and produce it. But by passing from one use of the term to the other without giving explicit warning, they have led to many misunderstandings and much barren controversy. The attack on Mill's doctrine of Cost of Production in relation to Value, which is made in Cairnes' *Leading Principles*, was published just after Mill's death; and unfortunately his interpretation of Mill's words was generally accepted as authoritative, because he was regarded as a follower of Mill. But in an article by the present writer on "Mill's Theory of Value" (*Fortnightly Review*, April, 1876) it is argued that Cairnes had mistaken Mill's meaning, and had really seen not more but less of the truth than Mill had done.

The expenses of production of any amount of a raw commodity may best be estimated with reference to the "margin of production" at which no rent is paid. But this method of speaking has great difficulties with regard to commodities that obey the law of increasing return.

very far. It is for instance often sufficient to take the supply prices of the different kinds of raw materials used in any manufacture as ultimate facts, without analysing these supply prices into the several elements of which they are composed; otherwise indeed the analysis would never end. We may then arrange the things that are required for making a commodity into whatever groups are convenient, and call them its *factors of production*. Its expenses of production when any given amount of it is produced are thus the supply prices of the corresponding quantities of its factors of production. And the sum of these is the supply price of that amount of the commodity.

. . .

§ 6. When therefore the amount produced (in a unit of time) is such that the demand price is greater than the supply price, then sellers receive more than is sufficient to make it worth their while to bring goods to market to that amount; and there is at work an active force tending to increase the amount brought forward for sale. On the other hand, when the amount produced is such that the demand price is less than the supply price, sellers receive less than is sufficient to make it worth their while to bring goods to market on that scale; so that those who were just on the margin of doubt as to whether to go on producing are decided not to do so, and there is an active force at work tending to diminish the amount brought forward for sale. When the demand price is equal to the supply price, the amount produced has no tendency either to be increased or to be diminished; it is in equilibrium.

When demand and supply are in equilibrium, the amount of the commodity which is being produced in a unit of time may be called the *equilibrium-amount*, and the price at which it is being sold may be called the *equilibrium-price*.

Such an equilibrium is *stable*; that is, the price, if displaced a little from it, will tend to return, as a pendulum oscillates about its lowest point; and it will be found to be a characteristic of stable equilibria that in them the demand price is greater than the supply price for amounts just less than the equilibrium amount, and *vice versâ*. For when the demand price is greater than the supply price, the amount produced tends to increase. Therefore, if the demand price is greater than the supply price for amounts just less than an equilibrium amount; then, if the scale of production is temporarily diminished somewhat below that equilibrium amount, it will tend to return; thus the equilibrium is stable for displacements in that direction. If the demand price is greater than the supply price for amounts just less than the equilibrium amount, it is sure to be less than the supply price for amounts just greater: and therefore, if the scale of production is somewhat increased beyond the equilibrium position, it will tend to return;

and the equilibrium will be stable for displacements in that direction also.

When demand and supply are in stable equilibrium, if any accident should move the scale of production from its equilibrium position, there will be instantly brought into play forces tending to push it back to that position; just as, if a stone hanging by a string is displaced from its equilibrium position, the force of gravity will at once tend to bring it back to its equilibrium position. The movements of the scale of production about its position of equilibrium will be of a somewhat similar kind.[2]

But in real life such oscillations are seldom as rhythmical as those of a stone hanging freely from a string; the comparison would be more exact if the string were supposed to hang in the troubled waters of a mill-race, whose stream was at one time allowed to flow freely, and at another partially cut off. Nor are these complexities sufficient to illustrate all the disturbances with which the economist and the merchant alike are forced to concern themselves. If the person holding the string swings his hand with movements partly rhythmical and partly arbitrary, the illustration will not outrun the difficulties of some very real and practical problems of value. For indeed the demand and supply schedules do not in practice remain unchanged for a long time together, but are constantly being changed; and every change in them alters the equilibrium amount and the equilibrium price, and thus gives new positions to the centres about which the amount and the price tend to oscillate.

These considerations point to the great importance of the element of time in relation to demand and supply, to the study of which we now proceed. We shall gradually discover a great many different limitations of the doctrine that the price at which a thing can be produced represents its real cost of production, that is, the efforts and sacrifices which have been directly and indirectly devoted to its production. For, in an age of rapid change such as this, the equilibrium of normal demand and supply

---

[2] To represent the equilibrium of demand and supply geometrically we may draw the demand and supply curves together. If then OR represents the rate at which production is being actually carried on, and Rd the demand price is greater than Rs the supply

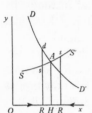

price, the production is exceptionally profitable, and will be increased. R, the *amount-index*, as we may call it, will move to the right. On the other hand, if Rd is less than Rs, R will move to the left. If Rd is equal to Rs, that is, if R is vertically under a point of intersection of the curves, demand and supply are in equilibrium.

This may be taken as the typical diagram for stable equilibrium for a commodity that obeys the law of diminishing return. But if we had made SS' a horizontal straight line, we should have represented the case of "constant return," in which the supply price is the same for all amounts of the commodity. And if we had made SS' inclined negatively, but less steeply than DD' (the necessity for this condition will appear more fully later on), we should have got a case of stable equilibrium for a commodity which obeys the law of increasing return. In either case the above reasoning remains unchanged without the alteration of a word or a letter; but the last case introduces difficulties which we have arranged to postpone.

does not thus correspond to any distinct relation of a certain aggregate of pleasures got from the consumption of the commodity and an aggregate of efforts and sacrifices involved in producing it: the correspondence would not be exact, even if normal earnings and interest were exact measures of the efforts and sacrifices for which they are the money payments. This is the real drift of that much quoted, and much-misunderstood doctrine of Adam Smith and other economists that the normal, or "natural," value of a commodity is that which economic forces tend to bring about *in the long run*. It is the average value which economic forces would bring about if the general conditions of life were stationary for a run of time long enough to enable them all to work out their full effect.[3]

But we cannot foresee the future perfectly. The unexpected may happen; and the existing tendencies may be modified before they have had time to accomplish what appears now to be their full and complete work. The fact that the general conditions of life are not stationary is the source of many of the difficulties that are met with in applying economic doctrines to practical problems.

Of course Normal does not mean Competitive. Market prices and Normal prices are alike brought about by a multitude of influences, of which some rest on a moral basis and some on a physical; of which some are competitive and some are not. It is to the persistence of the influences considered, and the time allowed for them to work out their effects that we refer when contrasting Market and Normal price, and again when contrasting the narrower and the broader use of the term Normal price.

§ 7. The remainder of the present volume will be chiefly occupied with interpreting and limiting this doctrine that the value of a thing tends in the long run to correspond to its cost of production.

We might as reasonably dispute whether it is the upper or the under blade of a pair of scissors that cuts a piece of paper, as whether value is governed by utility or cost of production. It is true that when one blade is held still, and the cutting is effected by moving the other, we may say with careless brevity that the cutting is done by the second; but the statement is not strictly accurate, and is to be excused only so long as it claims to be merely a popular and not a strictly scientific account of what happens.

In the same way, when a thing already made has to be sold, the price which people will be willing to pay for it will be governed by their desire to have it, together with the amount they can afford to spend on it. Their desire to have it depends partly on the chance that, if they do not buy it, they will be able to get another thing like it at as low a price: this depends on the causes that govern the supply of it, and this again upon cost of production. But it may so happen that the stock to be sold is practically fixed. This, for instance, is the case with a fish market, in which the value of fish for the day is governed almost exclusively by the stock on the slabs

[3] Bk. V, Chap. 5, § 2.

in relation to the demand: and if a person chooses to take the stock for granted, and say that the price is governed by demand, his brevity may perhaps be excused so long as he does not claim strict accuracy. So again it may be pardonable, but it is not strictly accurate to say that the varying prices which the same rare book fetches, when sold and resold at Christie's auction room, are governed exclusively by demand.

Taking a case at the opposite extreme, we find some commodities which conform pretty closely to the law of constant return; that is to say, their average cost of production will be very nearly the same whether they are produced in small quantities or in large. In such a case the normal level about which the market price fluctuates will be this definite and fixed (money) cost of production. If the demand happens to be great, the market price will rise for a time above the level; but as a result production will increase and the market price will fall: and conversely, if the demand falls for a time below its ordinary level.

In such a case, if a person chooses to neglect market fluctuations, and to take it for granted that there will anyhow be enough demand for the commodity to insure that some of it, more or less, will find purchasers at a price equal to this cost of production, then he may be excused for ignoring the influence of demand, and speaking of (normal) price as governed by cost of production—provided only he does not claim scientific accuracy for the wording of his doctrine, and explains the influence of demand in its right place.

Thus we may conclude that, *as a general rule*, the shorter the period which we are considering, the greater must be the share of our attention which is given to the influence of demand on value; and the longer the period, the more important will be the influence of cost of production on value. For the influence of changes in cost of production takes as a rule a longer time to work itself out than does the influence of changes in demand. The actual value at any time, the market value as it is often called, is often more influenced by passing events and by causes whose action is fitful and short lived, than by those which work persistently. But in long periods these fitful and irregular causes in large measure efface one another's influence; so that in the long run persistent causes dominate value completely. Even the most persistent causes are however liable to change. For the whole structure of production is modified, and the relative costs of production of different things are permanently altered, from one generation to another.

When considering costs from the point of view of the capitalist employer, we of course measure them in money; because his direct concern with the efforts needed for the work of his employees lies in the money payments he must make. His concern with the real costs of their effort and of the training required for it is only indirect, though a monetary assessment of his own labour is necessary for some problems, as will be seen later on. But when considering costs from the social point of view, when inquiring whether the cost of attaining a given result is increasing or diminishing with changing economic conditions, then we are concerned with the real costs of efforts of various qualities, and with the real cost of waiting. If the purchasing power of money, in terms of effort has remained about constant, and if the rate of remuneration for waiting has remained about constant, then the money measure of costs corresponds to the real costs: but such a correspondence is never to be assumed lightly. These considerations will generally suffice for the interpretation of the term Cost in what follows, even where no distinct indication is given in the context.

Chapter 5: EQUILIBRIUM OF NORMAL DEMAND AND SUPPLY, CONTINUED, WITH REFERENCE TO LONG AND SHORT PERIODS

. . .

§ 2. The element of time is a chief cause of those difficulties in economic investigations which make it necessary for man with his limited powers to go step by step; breaking up a complex question, studying one bit at a time, and at last combining his partial solutions into a more or less complete solution of the whole riddle. In breaking it up, he segregates those disturbing causes, whose wanderings happen to be inconvenient, for the time in a pound called *Cœteris Paribus*. The study of some group of tendencies is isolated by the assumption *other things being equal:* the existence of other tendencies is not denied, but their disturbing effect is neglected for a time. The more the issue is thus narrowed, the more exactly can it be handled: but also the less closely does it correspond to real life. Each exact and firm handling of a narrow issue, however, helps towards treating broader issues, in which that narrow issue is contained, more exactly than would otherwise have been possible. With each step more things can be let out of the pound; exact discussions can be made less abstract, realistic discussions can be made less inexact than was possible at an earlier stage.[1]

Our first step towards studying the influences exerted by the element of time on the relations between cost of production and value may well be to consider the famous fiction of the "Stationary state" in which those influences would be but little felt; and to contrast the results which would be found there with those in the modern world.

[1] This volume is concerned mainly with normal conditions; and these are sometimes described as Statical. But in the opinion of the present writer the problem of normal value belongs to economic Dynamics: partly because Statics is really but a branch of Dynamics, and partly because all suggestions as to economic rest, of which the hypothesis of a Stationary state is the chief, are merely provisional, used only to illustrate particular steps in the argument, and to be thrown aside when that is done.

This state obtains its name from the fact that in it the general conditions of production and consumption, of distribution and exchange remain motionless; but yet it is full of movement; for it is a mode of life. The average age of the population may be stationary; though each individual is growing up from youth towards his prime, or downwards to old age. And the same amount of things per head of the population will have been produced in the same ways by the same classes of people for many generations together; and therefore this supply of the appliances for production will have had full time to be adjusted to the steady demand.

Of course we might assume that in our stationary state every business remained always of the same size, and with the same trade connection. But we need not go so far as that; it will suffice to suppose that firms rise and fall, but that the "representative" firm remains always of about the same size, as does the representative tree of a virgin forest, and that therefore the economies resulting from its own resources are constant: and since the aggregate volume of production is constant, so also are those economies resulting from subsidiary industries in the neighbourhood, etc. [That is, its internal and external economies are both constant. The price, the expectation of which just induced persons to enter the trade, must be sufficient to cover in the long run the cost of building up a trade connection; and a proportionate share of it must be added in to make up the total cost of production.]

In a stationary state then the plain rule would be that cost of production governs value. Each effect would be attributable mainly to one cause; there would not be much complex action and reaction between cause and effect. Each element of cost would be governed by "natural" laws, subject to some control from fixed custom. There would be no reflex influence of demand; no fundamental difference between the immediate and the later effects of economic causes. There would be no distinction between long-period and short-period normal value, at all events if we supposed that in that monotonous world the harvests themselves were uniform: for the representative firm being always of the same size, and always doing the same class of business to the same extent and in the same way, with no slack times, and no specially busy times, its normal expenses by which the normal supply price is governed would be always the same. The demand lists of prices would always be the same, and so would the supply lists; and normal price would never vary.

But nothing of this is true in the world in which we live. Here every economic force is constantly changing its action, under the influence of other forces which are acting around it. Here changes in the volume of production, in its methods, and in its cost are ever mutually modifying one another; they are always affecting and being affected by the character and the extent of demand. Further all these mutual influences take time to work themselves out, and, as a rule, no two influences move at equal pace. In this world therefore every plain and simple doctrine as to the relations between cost of production, demand and value is necessarily false: and the greater the appearance of lucidity which is given to it by skilful exposition, the more mischievous it is. A man is likely to be a better economist if he trusts to his common sense, and practical instincts, than if he professes to study the theory of value and is resolved to find it easy.

§ 3. The Stationary state has just been taken to be one in which population is stationary. But nearly all its distinctive features may be exhibited in a place where population and wealth are both growing, provided they are growing at about the same rate, and there is no scarcity of land: and provided also the methods of production and the conditions of trade change but little; and above all, where the character of man himself is a constant quantity. For in such a state by far the most important conditions of production and consumption, of exchange and distribution will remain of the same quality, and in the same general relations to one another, though they are all increasing in volume.[2]

This relaxation of the rigid bonds of a purely stationary state brings us one step nearer to the actual conditions of life: and by relaxing them still further we get nearer still. We thus approach by gradual steps towards the difficult problem of the interaction of countless economic causes. In the stationary state all the conditions of production and consumption are reduced to rest: but less violent assumptions are made by what is, not quite accurately, called the *statical* method. By that method we fix our minds on some central point: we suppose it for the time to be reduced to a *stationary* state; and we then study in relation to it the forces that affect the things by which it is surrounded, and any tendency there may be to equilibrium of these forces. A number of these partial studies may lead the way towards a solution of problems too difficult to be grasped at one effort.

§ 4. We may roughly classify problems connected with fishing industries as those which are affected by very quick changes, such as uncertainties of the weather; or by changes of moderate length, such as the increased demand for fish caused by the scarcity of meat during the year or two following a cattle plague; or lastly, we may consider the great increase during a whole generation of the demand for fish which might result from the rapid growth of a high-strung artisan population making little use of their muscles.

The day to day oscillations of the price of fish resulting from uncertainties of the weather, etc., are governed by practically the same causes in modern England as in the supposed stationary state. The changes in the general economic conditions around us are quick; but they are not quick enough to affect perceptibly the short-period normal level about which the

[2] Compare Keynes, *Scope and Method of Political Economy*, VI, 2.

price fluctuates from day to day: and they may be neglected [impounded in *cœteris paribus*] during a study of such fluctuations.

Let us then pass on; and suppose a great increase in the general demand for fish, such for instance as might arise from a disease affecting farm stock, by which meat was made a dear and dangerous food for several years together. We now impound fluctuations due to the weather in *cœteris paribus*, and neglect them provisionally: they are so quick that they speedily obliterate one another, and are therefore not important for problems of this class. And for the opposite reason we neglect variations in the numbers of those who are brought up as seafaring men: for these variations are too slow to produce much effect in the year or two during which the scarcity of meat lasts. Having impounded these two sets for the time, we give our full attention to such influences as the inducements which good fishing wages will offer to sailors to stay in their fishing homes for a year or two, instead of applying for work on a ship. We consider what old fishing boats, and even vessels that were not specially made for fishing, can be adapted and sent to fish for a year or two. The normal price for any given daily supply of fish, which we are now seeking, is the price which will *quickly* call into the fishing trade capital and labour enough to obtain that supply in a day's fishing of average good fortune; the influence which the price of fish will have upon capital and labour available in the fishing trade being governed by rather narrow causes such as these. This new level about which the price oscillates during these years of exceptionally great demand, will obviously be higher than before. Here we see an illustration of the almost universal law that the term Normal being taken to refer to a short period of time *an increase in the amount demanded raises the normal supply* price. This law is almost universal even as regards industries which in long periods follow the tendency to increasing return.

But if we turn to consider the normal supply price with reference to a *long period* of time, we shall find that it is governed by a different set of causes, and with different results. For suppose that the disuse of meat causes a permanent distaste for it, and that an increased demand for fish continues long enough to enable the forces by which its supply is governed to work out their action fully (of course oscillation from day to day and from year to year would continue: but we may leave them on one side). The source of supply in the sea might perhaps show signs of exhaustion, and the fishermen might have to resort to more distant coasts and to deeper waters, Nature giving a Diminishing Return to the increased application of capital and labour of a given order of efficiency. On the other hand, those might turn out to be right who think that man is responsible for but a very small part of the destruction of fish that is constantly going on; and in that case a boat starting with equally good appliances and an equally efficient crew would be likely to get nearly as good a haul after the increase in the total volume of the fishing trade as before. In any case the normal cost of equipping a good boat with an efficient crew would certainly not be higher, and probably be a little lower after the trade had settled down to its now increased dimensions than before. For since fishermen require only trained aptitudes, and not any exceptional natural qualities, their number could be increased in less than a generation to almost any extent that was necessary to meet the demand; while the industries connected with building boats, making nets, etc. being now on a larger scale would be organized more thoroughly and economically. If therefore the waters of the sea showed no signs of depletion of fish, an increased supply could be produced at a lower price after a time sufficiently long to enable the normal action of economic causes to work itself out: and, the term Normal being taken to refer to a long period of time, the normal price of fish would decrease with an increase in demand.[3]

Thus we may emphasize the distinction already made between average price and normal price. An average may be taken of the prices of any set of sales extending over a day or a week or a year or any other time: or it may be the average of sales at any time in many markets; or it may be the average of many such averages. But the conditions which are normal to any one set of sales are not likely to be exactly those which are normal to the others: and therefore it is only by accident that an average price will be a normal price; that is, the price which any one set of conditions tends to produce. In a stationary state alone, as we have just seen, the term normal always means the same thing: there, but only there, "average price" and "normal price" are convertible terms.[4]

. . .

The general drift of the term normal supply price is always the same whether the period to which it refers is short or long; but there are great

[3] Tooke (*History of Prices*, Vol. I, p. 104) tells us: "There are particular articles of which the demand for naval and military purposes forms so large a proportion to the total supply, that no diminution of consumption by individuals can keep pace with the immediate increase of demand by government; and consequently, the breaking out of a war tends to raise the price of such articles to a great relative height. But even of such articles, if the consumption were not on a progressive scale of increase so rapid that the supply, with all the encouragement of a relatively high price, could not keep pace with the demand, the tendency is (supposing no impediment, natural or artificial, to production or importation) to occasion such an increase of quantity, as to reduce the price to nearly the same level as that from which it had advanced. And accordingly it will be observed, by reference to the table of prices, that salt-petre, hemp, iron, etc., after advancing very considerably under the influence of a greatly extended demand for military and naval purposes, tended downwards again whenever that demand was not progressively and rapidly increasing." Thus a continuously progressive increase in demand may raise the supply price of a thing even for several years together; though a steady increase of demand for that thing, at a rate not too great for supply to keep pace with it, would lower price.

[4] See Bk. V, Chap. 3, § 6. See also Keynes, *Scope and Method of Political Economy*, Chap. VII.

differences in detail. In every case reference is made to a certain given rate of aggregate production; that is, to the production of a certain aggregate amount daily or annually. In every case the price is that the expectation of which is sufficient and only just sufficient to make it worth while for people to set themselves to produce that aggregate amount; in every case the cost of production is marginal; that is, it is the cost of production of those goods which are on the margin of not being produced at all, and which would not be produced if the price to be got for them were expected to be lower. But the causes which determine this margin vary with the length of the period under consideration. For short periods people take the stock of appliances for production as practically fixed; and they are governed by their expectations of demand in considering how actively they shall set themselves to work those appliances. In long periods they set themselves to adjust the flow of these appliances to their expectations of demand for the goods which the appliances help to produce. Let us examine this difference closely.

§ 6. The immediate effect of the expectation of a high price is to cause people to bring into active work all their appliances of production, and to work them full time and perhaps overtime. The supply price is then the money cost of production of that part of the produce which forces the undertaker to hire such inefficient labour (perhaps tired by working overtime) at so high a price, and to put himself and others to so much strain and inconvenience that he is on the margin of doubt whether it is worth his while to do it or not. The immediate effect of the expectation of a low price is to throw many appliances for production out of work, and slacken the work of others; and if the producers had no fear of spoiling their markets, it would be worth their while to produce for a time for any price that covered the prime costs of production and rewarded them for their own trouble.

But, as it is, they generally hold out for a higher price; each man fears to spoil his chance of getting a better price later on from his own customers; or, if he produces for a large and open market, he is more or less in fear of incurring the resentment of other producers, should he sell needlessly at a price that spoils the common market for all. The marginal production in this case is the production of those whom a little further fall of price would cause, either from a regard to their own interest or by formal or informal agreement with other producers, to suspend production for fear of further spoiling the market. The price which, for these reasons, producers are just on the point of refusing, is the true marginal supply price for short periods. It is nearly always above, and generally very much above the special or prime cost for raw materials, labour and wear-and-tear of plant, which is immediately and directly involved by getting a little further use out of appliances which are not fully employed. This point needs further study.

In a trade which uses very expensive plant, the prime cost of goods is but a small part of their total cost; and an order at much less than their normal price may leave a large surplus above their prime cost. But if producers accept such orders in their anxiety to prevent their plant from being idle, they glut the market and tend to prevent prices from reviving. In fact however they seldom pursue this policy constantly and without moderation. If they did, they might ruin many of those in the trade, themselves perhaps among the number; and in that case a revival of demand would find little response in supply, and would raise violently the prices of the goods produced by the trade. Extreme variations of this kind are in the long run beneficial neither to producers nor to consumers; and general opinion is not altogether hostile to that code of trade morality which condemns the action of anyone who "spoils the market" by being too ready to accept a price that does little more than cover the prime cost of his goods, and allows but little on account of his general expenses.[5]

For example, if at any time the prime cost, in the narrowest sense of the word, of a bale of cloth is £100; and if another £100 are needed to make the cloth pay its due share of the general expenses of the establishment, including normal profits to its owners, then the practically effective supply price is perhaps not very likely to fall below £150 under ordinary conditions, even for short periods; though of course a few special bargains may be made at lower prices without much affecting the general market.

Thus, although nothing but prime cost enters *necessarily and directly* into the supply price for short periods, it is yet true that supplementary costs also exert some influence indirectly. A producer does not often isolate the cost of each separate small parcel of his output; he is apt to treat a considerable part of it, even in some cases the whole of it, more or less as a unit. He inquires whether it is worth his while to add a certain new line to his present undertakings, whether it is worth while to introduce a new machine and so on. He treats the extra output that would result from the change more or less as a unit beforehand; and afterwards he quotes the lowest prices, which he is willing to accept, with more or less reference to the whole cost of that extra output regarded as a unit.

In other words he regards an increase in his processes of production, rather than an individual parcel of his products, as a unit in most of his

---

[5] Where there is a strong combination, tacit or overt, producers may sometimes regulate the price for a considerable time together with very little reference to cost of production. And if the leaders in that combination were those who had the best facilities for production, it might be said, in apparent though not in real contradiction to Ricardo's doctrines, that the price was governed by that part of the supply which was most easily produced. But as a fact, those producers whose finances are weakest, and who are bound to go on producing to escape failure, often impose their policy on the rest of the combination: insomuch that it is a common saying, both in America and England, that the weakest members of a combination are frequently its rulers.

transactions. And the analytical economist must follow suit, if he would keep in close touch with actual conditions. These considerations tend to blur the sharpness of outline of the theory of value: but they do not affect its substance.[6]

To sum up then as regards short periods. The supply of specialized skill and ability, of suitable machinery and other material capital, and of the appropriate industrial organization has not time to be fully adapted to demand; but the producers have to adjust their supply to the demand as best they can with the appliances already at their disposal. On the one hand there is not time materially to increase those appliances if the supply of them is deficient; and on the other, if the supply is excessive, some of them must remain imperfectly employed, since there is not time for the supply to be much reduced by gradual decay, and by conversion to other uses. Variations in the particular income derived from them do not *for the time* affect perceptibly the supply; and do not directly affect the price of the commodities produced by them. The income is a surplus of total receipts over prime cost; [that is, it has something of the nature of a rent as will be seen more clearly in chapter viii.]. But unless it is sufficient to cover in the long run a fair share of the general costs of the business, production will gradually fall off. In this way a controlling influence over the relatively quick movements of supply price during short periods is exercised by causes in the background which range over a long period; and the fear of "spoiling the market" often makes those causes act more promptly than they otherwise would.

· · ·

Chapter 8: MARGINAL COSTS IN RELATION TO VALUES: GENERAL PRINCIPLES

§ 1. This Chapter and the three following are given to a study of the marginal costs of products in relation to the values of those products on the one hand, and on the other hand to the values of the land, machinery, and other appliances used in making them. *The study relates to normal conditions and long period results.* This fact must ever be borne in mind. The market value of anything may be much above or much below the normal cost of production: and the marginal costs of a particular producer

---

[6] This general description may suffice for most purposes: but in chapter xi. there will be found a more detailed study of that extremely complex notion, a marginal increment in the processes of production by a representative firm; together with a fuller explanation of the necessity of referring our reasonings to the circumstances of a representative firm, especially when we are considering industries which show a tendency to increasing return.

at any time may stand in no close relation to marginal costs under normal conditions.[1]

It was indicated at the end of Chapter VI. that no one part of the problem can be isolated from the rest. There are comparatively few things the demand for which is not greatly affected by the demand for other things to the usefulness of which they contribute; and it may even be said that the demand for the majority of articles of commerce is not direct but is derived from the demand for those commodities to the making of which they contribute, as materials or as implements. And again this demand, because it is so derived, is largely dependent on the supply of other things which will work with them in making those commodities. And again the supply of anything available for use in making any commodity is apt to be greatly influenced by the demand for that thing derived from its uses in making other commodities: and so on. These inter-relations can be and must be ignored in rapid and popular discussions on the business affairs of the world. But no study that makes any claim to thoroughness can escape from a close investigation of them. This requires many things to be borne in mind at the same time: and for that reason economics can never become a simple science.

The contribution which this group of chapters aims at making covers little ground: but that ground is difficult: and we shall need to work over it carefully, and from more than one point of view; for it is thickly strewn with pitfalls and stumbling blocks. It deals primarily with the earnings of land, machinery, and other material agents of production. Its main argument applies to the earnings of human beings; but they are influenced by some causes which do not affect the earnings of material agents of production: and the matter in hand is sufficiently difficult without further complicating it by side issues.

§ 2. Let us begin by recalling the action of the principle of substitution. In the modern world nearly all the means of production pass through the hands of employers and other business men, who specialize themselves in organizing the economic forces of the population. Each of them chooses in every case those factors of production which seem best for his purpose. And the sum of the prices which he pays for those factors which he uses is, as a rule, less than the sum of the prices which he would have to pay for any other set of factors which could be substituted for them: for, whenever it appears that this is not the case, he will, as a rule, set to work to substitute the less expensive arrangement or process.

This statement is in close harmony with such common sayings of every-

---

[1] Numerous objections have been urged against the important place assigned to marginal costs in modern analysis. But it will be found that most of them rely on arguments, in which statements referring to normal conditions and normal value are controverted by statements relating to abnormal or particular conditions.

day life, as that "everything tends to find its own level," that "most men earn just about what they are worth," that "if one man can earn twice as much as another, that shows that his work is worth twice as much," that "machinery will displace manual labour whenever it can do the work cheaper." The principle does not indeed act without hindrance. It may be restricted by custom or law, by professional etiquette or trade-union regulation: it may be weakened by want of enterprise, or it may be softened by a generous unwillingness to part with old associates. But it never ceases to act, and it permeates all the economic adjustments of the modern world.

Thus there are some kinds of field work for which horse-power is clearly more suitable than steam-power, and *vice versâ*. If we may now suppose that there have been no great recent improvements in horse or steam machinery, and that therefore the experience of the past has enabled farmers gradually to apply the law of substitution; then, on this supposition the application of steam-power will have been pushed just so far that any further use of it in the place of horse-power would bring no net advantage. There will however remain a margin on which they could be *indifferently* applied (as Jevons would have said); and on that margin the net efficiency of either in adding to the money value of the total product will be proportionate to the cost of applying it.[2]

Similarly, if there are two methods of obtaining the same result, one by skilled and the other by unskilled labour, that one will be adopted which is the more efficient in proportion to its cost. There will be a margin on which either will be indifferently applied.[3] On that line the efficiency of each will be in proportion to the price paid for it, account being taken of the special circumstances of different districts and of different workshops in the same district. In other words, the wages of skilled and unskilled labour will bear to one another the same ratio that their efficiencies do at the margin of indifference.

Again, there will be a rivalry between hand-power and machine-power similar to that between two different kinds of hand-power or two different kinds of machine-power. Thus hand-power has the advantage for some operations, as, for instance, for weeding out valuable crops that have an irregular growth; horse-power in its turn has a clear advantage for weeding an ordinary turnip field; and the application of each of them will be pushed

2 This margin will vary with local circumstances, as well as with the habits, inclinations, and resources of individual farmers. The difficulty of applying steam machinery in small fields and on rugged ground is overcome more generally in those districts in which labour is scarce than in those in which it is plentiful; especially if, as is probable, coal is cheaper, and the feed of horses dearer in the former than the latter.

3 Skilled manual labour being generally used for special orders and for things of which not many are required of the same pattern; and unskilled labour aided by specialized machinery being used for others. The two methods are to be seen side by side on similar work in every large workshop: but the position of the line between them will vary a little from one workshop to another.

in each district till any further use of it would bring no net advantage there. On the margin of indifference between hand-power and horse-power their prices must be proportionate to their efficiency; and thus the influence of substitution will tend to establish a direct relation between the wages of labour and the price that has to be paid for horse-power.

§ 3. As a rule many kinds of labour, of raw material, of machinery and other plant, and of business organization, both internal and external, go to the production of a commodity: and the advantages of economic freedom are never more strikingly manifest than when a business man endowed with genius is trying experiments, at his own risk, to see whether some new method, or combination of old methods, will be more efficient than the old. Every business man indeed, according to his energy and ability, is constantly endeavouring to obtain a notion of the relative efficiency of every agent of production that he employs; as well as of others that might possibly be substituted for some of them. He estimates as best he can how much *net product* (*i.e.* net addition to the value of his total product) will be caused by a certain extra use of any one agent; *net* that is after deducting for any extra expenses that may be indirectly caused by the change, and adding for any incidental savings. He endeavours to employ each agent up to that margin at which its net product would no longer exceed the price he would have to pay for it. He works generally by trained instinct rather than formal calculation; but his processes are substantially similar to those indicated in our study of derived demand; and, from another point of view, they may be described as those which might be reaped by a complex and refined system of book-keeping by double entry.[4]

We have already followed some simple estimates of this sort. We have noticed, for instance, how the proportion of hops and malt in ale can be varied, how the extra price which can be got for ale by increasing the quantity of hops in it is a representative of the causes which govern the demand price for hops. Assuming that no further trouble or expense of any kind is involved by this additional use of hops, and that the expediency of using this extra amount is doubtful, the extra value thus given to the ale is the marginal net product of the hops of which we are in search. In this case, as in most others, the net product is an improvement in quality or a general contribution to the value of the product; it is not a definite

---

[4] The changes, which he desires, may be such as could only be made on a large scale; as for instance the substitution of steam-power for hand-power in a certain factory; and in that case there would be a certain element of uncertainty and risk in the change. Such breaches of continuity are however inevitable both in production and consumption if we regard the action of single individuals. But as there is a continuous demand in a large market for hats and watches and wedding cakes, though no individual buys many of them (see Bk. III, Chap. III, § 5), so there will always be trades in which small businesses are most economically conducted without steam-power, and larger businesses with; while businesses of intermediate size are on the margin. Again, even in large establishments in which steam is already in use, there will always be some things done by hand-power which are done by steam-power elsewhere; and so on.

part of the produce which can be separated from the rest. But in exceptional instances that can be done.

§ 4. The notion of the marginal employment of any agent of production implies a possible tendency to diminishing return from its increased employment.

Excessive applications of any means to the attainment of any end are indeed sure to yield diminishing returns in every branch of business; and, one may say, in all the affairs of life. We may take some additional examples of a principle that has already been illustrated. In the manufacture of sewing machines some parts may well be made of cast iron; for others a common kind of steel will suffice; there are yet others for which a specially expensive steel-compound is needed; and all parts should be finished off more or less smoothly, so that the machine may work easily. Now if any one devoted a disproportionate care and expense to the selection of materials for the less important uses, it might truly be said that the expenditure was yielding a rapidly diminishing return; and that he would have done better to give some of it to making his machines work smoothly, or even to producing more machines: and the case might be even worse if he devoted an excessive expenditure to mere brilliancy of finish, and put low grade metal to work for which a higher grade was needed.

This consideration seems at first to simplify economic problems; but on the contrary it is a chief source of difficulty and confusion. For though there is some analogy between all these various tendencies to diminishing return, they yet are not identical. Thus the diminishing return which arises from an ill-proportioned application of the various agents of production into a particular task has little in common with that broad tendency to the pressure of a crowded and growing population on the means of subsistence. The great classical Law of Diminishing Return has its chief application, not to any one particular crop, but to all the chief food crops. It takes for granted that farmers raise, as a rule, those crops for which their land and other resources are best adapted, account being taken of the relative demands for the several crops; and that they distribute their resources appropriately between different routes. It does not attribute to them unlimited intelligence and wisdom, but it assumes that, taking one with another, they have shown a reasonable amount of care and discretion in the distribution of these resources. It refers to a country the whole land of which is already in the hands of active business men, who can supplement their own capital by loans from banks wherever they can show it is likely to be well applied; and asserts that an increase in the total amount of capital applied to agriculture in that country will yield diminishing returns of produce in general. This statement is akin to, but yet quite distinct from, the statement that if any farmer makes a bad distribution of his resources between different plans of cultivation, he will get a markedly diminishing return from those elements of expenditure which he has driven to excess.

For instance, in any given case, there is a certain proportion between the amounts which may with best advantage be spent on ploughing and harrowing, or manuring. There might be some differences of opinion on the matter, but only within narrow limits. An inexperienced person who ploughed many times over land, which was already in fairly good mechanical condition, while he gave it little or none of the manure which it was craving, would be generally condemned as having so over applied ploughing as to make it yield a rapidly diminishing return. But this result of the misapplication of resources has no very close connection with the tendency of agriculture in an old country to yield a diminishing return to a general increase of resources well applied in cultivation: and indeed exactly parallel cases can be found of a diminishing return to particular resources when applied in undue proportion, even in industries which yield an increasing return to increased applications of capital and labour when appropriately distributed.[5]

§ 5. The part played by the net product at the margin of production in the modern doctrine of Distribution is apt to be misunderstood. In particular many able writers have supposed that it represents the marginal use

[5] See Carver, *Distribution of Wealth*, Chap. II. Mr J. A. Hobson is a vigorous and suggestive writer on the realistic and social sides of economics: but, as a critic of Ricardian doctrines, he is perhaps apt to underrate the difficulty of the problems which he discusses. He argues that if the marginal application of any agent of production be curtailed, that will so disorganize production that every other agent will be working to less effect than before; and that therefore the total resulting loss will include not only the true marginal product of that agent, but also a part of the products due to the other agents: but he appears to have overlooked the following points:—(1) There are forces constantly at work tending so to readjust the distribution of resources between their different uses, that any maladjustment will be arrested before it has gone far: and the argument does not profess to apply to exceptional cases of violent maladjustment (2) When the adjustment is such as to give the best results, a slight change in the proportions in which they are applied diminishes the efficiency of that adjustment by a quantity which is very small relatively to that change—in technical language it is of "the second order of smalls"—; and it may therefore be neglected relatively to that change. (In pure mathematical phrase, efficiency being regarded as a function of the proportions of the agents; when the efficiency is at its maximum, its differential coefficient with regard to any one of these proportions is zero.) A grave error would therefore have been involved, if any allowance had been made for those elements which Mr Hobson asserts to have been overlooked. (3) In economics, as in physics, changes are generally continuous. Convulsive changes may indeed occur, but they must be dealt with separately: and an illustration drawn from a convulsive change can throw no true light on the processes of normal steady evolution. In the particular problem before us, this precaution is of special importance: for a violent check to the supply of any one agent of production, may easily render the work of all other agents practically useless; and therefore it may inflict a loss out of all proportion to the harm done by a small check to the supply of that agent when applied up to that margin, at which there was doubt whether the extra net product due to a small additional application of it would be remunerative. The study of changes in complex quantitative relations is often vitiated by a neglect of this consideration, to which Mr Hobson seems to be prone; as indeed is instanced by his remarks on a "marginal shepherd" in *The Industrial System*, p. 110. See Professor Edgeworth's masterly analyses of the two instances mentioned in this note, *Quarterly Journal of Economics*, 1904, p. 167; and *Scientia*, 1910, pp. 95–100.

of a thing as *governing* the value of the whole. It is not so; the doctrine says we must *go to the margin to study the action of those forces which govern* the value of the whole: and that is a very different affair. Of course the withdrawal of (say) iron from any of its necessary uses would have just the same influence on its value as its withdrawal from its marginal uses; in the same way as the pressure in a boiler for cooking under high pressure would be affected by the escape of any other steam just as it would by the escape of the steam in one of the safety valves: but in fact the steam does not escape except through the safety valves. In like manner iron, or any other agent of production, is not (under ordinary circumstances) thrown out of use except at points at which its use yields no clear surplus of profit; that is, it is thrown out from its marginal uses only.

Again, the finger of an automatic weighing machine determines, in the sense of *indicating*, the weight sought for. So the escape of steam from a safety valve, governed by a spring representing a pressure of a hundred pounds to the square inch, determines the pressure of steam in the boiler, in the sense of indicating that it has reached a hundred pounds to the inch. The pressure is caused by the heat; the spring in the valve governs the pressure by yielding and letting out some of the steam when its amount is so great, at the existing heat, as to overbear the resistance of the spring.

Similarly, with regard to machinery and other appliances of production made by man, there is a margin through which additional supplies come in after overcoming the resistance of a spring called "cost of production." For when the supply of those appliances is so small relatively to the demand that the earnings expected from new supplies are more than sufficient to yield normal interest (or profits, if earnings of management are reckoned in) on their cost of production, besides allowing for depreciation, etc., then the valve opens, and the new supplies come in. When the earnings are less than this, the valve remains shut: and as anyhow the existing supply is always in process of slow destruction by use and the lapse of time, the supply is always shrinking when the valve is closed. The valve is that part of the machinery by which the general relations of demand and supply govern value. But marginal uses do not govern value; because they, together with value, are themselves governed by those general relations.

§ 6. Thus, so long as the resources of an individual producer are in the form of general purchasing power, he will push every investment up to the margin at which he no longer expects from it a higher net return than he could get by investing in some other material, or machine, or advertisement, or in the hire of some additional labour: every investment will, as it were, be driven up to a valve which offers to it a resistance equal to its own expanding force. If he invests in material or in labour, that is soon embodied in some saleable product: the sale replenishes his fluid capital, and that again is invested up to the margin at which any further investment would yield a return so diminished as not to be profitable.

But if he invests in land, or in a durable building or machine, the return which he gets from his investment may vary widely from his expectation. It will be governed by the market for his products, which may change its character largely through new inventions, changes in fashion, etc., during the life of a machine, to say nothing of the perpetual life of land. The incomes which he thus may derive from investments in land and in machinery differ from his individual point of view mainly in the longer life of the land. But in regard to production in general, a dominant difference between the two lies in the fact that the supply of land is fixed (though in a new country, the supply of land utilized in man's service may be increased); while the supply of machines may be increased without limit. And this difference reacts on the individual producer. For if no great new invention renders his machines obsolete, while there is a steady demand for the things made by them, they will be constantly on sale at about their cost of production; and his machines will generally yield him normal profits on that cost of production, with deductions corresponding to their wear and tear.

Thus the rate of interest is a ratio: and the two things which it connects are both sums of money. So long as capital is "free," and the sum of money or general purchasing power over which it gives command is known, the net money income, expected to be derived from it, can be represented at once as bearing a given ratio (four or five or ten per cent.) to that sum. But when the free capital has been invested in a particular thing, its money value cannot as a rule be ascertained except by capitalizing the net income which it will yield: and therefore the causes which govern it are likely to be akin in a greater or less degree to those which govern rents.

We are thus brought to the central doctrine of this part of economics, viz.:—"That which is rightly regarded as interest on 'free' or 'floating' capital, or on new investments of capital, is more properly treated as a sort of rent—a *Quasi-rent*—on old investments of capital. And there is no sharp line of division between floating capital and that which has been 'sunk' for a special branch of production, nor between new and old investments of capital; each group shades into the other gradually. And thus even the rent of land is seen, not as a thing by itself, but as the leading species of a large genus; though indeed it has peculiarities of its own which are of vital importance from the point of view of theory as well as of practice."

Chapter 9: MARGINAL COSTS IN RELATION TO VALUE: CONTINUED

. . .

§ 2. Let us suppose that a meteoric shower of a few thousand large stones harder than diamonds fell all in one place; so that they were all picked up at once, and no amount of search could find any more. These stones, able to cut every material, would revolutionize many branches of industry; and the owners of them would have a differential advantage in production, that would afford a large producer's surplus. This surplus would be governed wholly by the urgency and volume of the demand for their services on the one hand and the number of the stones on the other hand: it could not be affected by the cost of obtaining a further supply, because none could be had at any price. A cost of production might indeed influence their value indirectly: but it would be the cost of tools made of hard steel and other materials of which the supply can be increased to keep pace with demand. So long as any of the stones were habitually used by intelligent producers for work which could be done equally well by such tools, the value of a stone could not much exceed the cost of producing tools (allowance being made for wear and tear) equally efficient with it in these inferior uses.

The stones, being so hard as not to be affected by wear, would probably be kept in operation during all the working hours of the day. And if their services were very valuable, it might be worth while to keep people working overtime, or even in double or triple shifts, in order to extract the utmost service from them. But the more intensively they were applied, the less net return would be reaped from each additional service forced from them; thus illustrating the law that the intensive working not only of land, but of every other appliance of production is likely to yield a diminishing return if pressed far enough.

The total supply of stones is fixed. But of course any particular manufacturer might obtain almost as many as he liked to pay for: and in the long run he would expect his outlay on them to be returned with interest (or profits, if the remuneration for his own work were not reckoned separately), just in the same way as if he were buying machinery, the total stock of which could be increased indefinitely, so that its price conformed pretty closely to its cost of production.

But when he had once bought the stones, changes in the processes of production or of demand for the things made by their aid, might cause the income yielded by them to become twice as great or only half as great as he had expected. In the latter case it would resemble the income derived from a machine, which had not the latest improvements and could earn only half as much as a new machine of equal cost. The values of the stone and of the machine alike would be reached by capitalizing the income which they were capable of earning, and that income would be governed by the net value of the services rendered by them. The income earning power and therefore the value of each would be independent of its own costs of production, but would be governed by the general demand for its products in relation to the general supply of those products. But in the case of the machine that supply would be controlled by the cost of supply of new machines equally efficient with it; and in the case of the stone there would be no such limit, so long as all the stones in existence were employed on work that could not be done by anything else.

This argument may be put in another way. Since any one, who bought stones, would take them from other producers, his purchase would not materially affect the general relations of demand for the services of the stones to the supply of those services. It would not therefore affect the price of the stones; which would still be the capitalized value of the services which they rendered in those uses, in which the need for them was the least urgent: and to say that the purchaser expected normal interest on the price which represented the capitalized value of the services, would be a circular statement that the value of the services rendered by stones is governed by the value of those very services.[1]

Next let us suppose that the stones were not all found at once but were scattered over the surface of the earth on public ground, and that a laborious search might expect to be rewarded by finding one here and there. Then people would hunt for the stones only up to that point, or margin, at which the probable gain of so doing would in the long run just reward the outlay of labour and capital involved; and in the long run, the normal value of the stones would be such as to maintain equilibrium between demand and supply, the number of the stones gathered annually being in the long run just that for which the normal demand price was equal to the normal supply price.

Finally, let us bring the case of the stones into accord with that of the lighter machinery and other plant ordinarily used in manufacture, by supposing that the stones were brittle, and were soon destroyed; and that an inexhaustible store existed from which additional supplies could be obtained quickly and certainly at a nearly uniform cost. In this case the value of the stones would always correspond closely to that cost: variations in

---

[1] Such circular reasonings are sometimes nearly harmless: but they always tend to overlay and hide the real issues. And they are sometimes applied to illegitimate uses by company promoters; and by advocates of special interests, who desire to influence the course of legislation in their own favour. For instance a semi-monopolistic business aggregation or trust is often "over-capitalized." To effect this a time is chosen, at which the branch of production with which it is concerned is abnormally prosperous: when perhaps some solid firms are earning fifty per cent. net on their capital in a single year, and thus making up for lean years past and to come in which their receipts will do little more than cover prime costs. Financiers connected with the flotation sometimes even arrange that the businesses to be offered to the public shall have a good many orders to fill at specially favourable prices: the loss falling on themselves, or on other companies which they control. The gains to be secured by semi-monopolistic selling, and possibly by some further economies in production are emphasized: and the stock of the trust is absorbed by the public. If ultimately objection to the conduct of the trust is raised, and especially to the strengthening of its semi-monopolistic position by a high tariff or any other public favour, the answer is given that the shareholders are receiving but a moderate return on their investments. Such cases are not uncommon in America. In this country a more moderate watering of the stock of some railways has been occasionally used indirectly as a defence of the shareholders against a lowering of rates, that threatens to reduce dividends on inflated capital below what would be a fair return on solid capital.

demand would have but little influence on their price, because even a
slight change in price would quickly effect a great change in the stock of
them in the market. In this case the income derived from a stone (allowance being made for wear-and-tear) would always adhere closely to interest on its cost of production.

§ 3. This series of hypotheses stretches continuously from the one extreme in which the income derived from the stones is a rent in the strictest
sense of the term, to the other extreme in which it is to be classed rather
with interest on free or floating capital. In the first extreme case the stones
cannot be worn out or destroyed, and no more can be found. They of course
tend to be distributed among the various uses to which they are applicable
in such a way that there is no use to which an increased supply of them
could be applied, without taking them away from some other use in which
they were rendering net services at least as valuable. These margins of
application of the several uses are thus *governed* by the relation in which
the fixed stock of stones stands to the aggregate of demands for them in
different uses. And the margins being thus governed, the prices that will
be paid for their use are *indicated* by the value of the services which they
render at any one of those margins.

A uniform tax on them, collected from the user, will lower their net
service in each use by the same amount: it will not affect their distribution
between several uses; and it will fall wholly on the owner, after perhaps
some little delay caused by a frictional resistance to readjustments.

At the opposite extreme of our chain of hypotheses, the stones perish so
quickly, and are so quickly reproduced at about a uniform cost, that variations in the urgency and volume of the uses to which the stones can be
put will be followed so promptly by changes in the stock of them available,
that those services can never yield much more or much less than normal
interest on the money cost of obtaining additional stones. In this case a
business man, when making his estimates for the cost of any undertaking
in which stones will be used, may enter *interest* (or if he is counting his
own work in, *profits*), for the time during which those stones will be used
(together with wear-and-tear), as part of the prime, special, or direct expenses of his undertaking. A tax on the stones under these conditions
would fall entirely on any one who even a little while after the tax had
come into force, gave out a contract for anything in making which the
stones would be used.

Taking an intermediate hypothesis as to the length of life of the stones
and the rapidity with which new supplies could be obtained; we find that
the charges which the borrower of stones must expect to pay, and the
revenue which the owner of the stones could reckon on deriving from them
at any time, might temporarily diverge some way from interest (or profits)
on their cost. For changes in the urgency and volume of the uses to which
they could be applied, might have caused the value of the services rendered

by them in their marginal uses to rise or fall a great deal, even though there had been no considerable change in the difficulty of obtaining them. And if this rise or fall, arising from variations in demand, and not from variations in the cost of the stones, is likely to be great during the period of any particular enterprise, or any particular problem of value that is under discussion; then for that discussion the income yielded by the stones is to be regarded as more nearly akin to a rent than to interest on the cost of producing the stones. A tax upon the stones in such a case would tend to diminish the rental which people would pay for their use, and therefore to diminish the inducements towards investing capital and effort in obtaining additional supplies. It would therefore check the supply, and compel those who needed the stones to pay gradually increasing rentals for their use, up to the point at which the rentals fully covered the costs of producing the stones. But the time needed for this readjustment might be long: and in the interval a great part of the tax would fall upon the owners of the stones.

If the life of the stones was long relatively to that process of production in which the stones were used which was under discussion, the stock of stones might be in excess of that needed to do all the work for which they were specially fitted. Some of them might be lying almost idle, and the owner of these stones might make up his estimate of the marginal price for which he was just willing to work without entering in that estimate interest on the value of the stones. That is to say, some costs which would have been classed as prime costs in relation to contracts, or other affairs, which lasted over a long period, would be classed as supplementary costs in relation to a particular affair which would last but a short time, and which came under consideration when business was slack.

It is of course just as essential in the long run that the price obtained should cover general or supplementary costs as that it should cover prime costs. An industry will be driven out of existence in the long run as certainly by failing to return even a moderate interest on capital invested in steam engines, as by failing to replace the price of the coal or the raw material used up from day to day: just as a man's work will be stopped as certainly by depriving him of food as by putting him in chains. But the man can go on working fairly well for a day without food; while if he is put in chains the check to his work comes at once. So an industry may, and often does, keep tolerably active during a whole year or even more, in which very little is earned beyond prime costs, and the fixed plant has "to work for nothing." But when the price falls so low that it does not pay for the out of pocket expenses during the year for wages and raw material, for coal and for lighting, etc., then the production is likely to come to a sharp stop.

This is the fundamental difference between those incomes yielded by agents of production which are to be regarded as rents or quasi-rents and those which (after allowing for the replacement of wear-and-tear and other destruction) may be regarded as interest (or profits) on current investments. The difference is fundamental, but it is only one of degree. Biology tends to show that the animal and vegetable kingdoms have a common origin. But yet there are fundamental differences between mammals and trees; while in a narrower sense the differences between an oak tree and an apple tree are fundamental; and so are in a still narrower sense those between an apple tree and a rose bush, though they are both classed as *rosaceæ*. Thus our central doctrine is that interest on free capital and quasi-rent on an old investment of capital shade into one another gradually; even the rent of land being not a thing by itself, but the leading species of a large genus.

§ 4. Again, pure elements are seldom isolated from all others by nature either in the physical or moral world. Pure rent in the strict sense of the term is scarcely ever met with: nearly all income from land contains more or less important elements which are derived from efforts invested in building houses and sheds, in draining the land and so on. But economists have learnt to recognize diversity of nature in those composite things to which the names of rent, profits, wages etc. are given in popular language; they have learnt that there is an element of true rent in the composite product that is commonly called wages, an element of true earnings in what is commonly called rent and so on. They have learnt in short to follow the example of the chemist who seeks for the true properties of each element; and who is thus prepared to deal with the common oxygen or soda of commerce, though containing admixtures of other elements.[2]

They recognize that nearly all land in actual use contains an element of capital; that separate reasonings are required for those parts of its value

[2] Professor Fetter seems to ignore this lesson in an article on "The passing of the concept of rent" in the *Quarterly Journal of Economics*, May 1901, p. 419; where he argues that "if only those things which owe nothing to labour are classed as land, and if it is then shown that there is no material thing in settled countries of which this can be said, it follows that everything must be classed as capital." Again he appears to have missed the true import of the doctrines which he assails, when he argues (*ib*. pp. 423–9) against "Extension as the fundamental attribute of land, and the basis of rent." The fact is that its extension (or rather the aggregate of "its space relations") is the chief, though not the only property of land, which causes the income derived from it (in an old country) to contain a large element of true rent: and that the element of true rent, which exists in the income derived from land, or the "rent of land" in the popular use of the term, is in practice so much more important than any others that it has given a special character to the historical development of the Theory of Rent. If meteoric stones of absolute hardness, in high demand and incapable of increase, had played a more important part in the economic history of the world than land, then the elements of true rent which attracted the chief attention of students, would have been associated with the property of hardness; and this would have given a special tone and character to the development of the Theory of Rent. But neither extension nor hardness is a fundamental attribute of all things which yield a true rent. Professor Fetter seems also to have missed the point of the central doctrine as to rents, quasi-rents and interest, given above.

which are, and those which are not, due to efforts of man invested in the land for the purposes of production; and that the results of these reasonings must be combined in dealing with any particular case of that income which commonly goes by the name "rent," but not all of which is rent in the narrower sense of the term. The manner in which the reasonings are to be combined depends on the nature of the problem. Sometimes the mere mechanical "composition of forces" suffices; more often allowance must be made for a quasi-chemical interaction of the various forces; while in nearly all problems of large scope and importance, regard must be had to biological conceptions of growth.

§ 5. Finally a little may be said on a distinction that is sometimes made between "scarcity rents" and "differential rents." In a sense all rents are scarcity rents, and all rents are differential rents. But in some cases it is convenient to estimate the rent of a particular agent by comparing its yield to that of an inferior (perhaps a marginal) agent, when similarly worked with appropriate appliances. And in other cases it is best to go straight to the fundamental relations of demand to the scarcity or abundance of the means for the production of those commodities for making which the agent is serviceable.

Suppose for instance that all the meteoric stones in existence were equally hard and imperishable; and that they were in the hands of a single authority: further that this authority decided, not to make use of its monopolistic power to restrict production so as to raise the price of its services artificially, but to work each of the stones to the full extent it could be profitably worked (that is up to the margin of pressure so intensive that the resulting product could barely be marketed at a price which covered, with profits, its expenses without allowing anything for the use of the stone). Then the price of the services rendered by the stones would have been governed by the natural scarcity of the aggregate output of their services in relation to the demand for those services; and the aggregate surplus or rent would most easily be reckoned as the excess of this scarcity price over the aggregate expenses of working the stones. It would therefore generally be regarded as a scarcity rent. But on the other hand it could have been reckoned as the differential excess of the aggregate value of the net services of the stones over that which would have been reached if all their uses had been as unproductive as their marginal uses. And exactly the same would be true if the stones were in the hands of different producers, impelled by competition with one another to work each stone up to the margin at which its further use ceased to be profitable.

This last instance has been so chosen as to bring out the fact that the "differential" as well as the "scarcity" routes for estimating rent are independent of the existence of inferior agents of production: for the differential comparison in favour of the more advantageous uses of the stones can be made by reference to the marginal uses of good stones, as clearly as by reference to the use of inferior stones which are on the margin of not being worth using at all.

In this connection it may be noted that the opinion that the existence of inferior land, or other agents of production, tends to raise the rents of the better agents is not merely untrue. It is the reverse of the truth. For, if the bad land were to be flooded and rendered incapable of producing anything at all, the cultivation of other land would need to be more intensive; and therefore the price of the product would be higher, and rents generally would be higher, than if that land had been a poor contributor to the total stock of produce.[3]

Chapter 13: THEORY OF CHANGES OF NORMAL DEMAND AND
SUPPLY IN RELATION TO THE DOCTRINE OF
MAXIMUM SATISFACTION

§ 1. In earlier chapters of this Book, we have considered gradual changes in the adjustment of demand and supply. But any great and lasting change in fashion; any substantive new invention; any diminution of population by war or pestilence; or the development or dwindling away of a source of supply of the commodity in question, or of a raw material used in it, or

[3] Compare Cassel, *Das Recht auf den vollen Arbeitsertrag*, p. 81.

The many misconceptions, that have appeared in the writings even of able economists, as to the nature of a quasi-rent, seem to arise from an inadequate attention to the differences between short periods and long in regard to value and costs. Thus it has been said that a quasi-rent is an "unnecessary profit," and that it is "no part of cost." Quasi-rent is correctly described as an unnecessary profit in regard to short periods, because no "special" or "prime" costs have to be incurred for the production of a machine that, by hypothesis, is already made and waiting for its work. But it is a necessary profit in regard to those other (supplementary) costs which must be incurred in the long run in addition to prime costs; and which in some industries, as for instance sub-marine telegraphy, are very much more important than prime costs. It is no part of cost under any conditions: but the confident expectation of coming quasi-rents is a necessary condition for the investment of capital in machinery, and for the incurring of supplementary costs generally.

Again a quasi-rent has been described as a sort of "conjuncture" or "opportunity" profit; and, almost in the same breath, as no profit or interest at all, but only a rent. For the time being, it is a conjuncture or opportunity income: while in the long run it is expected to, and it generally does, yield a normal rate of interest (or if earnings of management are counted in, of profit) on the free capital, represented by a definite sum of money that was invested in producing it. By definition the rate of interest is a percentage; that is a relation between two numbers (see above, p. 299). A machine is not a number: its value may be a certain number of pounds or dollars: but that value is estimated, unless the machine be a new one, as the aggregate of its (discounted) earnings, or quasi-rents. If the machine is new, its makers have calculated that this aggregate will appear to probable purchasers as the equivalent of a price which will repay the makers for it: in that case therefore it is as a rule, *both* a cost price, *and* a price which represents an aggregate of (discounted) future incomes. But when the machine is old and partially obsolete in pattern, there is no close relation between its value and its cost of production: its value is then simply the aggregate of the discounted values of the future quasi-rents, which it is expected to earn.

of another commodity which is a rival and possible substitute for it:—such a change as any of these may cause the prices set against any given annual (or daily) consumption and production of the commodity to cease to be its normal demand and supply prices for that volume of consumption and production; or, in other words, they may render it necessary to make out a new demand schedule or a new supply schedule, or both of them. We proceed to study the problems thus suggested.

An increase of normal demand for a commodity involves an increase in the price at which each several amount can find purchasers; or, which is the same thing, an increase of the quantity which can find purchasers at any price. This increase of demand may be caused by the commodity's coming more into fashion, by the opening out of a new use for it or of new markets for it, by the permanent falling off in the supply of some commodity for which it can be used as a substitute, by a permanent increase in the wealth and general purchasing power of the community, and so on. Changes in the opposite direction will cause a falling off in demand and a sinking of the demand prices. Similarly an increase of normal supply means an increase of the amounts that can be supplied at each several price, and a diminution of the price at which each separate amount can be supplied.[1] This change may be caused by the opening up of a new source of supply, whether by improved means of transport or in any other way, by an advance in the arts of production, such as the invention of a new process or of new machinery, or again, by the granting of a bounty on production. Conversely, a diminution of normal supply (or a raising of the supply schedule) may be caused by the closing up of a new source of supply or by the imposition of a tax.

§ 2. We have, then, to regard the effects of an increase of normal demand from three points of view, according as the commodity in question obeys the law of constant or of diminishing or of increasing return: that is, its supply price is practically constant for all amounts, or increases or diminishes with an increase in the amount produced.

In the first case an increase of demand simply increases the amount produced without altering its price; for the normal price of a commodity

[1] A rise or fall of the demand or supply prices involves of course a rise or fall of the demand or supply curve.

If the change is gradual, the supply curve will assume in succession a series of positions, each of which is a little below the preceding one; and in this way we might have represented the effects of that gradual improvement of industrial organization which arises from an increase in the scale of production, and which we have represented by assigning to it an influence upon the supply price for long-period curves. In an ingenious paper privately printed by Sir H. Cunynghame, a suggestion is made, which seems to come in effect to proposing that a long-period supply curve should be regarded as in some manner representing a series of short-period curves; each of these curves would assume throughout its whole length that development of industrial organization which properly belongs to the scale of production represented by the distance from Oy of the point in which that curve cuts the long-period supply curve and similarly with regard to demand.

which obeys the law of constant return is determined absolutely by its expenses of production: demand has no influence in the matter beyond this, that the thing will not be produced at all unless there is some demand for it at this fixed price.

If the commodity obeys the law of diminishing return an increase of demand for it raises its price and causes more of it to be produced; but not so much more as if it obeyed the law of constant return.

On the other hand, if the commodity obeys the law of increasing return, an increase of demand causes much more of it to be produced,—more than if the commodity obeyed the law of constant return,—and at the same time lowers its price. If, for instance, a thousand things of a certain kind have been produced and sold weekly at a price of 10s., while the supply price for two thousand weekly would be only 9s., a small rate of increase in normal demand may gradually cause this to become the normal price; since we are considering periods long enough for the full normal action of the causes that determine supply to work itself out. The converse holds in each case should normal demand fall off instead of increasing.[2]

The argument of this section has been thought by some writers to lend support to the claim that a Protective duty on manufactured imports in general increases the home market for those imports; and, by calling into

[2] Diagrams are of especial aid in enabling us to comprehend clearly the problems of this chapter.

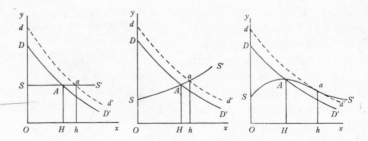

The three figures represent the three cases of constant, diminishing and increasing return respectively. The return in the last case is a diminishing one in the earlier stages of the increase of production, but an increasing one in those subsequent to the attainment of the original position of equilibrium, i.e. for amounts of the commodity greater than OH. In each case SS' is the supply curve, DD' the old position of the demand curve, and dd' its position after there has been increase of normal demand. In each case A and a are the old and new positions of equilibrium respectively, AH and ah are the old and new normal or equilibrium prices, and OH and Oh the old and new equilibrium amounts. Oh is in every case greater than OH, but in the second figure it is only a little greater, while in the third figure it is much greater. (This analysis may be carried further on the plan adopted later on in discussing the similar but more important problem of the effects of changes in the conditions of normal supply.) In the first figure ah is equal to AH, in the second it is greater, in the third it is less.

The effect of a falling-off of normal demand can be traced with the same diagrams, dd' being now regarded as the old and DD' as the new position of this demand curve; ah being the old equilibrium price, and AH the new one.

play the Law of Increasing Return, *ultimately* lowers their price to the home consumer. Such a result may indeed ultimately be reached by a wisely chosen system of "Protection to nascent industries" in a new country; where manufactures, like young children, have a power of rapid growth. But even there the policy is apt to be wrenched from its proper uses, to the enrichment of particular interests: for those industries which can send the greatest number of votes to the poll, are those which are already on so large a scale, that a further increase would bring very few new economies. And of course the industries in a country so long familiar with machinery as England is, have generally passed the stage at which they can derive much real help from such Protection: while Protection to any one industry nearly always tends to narrow the markets, especially the foreign markets, for other industries. These few remarks show that the question is complex: they do not pretend to reach further than that.

§ 3. We have seen that an increase in normal demand, while leading in every case to an increased production, will in some cases raise and in others lower prices. But now we are to see that increased facilities for supply (causing the supply schedule to be lowered) will always lower the normal price at the same time that it leads to an increase in the amount produced. For so long as the normal demand remains unchanged an increased supply can be sold only at a diminished price; but the fall of price consequent on a given increase of supply will be much greater in some cases than in others. It will be small if the commodity obeys the law of diminishing return; because then the difficulties attendant on an increased production will tend to counteract the new facilities of supply. On the other hand, if the commodity obeys the law of increasing return, the increased production will bring with it increased facilities, which will co-operate with those arising from the change in the general conditions of supply; and the two together will enable a great increase in production and consequent fall in price to be attained before the fall of the supply price is overtaken by the fall of the demand price. If it happens that the demand is very elastic, then a small increase in the facilities of normal supply, such as a new invention, a new application of machinery, the opening up of new and cheaper sources of supply, the taking off a tax or granting a bounty, may cause an enormous increase of production and fall of price.[3]

If we take account of the circumstances of composite and joint supply and demand, we have suggested to us an almost endless variety of problems which can be worked out by the methods adopted in these two chapters.

§ 4. We may now consider the effects which a change in the conditions of supply may exert on consumers' surplus or rent. For brevity of language

[3] All this can be most clearly seen by the aid of diagrams, and indeed there are some parts of the problem which cannot be satisfactorily treated without their aid. The three figures represent the three cases of constant and diminishing and increasing returns, respectively. In each case *DD'* is the demand curve, *SS'* the old position, and *ss'* the new position of the supply curve. A is the old, and *a* the new position of stable equilib-

a tax may be taken as representative of those changes which may cause a general increase, and a bounty as representative of those which may cause a general diminution in the normal supply price for each several amount of the commodity.

Firstly, if the commodity is one, the production of which obeys the law of constant return, so that the supply price is the same for all amounts of the commodity, consumers' surplus will be diminished by more than the increased payments to the producer; and therefore, in the special case of a tax, by more than the gross receipts of the State. For on that part of the consumption of the commodity, which is maintained, the consumer loses what the State receives: and on that part of the consumption which is destroyed by the rise in price, the consumers' surplus is destroyed; and of

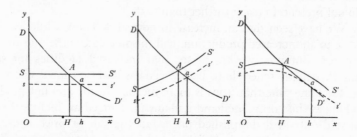

rium. *Oh* is greater than *OH*, and *ah* is less than *AH* in every case: but the changes are small in the second figure and great in the third. Of course the demand curve must lie below the old supply curve to the right of A, otherwise A would be a point not of stable; but of unstable equilibrium. But subject to this condition the more elastic the demand is, that is, the more nearly horizontal the demand curve is at A the further off will *a* be from A, and the greater therefore will be the increase of production and the fall of price.

The whole result is rather complex. But it may be stated thus. Firstly, given the elasticity of demand at A, the increase in the quantity produced and the fall in price will both be the greater, the greater be the return got from additional capital and labour applied to the production. That is, they will be the greater, the more nearly horizontal the supply curve is at A in the second figure, and the more steeply inclined it is in the third figure (subject to the condition mentioned above, that it does not lie below the demand curve to the right of A, and thus turn A into a position of unstable equilibrium). Secondly, given the position of the supply curve at A, the greater the elasticity of demand the greater will be the increase of production in every case; but the smaller will be the fall of price in the second figure, and the greater the fall of price in the third. The first figure may be regarded as a limiting case of either the second or third.

All this reasoning assumes that the commodity either obeys the law of diminishing return or obeys the law of increasing return throughout. If it obeys first one, and then the other, so that the supply curve is at one part inclined positively and at another negatively, no general rule can be laid down as to the effect on price of increased facilities of supply, though in every case this must lead to an increased volume of production. A great variety of curious results may be got by giving the supply curve different shapes, and in particular such as cut the demand curve more than once.

This method of inquiry is not applicable to a tax on wheat in so far as it is consumed by a labouring class which spends a great part of its income on bread; and it is not applicable to a general tax on all commodities: for in neither of these cases can it be assumed that the marginal value of money to the individual remains approximately the same after the tax has been levied as it was before.

course there is no payment for it to the producer or to the State.[4] Conversely, the gain of consumers' surplus caused by a bounty on a commodity that obeys the law of constant return, is less than the bounty itself. For on that part of the consumption which existed before the bounty, consumers' surplus is increased by just the amount of the bounty; while on the new consumption that is caused by the bounty, the gain of the consumers' surplus is less than the bounty.[5]

If however the commodity obeys the law of diminishing return; a tax by raising its price, and diminishing its consumption, will lower its expenses of production other than the tax: and the result will be to raise the supply price by something less than the full amount of the tax. In this case the gross receipts from the tax *may* be greater than the resulting loss of consumers' surplus, and they *will* be greater if the law of diminishing return acts so sharply that a small diminution of consumption causes a great falling-off in the expenses of production other than the tax.[6]

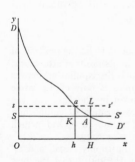

[4] This is most clearly seen by aid of a diagram. SS', the old constant return supply curve, cuts DD' the demand curve in A: DSA is the consumers' surplus. Afterwards a tax Ss being imposed the new equilibrium is found at a, and consumers' surplus is Dsa. The gross tax is only the rectangle $sSKa$, that is, a tax at the rate of Ss on an amount sa of the commodity. And this falls short of the loss of consumers' surplus by the area aKA. The net loss aKA is small or great, other things being equal, as aA is or is not inclined steeply. Thus it is smallest for those commodities the demand for which is most inelastic, that is, for necessaries. If therefore a given aggregate taxation has to be levied ruthlessly from any class it will cause less loss of consumers' surplus if levied on necessaries than if levied on comforts; though of course the consumption of luxuries and in a less degree of comforts indicates ability to bear taxation.

[5] If we now regard ss' as the old supply curve which is lowered to the position SS' by the granting of a bounty, we find the gain of consumers' surplus to be $sSAa$. But the bounty paid is Ss on an amount SA, which is represented by the rectangle $sSAL$: and this exceeds the gain of consumers' surplus by the area aLA.

[6] Let the old supply curve be SS', and let the imposition of a tax raise it to ss'; let A and a be the old and new positions of equilibrium, and let straight lines be drawn through them parallel to Ox and Oy, as in the figure. Then the tax being levied, as shown by the figure, at the rate of aE on each unit; and Oh, that is, CK units, being produced in the new position of equilibrium, the gross receipts of the tax will be $cFEa$, and the loss of consumers' surplus will be $cCAa$; that is, the gross receipts from the tax will be greater or less than the loss of consumers' surplus as $CFEK$ is greater or less than aKA; and in the figure as it stands it is much greater. If SS' had been so drawn as to indicate only very slight action of the law of diminishing return, that is, if it had been nearly horizontal in the neighbourhood of A, then EK would have been very small; and $CFEK$ would have become less than aKA.

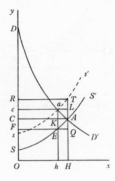

On the other hand, a bounty on a commodity which obeys the law of diminishing return will lead to increased production, and will extend the margin of cultivation to places and conditions in which the expenses of production, exclusive of the bounty, are greater than before. Thus it will lower the price to the consumer and increase consumers' surplus less than if it were given for the production of a commodity which obeyed the law of constant return. In that case the increase of consumers' surplus was seen to be less than the direct cost of the bounty to the State; and therefore in this case it is much less.[7]

By similar reasoning it may be shown that a tax on a commodity which obeys the law of increasing return is more injurious to the consumer than if levied on one which obeys the law of constant return. For it lessens the demand and therefore the output. It thus probably increases the expenses of manufacture somewhat: sends up the price by more than the amount of the tax; and finally diminishes consumers' surplus by much more than the total payments which it brings in to the exchequer.[8] On the other hand, a bounty on such a commodity causes so great a fall in its price to the consumer, that the consequent increase of consumers' surplus may exceed the total payments made by the State to the producers; and certainly will do so in case the law of increasing return acts at all sharply.

---

[7] To illustrate this case we may take ss' in the figure in footnote 6 to be the position of the supply curve before the granting of the bounty, and SS' to be its position afterwards. Thus a was the old equilibrium point, and A is the point to which the equilibrium moves when the bounty is awarded. The increase of consumers' surplus is only $cCAa$, while the payments made by the State under the bounty are, as shown by the figure, at the rate of AT on each unit of the commodity; and as in the new position of equilibrium there are produced OH, that is, CA units, they amount altogether to $RCAT$ which includes and is necessarily greater than the increase of consumers' surplus.

[8] Thus taking SS' in this figure to be the old position of the supply curve, and ss' its position after the tax, A to be the old and a the new positions of equilibrium, we have, as in the case of the preceding figure, the total tax represented by $cFEa$, and the loss of consumers' surplus by $cCAa$; the former being always less than the latter.

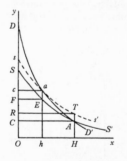

The statement in the text is put broadly and in simple outline. If it were applied to practical problems account would need to be taken of several considerations which have been ignored. An industry which yields an increasing return, is nearly sure to be growing, and therefore to be acquiring new economies of production on a large scale. If the tax is a small one, it may merely retard this growth and not cause a positive shrinking. Even if the tax is heavy and the industry shrinks, many of the economies gained will be in part at least preserved. In consequence ss' ought properly not to have the same shape as SS', and the distance aE ought to be less than AT.

JOAN ROBINSON

(1 9 0 3 –   )

It would be safe to say without fear of contradiction that Joan Robinson has been England's outstanding woman economic theorist of this or any other century and that she is equally well known elsewhere in the world. It is quite appropriate that England, which has been the home of so many distinguished economists, should also be the home of the leading female economic theoretician, and that a sample of her work be included in this volume.

The selections that follow are taken from The Economics of Imperfect Competition; however, her writing has explored not only the area of value and price theory, but also the macro-economic field as well. Among some of her better known books are Essays in the Theory of Employment (1937), Introduction to the Theory of Employment (1937), The Accumulation of Capital (1954), and Economic Philosophy (1963). Married to another famous British economist, E. A. G. Robinson, Mrs. Robinson has achieved her reputation on her own merits through the brilliant theoretical contributions contained in her many books as well as in numerous journal articles. In the field of macro-economics, she has been both a sympathetic critic of Marx's writings and an early interpreter of Keynes' General Theory in a day when this book had to be explained to economists and lay readers alike.

As enduring as anything she has written, however, has been The Economics of Imperfect Competition. Built "on the foundations laid by Marshall and Pigou," Mrs. Robinson's book went far beyond the analysis provided by either of these two distinguished economists in explaining the real world of business populated by numerous firms which had some power to set prices and determine output on their own. The reader will remember that the earlier economists had tended to emphasize the competitiveness of the market and the relative importance of the individual seller trapped in the grip of market forces.

Credit for exploring imperfections in the real market had to be shared with Professor Edward Chamberlin who came forth with the

equally famous Theory of Monopolistic Competition at about the
same time that Mrs. Robinson's book appeared in print. Although
many economists have tended to treat the two books as if they contained precisely the same message, that is only partially true because
important differences in emphasis and analysis exist between them.
Certainly, the magnitude of the contribution involved was sufficiently
great to admit ample recognition for both authors.

The chief omission from Mrs. Robinson's book that is of major importance to Professor Chamberlin's analysis is the concept of product
differentiation. Also, unlike Chamberlin, Mrs. Robinson placed little
or no emphasis on the blending of monopoly and competition—a condition Chamberlin regarded as the essence of "monopolistic competition."

Instead, Mrs. Robinson analyzed, by extensive use of geometry, the
ways in which price and output might vary from the picture given in
the perfectly competitive model and introduced the concepts of the
discriminating monopolist and of monopsony. A comparison of perfect and imperfect competition led Mrs. Robinson to conclude that
price and output would tend to be less satisfactory when competition is imperfect. The discriminating monopolist, by keeping his markets separate, could make greater profits by charging higher prices in
some markets than in others; the price he charged depended on the
level and elasticity of demand in a particular market. To select the
proper output in each market, the discriminating monopolist had to
compare his aggregate marginal revenue curve (the sum of the marginal revenue curves in each market) to his marginal cost curve and
then read back to his particular MR curves.

A particularly interesting bit of analysis concerned the monopsonist
whose power to control the price he paid for a factor of production
was the counterpart of the monopolist with his control over the price
of the things he sold. Since under a situation of monopsony it is possible for both the price and the quantity demanded to rise, the analysis
has been a natural defense of the demands of trade unions for higher
wages.

Although some of the most important sections of The Economics
of Imperfect Competition are reproduced below, the reader should be
aware that the book contains numerous other passages of ingenious
analysis which could not be included.

THE ECONOMICS OF
IMPERFECT COMPETITION

BOOK II / Monopoly Equilibrium

Chapter 3: MONOPOLY EQUILIBRIUM

1

The first problem to be solved is the determination of the output of the individual seller, given his costs of production, and given the conditions of demand for his commodity.

The problem may be considered either from the point of view of the *short period*, or the *quasi-long period*. In the short period the productive equipment of the firm is fixed, and part of the cost of production is fixed irrespective of output. The costs which need not be incurred if no output is produced (for instance, the cost of labour, raw material, and power) are known as *prime costs*. In the quasi-long period the productive equipment is conceived to be adapted to changes of output, and all costs except the minimum reward of the entrepreneur may vary with output. In the true *long period* the firm itself may be created or may disappear.

The cost curve which will be relevant to this inquiry is the curve of marginal cost to the individual firm.

The curve of marginal cost may be adapted to deal with short period or quasi-long period problems, and from the point of view of a firm already in existence long-period and quasi-long-period marginal costs are the same. The difference between the long period and the quasi-long period only arises from the fact that in the long period the number of firms producing a given commodity may alter, while in the quasi-long period it cannot alter.

In given conditions of demand, price and output will be determined by marginal cost, and the function of average cost will be to show whether, with a given price and output, the entrepreneur is earning a profit or not, and therefore whether he will continue to produce. As long as he continues in business at all, the level of average cost will not affect the amount of his output.

The importance of average costs in determining the profitability of production often leads, by a confusion of thought, to the view that they are also important, in a given situation, in determining price. For instance, business men often complain that some foreign rival has an advantage in competition because his overhead costs are lower. It is true that a firm whose overhead costs are low will be able to survive when low prices are ruling, while one with high overhead costs would be ruined, but as long as both continue to produce, the price is unaffected by the overhead costs.

A more sophisticated observer would be accustomed to look not at average total cost but at prime cost, as influencing price at any moment. Yet clearly it is not average but marginal prime cost that governs short-period price. Thus the rule that price is governed by marginal cost applies equally in the short period, when productive capacity is fixed, and in the quasi-long period, when it may be altered. In the short period marginal total cost is simply marginal prime cost, for it is only prime cost which alters when output alters. The distinction between prime and overhead costs is thus not of much significance in itself;[1] it is the distinction between average and marginal cost that is important, whatever the period may be which is under discussion.

2

Marginal cost may either fall or rise, as output increases, or it may be constant. In general we should expect that marginal cost for an individual concern would at first fall, and then rise or remain constant as output increases. This is likely to be true whether the technique of production is adapted to the change in output or not. In the quasi-long period, when the technique of production may be altered, there are likely to be economies of large-scale production. When there are no further economies of large scale to be gained from an increase in output, then, in the absence of scarce factors, marginal costs will be constant, so long as it is possible for the entrepreneur to increase his output without incurring diseconomies of large-scale management. Or marginal cost may be constant for a certain range of output if there is an exact balance between the economies and diseconomies entailed by increasing output. After a certain point diseconomies of large scale may outweigh the economies, and marginal costs may rise.[2]

[1] Average prime cost is important in determining whether (with given equipment) a business will produce something or nothing in any given conditions of demand.

[2] This treatment of the cost curves of a firm is based upon Mr. E. A. G. Robinson's *Structure of Competitive Industry*.

In many cases when marginal cost is constant, or even rising, average cost will be falling. There will always be a fixed element in total cost, the reward of the entrepreneur, and in many types of production, such as railways, the distribution of gas or wireless broadcasting, the minimum unit of plant necessary for the smallest output has a very large capacity. In such cases average costs must necessarily be falling, over a considerable range, with increases of output, and this has led some writers to suppose that in such cases price must necessarily fall with increases of demand. But this is a false deduction, for the fact that average cost is falling does not entail that marginal cost is falling, and it is marginal cost which determines output and price in any given situation.

A similar type of case is frequently met with in the short period when the capacity of the plant in existence in an industry is in excess of the output which is being produced, for the marginal prime cost is often constant up to capacity output. Consider, for instance, the case of a cotton mill which is working under capacity owing to a decline in demand. Either the whole mill may be worked for a few days a week, so that increases of output, up to the point at which a full week is being worked without over-time, bring about no rise in marginal cost. Or the mill may be worked every day, but part of the looms or spindles may be left idle; thus, if the machines are all equally good, there will again be no rise in marginal cost with increases of output up to the point where every machine is in use and further increases can only be made by working overtime or by reducing the number of machines tended by each worker. In either case marginal cost will be constant over a considerable range of output.[3]

Falling marginal costs in the short period are probably not so common as the frequent claim that an increase of output will lead to a lower price would lead us to expect. It is possible, however, that in some cases the technical efficiency of production is much impaired by working an organisation at less than the output for which it was designed, so that there are falling marginal costs up to the designed output. This may be the case, for instance, in the iron and steel industries, where there are large technical economies to be gained by working plant to its designed capacity. In general, however, it may be supposed that in the short period marginal costs begin to rise at a fairly low level of output, as a result of the limitation of plant and organisation, and in any case there must always be some level of output at which they begin to rise.

For our present purpose it makes no difference for what reason marginal costs are constant, or are rising or falling, though the nature of the average cost curve corresponding to any given marginal cost curve, and therefore the amount of profit, would be different in each case. And our analysis can be applied equally to quasi-long or to short-period cases provided that for

[3] In the second case, though not in the first, average prime cost will fall with increases of output, but this does not affect the argument.

each problem those curves are drawn which are relevant to the period under discussion.

3

The demand curve for the output of the individual firm will normally be falling. Its elasticity will depend upon many factors, of which the chief are the number of other firms selling the same commodity and the degree to which substitution is possible, from the point of view of buyers, between the output of other firms and the output of the firm in question. If there are few or no other firms producing closely similar commodities, the distribution of wealth among buyers, the conditions of supply of rival commodities, the conditions of supply of jointly-demanded commodities, and all the innumerable factors which affect the demand for any one commodity will influence the demand curve for the individual producer. But when the number of firms producing any one sufficiently homogeneous commodity is large it is the competition of these rival firms which will have the preponderating influence upon the demand curve for any one of them. The elasticity of demand for any one of them will be greater than the elasticity of demand for the commodity as a whole; for although each producer may have certain customers who prefer, for one reason or another, to buy from him, a rise in his price will drive some of them to buy from his competitors before it will drive them to give up buying the commodity altogether.

When, the number of firms being large, so that a change in the output of any one of them has a negligible effect upon the total output of the commodity, the commodity is perfectly homogeneous in the sense that the buyers are all alike in respect of their preferences (or indifference) between one firm and its rivals, then competition is perfect, and the elasticity of demand for the individual firm is infinite. That is to say, any one producer will be able to sell as much as he pleases at the current market price. If he lowers his price, by however little, he will be able to capture the whole market, while if he raises his price, by however little, he will be unable to sell at all.

Perfect competition is never likely to prevail in the production of any actual commodity, but it provides a limiting case of imperfect competition which is of considerable service in analysis. Conditions approximating closely to perfect competition are likely to occur, for instance, in an organised produce market, such as the corn exchange in a large market town.

4

It is assumed to be the aim of the producer to fix that price at which the excess of gross receipts or *revenue* over costs will be at a maximum. He will achieve this if he regulates output in such a way that the addition to his total revenue from selling an additional unit is exactly equal to the addition to his costs caused by producing that unit. If he sold one unit less, he would lose more of revenue than he saved of cost, and if he produced one unit more, he would incur more of cost than he gained of revenue.

The addition to total revenue produced by selling an additional unit of output is *marginal revenue*. The seller is assumed always to equate marginal revenue to marginal cost. He may be conceived to do this either by estimating the demand price and the cost of various outputs, or by a process of trial and error. For the sake of simplicity the individual producer may be referred to as a *monopolist*.

The marginal revenue curve of the monopolist is marginal to the demand curve for his product.

The demand curve represents his average revenue. If he can sell 1000 units at 10s. each, 10s. is his average revenue for 1000 units, and his total revenue from selling 1000 units is 10,000s. His marginal revenue will be the difference between his total revenue when he sells 1000 units and 1001 units. As output is increased selling price is reduced, so that average revenue declines as output increases. Marginal revenue will therefore be less than average revenue. Thus:

Units	Price or Average Revenue	Total Revenue	Marginal Revenue
10	20	200	—
11	19	209	9
12	18	216	7

The determination of output can be illustrated thus:

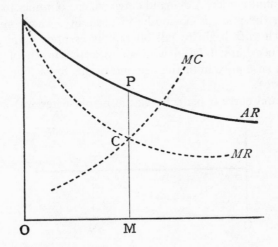

AR is the average revenue or demand curve.

MR is the marginal revenue curve.

MC is the marginal cost curve.

OM is the most remunerative output, and MP its price.

If the demand curve is inelastic, marginal revenue will be negative. Thus:

Units	Price	Total Revenue	Marginal Revenue
20	10	200	—
21	9	189	−11
22	8	176	−13

In such circumstances, it would pay the monopolist to contract output, for even if an addition to output costs him nothing, his revenue is reduced by each addition to his sales. If the demand curve were inelastic throughout its length, it would pay him best to produce an infinitesimal amount and

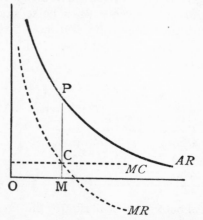

sell it for an infinite price. A demand curve which continues to be inelastic, however high the price, is obviously an absurdity. There must be some point at which sales begin to fall off rapidly as price is raised, and if a monopolist finds himself faced with an inelastic.stretch of the demand curve, he will raise price until the demand begins to become elastic (as in the figure above).

If the demand curve is perfectly elastic marginal revenue and price are

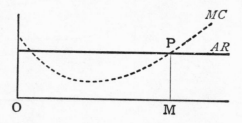

equal, and the output will be such that marginal cost is equal to price (as in the figure above).[4]

5

The price of the monopoly output will stand in a certain relation to its marginal cost.

If ϵ is the elasticity of demand, then we know that the price is equal to marginal revenue multiplied by $\epsilon/\epsilon - 1$. But for the monopoly output marginal revenue is equal to marginal cost. Thus monopoly price is equal to marginal cost multiplied by $\epsilon/\epsilon - 1$. This must be true whatever the shape of the cost curve, since marginal revenue will always be equal to marginal cost to the monopolist, at the monopoly output.

The same relationship can be expressed in another form:

> Let PM be the price of the monopoly output, OM, MC being the marginal cost and marginal revenue for the output OM.
> Let AP be the tangent to the demand curve at P. Then the correspondent AC is marginal to the tangent AP.

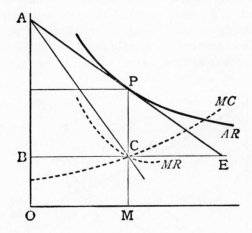

Draw BC perpendicular to the y axis, to cut it in B.
Let the tangent AP cut BC in E.
Then BC = ½BE.

---

[4] It is clear that the marginal method of analysis will produce exactly the same results as the method, used by Marshall, of finding the price at which the area representing "monopoly net revenue" is at a maximum, since net revenue is at a maximum when marginal revenue and marginal cost are equal. Both methods can be applied to problems of competition and of monopoly. Marshall introduced into his system of analysis an artificial cleavage between monopoly and competition, by treating competitive problems only by the "marginal" method, and monopoly problems only by the "areas" method.

AEB and PEC are similar triangles.

$\therefore$ CP = ½AB.

$\therefore$ MP = MC + ½AB.

Alternatively—

since MC = OB and AB = OA − OB,

MP = ½(OA + MC).

Thus monopoly price is equal to the marginal cost of the monopoly output *plus* half the distance cut off on the *y* axis by the marginal cost of that output and a tangent to the demand curve at that output. Or, alternatively, monopoly price is equal to half the sum of the intercept of the tangent on the *y* axis and the marginal cost. This relationship also will prove of service in the succeeding argument.

6

It remains to consider the amount of monopoly profit, or net receipts. This will be equal to the difference between the area lying under the marginal revenue curve (aggregate revenue) and the area lying under the marginal cost curve (aggregate costs). Monopoly profit can also be discovered by considering the average cost curve, which will be introduced at a later stage in the argument. Monopoly profit is the difference between average cost and average revenue, multiplied by output. Thus:

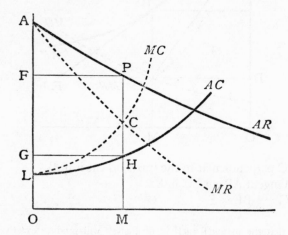

Monopoly profit is equal to the area ACL, and to the area FPHG, when MH is the average cost of the output OM.

. . .

BOOK IV / The Comparison of Monopoly and Competitive Output

Chapter 10: A DIGRESSION ON THE FOUR COST CURVES

1

The next task to which our technique may be applied is to make the comparison between competitive and monopoly output: that is to say, to contrast the output of an industry when it is composed of a number of independent producers, with the output of the same industry in the same conditions of demand when it is controlled by a single authority. We have already discussed the competitive supply curve, and we know that competitive output is the output at which demand price is equal to supply price. But the cost curve which governs monopoly output may obviously be something different from the supply curve which governs competitive output, and we cannot embark upon the comparison between monopoly and competitive output until we have examined this question more closely. The present chapter therefore is devoted to a digression on cost curves.[1]

2

We have seen that the supply curve of a commodity produced under perfect competition is the curve of average costs including rent. This proposition is no more than a tautology, since it follows from the definition of rent to the industry. Aggregate cost including rent is simply the total receipts of the industry, in equilibrium, and average cost including rent is necessarily equal to price. But this average cost curve is not the only curve which can be derived from the aggregate cost of the industry. There are four cost curves which can usefully be distinguished.

From aggregate cost including rent we can derive marginal cost including rent, that is, the increase in the total costs of the industry when output is increased by one unit. The curve of marginal cost including rent may be called α, and the curve of average cost including rent β. This curve, β, must coincide with the supply curve of the commodity, since supply price is equal to average cost including rent.

From aggregate cost excluding rent marginal and average cost excluding rent can be derived. Marginal cost excluding rent is the increase in the costs

---

[1] The treatment of the four cost curves here set out owes much to Mr. Shove, but he must not be held responsible for this exposition of them, which differs considerably from his own. Mr. Shove's article on "Varying Costs and Marginal Net Products" in the *Economic Journal*, June 1928, contains his first systematic treatment of the cost curves.

of the industry other than rent when output increases by one unit. Average cost excluding rent is the aggregate cost other than rent, divided by the output. The curve of marginal cost excluding rent may be called γ, and the curve of average cost excluding rent δ.

Then the α curve is marginal to the β curve and the γ curve is marginal to the δ curve, each pair obeying the various laws governing the behaviour of marginal and average curves.

The relationships between these four curves will be different according as the transfer price of any given unit of any factor is or is not independent of the amount of that factor employed in the industry. We will first consider the case where it is independent.

If we further assume that there are no economies of large-scale industry, so that not only the transfer cost, but also the efficiency, of each unit of a factor is independent of the amount of the factor employed, then marginal cost excluding rent is equal to the cost of the additional units of the factors required to make a unit increase of ouput. For the addition to the amount of each factor employed consists of marginal units, and the additional cost incurred includes no element of rent. But this additional cost is the same thing as cost at the margin and is equal to the supply price of the commodity. Thus the γ curve, showing marginal cost excluding rent, coincides (upon the two assumptions which we have made) with the supply curve of the commodity. And as we have seen, the β curve, showing average cost including rent, coincides with the supply curve. On our two assumptions, therefore, γ and β coincide. β and γ are then marginal to δ (average cost excluding rent) and α (marginal cost including rent) is marginal to β and γ.

A numerical example may help to make these relations clear.[2]

(1). Units of Output	(2). Total Cost excluding Rent	(3). Average Cost excluding Rent (2) ÷ (1)	(4). Marginal Cost excluding Rent Derived from (2)
		δ	$\gamma(= \beta)$
9	900	100	—
10	1020	102	120
11	1144	104	124
12	1272	106	128

The γ curve, which is marginal to δ, is derived by considering the increment of cost due to a unit increase of output. For instance, when output increases from 9 to 10 units total cost (excluding rent) rises from 900 to 1020. The marignal cost (excluding rent) of 10 units is therefore 120. On

---

[2] Once more the example is absurd but useful.

1020. The marginal cost (excluding rent) of 10 units is therefore 120. On supply curve of the commodity. Column 4 therefore gives the list of supply prices of the various outputs. Thus if 10 units are to be produced the price must be 120, if 11 units are to be produced the price must be 124 and so forth. We may therefore proceed with the example, assuming each amount of output to be sold at its appropriate price.

(1).	(5). Total Cost including Rent (4) × (1)	(6). Average Cost including Rent (5) ÷ (1) = (4)	(7). Marginal Cost including Rent Derived from (5)
		$\beta(=\gamma)$	a
10	1200	120	—
11	1364	124	164
12	1536	128	172

α is marginal to β, and the divergence between them represents the increase in the cost of producing the former output which is caused by a unit increase of output; that is, it shows the difference between the cost of n units when n are being produced and the cost of n units when $(n + 1)$ are being produced.[3] Thus when 11 units are being produced the difference between α and β is 40, because, when output increases from 10 units to 11, average cost is raised by 4, and the total cost of 10 units is therefore increased by 40. α is marginal cost including rent, and γ is marginal cost excluding rent: the increment of rent due to a unit increase of output is therefore shown by α *minus* γ. But γ here coincides with β. α *minus* β therefore shows the increment of rent. In other words, on the two assumptions which entail that γ and β coincide, the increase in the cost of producing a given output when output expands by one unit is equal to the increment of rent. Thus when 10 units are produced and sold at the appropriate price (120), total receipts are 1200 (column 5) and total costs excluding rent are 1020 (column 2). The rent is then 180. Similarly, when output is 11 units the rent is 220. The increase in rent brought about by

[3] If A is the average cost, M the marginal cost, and O the output,

$$M = \frac{d(AO)}{dO}$$

$$= A + O\frac{dA}{dO}.$$

$$\therefore \quad M - A = O\frac{dA}{dO},$$

which is the increase in the cost of the old output, O, when output is increased by one unit.

This relation is to be found, in a somewhat obscure form, in the *Economics of Welfare*, Macmillan, London, 1932, p. 803.

increasing output from 10 to 11 units is therefore 40, and this is the difference between α and β when 11 units are being produced.

The difference between β and δ is the average rent per unit of output. Thus when there is an output of 10 units the total rent is 180 and the difference between β and δ is 18. The total rent can thus be regarded either as total receipts *minus* total costs other than rent, or, since β and γ coincide, as marginal *minus* average cost (both excluding rent) multiplied by output.[4]

The marginal increment of rent obviously does not enter into the supply price of the commodity. Output will always be increased if price is greater than marginal cost to the individual producer, and this will be equal to cost at the margin for the whole industry. But every increase in output will raise the rent paid by all producers. Each individually will only be influenced by the rise in the rent of intra-marginal units of the scarce factors employed by himself, that is, by his share in the increment of rent. But since (on the assumption that competition is perfect) the proportion of the total output for which any one producer is responsible must be small, the share of any one producer in the increment of rent is negligible. The increment of rent to the whole industry will have no influence on the individual producer and will therefore not enter into supply price. It is marginal cost excluding rent which is equal to supply price, and marginal cost to the industry including rent is greater than supply price.

3

We have so far proceeded upon the assumption that there are no economies of large-scale industry. We must now remove this assumption, retaining the assumption that the transfer costs of units of the factors are independent of the amounts of the factors employed in the industry.

It is argued in the Appendix on Increasing and Diminishing Returns that the economies which arise from the increase in the scale of an industry can all be treated in the same terms as apply to the simple type of external economies which arise when some item in the productive equipment, for instance a machine, becomes cheaper (without altering in nature) when more of it is employed. We will therefore only deal, in the present context,

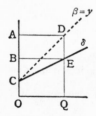

[4] In this figure DQ is the supply price of the output OQ. The rent can be shown either, as Marshall represents it, by the triangular area ADC, or by the rectangle ADEB. $DE(\beta - \delta)$ = rent per unit of output.

with economies of large-scale industry which are of this simple type. We will at first assume that there are no scarce factors. And we will suppose that decreasing costs arise from, say, buying machinery more cheaply when the industry expands, and so offers a larger market to machine makers, who, in turn, are producing under conditions of falling supply price.

The supply price of the commodity will be equal to the average cost of the industry, and to the average and marginal costs of each firm, and it will fall as the output of the industry expands. On the assumption that there is no scarce factor and therefore no payment of rent, the β curve will coincide with the δ curve, both showing average cost, and the γ curve will coincide with the α curve, both showing marginal cost.

Since δ (or β) is falling, γ (or α), which is marginal to it, must lie below it.

The divergence between γ and δ measures the difference between the cost of producing n units when n are being produced and the cost of n units when $(n + 1)$ are being produced. That is to say, it is the change in average cost, induced by a unit increase in output, multiplied by the former output. This difference may be described as the *induced economies* due to the unit increase in output. Thus if an increase in the output of the industry from 100 to 101 leads to economies which reduce average cost by 1, the induced economies due to the 101st unit of output are equal to 100.

Next we must consider the case where there are both economies of large-scale industry and scarce factors of production. As output increases, the cost of a marginal unit of a scarce factor increases, and consequently the cost including rent of all units of the factor increases, but, at the same time, each addition to output enlarges the scale of the industry, and reduces some other element in cost. To illustrate this case we may construct an imaginary example. Suppose, for instance, that land for growing hay is a scarce factor, but that every ton of hay added to the output of the hay-growing industry lowers the price of mowers by $0 \cdot 1$ of a shilling.[5] If 1000 new mowers are bought every year by the whole group of producers, then every additional ton of hay produced will reduce the aggregate expenditure on machinery by 100 shillings. That is to say, there are induced economies at the rate of 100 shillings, or £5, per ton. Suppose that the cost of producing a ton of hay on marginal land is £7. Then £7 will be the equilibrium supply price of a ton of hay, and its average cost, including rent, to all producers will be £7. But its marginal cost, excluding rent, to the industry as a whole is £7 *minus* the reduction in the cost of machinery brought about by adding a ton of hay to the total output. Thus its marginal cost, excluding rent, to the industry is £2. This artificial example illustrates the fact that when economies are present it is no longer true that marginal cost to the industry, excluding rent, is equal to the cost of the additional factors employed when output

---

[5] An absurdly high rate of induced economies is given for the sake of clarity.

increases. The cost of the additional factors employed, or cost at the margin, must necessarily be equal to supply price, but marginal cost to the industry, excluding rent, is now less than the supply price by the amount of the induced economies. The individual producer will only increase his output if price is greater than marginal cost to him, and marginal cost to the individual producer is equal to cost at the margin for the whole industry. But every increase in the output of one producer will have the effect of inducing economies which benefit all the other producers. The action of the individual will be influenced by his own share in these induced economies, but since we are discussing a perfectly competitive industry we must assume that the proportion of the total output controlled by any one producer is very small. His share in the induced economies will therefore be negligible, and they will not influence his conduct. It is the marginal cost to the individual which must be equal to supply price, and marginal cost to the industry, excluding rent, will be less than supply price when there are economies. β still coincides with the supply curve but γ now lies below β. α is marginal to β and γ is marginal to δ. The two pairs of curves are not connected by any marginal and average relationship, but if there are no scarce factors, α coincides with γ and β with δ. The divergence between γ and β measures the induced economies, and the divergence between γ and α measures the increment of rent, due to a unit increase of output.

4

The system of four cost curves may now be tabulated:

(1) α is marginal cost including rent;
   β is average cost including rent, and coincides with the supply curve of the commodity;
   γ is marginal cost excluding rent;
   δ is average cost excluding rent.

On the assumption that the transfer cost of any unit of a factor is independent of the amount of the factor employed, the relationships of these curves can be summarised as follows:

(2) When there are no economies of large-scale industry:
   γ coincides with β;
   α is marginal to γ and β;
   γ and β are marginal to δ.

(3) When there are no scarce factors:
   α coincides with γ;
   β coincides with δ;
   α and γ are marginal to β and δ.

(4) When there are no scarce factors and no economies:

  γ coincides with β;
  α coincides with γ;
  β coincides with δ;
  $\therefore$ all four curves coincide.

(5) When there are both scarce factors and economies:

  All four curves are separate.
  α is marginal to β;
  γ is marginal to δ.

(6) $\alpha - \gamma$ = marginal increment of rent;
  $\beta - \delta$ = average rent per unit of output;
  $\beta - \gamma$ = induced economies.

(7) When there are no economies but there is a scarce factor, supply price must be rising. β ($= \gamma$) must be rising, and α must lie above β. δ lies below β, and is also rising.

When there are economies but no scarce factor the supply price must be falling. β ($= \delta$) must be falling, and α ($= \gamma$) lies below β.

When there are neither economies nor scarce factors the supply price is constant and all four curves coincide and are horizontal.

(8) When there are both economies and scarce factors the supply price may be either rising, falling, or constant.

When the increment of rent ($\alpha - \gamma$) is greater than the induced economies ($\beta - \gamma$), supply price will be rising, β will be rising, and α will lie above β.

Conversely, when ($\alpha - \gamma$) is less than (B $- \gamma$), β will be falling, and α will lie below β.

If the increment of rent ($\alpha - \gamma$) is exactly equal to the induced economies ($\beta - \gamma$), supply price will be constant, and α and β will coincide in a horizontal straight line.[6]

Whether supply price is rising, falling, or constant, γ will lie below β to an extent determined by the induced economies.

5

We have so far assumed that the transfer cost of any unit of a factor is independent of the amount of the factor employed. It remains to study

---

[6] The difference between the type of constant supply price in which all four curves coincide, because there are no economies and no scarce factors, and the type of constant supply price in which only β and α coincide, because the rise in cost due to the scarce factors is just offset by the economies of large scale, corresponds to the difference between constant cost according to Mr. Sraffa and constant cost according to Marshall. See Sraffa, *Economic Journal*, December, 1926, p. 541, note.

the relationships between the four cost curves when this assumption is removed. If the factors are homogeneous, so that the transfer cost of all units is the same, there will be no rent. But the cost of the factor rises as more is employed, because its earnings in other industries increase as more of it is absorbed into the expanding industry. Since there is no rent β and δ coincide, and α and γ coincide, whether there are economies of large scale or not. β may be rising or falling, according as the rise in the cost of the scarce factors outweighs or is outweighed by economies of large scale. The divergence between α $(= \gamma)$ and β $(= \delta)$ will measure the difference between the cost of n units when n units are produced and the cost of n units when $(n + 1)$ are produced. When there are no economies this difference will be equal to the increased cost of the scarce factors already employed as a result of an increase in the amount employed sufficient to add a unit to output. And when there are no scarce factors it will be equal (as we found above) to the induced economies. But when there are both economies and scarce factors it will not measure either of these quantities separately.[7]

When the scarce factors are not homogeneous, so that there is rent, their cost will rise, as more is employed, both because the efficiency of a marginal unit, relatively to its price, is reduced as more of the factor is employed, and because the transfer cost of intra-marginal units is raised. β must still show cost will rise, as more is employed, both because the efficiency of a marginal excluding rent) coincides with β when there are no economies of large scale. When there are no economies β will be rising and γ will lie between β and α; $\gamma - \beta$ will show the change of costs, other than rent, incurred in producing n units when an $(n + 1)$th unit is added to output. That is to say, it will measure the change in the transfer costs of the factors already employed when the amount employed increases sufficiently to add one unit to output. When there are also economies of large scale, γ may lie above or below β, and will coincide with it if the change in the transfer costs of the factors already employed is exactly offset by the induced economies.

Chapter 11: COMPARISONS OF MONOPOLY AND COMPETITIVE
  OUTPUT

1

. . .

It is now possible to make the comparison of monopoly and competitive output. We shall take as our basis of comparison a perfectly competitive

[7] We are here studying the type of increasing cost contemplated by Professor Pigou, and these few hints may be of service in interpreting Appendix III. of the *Economics of Welfare* to a non-mathematical reader. The conclusions of the Appendix are of course independent of the relations between the four curves, but Professor Pigou himself appears to visualize a world in which α and γ always coincide.

industry. The conditions in which competition is perfect are not likely to
be completely fulfilled in any actual case. If we are contrasting conditions
of monopoly with conditions of competition in the real world—if we are
interested, for example, in the effect of rationalisation on a competitive
industry—we should in practice be comparing conditions of monopoly
with conditions of imperfect competition. But when we take absolutely
perfect competition for a starting-point we have a simple and definite
notion of what we mean by competitive output, and the comparison can
be made in its simplest form.

In order to make a valid theoretical comparison between competitive
output and monopoly output in a particular industry it is necessary to make
very severe assumptions. First, we must have a definite idea of what we
mean by the commodity that we are considering. Secondly, if we wish to
discuss what will happen to output and prices if a certain commodity,
hitherto produced by competing firms, is monopolised, we must assume
that neither the demand curve for the commodity nor the costs of production of any given output are altered by the change. These assumptions are
unlikely to be fulfilled in any actual situation, and in studying an actual
case changes in demand and in the efficiency of production must be
allowed for. On the assumption that they are unchanged, the relationship
between monopoly and competitive output can easily be discovered.

2

If there are no scarce factors and no economies of large scale, all four
cost curves coincide in a horizontal line. The monopolist equates marginal cost to him with marginal revenue; under competition average cost
is equal to price, and marginal cost to the monopolist is equal to average
cost to him and to the competitive industry. It follows from the geometrical relations set out in Chapter 2 that monopoly output is half competitive
output when the demand curve is a straight line, less than half when the
demand curve is concave, and more than half when the demand curve is
convex.

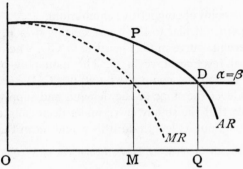

The above figure represents a case in which the demand curve is convex.

OM is the monopoly output, OQ the competitive output.

OM is greater than half OQ.

But complications are introduced into the comparison by the existence of increasing and decreasing cost. The statement that a monopolist will produce up to the point where marginal cost is equal to marginal revenue is perfectly general; it applies equally to constant, decreasing, and increasing costs. But we have now discovered that marginal cost is not a simple notion. The α, β, and γ curves each show marginal cost in a different sense. Which of them shows the marginal cost which a monopolist will take into account? Before we can decide this question, we must consider whether the monopolist is obliged to pay rent to the factors which he employs. In some cases, as we shall see in a moment, it is unlikely that he will do so. If the monopolist pays the full rent for any scarce factor, then, on the assumption that the introduction of a single control in no way alters methods of production, the monopolist's average costs are the same for each output as average costs under competition; that is to say, they are the same as the competitive supply price for each output, and the marginal cost curve of the monopolist is marginal to the competitive supply curve. The competitive supply curve is β (average cost including rent) and the curve marginal to it is α (marginal cost including rent). When the demand and supply curves are straight lines, monopoly output will be half competitive output, whether the supply curve is rising or falling.

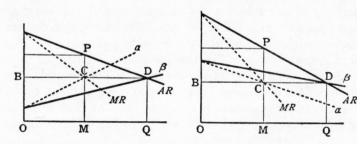

Let D be the point of competitive equilibrium.

Draw DB perpendicular to the y axis, cutting it in B, and cutting the marginal revenue curve in C. Then BC = CD. The α curve also cuts the marginal revenue curve in C. The monopoly output (OM) is then equal to half the competitive output (OQ).[1]

This is true whatever the slope of the demand and supply curves. It is of course impossible that the supply curve under decreasing cost should be a straight line throughout its length, for this would mean that after a certain

[1] This result is already familiar; see Pigou, *Economics of Welfare*, Macmillan, London, 1932, p. 807.

output marginal cost became negative. There is no absurdity, however, in supposing it to be a straight line for the range of outputs necessary to the comparison.

If the supply curve is concave, and the demand curve is a straight line, then monopoly output is greater than half the competitive output whether the supply curve is rising or falling.

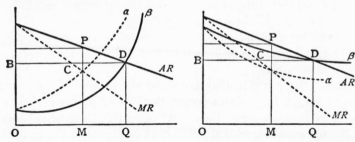

When the supply curve is rising, α will cut BD to the right of C, and when it is falling, to the left of C. In each case therefore it will cut MR below C and to the right of it. Therefore since BC = CD the monopoly output (OM) will be greater than half the competitive output (OQ).

Conversely, when the supply curve is convex, and the demand curve is a straight line, monopoly output will be less than half competitive output.

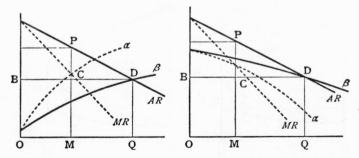

When the supply curve is rising, α will cut BD to the left of C, and when it is falling, to the right of C. Therefore in each case α will cut MR above C and to the left of it, and monopoly output (OM) will be less than half competitive output (OQ).

Similarly it can be seen that when the supply curve is a straight line (whether costs are rising, falling, or constant), monopoly output will be less than half competitive output for a concave demand curve, and it will be greater than half for a convex demand curve.

Thus we find that concavity of the supply curve and convexity of the demand curve lead to a high ratio of monopoly to competitive output.

And convexity of the supply curve and concavity of the demand curve lead to a small ratio.

When the demand curve is concave and the supply curve convex, monopoly output must be less than half competitive output. When the demand curve is convex and the supply curve concave, monopoly output must be more than half competitive output. In this case price is falling at an increasing rate and cost rising at an increasing rate as output increases. It is therefore a case that is likely to occur in practice.[2]

When both the demand curve and the supply curve are concave, and when both are convex, monopoly output may be half, or more or less than half, competitive output.

In all these cases it is clear that monopoly output cannot be greater than competitive output. For outputs greater than the competitive amount the demand curve must lie below the supply curve (which represents average cost to the monopolist), so that any output greater than the competitive output would have to be sold at a loss. At most the monopoly output may be equal to the competitive output. This may occur if either the demand or the supply curve after being sufficiently elastic becomes suddenly perfectly inelastic, as in the cases illustrated in the two succeeding figures.

These may be regarded as limiting cases of convexity of the demand curve and concavity of the supply curve, which each tend to produce a high ratio of monopoly to competitive output. Monopoly output would also be equal to competitive output if it so happened that the demand curve lay

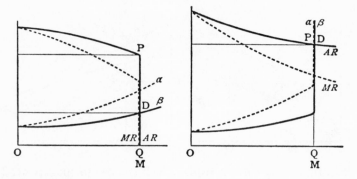

below the supply curve except at one point, where the two curves were tangential. There would then be only one output which could be produced without a loss,[3] and it must be this output which would be produced both under monopoly and under competition.

---

[2] In so far as any case in which monopolisation leaves the cost curves unchanged is ever likely to occur.

[3] Such a situation could only arise by chance for a competitive industry, but it is the ordinary situation of each individual firm in an industry which is earning normal profits.

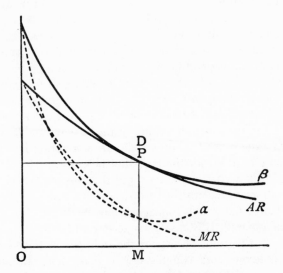

This may be regarded as the limiting case of the situation in which monopoly output must approach competitive output because the demand curve lies below the supply curve except for a small range of outputs, so that outputs outside this range could only be sold at a loss.

3

We have so far supposed that the monopolist is paying the full rent for the scarce factors which he employs. But this may not always be the case. If the scarce factor is land the monopolist will often omit rent from his calculations, and take account only of transfer costs, simply because he owns the land himself. Moreover, if the monopolist hires land but the land which he employs is owned by a large number of separate landlords, it is unlikely that he will be obliged to pay the full rent for it, since it will be possible for him to make a separate bargain with each landlord. The monopolist controls the whole demand for the land in its most profitable use. If it does not take service with him, it will have to earn a lower payment elsewhere. The monopolist therefore can offer to each landlord the transference earnings of the land, that is to say the payment which it could earn in its next best use; and, if the landlord rejects the monopolist's offer of the transference price for his piece of land, he will find that he can do no better by offering it to other producers, who must necessarily belong to some other industry for which the suitability of his land is not so great. It would be profitable to the monopolist on the other hand to pay for any individual site the full rent which it earns in his industry rather than to forgo the use of it. Thus for each piece of land there will be an upper and a lower limit to its earnings, which must lie somewhere between its full rent and its transference earnings. For land on the margin of transference the two limits coincide. The actual price which the monopolist will pay for each piece of land will depend upon his skill in bargaining relatively to the skill of the individual landlords.[4] In order to establish his reputation as a hard bargainer the monopolist may prefer to sacrifice the use of any site the owner of which resolutely stands out for a price greater than the transference earnings of his land, and by this means he may be able so to weaken the resistance of the other landlords (who are not acting in concert) that he need pay no rent at all for the land that he employs. In other cases he will be obliged to pay part of the rent, but it seems on the whole improbable that he will ever be compelled to pay the full rent for all the land.

When the scarce factor is labour it will not be so easy for the monopolist to avoid paying rent. It is customary to pay all labour, of a given grade of efficiency from the point of view of the industry, at the same rate, and it may be troublesome and complicated to make separate bargains with individual workers. Where unskilled labour is concerned, however, it may be possible to do so, and for the high-grade labour of salaried workers, since it is customary to make separate terms with each individual, the situation will be very similar to that of land, and the monopolist will often be able to acquire the services of each worker for no more than his transference earnings.

When the scarce factor is entrepreneurship, and the monopoly consists of a cartel formed by firms which were formerly competing, it will be the aim of the monopolist organisation to maximise the whole surplus which they receive, and the rent of entrepreneurship must clearly not be regarded as part of the expenses of production, but as part of the monopoly profit. Thus there will be many cases in which the monopolist pays no rent.

In order to discover monopoly output when the monopolist does not pay rent, it will be assumed that the transfer cost of individual productive units is independent of the scale of the industry.[5] We will first discuss the case in which there are no economies of large-scale industry.

In every case where the monopolist succeeds in avoiding the payment of the whole of the rent for any scarce factor that he employs, his marginal cost is the marginal cost to the industry excluding rent, and is shown by the γ curve. Now, as we have seen, when there are no economies of large-scale industry, γ and β coincide, for then average cost to the competitive industry is equal to marginal cost excluding rent. Marginal cost to the

[4] Cf. Pigou, *Economics of Welfare*, Macmillan, London, 1932, p. 280, for a discussion of the similar case of perfect price discrimination in selling.

[5] The relationship between the four cost curves shown in Section 4 of the last chapter will then obtain. For the sake of simplicity the assumption is retained in the rest of this chapter, but the comparisons can be made, when it is removed, by applying the results of Section 5 of the last chapter.

monopolist will therefore be shown by the β curve. If the monopolist pays part of the rent for any factor but not the whole of it, or if there are some scarce factors for which he pays the full rent, and others for which he pays none, his marginal cost will be somewhat greater than average cost to the competitive industry, but less than marginal cost including rent, and his marginal cost curve will lie somewhere between β and α. It is therefore clear that when the monopolist pays less than the full rent of any scarce factor the monopoly output will be a larger proportion of competitive output than when he does pay the full rent. For instance if the demand and supply curves are both straight lines he will produce more than half the competitive output. In the simple case where he pays no rent at all, so that his marginal costs are given by the β curve, it can further be seen that as long as the demand curve is a straight line he will produce more than half the competitive output whatever the shape of the supply curve. Thus:

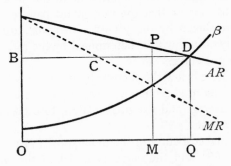

Since the demand curve is a straight line, BC = CD. But β must cut MR below C. Therefore OM is greater than half OQ.

We saw that in the cases where the monopolist pays the full rent (so that his marginal cost curve is marginal to the competitive supply curve), the ratio of monopoly output to competitive output for straight-line supply and demand curves is independent of their slope. In the case that we are now considering it can be seen that the ratio will tend to be greater the greater the elasticity of demand at the competitive point and the less the elasticity of supply.[6]

[6] The analysis of the case in which the monopolist pays no rent is of considerable importance, as it may be used to represent the case of short-period supply. In the short period the investment of capital in the industry, the number of entrepreneurs engaged in it, and the organisation of production, are all taken as given. The competitive supply curve is then the curve of marginal prime costs, and this is also the curve of marginal cost to the monopolist. The study of restriction of output in short-period conditions must therefore be made by means of the analysis, given above, in which the monopolist's marginal cost curve coincides with the competitive supply curve. Monopoly output will be that at which marginal prime cost is equal to marginal revenue, and the surplus above total prime costs is at a maximum; competitive output will be that at which marginal prime costs are equal to price, and the ratio between them will depend upon the elasticities of demand and supply.

But even if the monopolist is paying no rent his output cannot exceed competitive output. At the point of competitive equilibrium the supply curve, which shows the monopolist's marginal cost, cuts the demand curve from below, so that for any output greater than the competitive amount, the price (and *a fortiori* the marginal revenue) must be less than marginal cost. In the limiting case, monopoly output may be equal to competitive output if the supply is perfectly inelastic for a sufficient range of prices.

4

We must now consider the case in which there are both scarce factors for which the monopolist does not pay the full rent and economies of large-scale industry, retaining the assumption that the transfer costs of individual productive units are independent of the scale of the industry. For the sake of simplicity let us suppose that the monopolist pays no rent at all. Then marginal costs are shown by the γ curve (marginal cost excluding rent) and the monopoly output will be determined by the intersection of γ with the marginal revenue curve.

The γ curve will lie below the β curve to an extent which depends upon the amount of the induced economies at each point, and the two curves do not stand in the average and marginal relation to each other as long as a scarce factor is present.

Since the marginal cost curve of the monopolist (γ) now lies below both the supply curve (β) and the curve marginal to the supply curve (α), it is clear that, if the demand is sufficiently elastic at the competitive point, monopoly output may be greater than competitive output (as in the sec-

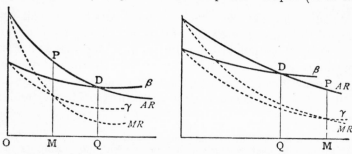

ond figure). This will be more likely to occur the greater the elasticity of demand at the competitive point and the greater the amount of induced economies.[7]

---

[7] The monopoly output will be equal to the competitive output when the amount of induced economies is such that if there were no scarce factor (and therefore no rent for the competitive industry) the elasticity of supply would be equal to the elasticity of demand. If the amount of the economies is greater than this, monopoly output will exceed competitive output, and conversely, whatever the actual elasticity of supply. With

5

It has now been shown that when the monopolist pays the full rent of the scarce factors, even if there are economies of large-scale industry, monopoly output cannot be greater than competitive output. And when there is a scarce factor for which the monopolist does not pay rent, but there are no economies, again monopoly output cannot be greater than competitive output. But if there are both economies and a scarce factor for which the monopolist does not pay the full rent, then it is possible for monopoly output to exceed competitive . output. Neither condition is sufficient by itself, but both together may lead to a situation in which monopoly output is greater than competitive output. This conclusion may appear strange, but upon reflection it is seen to be consonant with common sense. When there are economies, but the monopolist pays rent, then his average cost is equal to the supply price, so that for any output greater than the competitive output the price would be less than the average cost to the monopolist. And when the monopolist pays no rent, but there are no economies, the monopolist's marginal cost is equal to the supply price, so that for any output greater than the competitive output the price and, *a fortiori*, the marginal revenue would be less than marginal cost to the monopolist. But when there are both economies and a scarce factor for which rent is not paid, marginal and average cost to the monopolist are both less than the competitive supply price, and it is then possible that the monopolist will produce more than the competitive output.

Thus it is only when there is a scarce factor for which the full rent is not paid, and at the same time there are economies of large-scale industry, that it is possible that monopoly output may be greater than competitive output. In all other cases, as we have seen, monopoly output may (on extreme assumptions) be equal to competitive output, but it can never be greater.

BOOK V / Price Discrimination

Chapter 15: PRICE DISCRIMINATION

1

It often happens that a monopolist finds it possible and profitable to sell a single commodity at different prices to different buyers. This can occur when he is selling in several markets which are divided from one another in such a way that goods which are sold in the cheaper market cannot be

---

a given amount of economies (shown by a given vertical distance between the γ and β curves) the monopoly output will approximate more closely to the competitive output the less the elasticity of supply.

bought from the monopolist and resold in the dearer market; and when customers in the dearer market cannot transfer themselves into the cheaper market to get the benefit of the lower price. The act of selling the same article, produced under a single control, at different prices to different buyers is known as *price discrimination*.

Under conditions of perfect competition price discrimination could not exist even if the market could be easily divided into separate parts. In each section of the market the demand would be perfectly elastic, and every seller would prefer to sell his whole output in that section of the market in which he could obtain the highest price. The attempt to do so, of course, would drive the price down to the competitive level, and there would be only one price throughout the whole market. So long as the market is perfect it is only if all sellers are combined or are acting in agreement that they can take advantage of the barriers between one part of a market and another to charge different prices for the same thing.

But if there is some degree of market imperfection there can be some degree of discrimination. The market is imperfect because customers will not move readily from one seller to another, and if it is possible for an individual seller to divide his market into separate parts, price discrimination becomes practicable. But since under ordinary competitive conditions the demand curves for the individual sellers are likely to be very elastic, price discrimination will not usually lead to any very great differences in the prices charged to different buyers by any one seller.

When a single seller is not subject to close competition, or when there is an agreement between rival sellers, price discrimination is more likely to occur. The most usual case is in the sale of direct personal services, where there is no possibility of a transfer from one market to another. For instance surgeons commonly grade the fee for an operation according to the wealth of the patient. This practice is maintained by a tradition among doctors, and would break down if they chose to compete among themselves by underbidding one another in the fees charged to rich patients. Or discrimination may occur when the markets in which a monopolist is selling are divided from each other geographically or by tariff barriers, so that there would be a considerable expense in transferring goods from a cheaper market to be resold in a dearer market; when this type of discrimination leads to a concern selling at a lower price in an export market and a higher price at home it is commonly described as "dumping." Or discrimination may occur when several groups of buyers require the same service in connection with clearly differentiated commodities. Thus a railway can charge different rates for the transport of cotton goods and of coal without any fear that bales of cotton will be turned into loads of coal in order to enjoy a cheaper rate.

There is probably also a good deal of rather haphazard discrimination wherever goods are sold on special orders, so that the individual buyer has no means of knowing what price is being charged to other buyers for a similar commodity.

Even when there is no natural barrier between groups of customers there are various devices by which the market may be broken up so as to make price discrimination possible. Various brands of a certain article which in fact are almost exactly alike may be sold as different qualities under names and labels which induce rich and snobbish buyers to divide themselves from poorer buyers; and in this way the market is split up, and the monopolist can sell what is substantially the same thing at several prices. The device of making the same thing appear in different guises will also serve to save the monopolist from the reproaches of injustice between customers which sometimes put difficulties in the way of price discrimination.

2

In some cases the demand in one market will depend upon the price that is being charged in another market. The case of first- and third-class railway fares, analysed by Edgeworth,[1] is of this nature. In the following argument we shall only consider cases in which the demand curve in each separate market is independent of the prices charged in the other markets.

An analysis of price discrimination can then be built up from the analysis already given for simple monopoly when only one price can be charged for a single commodity. If it is possible for a monopolist to sell the same commodity in separate markets it will clearly be to his advantage to charge different prices in the different markets, provided that the elasticities of demand in the separate markets are not equal. For if he charges the same price in each market he will find that, at that price, the marginal revenue obtained by selling an increment of output in each market separately is greater in some markets than in others. He can therefore increase his profit by selling less in those markets where the elasticity of demand is less and the marginal revenue smaller, and selling more in those markets where the elasticity of demand is higher and the marginal revenue greater. He will therefore adjust his sales in such a way that the marginal revenue obtained from selling an additional unit of output in any one market is the same for all the markets. And his profits will be at a maximum when the marginal revenue in each market is equal to the marginal cost of the whole output.[2] The method by which prices will be determined can be shown by the following method.

Suppose that there are two markets, I and II, in which the conditions of

[1] *Papers Relating to Political Economy*, Vol. I, p. 174.

[2] Professor Pigou does not make use of this method, but he is evidently aware of the underlying fact, though he expresses it in a somewhat obscure mathematical form (*Economics of Welfare*, Macmillan, London, 1932, p. 302, note 1).

demand are different. With the same system of axes, draw the demand curves (D_1 and D_2) of the two markets with the corresponding marginal revenue curves, and sum them laterally, so as to obtain an aggregate demand curve showing the total amount that would be sold at each price if the price were the same in both markets, and an aggregate marginal revenue curve showing the amount of sales that would correspond to each value of the marginal revenue if the marginal revenue were the same in both markets. This curve will show the marginal revenue obtained by the discriminating monopolist.

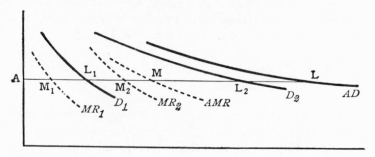

This construction can be exhibited thus:

Draw any line AL parallel to the x axis, to cut D_1 in L_1, D_2 in L_2, and the aggregate demand curve (AD) in L.
Let it cut MR_1 in M_1, MR_2 in M_2, and the aggregate marginal revenue curve (AMR) in M.
Then $AL = AL_1 + AL_2$, and $AM = AM_1 + AM_2$.

The monopoly output under price discrimination is determined by the intersection of the monopolist's marginal cost curve with the aggregate marginal revenue curve. This total output is made up of the amounts sold in the two markets, in each of which marginal revenue is equal to the marginal cost of the whole output. The price in each market will be the demand price for the amount of output sold there.[3]
OM is the total output, and is equal to $OM_1 + OM_2$.
MC is the marginal cost of the output OM.
OM_1 is sold at the price M_1P_1 in market I. OM_2 is sold at the price M_2P_2 in market II. The shaded area shows the monopoly revenue, which is equal to the area lying under the aggregate marginal revenue curve (total revenue) *minus* the area lying under the marginal cost curve (total costs).

[3] Professsor Yntema makes use of this construction (see "The Influence of Dumping on Monopoly Price," *Journal of Political Economy*, December, 1928), but he confines himself to establishing with its aid a proposition which can be proved without resort to any such complicated apparatus.

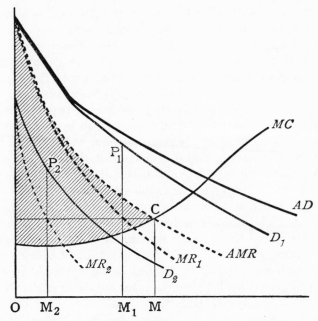

In the above figure marginal costs are rising, but whether marginal costs are constant, rising, or falling, output will be determined by the point at which the aggregate marginal revenue curve cuts the marginal cost curve, and the amount sold in each market will be the amount for which marginal revenue is equal to the marginal cost of the whole output.[4]

.   .   .

BOOK VI / Monopsony

Chapter 17: A DIGRESSION ON THE BUYER

.   .   .

2

It is necessary to find a name for the individual buyer which will correspond to the name *monopolist* for the individual seller. In the following pages an individual buyer is referred to as a *monopsonist*.[1]

The criterion of perfect competition among sellers is that the demand

---

[4] The points at which the separate marginal revenue curves cut the marginal cost curve have no significance, since these points (except when costs happen to be constant) do not show the marginal cost of the whole output which is actually being produced.

[1] The older phrase "monopoly buyer" is illogical. I am indebted to Mr. B. L. Hallward, of Peterhouse, Cambridge, for the word *monopsony*, which is derived from ὀψωνεῖν, to go marketing.

curve for the individual seller should be perfectly elastic; similarly the criterion for perfect competition among buyers is that the supply curve to the individual buyer should be perfectly elastic. This is the case in an ordinary competitive market. A buyer can walk into a shop and buy as much as he pleases at the current price. If he offers less he can buy nothing, and if he offered a little more he would engross the whole supply. Perfect competition among sellers requires two conditions, that the number of sellers shall be large, and that the customers shall all have the same preference (or the same indifference) between one firm and its rivals. Similarly perfect competition among buyers requires that the numbers of buyers composing a market shall be large, so that a change in the amount purchased by any one of them has a negligible effect upon the total purchases of the market, and that sellers are indifferent as to whom they provide with their wares. The second condition will not always be fulfilled—some firms will give special terms to certain customers either from sentiment, family connection, gratitude, or a "lively expectation of benefits to come" —but it is clearly more frequently fulfilled in the real world than are the conditions of a perfect market from the point of view of sellers.[2] So long as competition among buyers is perfect, marginal utility must be equal, for each buyer, to the price of the commodity. For price is equal to marginal cost to the buyer, and marginal utility is defined as some quantity which is equated to marginal cost. But the marginal utility curve for a buyer is not a demand curve. It does not represent a list of the amounts of a commodity which will be bought at various prices; it represents the amounts which will be bought at various marginal costs to the buyer. So long as the supply of the commodity is perfectly elastic to the buyer the marginal utility of each amount of it will be equal to its price (since its price is equal to its marginal cost). It is therefore formally correct to describe the marginal utility curve of a buyer as his demand curve upon the assumption that the competition among buyers is perfect, just as, under perfect sellers' competition, where marginal cost is equal to price, the marginal cost curve of a seller is the supply curve of his output. When competition among buyers is known to be perfect the demand curve of the market may be taken to represent the marginal utility curve of the buyers as a group. The total amount purchased is divided between the buyers in such a way that the marginal utility of the amount purchased by each one of them is equal to the price.[3]

It is impossible to draw up the supply curve of a commodity produced by

[2] Moreover, the supply to an individual may be perfectly elastic, even though the market is not perfect, since there are often a large number of buyers to each seller, so that the relevant amount of purchases for any one buyer can be had at a constant price.

[3] Even if all the problems connected with the definition of utility are assumed to be solved, the difficulty remains that the marginal utilities of different buyers composing a market are not measured on the same scale (see Marshall, *Principles of Economics*, Macmillan, London, 1946, 8th ed., p. 128), because the utility of money, in which the

a number of sellers without first postulating the conditions of demand for the individual sellers. Similarly it is impossible to draw up the demand curve for a commodity purchased by a number of buyers without postulating the conditions of supply to the individual buyers. But to postulate that competition among buyers is perfect is far more realistic than to postulate that competition among sellers is perfect, since the number of buyers in any ordinary market is large relatively to the number of sellers. In the following chapter, therefore, we shall only consider the case of a single buyer on the one side and a perfectly competitive market of buyers on the other, and ignore the problem of an imperfectly competitive market of buyers.

Chapter 18: MONOPSONY

1

The principle underlying the analysis of the decisions of a buyer as to how much of a commodity to buy is that he will equate marginal utility to marginal cost. As we have seen, this statement is no more than a tautology. If the supply of the commodity to him is perfectly elastic he will equate marginal utility to price. This will occur, first, if he is one of a large number of buyers, so that a change in his purchases has a negligible effect upon the total output of the commodity, and consequently a negligible effect upon its price; or, second, if the commodity is sold under conditions of constant supply price, so that even if a change in his purchases produces a significant change in output it causes no change in price.

Examples of a buying agency whose purchases represent the whole or a large proportion of the output of a commodity produced by a competitive[1] industry are found when the consumers of a certain commodity are organised, or when a socialist government regulates imports, or when a certain individual happens to have a taste for some commodity which no one else requires. An everyday example occurs when an individual orders note-paper with his address printed on it. In such cases, if the commodity is not produced under constant supply price, marginal utility will not be equal to price. The amount purchased will be regulated so that marginal utility is equal to marginal cost. The price will be the supply price of that amount of the commodity, which may be either greater or less than its marginal cost to the buyer.

---

utility of the commodity is measured, will be different for buyers who differ in respect of relevant social and psychological characteristics, or in respect of their money income. But it is convenient for some problems to regard the demand curve of a market as a collective marginal utility curve, and provided it is recognised that marginal utility is a purely formal conception which may be, in some circumstances, devoid of any real or interesting meaning, it appears legitimate to make use of it.

[1] The case of a monopsonist buying from a monopolist (usually called "bilateral monopoly") is not discussed here.

2

Our next task is to consider the change in the amount of a commodity purchased when the market changes from an indefinitely large number of competing buyers to a single buying agency. This may be described as the comparison between competitive and monopsony buying, just as the corresponding comparison for selling was called the comparison between competitive and monopoly output.

The present comparison is not subject to the formidable objections which were raised against the earlier comparison. The chief objections sprang from the fact that in order to give a definite basis to the comparison it was necessary to postulate conditions of perfect competition, which are rarely to be found in the real world. It is true that the demand curve only has an unambiguous meaning when buying is perfectly competitive, but this state of affairs is the rule rather than the exception in most ordinary markets, since there are usually a large number of buyers to each seller. The basis of our comparison, therefore, the competitive demand curve, can be used without hesitation. It is easy to imagine a group of buyers at first acting independently of each other, and then forming an agreement to act in concert without causing any change in the demand curve, which may be taken to represent the marginal utility curve of the monopsonist organisation, or any change in the conditions of supply of the commodity which they consume.[2] We can therefore set out the comparison between the amounts of a commodity that would be bought under competition and under monopsony when the marginal utility curve and supply curve are the same in the two cases, without being obliged to make the reservation that in practice they never will be the same.

The comparison will be in some respects similar to the comparison between monopoly and competition. A monopsonist has to pay the supply price of the output of the commodity which he buys, but he will regulate his purchases in such a way that marginal cost is equal to marginal utility; while under competition it is the price, or average cost to the buyer, which is equal to marginal utility. It follows that under constant supply price, when average and marginal cost are equal, the amount purchased under monopsony will be the same as under competition. But when an industry is working under increasing or diminishing supply price, marginal cost to the monopsonist will not be equal to the price of the commodity.

Under increasing supply price, since each additional purchase which the monopsonist makes raises the price which he must pay, the marginal cost

[2] It is important to notice, however, that a monopsonist organisation will reproduce the conditions of a perfect market. It will therefore enforce reorganisation upon an imperfectly competitive industry, in such a way as to ensure that any given output is produced in the most efficient manner.

to him is greater than the supply price of the commodity. Supply price is average cost to the monopsonist, but he will regulate his purchases by reference to marginal cost.

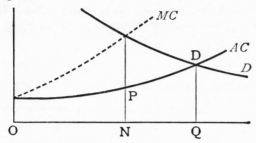

MC is the marginal cost curve to the industry, and this is the marginal cost curve from the point of view of the monopsonist.

AC is the average cost curve of the industry, or the supply curve.

The monopsonist will buy that output (ON) at which marginal utility (or competitive demand price) is equal to marginal cost, and he will pay NP, the supply price for that output, which is less than the competitive price (QD).

If the curves are straight lines, it can be seen that he will buy something more than half the competitive amount. If his demand were perfectly elastic (a case which it is hard to conceive), and the supply curve was a straight line, he would buy exactly half the competitive amount.

If the industry is working under decreasing supply price, he will find that every increase in his purchases lowers the supply price,[3] and marginal cost to him, which is the same thing as marginal cost to the industry, will be less than the supply price. He will therefore buy more than the competitive amount. Thus:

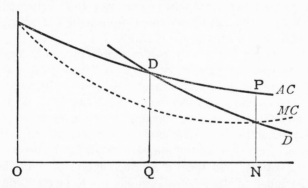

[3] Under conditions of decreasing supply price the monopsonist cannot proceed merely by declaring the price at which he will buy, for an unconditional offer of a certain price would call out an indefinitely large output from the industry. The monopsonist (who is conceived to know the course of the supply curve of the commodity) must decide upon the output that he will buy, and allot it between the different sellers.

ON will exceed OQ, and NP, the monopsony price, will be less than
QD, the competitive price.

ON may exceed OQ without limit, and with a given supply curve it
will be greater the less the slope of the demand curve. It will approach
more closely to the competitive amount the greater the slope of the
demand curve.

If the demand of the monopsonist is perfectly inelastic (as might occur
over the relevant range of prices) he will purchase the competitive amount
at the competitive price.

. . .

BOOK IX / Exploitation

Chapter 26: MONOPSONISTIC EXPLOITATION OF LABOUR

1

We must now examine the type of exploitation which arises because the
supply of labour is imperfectly elastic to the unit of control. The supply to
an industry may be less than perfectly elastic for any of the reasons discussed in Chapter 8. The nature of the limitation upon the supply of labour
is not relevant to our inquiry, for our analysis can be applied to limitations
of any type, but for the sake of simplicity we will first deal only with one
case: that in which all the workers employed are alike in their efficiency in
the industry in question, and yet progressively higher wages have to be
paid to all in order to attract fresh supplies of labour. This might occur
because it was necessary to tempt labour away from better paid occupations, to overcome the cost of movement from more distant regions, or to
overcome a preference for other occupations.

The notion of an imperfectly elastic supply of labour presents some
difficulties, because the elasticity of supply will vary greatly according to
the period of time under consideration. It is likely to be more elastic the
longer the period under consideration. And a supply of labour once attracted to a certain area or a certain industry by a rise in wages may not
immediately (or indeed ever) cease to be available when wages fall back
to their former level. But for the purposes of our formal analysis it is only
necessary to postulate that there is a rising supply curve of labour over a
period long enough to allow normal equilibrium to be established. In this,
as in all the problems with which this book attempts to deal, a very artificial
degree of simplification is necessary to the formal analysis. The most that
can be hoped from it is to indicate some of the considerations that have to
be taken into account in dealing with actual problems.

2

When the supply of labour is less than perfectly elastic to any employing agency, that amount of labour will be employed whose marginal cost is equal to its marginal net productivity, and the wage will be equal to the supply price of the amount of labour employed. The demand curve for labour of the employing agency may be of various forms. If it is an isolated monopoly the demand curve for labour must be drawn up on the principles discussed in Chapter 21. But if the employing agency is an industry composed of a number of independent firms they may act in concert in regulating wages although they compete in selling the commodity which they produce. In practice agreements to regulate wages are usually worked in a very rough and ready way, but it is worth while to consider the exact analysis of an agreement which follows some definite principle. It is possible to distinguish two principles upon which the demand curve for labour may be drawn up. First, if there is merely a "gentleman's agreement" not to spoil the market by bidding up wages, the individual firms composing the industry may be conceived to be in perfect competition in every respect except in hiring labour. Then the amount of capital employed with a given number of men will be such that the marginal productivity of capital to the firm is equal to its price, that is to say, the competitive amount of capital will be employed with any given number of men. And each firm will wish to employ that amount of labour whose marginal productivity to the firm is equal to the marginal cost of labour to the whole group, ignoring the effect upon the price of the commodity of an increase in output. The industry's demand curve for labour will then be shown, for any given number of men, by the value of the marginal physical product of labour. Second, a more far-reaching type of agreement amongst the firms, which still falls short of complete monopoly, will be found if the competitive amount of capital is employed with each number of men, but the organised group of firms take into account the fall in the price of the commodity due to an increase of output, and so employ that amount of labour whose marginal net productivity to the whole group is equal to its marginal cost. In any actual case neither of these principles is likely to be followed exactly, but this fact is not relevant to the analysis, for, however the demand curve for labour is drawn up, the analysis follows the same course once the demand curve for labour is given.

On whatever principle the demand curve is constructed it is necessary to assume that there are a fixed number of firms, that is to say, that the profits due to monopsony do not draw new firms into the industry; for the amount of the monopsony profit depends upon the conditions of supply of labour, and cannot be represented in the demand curve. If the existence of a monopsony profit, or its removal, are conceived to alter the number of

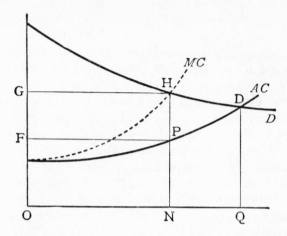

firms in the industry, a new monopsony demand curve must be drawn up
for each number of firms.[1]

The amount of employment given by the monopsonist organisation will
be restricted to the amount at which the marginal cost of labour to the
whole group is equal to its demand price for each particular type of organisation. The wage will be equal to the supply price of labour, and this, in
each case, will be less than the value of the marginal physical product of
labour. Thus exploitation will occur.

Monopsonistic exploitation of this type can be removed by the imposition of a minimum wage.

> In the above figure, let D be the demand curve for labour of the
> monopsonist organisation, upon whatever principle it may be drawn
> up. Then the amount of labour employed (ON) will be that at which
> MC (the marginal cost curve of labour) cuts the demand curve, D.

Now, suppose that a trade union or a trade board imposes a minimum wage
upon the industry; then the supply of labour to the industry becomes
perfectly elastic at the imposed wage, up to that number of men whose
supply price to the industry is in any case equal to that wage. Beyond this
number the new supply curve of labour must coincide with the old. If the
authority imposing the minimum wage is sufficiently strong to be able to
choose freely what wage to impose, there are several alternatives before it.
If, at the lower limit, the existing wage (NP) is imposed as a minimum
everything remains as before. If the wage (NH) is chosen, which is equal
to the demand price for the number of men employed in the exploited position, employment will remain unchanged and the wage will be raised. For
any higher wage employment will be reduced, and for any wage between

[1] This was first pointed out to me by Mr. P. M. Forrester, who was then reading for
the Economics Tripos.

NP and NH employment will increase. The maximum increase in employment will occur at the wage (QD) at which the old supply curve of labour cuts the demand curve of the monopsonist organisation.[2] Thus the rise in wages which reduces exploitation and transfers a part or the whole of the monopsony profit to labour will actually result in an increase of employment.

Even when the wage QD, or some higher wage, is imposed, exploitation does not wholly disappear except in the case where D, the demand curve for labour of the group of firms, represents the value of the marginal physical product of labour.[3] The element in exploitation due to monopoly cannot be eliminated merely by removing the inelasticity of the supply curve of labor. . . .

[2] I am indebted to Mr. Shove for this analysis, but my presentation of it is slightly different from his.

[3] This will be the case when a number of independent firms, acting in concert for the regulation of wages, arrange their employment of labour on the first of the principles described on p. 349.

JOHN MAYNARD
KEYNES
(1887–1946)

With the possible exception of Jevons, each of the economists we have encountered thus far had a profound effect not only upon economic theory, but on the thinking and policies of the statesmen and business leaders of his time. Both Smith and Ricardo helped to reduce the amount of government interference in the internal and external affairs of the country. Malthus helped to change the government's policies toward the poor. John Stuart Mill and Alfred Marshall were constantly called upon to help formulate governmental policy. Although never a consultant for any government, Marx's impact on economic policy is still being felt today! If anything, the effect of John Maynard Keynes on the thinking of those inside and outside the economics profession has been even more dramatic. Economic thinking has literally undergone a revolution as a result of Keynes' writing. It should be readily apparent to the reader that in the case of each of the preceding writers, the views they expressed were a reflection of the times in which the economist lived and the problems faced by the economy of which he was a member. As will become apparent in a moment, this generalization also applies with great force to the writings of Keynes.

Trained in the Classical doctrine under the tutelage of Alfred Marshall and Arthur Pigou (the latter was to serve as a prime target for Keynes' attacks), Keynes renounced one of the major tenets of Classical doctrine—the belief that the economy always tended to move toward an equilibrium assuring full employment. Keynes suggested instead that equilibrium might occur while the economy was operating at a level of national income far below the level necessary to assure full employment.

Reared in the Classical English tradition of economics, Keynes was perhaps overly conscious of the cleavage between his views and those who preceded him. He was well aware of Malthus' early dissent from the general formulation of Say's Law that supply creates its own demand, but apparently was ignorant of the work of the Swedish economist Wicksell who a short time before Keynes had developed an analysis closely parallel in some ways to Keynes' own.

The General Theory of Employment, Interest and Money is a difficult book to read even today when readers have available to them numerous guides which interpret the more difficult passages. New terms such as consumption function, marginal efficiency of capital, and liquidity preference still have to be mastered. But the central message of Keynes' book is clear—no longer can the economy assume that a laissez-faire market guided only by the forces of supply and demand will produce consistently high levels of employment.

In support of this conclusion, Keynes developed the concept of effective demand. In the absence of government intervention, effective demand was determined by the level of consumption plus the volume of investment. As an economy's output continued to grow, there was a tendency for a larger and larger absolute amount to be saved. Unless these savings were returned to the economy in the form of investment, not all of the output of the economy could be sold, and businessmen would reduce the scale of their operations, thereby reducing national income and level of employment.

The earlier Classical view that all savings automatically channeled themselves into investment was challenged by Keynes on two counts. First, the desire for liquidity by the public might be too high to make it possible to bring the interest rate down to the point where borrowing would be attractive. Interest, according to Keynes, was a price paid to get people to part with liquidity; willingness to part with liquidity might come only at very high rates of interest. Even if the interest rate could be driven down to a low level, however, businessmen might still be unwilling to borrow because their anticipated return on their investments (the marginal efficiency of capital) was too low and too inelastic. Because he was skeptical of the economy's ability to function properly on its own, Keynes recommended the application of both monetary and fiscal policy to ensure the economy's health.

The passages we have selected provide the reader with what one commentator has referred to as the "Keynesian building blocks." Nevertheless Keynes' book was a general theory, and not all parts of the edifice are contained herein. Missing, for example, are the distinctions Keynes drew between his theory of interest and Classical theory, the elaboration of his views on the futility of seeking to cure unemployment through cuts in wages, and his attempt to explain the business cycle in terms of shifts of the marginal efficiency of capital. Nor have we included Chapter 23 in which Keynes observed that perhaps the Mercantilists were sounder in their economic objectives of securing a healthy economy than most economists since that time had been willing to admit.

However, those sections we have been able to include will provide the reader with an understanding of why the General Theory has been the subject of an endless discussion among economists—one that still continues today over a quarter of a century after the book's publication. The unorthodox views set forth by this brilliant economist have been the stimulus for innumerable books and articles, voicing both criticism and praise.

Keynes' claim to fame does not rest with the General Theory alone. He was the author of numerous other articles and books. Among the latter were The Economic Consequences of the Peace, Tract on Monetary Reform, Treatise on Money, and How to Pay for the War. He was a success in all his endeavors. He was a brilliant teacher, a proficient businessman, and an eminent adviser to the British government for many years. It was in recognition of his manifest talents and contributions that he was awarded the title of Lord shortly before his death.

THE GENERAL THEORY OF EMPLOYMENT, INTEREST AND MONEY

BOOK I / Introduction

Chapter 1: THE GENERAL THEORY

I have called this book the *General Theory of Employment, Interest and Money*, placing the emphasis on the prefix *general*. The object of such a title is to contrast the character of my arguments and conclusions with those of the *classical* theory of the subject, upon which I was brought up and which dominates the economic thought, both practical and theoretical, of the governing and academic classes of this generation, as it has for a hundred years past. I shall argue that the postulates of the classical theory are applicable to a special case only and not to the general case, the situation which it assumes being a limiting point of the possible positions of equilibrium. Moreover, the characteristics of the special case assumed by the classical theory happen not to be those of the economic society in which we actually live, with the result that its teaching is misleading and disastrous if we attempt to apply it to the facts of experience.

Chapter 2: THE POSTULATES OF THE CLASSICAL ECONOMISTS

. . .

1

The classical theory of employment—supposedly simple and obvious—has been based, I think, on two fundamental postulates, though practically without discussion, namely:

I. *The wage is equal to the marginal product of labour.*

That is to say, the wage of an employed person is equal to the value which would be lost if employment were to be reduced by one unit (after deducting any other costs which this reduction of output would avoid); subject, however, to the qualification that the equality may be disturbed, in accordance with certain principles, if competition and markets are imperfect.

II. *The utility of the wage when a given volume of labour is employed is equal to the marginal disutility of that amount of employment.*

That is to say, the real wage of an employed person is that which is just sufficient (in the estimation of the employed persons themselves) to induce the volume of labour actually employed to be forthcoming; subject to the qualification that the equality for each individual unit of labour may be disturbed by combination between employable units analogous to the imperfections of competition which qualify the first postulate. Disutility must be here understood to cover every kind of reason which might lead a man, or a body of men, to withhold their labour rather than accept a wage which had to them a utility below a certain minimum.

This postulate is compatible with what may be called "frictional" unemployment. For a realistic interpretation of it legitimately allows for various inexactnesses of adjustment which stand in the way of continuous full employment: for example, unemployment due to a temporary want of balance between the relative quantities of specialised resources as a result of miscalculation or intermittent demand; or to time-lags consequent on unforeseen changes; or to the fact that the change-over from one employment to another cannot be effected without a certain delay, so that there will always exist in a non-static society a proportion of resources unemployed "between jobs." In addition to "frictional" unemployment, the postulate is also compatible with "voluntary" unemployment due to the refusal or inability of a unit of labour, as a result of legislation or social practices or of combination for collective bargaining or of slow response to change or of mere human obstinacy, to accept a reward corresponding to the value of the product attributable to its marginal productivity. But these two categories of "frictional" unemployment and "voluntary" unemployment are comprehensive. . . .

The classical postulates do not admit of the possibility of the third category, which I shall define below as "involuntary" unemployment.

Subject to these qualifications, the volume of employed resources is duly determined, according to the classical theory, by the two postulates. The first gives us the demand schedule for employment, the second gives us the supply schedule; and the amount of employment is fixed at the point where the utility of the marginal product balances the disutility of the marginal employment.

It would follow from this that there are only four possible means of increasing employment:

(a) An improvement in organisation or in foresight which diminishes "frictional" unemployment;

(b) a decrease in the marginal disutility of labour, as expressed by the real wage for which additional labour is available, so as to diminish "voluntary" unemployment;

(c) an increase in the marginal physical productivity of labour in the wage-goods industries (to use Professor Pigou's convenient term for goods upon the price of which the utility of the money-wage depends);

or (d) an increase in the price of non-wage-goods compared with the price of wage-goods, associated with a shift in the expenditure of non-wage-earners from wage-goods to non-wage-goods.

This, to the best of my understanding, is the substance of Professor Pigou's *Theory of Unemployment*—the only detailed account of the classical theory of employment which exists.

2

Is it true that the above categories are comprehensive in view of the fact that the population generally is seldom doing as much work as it would like to do on the basis of the current wage? For, admittedly, more labour would, as a rule, be forthcoming at the existing money-wage if it were demanded. The classical school reconcile this phenomenon with their second postulate by arguing that, while the demand for labour at the existing money-wage may be satisfied before everyone willing to work at this wage is employed, this situation is due to an open or tacit agreement amongst workers not to work for less, and that if labour as a whole would agree to a reduction of money-wages more employment would be forthcoming. If this is the case, such unemployment, though apparently involuntary, is not strictly so, and ought to be included under the above category of "voluntary" unemployment due to the effects of collective bargaining, etc.

This calls for two observations, the first of which relates to the actual attitude of workers towards real wages and money-wages respectively and is not theoretically fundamental, but the second of which is fundamental.

Let us assume, for the moment, that labour is not prepared to work for a lower money-wage and that a reduction in the existing level of money-wages would lead, through strikes or otherwise, to a withdrawal from the labour market of labour which is now employed. Does it follow from this that the existing level of real wages accurately measures the marginal dis-utility of labour? Not necessarily. For, although a reduction in the existing money-wage would lead to a withdrawal of labour, it does not follow that a fall in the value of the existing money-wage in terms of wage-goods would do so, if it were due to a rise in the price of the latter. In other words, it may be the case that within a certain range the demand of labour is for a minimum money-wage and not for a minimum real wage. The classical school have tacitly assumed that this would involve no significant change in their theory. But this is not so. For if the supply of labour is not a function of real wages as its sole variable, their argument breaks down entirely and leaves the question of what the actual employment will be quite indeterminate. They do not seem to have realised that, unless the supply of labour is a function of real wages alone, their supply curve for labour will shift bodily with every movement of prices. Thus their method is tied up with their very special assumptions, and cannot be adapted to deal with the more general case.

Now ordinary experience tells us, beyond doubt, that a situation where labour stipulates (within limits) for a money-wage rather than a real wage, so far from being a mere possibility, is the normal case. Whilst workers will usually resist a reduction of money-wages, it is not their practice to with-draw their labour whenever there is a rise in the price of wage-goods. It is sometimes said that it would be illogical for labour to resist a reduction of money-wages but not to resist a reduction of real wages. For reasons given below this might not be so illogical as it appears at first; and, as we shall see later, fortunately so. But, whether logical or illogical, experience shows that this is how labour in fact behaves.

Moreover, the contention that the unemployment which characterises a depression is due to a refusal by labour to accept a reduction of money-wages is not clearly supported by the facts. It is not very plausible to assert that unemployment in the United States in 1932 was due either to labour obstinately refusing to accept a reduction of money-wages or to its ob-stinately demanding a real wage beyond what the productivity of the economic machine was capable of furnishing. Wide variations are experi-enced in the volume of employment without any apparent change either in the minimum real demands of labour or in its productivity. Labour is not more truculent in the depression than in the boom—far from it. Nor is its physical productivity less. These facts from experience are a *prima facie* ground for questioning the adequacy of the classical analysis.

. . .

The traditional theory maintains, in short, *that the wage bargains be-tween the entrepreneurs and the workers determine the real wage;* so that, assuming free competition amongst employers and no restrictive combination amongst workers, the latter can, if they wish, bring their real wages into conformity with the marginal disutility of the amount of employment offered by the employers at that wage. If this is not true, then there is no longer any reason to expect a tendency towards equality between the real wage and the marginal disutility of labour.

The classical conclusions are intended, it must be remembered, to apply to the whole body of labour and do not mean merely that a single individual can get employment by accepting a cut in money-wages which his fellows refuse. They are supposed to be equally applicable to a closed system as to an open system, and are not dependent on the characteristics of an open system or on the effects of a reduction of money-wages in a single country on its foreign trade, which lie, of course, entirely outside the field of this discussion. Nor are they based on indirect effects due to a lower wages-bill in terms of money having certain reactions on the banking system and the state of credit. They are based on the belief that in a closed system a reduction in the general level of money-wages will be accompanied, at any rate in the short period and subject only to minor qualifications, by some, though not always a proportionate, reduction in real wages.

Now the assumption that the general level of real wages depends on the money-wage bargains between the employers and the workers is not obviously true. Indeed it is strange that so little attempt should have been made to prove or to refute it. For it is far from being consistent with the general tenor of the classical theory, which has taught us to believe that prices are governed by marginal prime cost in terms of money and that money-wages largely govern marginal prime cost. Thus if money-wages change, one would have expected the classical school to argue that prices would change in almost the same proportion, leaving the real wage and the level of unemployment practically the same as before, any small gain or loss to labour being at the expense or profit of other elements of marginal cost which have been left unaltered. They seem, however, to have been diverted from this line of thought, partly by the settled conviction that labour is in a position to determine its own real wage and partly, perhaps, by preoccupation with the idea that prices depend on the quantity of money. And the belief in the proposition that labour is always in a position to determine its own real wage, once adopted, has been maintained by its being confused with the proposition that labour is always in a position to determine what real wage shall correspond to *full* employment, *i.e.* the *maximum* quantity of employment which is compatible with a given real wage.

To sum up: there are two objections to the second postulate of the classical theory. The first relates to the actual behaviour of labour. A fall in real wages due to a rise in prices, with money-wages unaltered, does not, as a rule, cause the supply of available labour on offer at the current wage to fall below the amount actually employed prior to the rise of prices.

To suppose that it does is to suppose that all those who are now unemployed though willing to work at the current wage will withdraw the offer of their labour in the event of even a small rise in the cost of living. Yet this strange supposition apparently underlies Professor Pigou's *Theory of Unemployment*, and it is what all members of the orthodox school are tacitly assuming.

But the other, more fundamental, objection, which we shall develop in the ensuing chapters, flows from our disputing the assumption that the general level of real wages is directly determined by the character of the wage bargain. In assuming that the wage bargain determines the real wage the classical school have slipt in an illicit assumption. For there may be *no* method available to labour as a whole whereby it can bring the wage-goods equivalent of the general level of money-wages into conformity with the marginal disutility of the current volume of employment. There may exist no expedient by which labour as a whole can reduce its *real* wage to a given figure by making revised *money* bargains with the entrepreneurs. This will be our contention. We shall endeavour to show that primarily it is certain other forces which determine the general level of real wages. The attempt to elucidate this problem will be one of our main themes. We shall argue that there has been a fundamental misunderstanding of how in this respect the economy in which we live actually works.

3

Though the struggle over money-wages between individuals and groups is often believed to determine the general level of real wages, it is, in fact, concerned with a different object. Since there is imperfect mobility of labour, and wages do not tend to an exact equality of net advantage in different occupations, any individual or group of individuals, who consent to a reduction of money-wages relatively to others, will suffer a *relative* reduction in real wages, which is a sufficient justification for them to resist it. On the other hand it would be impracticable to resist every reduction of real wages, due to a change in the purchasing-power of money which affects all workers alike; and in fact reductions of real wages arising in this way are not, as a rule, resisted unless they proceed to an extreme degree. Moreover, a resistance to reductions in money-wages applying to particular industries does not raise the same insuperable bar to an increase in aggregate employment which would result from a similar resistance to every reduction in real wages.

In other words, the struggle about money-wages primarily affects the *distribution* of the aggregate real wage between different labour-groups, and not its average amount per unit of employment, which depends, as we shall see, on a different set of forces. The effect of combination on the part of a group of workers is to protect their *relative* real wage. The *general* level of real wages depends on the other forces of the economic system.

Thus it is fortunate that the workers, though unconsciously, are instinctively more reasonable economists than the classical school, inasmuch as they resist reductions of money-wages, which are seldom or never of an all-round character, even though the existing real equivalent of these wages exceeds the marginal disutility of the existing employment; whereas they do not resist reductions of real wages, which are associated with increases in aggregate employment and leave relative money-wages unchanged, unless the reduction proceeds so far as to threaten a reduction of the real wage below the marginal disutility of the existing volume of employment. Every trade union will put up some resistance to a cut in money-wages, however small. But since no trade union would dream of striking on every occasion of a rise in the cost of living, they do not raise the obstacle to any increase in aggregate employment which is attributed to them by the classical school.

4

We must now define the third category of unemployment, namely "involuntary" unemployment in the strict sense, the possibility of which the classical theory does not admit.

Clearly we do not mean by "involuntary" unemployment the mere existence of an unexhausted capacity to work. An eight-hour day does not constitute unemployment because it is not beyond human capacity to work ten hours. Nor should we regard as "involuntary" unemployment the withdrawal of their labour by a body of workers because they do not choose to work for less than a certain real reward. Furthermore, it will be convenient to exclude "frictional" unemployment from our definition of "involuntary" unemployment. My definition is, therefore, as follows: *Men are involuntarily unemployed if, in the event of a small rise in the price of wage-goods relatively to the money-wage, both the aggregate supply of labour willing to work for the current money-wage and the aggregate demand for it at that wage would be greater than the existing volume of employment.* An alternative definition, which amounts, however, to the same thing, will be given in the next chapter.

It follows from this definition that the equality of the real wage to the marginal disutility of employment presupposed by the second postulate, realistically interpreted, corresponds to the absence of "involuntary" unemployment. This state of affairs we shall describe as "full" employment, both "frictional" and "voluntary" unemployment being consistent with "full" employment thus defined. This fits in, we shall find, with other characteristics of the classical theory, which is best regarded as a theory of distribution in conditions of full employment. So long as the classical postulates hold good, unemployment, which is in the above sense involuntary, cannot occur. Apparent unemployment must, therefore, be the result either of temporary loss of work of the "between jobs" type or of intermittent demand for highly specialised resources or of the effect of a trade union "closed shop" on the employment of free labour. Thus writers in the classical tradition, overlooking the special assumption underlying their theory, have been driven inevitably to the conclusion, perfectly logical on their assumption, that apparent unemployment (apart from the admitted exceptions) must be due at bottom to a refusal by the unemployed factors to accept a reward which corresponds to their marginal productivity. A classical economist may sympathise with labour in refusing to accept a cut in its money-wage, and he will admit that it may not be wise to make it to meet conditions which are temporary; but scientific integrity forces him to declare that this refusal is, nevertheless, at the bottom of the trouble.

Obviously, however, if the classical theory is only applicable to the case of full employment, it is fallacious to apply it to the problems of involuntary unemployment—if there be such a thing (and who will deny it?). The classical theorists resemble Euclidean geometers in a non-Euclidean world who, discovering that in experience straight lines apparently parallel often meet, rebuke the lines for not keeping straight—as the only remedy for the unfortunate collisions which are occurring. Yet, in truth, there is no remedy except to throw over the axiom of parallels and to work out a non-Euclidean geometry. Something similar is required to-day in economics. We need to throw over the second postulate of the classical doctrine and to work out the behaviour of a system in which involuntary unemployment in the strict sense is possible.

5

In emphasising our point of departure from the classical system, we must not overlook an important point of agreement. For we shall maintain the first postulate as heretofore, subject only to the same qualifications as in the classical theory; and we must pause, for a moment, to consider what this involves.

It means that, with a given organisation, equipment and technique, real wages and the volume of output (and hence of employment) are uniquely correlated, so that, in general, an increase in employment can only occur to the accompaniment of a decline in the rate of real wages. Thus I am not disputing this vital fact which the classical economists have (rightly) asserted as indefeasible. In a given state of organisation, equipment and technique, the real wage earned by a unit of labour has a unique (inverse) correlation with the volume of employment. Thus *if* employment increases, then, in the short period, the reward per unit of labour in terms of wage-goods must, in general, decline and profits increase. This is simply the obverse of the familiar proposition that industry is normally working subject to decreasing returns in the short period during which equipment etc. is assumed to be constant; so that the marginal product in the wage-good industries (which governs real wages) necessarily diminishes as employment is increased. So long, indeed, as this proposition holds, *any* means of increasing employment must lead at the same time to a diminution of the marginal product and hence of the rate of wages measured in terms of this product.

But when we have thrown over the second postulate, a decline in employment, although necessarily associated with labour's *receiving* a wage equal in value to a larger quantity of wage-goods, is not necessarily due to labour's *demanding* a larger quantity of wage-goods; and a willingness on the part of labour to accept lower money-wages is not necessarily a remedy for unemployment.

. . .

Chapter 3: THE PRINCIPLE OF EFFECTIVE DEMAND

. . .

2

A brief summary of the theory of employment to be worked out in the course of the following chapters may, perhaps, help the reader at this stage, even though it may not be fully intelligible. The terms involved will be more carefully defined in due course. In this summary we shall assume that the money-wage and other factor costs are constant per unit of labour employed. But this simplification, with which we shall dispense later, is introduced solely to facilitate the exposition. The essential character of the argument is precisely the same whether or not money-wages, etc., are liable to change.

The outline of our theory can be expressed as follows. When employment increases, aggregate real income is increased. The psychology of the community is such that when aggregate real income is increased aggregate consumption is increased, but not by so much as income. Hence employers would make a loss if the whole of the increased employment were to be devoted to satisfying the increased demand for immediate consumption. Thus, to justify any given amount of employment there must be an amount of current investment sufficient to absorb the excess of total output over what the community chooses to consume when employment is at the given level. For unless there is this amount of investment, the receipts of the entrepreneurs will be less than is required to induce them to offer the given amount of employment. It follows, therefore, that, given what we shall call the community's propensity to consume, the equilibrium level of employment, *i.e.* the level at which there is no inducement to employers as a whole either to expand or to contract employment, will depend on the amount of current investment. The amount of current investment will depend, in turn, on what we shall call the inducement to invest; and the inducement to invest will be found to depend on the relation between the schedule of the marginal efficiency of capital and the complex of rates of interest on loans of various maturities and risks.

Thus, given the propensity to consume and the rate of new investment, there will be only one level of employment consistent with equilibrium; since any other level will lead to inequality between the aggregate supply price of output as a whole and its aggregate demand price. This level cannot be *greater* than full employment, *i.e.* the real wage cannot be less than the marginal disutility of labour. But there is no reason in general for expecting it to be *equal* to full employment. The effective demand associated with full employment is a special case, only realised when the propensity to consume and the .inducement to invest stand in a particular relationship to one another. This particular relationship, which corresponds to the assumptions of the classical theory, is in a sense an optimum relationship. But it can only exist when, by accident or design, current investment provides an amount of demand just equal to the excess of the aggregate supply price of the output resulting from full employment over what the community will choose to spend on consumption when it is fully employed.

This theory can be summed up in the following propositions:

(1) In a given situation of technique, resources and costs, income (both money-income and real income) depends on the volume of employment N.

(2) The relationship between the community's income and what it can be expected to spend on consumption, designated by D_1, will depend on the psychological characteristic of the community, which we shall call its *propensity to consume*. That is to say, consumption will depend on the level of aggregate income and, therefore, on the level of employment N, except when there is some change in the propensity to consume.

(3) The amount of labour N which the entrepreneurs decide to employ depends on the sum (D) of *two* quantities, namely D_1, the amount which the community is expected to spend on consumption, and D_2, the amount which it is expected to devote to new investment. D is what we have called above the *effective demand*.

(4) Since $D_1 + D_2 = D = \phi(N)$, where ϕ is the aggregate supply function, and since, as we have seen in (2) above, D_1 is a function of N, which

we may write $\chi(N)$, depending on the propensity to consume, it follows that $\phi(N) - \chi(N) = D_2$.

(5) Hence the volume of employment in equilibrium depends on (i) the aggregate supply function, ϕ, (ii) the propensity to consume, χ, and (iii) the volume of investment, D_2. This is the essence of the General Theory of Employment.

(6) For every value of N there is a corresponding marginal productivity of labour in the wage-goods industries; and it is this which determines the real wage. (5) is, therefore, subject to the condition that N cannot *exceed* the value which reduces the real wage to equality with the marginal disutility of labour. This means that not all changes in D are compatible with our temporary assumption that money-wages are constant. Thus it will be essential to a full statement of our theory to dispense with this assumption.

(7) On the classical theory, according to which $D = \phi(N)$ for *all* values of N, the volume of employment is in neutral equilibrium for all values of N less than its maximum value; so that the forces of competition between entrepreneurs may be expected to push it to this maximum value. Only at this point, on the classical theory, can there be stable equilibrium.

(8) *When employment increases, D_1 will increase, but not by so much as* D; since when our income increases our consumption increases also, but not by so much. The key to our practical problem is to be found in this psychological law. For it follows from this that the greater the volume of employment the greater will be the gap between the aggregate supply price (Z) of the corresponding output and the sum (D_1) which the entrepreneurs can expect to get back out of the expenditure of consumers. Hence, if there is no change in the propensity to consume, employment cannot increase, unless at the same time D_2 is increasing so as to fill the increasing gap between Z and D_1. Thus—except on the special assumptions of the classical theory according to which there is some force in operation which, when employment increases, always causes D_2 to increase sufficiently to fill the widening gap between Z and D_1—the economic system may find itself in stable equilibrium with N at a level below full employment, namely at the level given by the intersection of the aggregate demand function with the aggregate supply function.

Thus the volume of employment is not determined by the marginal disutility of labour measured in terms of real wages, except in so far as the supply of labour available at a given real wage sets a *maximum* level to employment. The propensity to consume and the rate of new investment determine between them the volume of employment, and the volume of employment is uniquely related to a given level of real wages—not the other way round. If the propensity to consume and the rate of new investment result in a deficient effective demand, the actual level of employment will fall short of the supply of labour potentially available at the existing real wage, and the equilibrium real wage will be *greater* than the marginal disutility of the equilibrium level of employment.

This analysis supplies us with an explanation of the paradox of poverty in the midst of plenty. For the mere existence of an insufficiency of effective demand may, and often will, bring the increase of employment to a standstill *before* a level of full employment has been reached. The insufficiency of effective demand will inhibit the process of production in spite of the fact that the marginal product of labour still exceeds in value the marginal disutility of employment.

Moreover the richer the community, the wider will tend to be the gap between its actual and its potential production; and therefore the more obvious and outrageous the defects of the economic system. For a poor community will be prone to consume by far the greater part of its output, so that a very modest measure of investment will be sufficient to provide full employment; whereas a wealthy community will have to discover much ampler opportunities for investment if the saving propensities of its wealthier members are to be compatible with the employment of its poorer members. If in a potentially wealthy community the inducement to invest is weak, then, in spite of its potential wealth, the working of the principle of effective demand will compel it to reduce its actual output, until, in spite of its potential wealth, it has become so poor that its surplus over its consumption is sufficiently diminished to correspond to the weakness of the inducement to invest.

But worse still. Not only is the marginal propensity to consume weaker in a wealthy community, but, owing to its accumulation of capital being already larger, the opportunities for further investment are less attractive unless the rate of interest falls at a sufficiently rapid rate. . . .

Thus the analysis of the Propensity to Consume, the definition of the Marginal Efficiency of Capital and the theory of the Rate of Interest are the three main gaps in our existing knowledge which it will be necessary to fill. When this has been accomplished, we shall find that the Theory of Prices falls into its proper place as a matter which is subsidiary to our general theory. We shall discover, however, that Money plays an essential part in our theory of the Rate of Interest; and we shall attempt to disentangle the peculiar characteristics of Money which distinguish it from other things.

3

The idea that we can safely neglect the aggregate demand function is fundamental to the Ricardian economics, which underlie what we have been taught for more than a century. Malthus, indeed, had vehemently opposed Ricardo's doctrine that it was impossible for effective demand to be deficient; but vainly. For, since Malthus was unable to explain clearly (apart from an appeal to the facts of common observation) how and why effective demand could be deficient or excessive, he failed to furnish an alternative construction; and Ricardo conquered England as completely as the Holy Inquisition conquered Spain. Not only was his theory accepted by the city, by statesmen and by the academic world. But controversy ceased; the other point of view completely disappeared; it ceased to be discussed. The great puzzle of Effective Demand with which Malthus had wrestled vanished from economic literature. You will not find it mentioned even once in the whole works of Marshall, Edgeworth and Professor Pigou, from whose hands the classical theory has received its most mature embodiment. It could only live on furtively, below the surface, in the underworlds of Karl Marx, Silvio Gesell or Major Douglas.

The completeness of the Ricardian victory is something of a curiosity and a mystery. It must have been due to a complex of suitabilities in the doctrine to the environment into which it was projected. That it reached conclusions quite different from what the ordinary uninstructed person would expect, added, I suppose, to its intellectual prestige. That its teaching, translated into practice, was austere and often unpalatable, lent it virtue. That it was adapted to carry a vast and consistent logical superstructure, gave it beauty. That it could explain much social injustice and apparent cruelty as an inevitable incident in the scheme of progress, and the attempt to change such things as likely on the whole to do more harm than good, commended it to authority. That it afforded a measure of justification to the free activities of the individual capitalist, attracted to it the support of the dominant social force behind authority.

. . .

BOOK II / Definitions and Ideas

Chapter 7: THE MEANING OF SAVING AND INVESTMENT FURTHER CONSIDERED

1

Saving and *Investment* have been so defined that they are necessarily equal in amount, being, for the community as a whole, merely different aspects of the same thing. Several contemporary writers (including myself in my *Treatise on Money*) have, however, given special definitions of these terms on which they are not necessarily equal. Others have written on the assumption that they may be unequal without prefacing their discussion with any definitions at all. It will be useful, therefore, with a view to relating the foregoing to other discussions of these terms, to classify some of the various uses of them which appear to be current.

So far as I know, everyone agrees in meaning by *Saving* the excess of income over what is spent on consumption. It would certainly be very inconvenient and misleading not to mean this. Nor is there any important difference of opinion as to what is meant by expenditure on consumption. Thus the differences of usage arise either out of the definition of *Investment* or out of that of *Income*.

2

Let us take *Investment* first. In popular usage it is common to mean by this the purchase of an asset, old or new, by an individual or a corporation. Occasionally, the term might be restricted to the purchase of an asset on the Stock Exchange. But we speak just as readily of investing, for example, in a house, or in a machine, or in a stock of finished or unfinished goods; and, broadly speaking, new investment, as distinguished from reinvestment, means the purchase of a capital asset of any kind out of income. If we reckon the sale of an investment as being negative investment, *i.e.* disinvestment, my own definition is in accordance with popular usage; since exchanges of old investments necessarily cancel out. We have, indeed, to adjust for the creation and discharge of debts (including changes in the quantity of credit or money); but since for the community as a whole the increase or decrease of the aggregate creditor position is alway exactly equal to the increase or decrease of the aggregate debtor position, this complication also cancels out when we are dealing with aggregate investment. Thus, assuming that income in the popular sense corresponds to my net income, aggregate investment in the popular sense coincides with my definition of net investment, namely the net addition to all kinds of capital equipment, after allowing for those changes in the value of the old capital equipment which are taken into account in reckoning net income.

Investment, thus defined, includes, therefore, the increment of capital equipment, whether it consists of fixed capital, working capital or liquid capital; and the significant differences of definition (apart from the distinction between investment and net investment) are due to the exclusion from investment of one or more of these categories.

Mr. Hawtrey, for example, who attaches great importance to changes in liquid capital, *i.e.* to undesigned increments (or decrements) in the stock of unsold goods, has suggested a possible definition of investment from which such changes are excluded. In this case an excess of saving over investment would be the same thing as an undesigned increment in the stock of unsold goods, *i.e.* as an increase of liquid capital. Mr. Hawtrey has not convinced me that this is the factor to stress; for it lays all the emphasis on the correction of changes which were in the first instance unforeseen, as compared with those which are, rightly or wrongly, anticipated. Mr. Hawtrey regards the daily decisions of entrepreneurs concerning their scale of output as being varied from the scale of the previous day by reference to the changes in their stock of unsold goods. Certainly, in the case of consumption goods, this plays an important part in their decisions. But I see no object in excluding the play of other factors on their decisions; and I prefer, therefore, to emphasise the total change of effective demand and not merely that part of the change in effective demand which reflects the increase or decrease of unsold stocks in the previous period. Moreover, in the case of fixed capital, the increase or decrease of unused capacity corresponds to the increase or decrease in unsold stocks in its effect on decisions to produce; and I do not see how Mr. Hawtrey's method can handle this at least equally important factor.

It seems probable that capital formation and capital consumption, as used by the Austrian school of economists, are not identical either with investment and disinvestment as defined above or with net investment and disinvestment. In particular, capital consumption is said to occur in circumstances where there is quite clearly no net decrease in capital equipment as defined above. I have, however, been unable to discover a reference to any passage where the meaning of these terms is clearly explained. The statement, for example, that capital formation occurs when there is a lengthening of the period of production does not much advance matters.

3

We come next to the divergences between Saving and Investment which are due to a special definition of income and hence of the excess of income over consumption. My own use of terms in my *Treatise on Money* is an example of this. For, as I have explained, the definition of income, which I there employed, differed from my present definition by reckoning as the income of entrepreneurs not their actually realised profits but (in some sense) their "normal profit." Thus by an excess of saving over investment I meant that the scale of output was such that entrepreneurs were earning a less than normal profit from their ownership of the capital equipment; and by an increased excess of saving over investment I meant that a decline was taking place in the actual profits, so that they would be under a motive to contract output.

As I now think, the volume of employment (and consequently of output and real income) is fixed by the entrepreneur under the motive of seeking to maximise his present and prospective profits (the allowance for user cost being determined by his view as to the use of equipment which will maximise his return from it over its whole life); whilst the volume of employment which will maximise his profit depends on the aggregate demand function given by his expectations of the sum of the proceeds resulting from consumption and investment respectively on various hypotheses. In my *Treatise on Money* the concept of *changes* in the excess of investment over saving, as there defined, was a way of handling changes in profit, though I did not in that book distinguish clearly between expected and realised results. I there argued that change in the excess of investment over saving was the motive force governing changes in the volume of output. Thus the new argument, though (as I now think) much more accurate and instructive, is essentially a development of the old. Expressed in the language of my *Treatise on Money*, it would run: the expectation of an increased excess of Investment over Saving, given the former volume of employment and output, will induce entrepreneurs to increase the volume of employment and output. The significance of both my present and my former arguments lies in their attempt to show that the volume of employment is determined by the estimates of effective demand made by the entrepreneurs, an expected increase of investment relatively to saving as defined in my *Treatise on Money* being a criterion of an increase in effective demand. But the exposition in my *Treatise on Money* is, of course, very confusing and incomplete in the light of the further developments here set forth.

Mr. D. H. Robertson has defined to-day's income as being equal to *yesterday's* consumption *plus* investment, so that to-day's saving, in his sense, is equal to yesterday's investment *plus* the excess of yesterday's consumption over to-day's consumption. On this definition saving can exceed investment, namely, by the excess of yesterday's income (in my sense) over to-day's income. Thus when Mr. Robertson says that there is an excess of saving over investment, he means literally the same thing as I mean when I say that income is falling, and the excess of saving in his sense is exactly equal to the decline of income in my sense. If it were true that current expectations were always determined by yesterday's realised results, to-day's effective demand would be equal to yesterday's income. Thus Mr. Robertson's method might be regarded as an alternative attempt to mine (being, perhaps, a first approximation to it) to make the same distinction, so vital for causal analysis, that I have tried to make by the contrast between effective demand and income.

. . .

The prevalence of the idea that saving and investment, taken in their straightforward sense, can differ from one another, is to be explained, I think, by an optical illusion due to regarding an individual depositor's relation to his bank as being a one-sided transaction, instead of seeing it as the two-sided transaction which it actually is. It is supposed that a depositor and his bank can somehow contrive between them to perform an operation by which savings can disappear into the banking system so that they are lost to investment, or, contrariwise, that the banking system can make it possible for investment to occur, to which no saving corresponds. But no one can save without acquiring an asset, whether it be cash or a debt or capital-goods; and no one can acquire an asset which he did not previously possess, unless *either* an asset of equal value is newly produced *or* someone else parts with an asset of that value which he previously had. In the first alternative there is a corresponding new investment: in the second alternative someone else must be dis-saving an equal sum. For his loss of wealth must be due to his consumption exceeding his income, and not to a loss on capital account through a change in the value of a capital-asset, since it is not a case of his suffering a loss of value which his asset formerly had; he is duly receiving the current value of his asset and yet is not retaining this value in wealth of any form, *i.e.* he must be spending it on current consumption in excess of current income. Moreover, if it is the banking system which parts with an asset, someone must be parting with cash. It follows that the aggregate saving of the first individual and of others taken together must necessarily be equal to the amount of current new investment.

The notion that the creation of credit by the banking system allows investment to take place to which "no genuine saving" corresponds can only be the result of isolating one of the consequences of the increased bank-credit to the exclusion of the others. If the grant of a bank-credit to an entrepreneur additional to the credits already existing allows him to make an addition to current investment which would not have occurred otherwise, incomes will necessarily be increased and at a rate which will normally *exceed* the rate of increased investment. Moreover, except in conditions of full employment, there will be an increase of real income as well as of money-income. The public will exercise "a free choice" as to the proportion in which they divide their increase of income between saving and spending; and it is impossible that the intention of the entrepreneur who has borrowed in order to increase investment can become effective (except in substitution for investment by other entrepreneurs which would have occurred otherwise) at a faster rate than the public decide to increase their savings. Moreover, the savings which result from this decision are just as genuine as any other savings. No one can be compelled to own the additional money corresponding to the new bank-credit, unless he deliberately prefers to hold more money rather than some other form of wealth. Yet employment, incomes and prices cannot help moving in such a way that in the new situation someone does choose to hold the additional money. It is true that an unexpected increase of investment in a particular direction may cause an irregularity in the rate of aggregate saving and investment which would not have occurred if it has been sufficiently fore-seen. It is also true that the grant of the bank-credit will set up three tendencies—(1) for output to increase, (2) for the marginal product to rise in value in terms of the wage-unit (which in conditions of decreasing return must necessarily accompany an increase of output), and (3) for the wage-unit to rise in terms of money (since this is a frequent concomitant of better employment); and these tendencies may affect the distribution of real income between different groups. But these tendencies are character-istic of a state of increasing output as such, and will occur just as much if the increase in output has been initiated otherwise than by an increase in bank-credit. They can only be avoided by avoiding any course of action capable of improving employment. Much of the above, however, is antici-pating the result of discussions which have not yet been reached.

Thus the old-fashioned view that saving always involves investment, though incomplete and misleading, is formally sounder than the new-fangled view that there can be saving without investment or investment without "genuine" saving. The error lies in proceeding to the plausible inference that, when an individual saves, he will increase aggregate invest-ment by an equal amount. It is true, that, when an individual saves he increases his own wealth. But the conclusion that he also increases aggre-gate wealth fails to allow for the possibility that an act of individual saving may react on someone else's savings and hence on someone else's wealth.

The reconciliation of the identity between saving and investment with the apparent "free-will" of the individual to save what he chooses irre-spective of what he or others may be investing, essentially depends on sav-ing being, like spending, a two-sided affair. For although the amount of his own saving is unlikely to have any significant influence on his own income, the reactions of the amount of his consumption on the incomes of others makes it impossible for all individuals simultaneously to save any given sums. Every such attempt to save more by reducing consumption will so affect incomes that the attempt necessarily defeats itself. It is, of course, just as impossible for the community as a whole to save *less* than the amount of current investment, since the attempt to do so will necessarily raise incomes to a level at which the sums which individuals choose to save add up to a figure exactly equal to the amount of investment.

The above is closely analogous with the proposition which harmonises the liberty, which every individual possesses, to change, whenever he chooses, the amount of money he holds, with the necessity for the total amount of money, which individual balances add up to, to be exactly equal to the amount of cash which the banking system has created. In this latter case the equality is brought about by the fact that the amount of money which people choose to hold is not independent of their incomes or of the prices of the things (primarily securities), the purchase of which is the natural alternative to holding money. Thus incomes and such prices necessarily change until the aggregate of the amounts of money which individuals choose to hold at the new level of incomes and prices thus brought about has come to equality with the amount of money created by the banking system. This, indeed, is the fundamental proposition of monetary theory.

Both these propositions follow merely from the fact that there cannot be a buyer without a seller or a seller without a buyer. Though an individual whose transactions are small in relation to the market can safely neglect the fact that demand is not a one-sided transaction, it makes nonsense to neglect it when we come to aggregate demand. This is the vital difference between the theory of the economic behaviour of the aggregate and the theory of the behaviour of the individual unit, in which we assume that changes in the individual's own demand do not affect his income.

BOOK III / The Propensity to Consume

Chapter 8: THE PROPENSITY TO CONSUME: THE OBJECTIVE FACTORS

1

We are now in a position to return to our main theme, from which we broke off at the end of Book I in order to deal with certain general problems of method and definition. The ultimate object of our analysis is to discover what determines the volume of employment. So far we have established the preliminary conclusion that the volume of employment is determined by the point of intersection of the aggregate supply function with the aggregate demand function. The aggregate supply function, however, which depends in the main on the physical conditions of supply, involves few considerations which are not already familiar. The form may be unfamiliar but the underlying factors are not new. . . . But, in the main, it is the part played by the aggregate demand function which has been overlooked; and it is to the aggregate demand function that we shall devote Books III and IV.

The aggregate demand function relates any given level of employment to the "proceeds" which that level of employment is expected to realise. The "proceeds" are made up of the sum of two quantities—the sum which will be spent on consumption when employment is at the given level, and the sum which will be devoted to investment. The factors which govern these two quantities are largely distinct. In this book we shall consider the former, namely what factors determine the sum which will be spent on consumption when employment is at a given level; and in Book IV we shall proceed to the factors which determine the sum which will be devoted to investment.

Since we are here concerned in determining what sum will be spent on consumption when employment is at a given level, we should, strictly speaking, consider the function which relates the former quantity (C) to the latter (N). It is more convenient, however, to work in terms of a slightly different function, namely, the function which relates the consumption in terms of wage-units (C_w) to the income in terms of wage-units (Y_w) corresponding to a level of employment N. This suffers from the objection that Y_w is not a unique function of N, which is the same in all circumstances. For the relationship between Y_w and N may depend (though probably in a very minor degree) on the precise nature of the employment. That is to say, two different distributions of a given aggregate employment N between different employments might (owing to the different shapes of the individual employment functions) lead to different values of Y_w. In conceivable circumstances a special allowance might have to be made for this factor. But in general it is a good approximation to regard Y_w as uniquely determined by N. We will therefore define what we shall call *the propensity to consume* as the functional relationship χ between Y_w, a given level of income in terms of wage-units, and C_w the expenditure on consumption out of that level of income, so that

$$C_w = \chi(Y_w) \text{ or } C = W \cdot \chi(Y_w).$$

The amount that the community spends on consumption obviously depends (i) partly on the amount of its income, (ii) partly on the other objective attendant circumstances, and (iii) partly on the subjective needs and the psychological propensities and habits of the individuals composing it and the principles on which the income is divided between them (which may suffer modification as output is increased). The motives to spending interact and the attempt to classify them runs the danger of false division. Nevertheless it will clear our minds to consider them separately under two broad heads which we shall call the subjective factors and the objective factors. The subjective factors include those psychological characteristics of human nature and those social practices and institutions which, though not unalterable, are unlikely to undergo a material change over a short period of time except in abnormal or revolutionary circumstances. In an historical enquiry or in comparing one social system with another of a different type, it is necessary to take account of the manner in which changes in the subjective factors may affect the propensity to consume. But, in general, we shall in what follows take the subjective factors as given; and we shall assume that the propensity to consume depends only on changes in the objective factors.

2

The principal objective factors which influence the propensity to consume appear to be the following:

(1) *A change in the wage-unit.*—Consumption (C) is obviously much more a function of (in some sense) *real* income than of money-income. In a given state of technique and tastes and of social conditions determining the distribution of income, a man's real income will rise and fall with the amount of his command over labour-units, *i.e.* with the amount of his income measured in wage-units; though when the aggregate volume of output changes, his real income will (owing to the operation of decreasing returns) rise less than in proportion to his income measured in wage-units. As a first approximation, therefore, we can reasonably assume that, if the wage-unit changes, the expenditure on consumption corresponding to a given level of employment will, like prices, change in the same proportion; though in some circumstances we may have to make an allowance for the possible reactions on aggregate consumption of the change in the distribution of a given real income between entrepreneurs and rentiers resulting from a change in the wage-unit. Apart from this, we have already allowed for changes in the wage-unit by defining the propensity to consume in terms of income measured in terms of wage-units.

(2) *A change in the difference between income and net income.*—We have shown above that the amount of consumption depends on net income rather than on income, since it is, by definition, his net income that a man has primarily in mind when he is deciding his scale of consumption. In a given situation there may be a somewhat stable relationship between the two, in the sense that there will be a function uniquely relating different levels of income to the corresponding levels of net income. If, however, this should not be the case, such part of any change in income as is not reflected in net income must be neglected since it will have no effect on consumption; and, similarly, a change in net income, not reflected in income, must be allowed for. Save in exceptional circumstances, however, I doubt the practical importance of this factor. We will return to a fuller discussion of the effect on consumption of the difference between income and net income in the fourth section of this chapter.

(3) *Windfall changes in capital-values not allowed for in calculating net income.*—These are of much more importance in modifying the propensity to consume, since they will bear no stable or regular relationship to the amount of income. The consumption of the wealth-owning class may be extremely susceptible to unforeseen changes in the money-value of its wealth. This should be classified amongst the major factors capable of causing short-period changes in the propensity to consume.

(4) *Changes in the rate of time-discounting, i.e. in the ratio of exchange*

between present goods and future goods.—This is not quite the same thing as the rate of interest, since it allows for future changes in the purchasing power of money in so far as these are foreseen. Account has also to be taken of all kinds of risks, such as the prospect of not living to enjoy the future goods or of confiscatory taxation. As an approximation, however, we can identify this with the rate of interest.

The influence of this factor on the rate of spending out of a given income is open to a good deal of doubt. For the classical theory of the rate of interest, which was based on the idea that the rate of interest was the factor which brought the supply and demand for savings into equilibrium, it was convenient to suppose that expenditure on consumption is *cet. par.* negatively sensitive to changes in the rate of interest, so that any rise in the rate of interest would appreciably diminish consumption. It has long been recognised, however, that the total effect of changes in the rate of interest on the readiness to spend on present consumption is complex and uncertain, being dependent on conflicting tendencies, since some of the subjective motives towards saving will be more easily satisfied if the rate of interest rises, whilst others will be weakened. Over a long period, substantial changes in the rate of interest probably tend to modify social habits considerably, thus affecting the subjective propensity to spend—though in which direction it would be hard to say, except in the light of actual experience. The usual type of short-period fluctuation in the rate of interest is not likely, however, to have much *direct* influence on spending either way. There are not many people who will alter their way of living because the rate of interest has fallen from 5 to 4 per cent, if their aggregate income is the same as before. Indirectly there may be more effects, though not all in the same direction. Perhaps the most important influence, operating through changes in the rate of interest, on the readiness to spend out of a given income, depends on the effect of these changes on the appreciation or depreciation in the price of securities and other assets. For if a man is enjoying a windfall increment in the value of his capital, it is natural that his motives towards current spending should be strengthened, even though in terms of income his capital is worth no more than before; and weakened if he is suffering capital losses. But this indirect influence we have allowed for already under (3) above. Apart from this, the main conclusion suggested by experience is, I think, that the short-period influence of the rate of interest on individual spending out of a given income is secondary and relatively unimportant, except, perhaps, where unusually large changes are in question. When the rate of interest falls very low indeed, the increase in the ratio between an annuity purchasable for a given sum and the annual interest on that sum may, however, provide an important source of negative saving by encouraging the practice of providing for old age by the purchase of an annuity.

The abnormal situation, where the propensity to consume may be sharply affected by the development of extreme uncertainty concerning the future and what it may bring forth, should also, perhaps, be classified under this heading.

(5) *Changes in fiscal policy.*—In so far as the inducement to the individual to save depends on the future return which he expects, it clearly depends not only on the rate of interest but on the fiscal policy of the Government. Income taxes, especially when they discriminate against "unearned" income, taxes on capital-profits, death-duties and the like are as relevant as the rate of interest; whilst the range of possible changes in fiscal policy may be greater, in expectation at least, than for the rate of interest itself. If fiscal policy is used as a deliberate instrument for the more equal distribution of incomes, its effect in increasing the propensity to consume is, of course, all the greater.

We must also take account of the effect on the aggregate propensity to consume of Government sinking funds for the discharge of debt paid for out of ordinary taxation. For these represent a species of corporate saving, so that a policy of substantial sinking funds must be regarded in given circumstances as reducing the propensity to consume. It is for this reason that a change-over from a policy of Government borrowing to the opposite policy of providing sinking funds (or *vice versa*) is capable of causing a severe contraction (or marked expansion) of effective demand.

(6) *Changes in expectations of the relation between the present and the future level of income.*—We must catalogue this factor for the sake of formal completeness. But, whilst it may affect considerably a particular individual's propensity to consume, it is likely to average out for the community as a whole. Moreover, it is a matter about which there is, as a rule, too much uncertainty for it to exert much influence.

We are left therefore, with the conclusion that in a given situation the propensity to consume may be considered a fairly stable function, provided that we have eliminated changes in the wage-unit in terms of money. Windfall changes in capital-values will be capable of changing the propensity to consume, and substantial changes in the rate of interest and in fiscal policy may make some difference; but the other objective factors which might affect it, whilst they must not be overlooked, are not likely to be important in ordinary circumstances.

The fact that, given the general economic situation, the expenditure on consumption in terms of the wage-unit depends in the main, on the volume of output and employment is the justification for summing up the other factors in the portmanteau function "propensity to consume." For whilst the other factors are capable of varying (and this must not be forgotten), the aggregate income measured in terms of the wage-unit is, as a rule, the principal variable upon which the consumption-constituent of the aggregate demand function will depend.

3

Granted, then, that the propensity to consume is a fairly stable function so that, as a rule, the amount of aggregate consumption mainly depends on the amount of aggregate income (both measured in terms of wage-units), changes in the propensity itself being treated as a secondary influence, what is the normal shape of this function?

The fundamental psychological law, upon which we are entitled to depend with great confidence both *a priori* from our knowledge of human nature and from the detailed facts of experience, is that men are disposed, as a rule and on the average, to increase their consumption as their income increases, but not by as much as the increase in their income. That is to say, if C_w is the amount of consumption and Y_w is income (both measured in wage-units) ΔC_w has the same sign as ΔY_w but is smaller in amount, *i.e.* dC_w/dY_w is positive and less than unity.

This is especially the case where we have short periods in view, as in the case of the so-called cyclical fluctuations of employment during which habits, as distinct from more permanent psychological propensities, are not given time enough to adapt themselves to changed objective circumstances. For a man's habitual standard of life usually has the first claim on his income, and he is apt to save the difference which discovers itself between his actual income and the expense of his habitual standard; or, if he does adjust his expenditure to changes in his income, he will over short periods do so imperfectly. Thus a rising income will often be accompanied by increased saving, and a falling income by decreased saving, on a greater scale at first than subsequently.

But, apart from short-period *changes* in the level of income, it is also obvious that a higher absolute level of income will tend, as a rule, to widen the gap between income and consumption. For the satisfaction of the immediate primary needs of a man and his family is usually a stronger motive than the motives towards accumulation, which only acquire effective sway when a margin of comfort has been attained. These reasons will lead, as a rule, to a greater *proportion* of income being saved as real income increases. But whether or not a greater proportion is saved, we take it as a fundamental psychological rule of any modern community that, when its real income is increased, it will not increase its consumption by an equal *absolute* amount, so that a greater absolute amount must be saved, unless a large and unusual change is occurring at the same time in other factors. As we shall show subsequently, the stability of the economic system essentially depends on this rule prevailing in practice. This means that, if employment and hence aggregate income increase, *not all* the additional employment will be required to satisfy the needs of additional consumption.

On the other hand, a decline in income due to a decline in the level of employment, if it goes far, may even cause consumption to exceed income not only by some individuals and institutions using up the financial reserves which they have accumulated in better times, but also by the Government, which will be liable, willingly or unwillingly, to run into a budgetary deficit or will provide unemployment relief, for example, out of borrowed money. Thus, when employment falls to a low level, aggregate consumption will decline by a smaller amount than that by which real income has declined, by reason both of the habitual behaviour of individuals and also of the probable policy of governments; which is the explanation why a new position of equilibrium can usually be reached within a modest range of fluctuation. Otherwise a fall in employment and income, once started, might proceed to extreme lengths.

This simple principle leads, it will be seen, to the same conclusion as before, namely, that employment can only increase *pari passu* with an increase in investment; unless, indeed, there is a change in the propensity to consume. For since consumers will spend less than the increase in aggregate supply price when employment is increased, the increased employment will prove unprofitable unless there is an increase in investment to fill the gap.

. . .

Chapter 10: THE MARGINAL PROPENSITY TO CONSUME

1

. . .

The fluctuations in real income under consideration in this book are those which result from applying different quantities of employment (*i.e.* of labour-units) to a given capital equipment, so that real income increases and decreases with the number of labour-units employed. If, as we assume in general, there is a decreasing return at the margin as the number of labour-units employed on the given capital equipment is increased, income measured in terms of wage-units will increase more than in proportion to the amount of employment, which, in turn, will increase more than in proportion to the amount of real income measured (if that is possible) in terms of product. Real income measured in terms of product and income measured in terms of wage-units will, however, increase and decrease together (in the short period when capital equipment is virtually unchanged). Since, therefore, real income, in terms of product, may be incapable of precise numerical measurement, it is often convenient to regard income in terms of wage-units (Y_w) as an adequate working index of changes in real income. In certain contexts we must not overlook the fact that, in general, Y_w increases and decreases in a greater proportion than real income; but in other contexts the fact that they always increase and decrease together renders them virtually interchangeable.

Our normal psychological law that, when the real income of the community increases or decreases, its consumption will increase or decrease but not so fast, can, therefore, be translated—not, indeed, with absolute accuracy but subject to qualifications which are obvious and can easily be stated in a formally complete fashion—into the propositions that ΔC_w and ΔY_w have the same sign, but $\Delta Y_w > \Delta C_w$, where C_w is the consumption in terms of wage-units. This is merely a repetition of the proposition already established. Let us define, then, dC_w/dY_w as the *marginal propensity to consume*.

This quantity is of considerable importance, because it tells us how the next increment of output will have to be divided between consumption and investment. For $\Delta Y_w = \Delta C_w + \Delta I_w$, where ΔC_w and ΔI_w are the increments of consumption and investment; so that we can write $\Delta Y_w = k\Delta I_w$, where $I - I/k$ is equal to the marginal propensity to consume.

Let us call k the *investment multiplier*. It tells us that, when there is an increment of aggregate investment, income will increase by an amount which is k times the increment of investment.

. . .

We have been dealing so far with a *net* increment of investment. If, therefore, we wish to apply the above without qualification to the effect of (*e.g.*) increased public works, we have to assume that there is no offset through decreased investment in other directions,—and also, of course, no associated change in the propensity of the community to consume. Mr. Kahn was mainly concerned in the article referred to above in considering what offsets we ought to take into account as likely to be important, and in suggesting quantitative estimates. For in an actual case there are several factors besides some specific increase of investment of a given kind which enter into the final result. If, for example, a Government employs 100,000 additional men on public works, and if the multiplier (as defined above) is 4, it is not safe to assume that aggregate employment will increase by 400,000. For the new policy may have adverse reactions on investment in other directions.

It would seem (following Mr. Kahn) that the following are likely in a modern community to be the factors which it is most important not to overlook (though the first two will not be fully intelligible until after Book IV. has been reached):

(i) The method of financing the policy and the increased working cash, required by the increased employment and the associated rise of prices, may have the effect of increasing the rate of interest and so retarding investment in other directions, unless the monetary authority takes steps to the contrary; whilst, at the same time, the increased cost of capital goods will reduce their marginal efficiency to the private investor, and this will require an actual *fall* in the rate of interest to offset it.

(ii) With the confused psychology which often prevails, the Government programme may, through its effect on "confidence," increase liquidity-preference or diminish the marginal efficiency of capital, which, again, may retard other investment unless measures are taken to offset it.

(iii) In an open system with foreign-trade relations, some part of the multiplier of the increased investment will accrue to the benefit of employment in foreign countries, since a proportion of the increased consumption will diminish our own country's favourable foreign balance; so that, if we consider only the effect on domestic employment as distinct from world employment, we must diminish the full figure of the multiplier. On the other hand our own country may recover a portion of this leakage through favourable repercussions due to the action of the multiplier in the foreign country in increasing its economic activity.

Furthermore, if we are considering changes of a substantial amount, we have to allow for a progressive change in the marginal propensity to consume, as the position of the margin is gradually shifted; and hence in the multiplier. The marginal propensity to consume is not constant for all levels of employment, and it is probable that there will be, as a rule, a tendency for it to diminish as employment increases; when real income increases, that is to say, the community will wish to consume a gradually diminishing proportion of it.

There are also other factors, over and above the operation of the general rule just mentioned, which may operate to modify the marginal propensity to consume, and hence the multiplier; and these other factors seem likely, as a rule, to accentuate the tendency of the general rule rather than to offset it. For, in the first place, the increase of employment will tend, owing to the effect of diminishing returns in the short period, to increase the proportion of aggregate income which accrues to the entrepreneurs, whose individual marginal propensity to consume is probably less than the average for the community as a whole. In the second place, unemployment is likely to be associated with negative saving in certain quarters, private or public, because the unemployed may be living either on the savings of themselves and their friends or on public relief which is partly financed out of loans; with the result that re-employment will gradually diminish these particular acts of negative saving and reduce, therefore, the marginal propensity to consume more rapidly than would have occurred from an equal increase in the community's real income accruing in different circumstances.

In any case, the multiplier is likely to be greater for a small net increment of investment than for a large increment; so that, where substantial changes are in view, we must be guided by the average value of the multiplier based on the average marginal propensity to consume over the range in question.

. . .

We have seen that the greater the marginal propensity to consume, the greater the multiplier, and hence the greater the disturbance to employment corresponding to a given change in investment. This might seem to lead to the paradoxical conclusion that a poor community in which saving is a very small proportion of income will be more subject to violent fluctuations than a wealthy community where saving is a larger proportion of income and the multiplier consequently smaller.

This conclusion, however, would overlook the distinction between the effects of the marginal propensity to consume and those of the average propensity to consume. For whilst a high marginal propensity to consume involves a larger *proportionate* effect from a given percentage change in investment, the *absolute* effect will, nevertheless, be small if the *average* propensity to consume is also high. This may be illustrated as follows by a numerical example.

Let us suppose that a community's propensity to consume is such that, so long as its real income does not exceed the output from employing 5,000,000 men on its existing capital equipment, it consumes the whole of its income; that of the output of the next 100,000 additional men employed it consumes 99 per cent., of the next 100,000 after that 98 per cent., of the third 100,000 97 per cent. and so on; and that 10,000,000 men employed represents full employment. It follows from this that, when $5,000,000 + n \times 100,000$ men are employed, the multiplier at the margin is $100/n$, and $n(n + 1)/2.(50 + n)$ per cent. of the national income is invested.

Thus when 5,200,000 men are employed the multiplier is very large, namely 50, but investment is only a trifling proportion of current income, namely, 0.06 per cent.; with the result that if investment falls off by a large proportion, say about two-thirds, employment will only decline to 5,100,000, *i.e.* by about 2 per cent. On the other hand, when 9,000,000 men are employed, the marginal multiplier is comparatively small, namely 2½, but investment is now a substantial proportion of current income, namely 9 per cent.; with the result that if investment falls by two-thirds, employment will decline to 6,900,000, namely, by 23 per cent. In the limit where investment falls off to zero, employment will decline by about 4 per cent. in the former case, whereas in the latter case it will decline by 44 per cent.[1]

---

[1] Quantity of investment is measured, above, by the number of men employed in producing it. Thus if there are diminishing returns per unit of employment as employment increases, what is double the quantity of investment on the above scale will be less than double on a physical scale (if such a scale is available).

In the above example, the poorer of the two communities under comparison is poorer by reason of under-employment. But the same reasoning applies by easy adaptation if the poverty is due to inferior skill, technique or equipment. Thus whilst the multiplier is larger in a poor community, the effect on employment of fluctuations in investment will be much greater in a wealthy community, assuming that in the latter current investment represents a much larger proportion of current output.[2]

It is also obvious from the above that the employment of a given number of men on public works will (on the assumptions made) have a much larger effect on aggregate employment at a time when there is severe unemployment, than it will have later on when full employment is approached. In the above example, if, at a time when employment has fallen to 5,200,000, an additional 100,000 men are employed on public works, total employment will rise to 6,400,000. But if employment is already 9,000,000 when the additional 100,000 men are taken on for public works, total employment will only rise to .9,200,000. Thus public works even of doubtful utility may pay for themselves over and over again at a time of severe unemployment, if only from the diminished cost of relief expenditure, provided that we can assume that a smaller proportion of income is saved when unemployment is greater; but they may become a more doubtful proposition as a state of full employment is approached. Furthermore, if our assumption is correct that the marginal propensity to consume falls off steadily as we approach full employment, it follows that it will become more and more troublesome to secure a further given increase of employment by further increasing investment.

. . .

BOOK IV / The Inducement to Invest

Chapter 11: THE MARGINAL EFFICIENCY OF CAPITAL

1

When a man buys an investment or capital-asset, he purchases the right to the series of prospective returns, which he expects to obtain from selling

[2] More generally, the ratio of the proportional change in total demand to the proportional change in investment

$$= \frac{\Delta Y}{Y} \Big/ \frac{\Delta I}{I} = \frac{\Delta Y}{Y} \cdot \frac{Y - C}{\Delta Y - \Delta C} = \frac{I - \dfrac{C}{Y}}{I - \dfrac{dC}{dY}}.$$

As wealth increases dC/dY diminishes, but C/Y also diminishes. Thus the fraction increases or diminishes according as consumption increases or diminishes in a smaller or greater proportion than income.

its output, after deducting the running expenses of obtaining that output, during the life of the asset. This series of annuities $Q_1, Q_2 \ldots Q_n$ it is convenient to call the *prospective yield* of the investment.

Over against the prospective yield of the investment we have the *supply price* of the capital-asset, meaning by this, not the market-price at which an asset of the type in question can actually be purchased in the market, but the price which would just induce a manufacturer newly to produce an additional unit of such assets, *i.e.* what is sometimes called its *replacement cost*. The relation between the prospective yield of a capital-asset and its supply price or replacement cost, *i.e.* the relation between the prospective yield of one more unit of that type of capital and the cost of producing that unit, furnishes us with the *marginal efficiency of capital* of that type. More precisely, I define the marginal efficiency of capital as being equal to that rate of discount which would make the present value of the series of annuities given by the returns expected from the capital-asset during its life just equal to its supply price. This gives us the marginal efficiencies of particular types of capital-assets. The greatest of these marginal efficiencies can then be regarded as the marginal efficiency of capital in general.

The reader should note that the marginal efficiency of capital is here defined in terms of the *expectation* of yield and of the *current* supply price of the capital-asset. It depends on the rate of return expected to be obtainable on money if it were invested in a *newly* produced asset; not on the historical result of what an investment has yielded on its original cost if we look back on its record after its life is over.

If there is an increased investment in any given type of capital during any period of time, the marginal efficiency of that type of capital will diminish as the investment in it is increased, partly because the prospective yield will fall as the supply of that type of capital is increased, and partly because, as a rule, pressure on the facilities for producing that type of capital will cause its supply price to increase; the second of these factors being usually the more important in producing equilibrium in the short run, but the longer the period in view the more does the first factor take its place. Thus for each type of capital we can build up a schedule, showing by how much investment in it will have to increase within the period, in order that its marginal efficiency should fall to any given figure. We can then aggregate these schedules for all the different types of capital, so as to provide a schedule relating the rate of aggregate investment to the corresponding marginal efficiency of capital in general which that rate of investment will establish. We shall call this the investment demand-schedule; or, alternatively, the schedule of the marginal efficiency of capital.

Now it is obvious that the actual rate of current investment will be pushed to the point where there is no longer any class of capital-asset of which the marginal efficiency exceeds the current rate of interest. In other words, the rate of investment will be pushed to the point on the investment demand-schedule where the marginal efficiency of capital in general is equal to the market rate of interest.[1]

The same thing can also be expressed as follows. If Q_r is the prospective yield from an asset at time r, and d_r is the present value of £1 deferred r years *at the current rate of interest*, $\Sigma Q_r d_r$ is the demand price of the investment; and investment will be carried to the point where $\Sigma Q_r d_r$ becomes equal to the supply price of the investment as defined above. If, on the other hand, $\Sigma Q_r d_r$ falls short of the supply price, there will be no current investment in the asset in question.

It follows that the inducement to invest depends partly on the investment demand-schedule and partly on the rate of interest. Only at the conclusion of Book IV. will it be possible to take a comprehensive view of the factors determining the rate of investment in their actual complexity. I would, however, ask the reader to note at once that neither the knowledge of an asset's prospective yield nor the knowledge of the marginal efficiency of the asset enables us to deduce either the rate of interest or the present value of the asset. We must ascertain the rate of interest from some other source, and only then can we value the asset by "capitalising" its prospective yield.

2

How is the above definition of the marginal efficiency of capital related to common usage? The *Marginal Productivity* or *Yield* or *Efficiency* or *Utility* of Capital are familiar terms which we have all frequently used. But it is not easy by searching the literature of economics to find a clear statement of what economists have usually intended by these terms.

There are at least three ambiguities to clear up. There is, to begin with, the ambiguity whether we are concerned with the increment of physical product per unit of time due to the employment of one more physical unit of capital, or with the increment of value due to the employment of one more value unit of capital. The former involves difficulties as to the definition of the physical unit of capital, which I believe to be both insoluble and unnecessary. It is, of course, possible to say that ten labourers will raise more wheat from a given area when they are in a position to make use of certain additional machines; but I know no means of reducing this to an intelligible arithmetical ratio which does not bring in values. Nevertheless many discussions of this subject seem to be mainly concerned with the

---

[1] For the sake of simplicity of statement I have slurred the point that we are dealing with complexes of rates of interest and discount corresponding to the different lengths of time which will elapse before the various prospective returns from the asset are realised. But it is not difficult to re-state the argument so as to cover this point.

physical productivity of capital in some sense, though the writers fail to make themselves clear.

Secondly, there is the question whether the marginal efficiency of capital is some absolute quantity or a ratio. The contexts in which it is used and the practice of treating it as being of the same dimension as the rate of interest seem to require that it should be a ratio. Yet it is not usually made clear what the two terms of the ratio are supposed to be.

Finally, there is the distinction, the neglect of which has been the main cause of confusion and misunderstanding, between the increment of value obtainable by using an additional quantity of capital in the *existing* situation, and the series of increments which it is expected to obtain *over the whole life* of the additional capital asset;—*i.e.* the distinction between Q_1 and the complete series $Q_1, Q_2 \ldots Q_r \ldots$ This involves the whole question of the place of expectation in economic theory. Most discussions of the marginal efficiency of capital seem to pay no attention to any member of the series except Q_1. Yet this cannot be legitimate except in a static theory, for which all the Q's are equal. The ordinary theory of distribution, where it is assumed that capital is getting *now* its marginal productivity (in some sense or other), is only valid in a stationary state. The aggregate current return to capital has no direct relationship to its marginal efficiency; whilst its current return at the margin of production (*i.e.* the return to capital which enters into the supply price of output) is its marginal user cost, which also has no close connection with its marginal efficiency.

There is, as I have said above, a remarkable lack of any clear account of the matter. At the same time I believe that the definition which I have given above is fairly close to what Marshall intended to mean by the term. The phrase which Marshall himself uses is "marginal net efficiency" of a factor of production; or, alternatively, the "marginal utility of capital." The following is a summary of the most relevant passage which I can find in his *Principles* (6th ed., pp. 519–520). I have run together some non-consecutive sentences to convey the gist of what he says:

> "In a certain factory an extra £100 worth of machinery can be applied so as not to involve any other extra expense, and so as to add annually £3 worth to the net output of the factory after allowing for its own wear and tear. If the investors of capital push it into every occupation in which it seems likely to gain a high reward; and if, after this has been done and equilibrium has been found, it still pays and only just pays to employ this machinery, we can infer from this fact that the yearly rate of interest is 3 per cent. But illustrations of this kind merely indicate part of the action of the great causes which govern value. They cannot be made into a theory of interest, any more than into a theory of wages, without reasoning in a circle. . . . Suppose that the rate of interest is 3 per cent. per annum on perfectly good security; and that the hat-making trade absorbs a capital of one million pounds. This implies that the hat-making trade can turn the whole

million pounds' worth of capital to so good account that they would pay
3 per cent. per annum net for the use of it rather than go without any
of it. There may be machinery which the trade would have refused to
dispense with if the rate of interest had been 20 per cent. per annum. If
the rate had been 10 per cent., more would have been used; if it had been
6 per cent., still more; if 4 per cent. still more; and finally, the rate being
3 per cent., they use more still. When they have this amount, the marginal utility of the machinery, *i.e.* the utility of that machinery which it is
only just worth their while to employ, is measured by 3 per cent."

It is evident from the above that Marshall was well aware that we are
involved in a circular argument if we try to determine along these lines
what the rate of interest actually is.[2] In this passage he appears to accept
the view set forth above, that the rate of interest determines the point to
which new investment will be pushed, given the schedule of the marginal
efficiency of capital. If the rate of interest is 3 per cent., this means that
no one will pay £100 for a machine unless he hopes thereby to add £3 to
his annual net output after allowing for costs and depreciation. In other
passages Marshall was less cautious—though still drawing back when his
argument was leading him on to dubious ground.

Although he does not call it the "marginal efficiency of capital," Professor Irving Fisher has given in his *Theory of Interest* (1930) a definition of
what he calls "the rate of return over cost" which is identical with my
definition. "The rate of return over cost," he writes,[3] "is that rate which,
employed in computing the present worth of all the costs and the present
worth of all the returns, will make these two equal." Professor Fisher explains that the extent of investment in any direction will depend on a
comparison between the rate of return over cost and the rate of interest. To
induce new investment "the rate of return over cost must exceed the rate
of interest."[4] "This new magnitude (or factor) in our study plays the central rôle on the investment opportunity side of interest theory."[5] Thus
Professor Fisher uses his "rate of return over cost" in the same sense and
for precisely the same purpose as I employ "the marginal efficiency of
capital."

3

The most important confusion concerning the meaning and significance
of the marginal efficiency of capital has ensued on the failure to see that

[2] But was he not wrong in supposing that the marginal productivity theory of wages
is equally circular?
[3] *Op. cit.*, p. 168.
[4] *Op. cit.*, p. 159.
[5] *Op. cit.*, p. 155.

it depends on the *prospective* yield of capital, and not merely on its current yield. This can be best illustrated by pointing out the effect on the marginal efficiency of capital of an expectation of changes in the prospective cost of production, whether these changes are expected to come from changes in labour cost, *i.e.* in the wage-unit, or from inventions and new technique. The output from equipment produced to-day will have to compete, in the course of its life, with the output from equipment produced subsequently, perhaps at a lower labour cost, perhaps by an improved technique, which is content with a lower price for its output and will be increased in quantity until the price of its output has fallen to the lower figure with which it is content. Moreover, the entrepreneur's profit (in terms of money) from equipment, old or new, will be reduced, if all output comes to be produced more cheaply. In so far as such developments are foreseen as probable, or even as possible, the marginal efficiency of capital produced to-day is appropriately diminished.

This is the factor through which the expectation of changes in the value of money influences the volume of current output. The expectation of a fall in the value of money stimulates investment, and hence employment generally, because it raises the schedule of the marginal efficiency of capital, *i.e.* the investment demand-schedule; and the expectation of a rise in the value of money is depressing, because it lowers the schedule of the marginal efficiency of capital.

. . .

Chapter 13: THE GENERAL THEORY OF THE RATE OF INTEREST

1

We have shown that, whilst there are forces causing the rate of investment to rise or fall so as to keep the marginal efficiency of capital equal to the rate of interest, yet the marginal efficiency of capital is, in itself, a different thing from the ruling rate of interest. The schedule of the marginal efficiency of capital may be said to govern the terms on which loanable funds are demanded for the purpose of new investment; whilst the rate of interest governs the terms on which funds are being currently supplied. To complete our theory, therefore, we need to know what determines the rate of interest.

In Chapter 14 and its Appendix we shall consider the answers to this question which have been given hitherto. Broadly speaking, we shall find that they make the rate of interest to depend on the interaction of the schedule of the marginal efficiency of capital with the psychological propensity to save. But the notion that the rate of interest is the balancing factor which brings the demand for saving in the shape of new investment forthcoming at a given rate of interest into equality with the supply of saving which results at that rate of interest from the community's psychological propensity to save, breaks down as soon as we perceive that it is impossible to deduce the rate of interest merely from a knowledge of these two factors.

What, then, is our answer to this question?

2

The psychological time-preferences of an individual require two distinct sets of decisions to carry them out completely. The first is concerned with that aspect of time-preference which I have called the *propensity to consume*, which, operating under the influence of the various motives, determines for each individual how much of his income he will consume and how much he will reserve in *some* form of command over future consumption.

But this decision having been made, there is a further decision which awaits him, namely, in *what form* he will hold the command over future consumption which he has reserved, whether out of his current income or from previous savings. Does he want to hold it in the form of immediate, liquid command (*i.e.* in money or its equivalent)? Or is he prepared to part with immediate command for a specified or indefinite period, leaving it to future market conditions to determine on what terms he can, if necessary, convert deferred command over specific goods into immediate command over goods in general? In other words, what is the degree of his *liquidity-preference*—where an individual's liquidity-preference is given by a schedule of the amounts of his resources, valued in terms of money or of wage-units, which he will wish to retain in the form of money in different sets of circumstances?

We shall find that the mistake in the accepted theories of the rate of interest lies in their attempting to derive the rate of interest from the first of these two constituents of psychological time-preference to the neglect of the second; and it is this neglect which we must endeavour to repair.

It should be obvious that the rate of interest cannot be a return to saving or waiting as such. For if a man hoards his savings in cash, he earns no interest, though he saves just as much as before. On the contrary, the mere definition of the rate of interest tells us in so many words that the rate of interest is the reward for parting with liquidity for a specified period. For the rate of interest is, in itself, nothing more than the inverse proportion between a sum of money and what can be obtained for parting with control over the money in exchange for a debt[1] for a stated period of time.[2]

Thus the rate of interest at any time, being the reward for parting with liquidity, is a measure of the unwillingness of those who possess money to part with their liquid control over it. The rate of interest is not the "price" which brings into equilibrium the demand for resources to invest with the readiness to abstain from present consumption. It is the "price" which equilibrates the desire to hold wealth in the form of cash with the available quantity of cash;—which implies that if the rate of interest were lower, *i.e.* if the reward for parting with cash were diminished, the aggregate amount of cash which the public would wish to hold would exceed the available supply, and that if the rate of interest were raised, there would be a surplus of cash which no one would be willing to hold. If this explanation is correct, the quantity of money is the other factor, which, in conjunction with liquidity-preference, determines the actual rate of interest in given circumstances. Liquidity-preference is a potentiality or functional tendency, which fixes the quantity of money which the public will hold when the rate of interest is given; so that if r is the rate of interest, M the quantity of money and L the function of liquidity-preference, we have $M = L(r)$. This is where, and how, the quantity of money enters into the economic scheme.

At this point, however, let us turn back and consider why such a thing as liquidity-preference exists. In this connection we can usefully employ the ancient distinction between the use of money for the transaction of current business and its use as a store of wealth. As regards the first of these two uses, it is obvious that up to a point it is worth while to sacrifice a certain amount of interest for the convenience of liquidity. But, given that the rate of interest is never negative, why should anyone prefer to hold his wealth in a form which yields little or no interest to holding it in a form which yields interest (assuming, of course, at this stage, that the risk of default is the same in respect of a bank balance as of a bond)? There

---

[1] Without disturbance to this definition, we can draw the line between "money" and "debts" at whatever point is most convenient for handling a particular problem. For example, we can treat as *money* any command over general purchasing power which the owner has not parted with for a period in excess of three months, and as *debt* what cannot be recovered for a longer period than this; or we can substitute for "three months" one month or three days or three hours or any other period; or we can exclude from *money* whatever is not legal tender on the spot. It is often convenient in practice to include in *money* time-deposits with banks and, occasionally, even such instruments as (*e.g.*) treasury bills. As a rule, I shall, as in my *Treatise on Money*, assume that money is co-extensive with bank deposits.

[2] In general discussion, as distinct from specific problems where the period of the debt is expressly specified, it is convenient to mean by the rate of interest the complex of the various rates of interest current for different periods of time, *i.e.* for debts of different maturities.

is, however, a necessary condition failing which the existence of a liquidity-preference for money as a means of holding wealth could not exist.

This necessary condition is the existence of *uncertainty* as to the future of the rate of interest, *i.e.* as to the complex of rates of interest for varying maturities which will rule at future dates. For if the rates of interest ruling at all future times could be foreseen with certainty, all future rates of interest could be inferred from the *present* rates of interest for debts of different maturities, which would be adjusted to the knowledge of the future rates. For example, if $_1d_r$ is the value in the present year 1 of £1 deferred r years and it is known that $_nd_r$ will be the value in the year n of £1 deferred r years from that date, we have

$$_nd_r = \frac{_1d_{n+r}}{_1d_n} \; ;$$

whence it follows that the rate at which any debt can be turned into cash n years hence is given by two out of the complex of current rates of interests. If the current rate of interest is positive for debts of every maturity, it must always be more advantageous to purchase a debt than to hold cash as a store of wealth.

If, on the contrary, the future rate of interest is uncertain we cannot safely infer that $_nd_r$ will prove to be equal to $_1d_{n+r}/_1d_n$ when the time comes. Thus if a need for liquid cash may conceivably arise before the expiry of n years, there is a risk of a loss being incurred in purchasing a long-term debt and subsequently turning it into cash, as compared with holding cash. The actuarial profit or mathematical expectation of gain calculated in accordance with the existing probabilities—if it can be so calculated, which is doubtful—must be sufficient to compensate for the risk of disappointment.

There is, moreover, a further ground for liquidity-preference which results from the existence of uncertainty as to the future of the rate of interest, provided that there is an organised market for dealing in debts. For different people will estimate the prospects differently and anyone who differs from the predominant opinion as expressed in market quotations may have a good reason for keeping liquid resources in order to profit, if he is right, from its turning out in due course that the $_1d_r$'s were in a mistaken relationship to one another.[3]

This is closely analogous to what we have already discussed at some length in connection with the marginal efficiency of capital. Just as we found that the marginal efficiency of capital is fixed, not by the "best" opinion, but by the market valuation as determined by mass psychology, so also expectations as to the future of the rate of interest as fixed by mass psychology have their reactions on liquidity-preference;—but with this addi-

---

[3] This is the same point as I discussed in my *Treatise on Money* under the designation of the two views and the "bull-bear" position.

tion that the individual, who believes that future rates of interest will be above the rates assumed by the market, has a reason for keeping actual liquid cash,[4] whilst the individual who differs from the market in the other direction will have a motive for borrowing money for short periods in order to purchase debts of longer term. The market price will be fixed at the point at which the sales of the "bears" and the purchases of the "bulls" are balanced.

The three divisions of liquidity-preference which we have distinguished above may be defined as depending on (i) the transactions-motive, *i.e.* the need of cash for the current transaction of personal and business exchanges; (ii) the precautionary-motive, *i.e.* the desire for security as to the future cash equivalent of a certain proportion of total resources; and (iii) the speculative-motive, *i.e.* the object of securing profit from knowing better than the market what the future will bring forth. As when we were discussing the marginal efficiency of capital, the question of the desirability of having a highly organised market for dealing with debts presents us with a dilemma. For, in the absence of an organised market, liquidity-preference due to the precautionary-motive would be greatly increased; whereas the existence of an organised market gives an opportunity for wide fluctuations in liquidity-preference due to the speculative-motive.

It may illustrate the argument to point out that, if the liquidity-preferences due to the transactions-motive and the precautionary-motive are assumed to absorb a quantity of cash which is not very sensitive to changes in the rate of interest as such and apart from its reactions on the level of income, so that the total quantity of money, less this quantity, is available for satisfying liquidity-preferences due to the speculative-motive, the rate of interest and the price of bonds have to be fixed at the level at which the desire on the part of certain individuals to hold cash (because at that level they feel "bearish" of the future of bonds) is exactly equal to the amount of cash available for the speculative-motive. Thus each increase in the quantity of money must raise the price of bonds sufficiently to exceed the expectations of some "bull" and so influence him to sell his bond for cash and join the "bear" brigade. If, however, there is a negligible demand for cash from the speculative-motive except for a short transitional interval, an increase in the quantity of money will have to lower the rate of interest almost forthwith, in whatever degree is necessary to raise employment and the wage-unit sufficiently to cause the additional cash to be absorbed by the transactions-motive and the precautionary-motive.

As a rule, we can suppose that the schedule of liquidity-preference relat-

[4] It might be thought that, in the same way, an individual, who believed that the prospective yield of investments will be below what the market is expecting, will have a sufficient reason for holding liquid cash. But this is not the case. He has a sufficient reason for holding cash or debts in preference to equities; but the purchase of debts will be a preferable alternative to holding cash, unless he also believes that the future rate of interest will prove to be higher than the market is supposing.

ing the quantity of money to the rate of interest is given by a smooth curve which shows the rate of interest falling as the quantity of money is increased. For there are several different causes all leading towards this result.

In the first place, as the rate of interest falls, it is likely, *cet. par.*, that more money will be absorbed by liquidity-preferences due to the transactions-motive. For if the fall in the rate of interest increases the national income, the amount of money which it is convenient to keep for transactions will be increased more or less proportionately to the increase in income; whilst, at the same time, the cost of the convenience of plenty of ready cash in terms of loss of interest will be diminished. Unless we measure liquidity-preference in terms of wage-units rather than of money (which is convenient in some contexts), similar results follow if the increased employment ensuing on a fall in the rate of interest leads to an increase of wages, *i.e.* to an increase in the money value of the wage-unit. In the second place, every fall in the rate of interest may, as we have just seen, increase the quantity of cash which certain individuals will wish to hold because their views as to the future of the rate of interest differ from the market views.

Nevertheless, circumstances can develop in which even a large increase in the quantity of money may exert a comparatively small influence on the rate of interest. For a large increase in the quantity of money may cause so much uncertainty about the future that liquidity-preferences due to the security-motive may be strengthened; whilst opinion about the future of the rate of interest may be so unanimous that a small change in present rates may cause a mass movement into cash. It is interesting that the stability of the system and its sensitiveness to changes in the quantity of money should be so dependent on the existence of a *variety* of opinion about what is uncertain. Best of all that we should know the future. But if not, then, if we are to control the activity of the economic system by changing the quantity of money, it is important that opinions should differ. Thus this method of control is more precarious in the United States, where everyone tends to hold the same opinion at the same time, than in England where differences of opinion are more usual.

. . .

INDEX